Selling:
The Profession

Focusing on Building Relationships

David J. Lill

Jennifer K. Lill

6th Edition

Project Manager: Martha Lill

Creative Directors: Jennifer Lill and David Lill

Cover Design/Book Layout: Jay Arnold

Creative Design: iDesign, Inc.

Technical Consultants: Don Evans, Barb Evans

Image Consultants: Jimmie Carter, Linda Carter

Editorial Assistance: Rebecca Henderson, Brenda Liefso, Kristina Smiley

Case Studies and Role Plays: Dr. William Barnett

Feel free to contact the authors if you want specific information on how to access all aspects of the website developed exclusively to assist you in the preparation of lecture material, tests, case studies, and other sales-related classroom activities.

Website: www.sellingtheprofession.com

This book may be purchased for educational, business, or sales promotional use. For information or to order, please contact:

DM Bass Publications
6635 Broken Bow Drive
Antioch, TN 37013
615.941.2747 (work)
615.476.5035 (mobile)
615.941.2458 (fax)
dlill48@comcast.net

ISBN-13: 978-0-692-01427-1

ISBN-10: 0-6920142-7-6

SIXTH EDITON

The Library of Congress Cataloging-in-Publication data

Lill, David J. and Jennifer K. Lill

Selling: The Profession / Focusing on Building Relationships / Dr. David J. Lill and Jennifer K. Lill

6th ed. ISBN 978-0-692-01427-1 (paper)

1. Business 2. Sales Training 3. Career Development 4. Self-Help

PRINTED IN CHINA

Dedication

To Martha - The best wife, mom,
and grandma on the planet! We
love you so much!

CREDITS

Written permission to use the following materials has been obtained from the appropriate rights holders:

Sales & Marketing Management

Categories of Salespeople, VNU Business Publications USA, formerly Bill Communications, Inc.

Journal of Personal Selling & Sales Management
Rapport Building for Salespeople: A Neurolinguistic Approach, Nickels, William G, Robert F Everett and Robert Klein; Dr. Ron Michaels, Dept. of Marketing

How Important it is to Listen – pamphlet cartoon, Unisys Corporation

Andy Capp cartoon, North America Syndicate

iStock Photos—All photos in the text were purchased through this company and used with permission.

A special thanks and acknowledgement to Barbara Grieninger, former Permissions Manager, and to Michael Reaggs and Lisa Abelson, former Reprint Managers, for *Sales & Marketing Management* magazine for giving us permission to modify and adapt exhibits, charts, articles, and pictures from issues of the magazine. The pages listed here have items used from various issues of *Sales & Marketing Management* magazine: 17, 27, 65, 81, 137, 139, 160, 205, 254, 315, 364.

BRIEF CONTENTS

PART 1

Relationship Building and the Sales Cycle Framework

PART 2

Cultivating an Ethics Climate and Developing Communication Skills

PART 3

Gaining Knowledge, Preparing, and Planning for the Presentation

PART 4

The Face-to-Face Relationship Model of Selling

PART 5

Management Aspects: Personal and Organizational

TABLE OF CONTENTS

PART 1

Relationship Building and the Sales Cycle Framework

1 A Career in Professional Selling   5

2 Relationship Selling   25

PART 2

Cultivating an Ethics Climate and Developing Communication Skills

PART 3

Gaining Knowledge, Preparing, and Planning for the Presentation

PART 4
The Face-to-Face Relationship Model of Selling

PART 5

Management Aspects: Personal and Organizational

PREFACE

Approach and Purpose

The ideas, concepts, and style of this text are the result of years spent teaching professional selling to college and university students, conducting seminars for sales professionals, and professional business consulting, combined with over thirty five years of personal experience in various phases of the business of selling. As professionals and seasoned salespeople who love the sales environment and desire to see an improvement in the ethical business climate, we wanted a text that would: 1) Show that selling can be an honest, respected profession; 2) convince motivated, creative students that selling is a profession to consider—not just something you do until something better comes along; and 3) demonstrate that, if practiced as explained in this text, a sales career will be a source of financial and personal satisfaction.

Selling: The Profession focuses on building relationships. It is this relationship-building style that spells success for salespeople operating in a highly competitive business environment and dealing with today's sophisticated buyers who demand correct answers to complex problems. The book's style and organization makes it fun to read, easy to comprehend, and highly practical as a training tool for anyone really interested in developing their skills as a salesperson. The sales process is broken down into its most basic components, in an attempt to simplify the complex buyer-seller interaction that takes place in an actual selling situation, with the result being an *eight-step sales cycle model* that we explore in depth in over one-half of the book.

Because attitude is so important for achieving success in selling, verbal and nonverbal communication and social style technology chapters are included as foundation stones. An understanding of these concepts allows you to more readily appreciate the complex, dynamic behavioral relationships that take place in selling. You will be introduced to the availability and usefulness of sales force automation and the numerous technology products available. Global competition has enlarged the playing field. As global competition brings new challenges, technology brings new tools that help sales professionals sell more effectively and efficiently.

Throughout the text, you see the "real world" of selling through review of the current sales literature, personal experience, and interviews with successful active sales professionals who put the theory contained in the book into everyday practice. As one top salesperson said, *"Practice without theory is blind and theory without practice is sterile."*

Selling: The Profession is your guide for success in today's selling environment. Becoming a great salesperson involves no less a commitment to your profession than does becoming a great student, physician, lawyer, or teacher. Success begins by taking a single step. It begins by learning the correct principles and gaining the proper knowledge to lead you down the right path to success.

Your ability to develop and maintain long-term relationships is the key to your success as a person, a student, and a business professional. For customers, a buying decision means a decision to enter into a relationship with a salesperson and their company. It is very much like a "business marriage." *Selling: The Profession* shows you how to bring about that union.

Relationships can be more important than the actual product being sold. Customers don't always know the ingredients or components of a product, how a company functions, or how they will be treated after money changes hands, but they can make an assessment about a salesperson and about the relationship that has occurred over the course of the selling process. Ultimately, customers' decisions are based on the fact that they trust and believe in what a salesperson says. Therefore, the quality of the relationship with a customer is the competitive advantage that enables salespeople to succeed over rivals who may have similar products and services.

Just as optometrists help improve their patients' vision, this textbook serves as a "prescription" for the study of professional selling. You wouldn't expect to enhance your eyesight without the right corrective lenses. So why would you expect your understanding of relationship selling to improve without having the right tools for success?

Read the following five part descriptions so that you can see the logic of the chapter sequence and how you can get the most out of the organization of the book. Remember, this is *your* textbook, your personal prescription for sharpened focus and success in relationship selling.

PART 1   Relationship Building and the Sales Cycle Framework

Chapter 1 discusses the consultative nature and problem-solving approach to professional selling and details the characteristics that successful salespeople possess. Relationship selling is interactive, involves two-way communication, encourages prospect participation, employs empathy, and promotes a win-win environment. Today's style of selling favors building close and trusting long-term relationships. Positioning yourself as a consultant creates a partnership with customers. You are peers working to solve problems together.

You gain a better understanding of the complete selling situation and the problems it generates by breaking the sale into its basic tasks. There are several steps to achieving a successful sale. An eight-step sales cycle is introduced in **chapter 2** and explained in detail in chapters 7 to 14. It just makes sense that if you understand what the steps are in the *Sales Cycle Framework for Relationship Selling*, and what is required to make each step a successful endeavor, you will become a professional in selling much quicker than those who are simply stumbling through the process trying to figure it out. The chapters included in this section are:

1. A Career in Professional Selling
2. Relationship Selling

PART 2   Cultivating an Ethical Climate and Developing Communication Skills

Few professions give you more opportunities for rejection on a daily basis than does the field of sales. **Chapter 3** discusses the need for a strong ethical and moral character to sustain a sales career. Honest and caring service brings customers back and assures success.

Success in professional selling also depends upon your ability to have a productive exchange of information with prospects and customers. As detailed in **chapter 4**, the more you understand about prospects and their decision-making process, the more readily you can discover what they need and want. Because success in relationship selling depends on accurately getting your message across to prospects, chapter 4 also describes how to break through communication barriers.

An especially useful tool for gaining insight into how the prospect is thinking is knowledge of the social styles model, presented in **chapter 5**. A social style is the way a person sends and receives information. It is a method for finding the best way to approach a prospect and to set up a working relationship with that person. The chapters included in this section are:

3. Ethical and Legal Issues in Selling
4. Purchase Behavior and Communication
5. Finding Your Selling Style

PART 3   Gaining Knowledge, Preparing, and Planning for the Presentation

The information in **chapter 6** prepares you for success in a sales career by focusing on gaining product knowledge, developing a plan for self-motivation and goal setting, and introducing the use of sales force technology.

Chapters 7 and 8 discuss the procedures for locating and qualifying prospects and identifying the information needed to prepare for an effective presentation. **Chapter 7** is a thorough look at prospecting. As the saying goes, "I'd rather be a master prospector than a wizard of speech and have no one to tell my story to." **Chapter 8** discusses the process of gathering preapproach information and presents a *six-step telephone track* for making appointments for that all-important personal interview. The chapters in this section are:

6. Preparation For Success in Selling
7. Becoming a Master Prospector
8. Preapproach and Telephone Techniques

PART 4   The Face-to-Face Relationship Model of Selling

Chapters 9 to 13 are the very heart of professional selling. This is considered the "how to" portion of the textbook. This is referred to as the face-to-face portion of the sales cycle. It is the valuable time spent in the actual sales interview—the time when a commitment is obtained and kept.

What happens in the opening minutes is crucial to the overall success of the sales interview, so **chapter 9** focuses on the approach. **Chapter 10** is devoted to the art of asking questions and listening effectively. Questioning and listening guidelines are presented to carry you through the entire sales interview. The SPIN® Selling technique is explained and dramatized using a very practical example. **Chapter 11** details the techniques to use in the actual presentation. Units of conviction are the building blocks for creating and making a meaningful sales presentation. The five elements that comprise a complete unit of conviction are explained and illustrated.

Chapters 12 and 13 present the psychology behind handling objections and closing the sale. A plan to handle objections is introduced, and a separate section in **chapter 12** explains several ways of dealing with the difficult price objection. **Chapter 13** stresses that closing the sale is the natural conclusion to a successful sales interview. The chapters in this section are:

9. Approaching the Prospect
10. Identifying Needs by Questioning and Listening
11. Making the Presentation
12. Handling Objections
13. Closing the Sale

PART 5   Management Aspect: Personal and Organizational

The service you give the customer after the sale has been completed can be as important, or even more important, than the sale itself. Keeping current customers happy and regaining lost clients is the focus of **chapter 14**. The customer absolutely defines quality in every transaction. Great salespeople don't talk customer service—*they live perfect service.*

Chapter 15 shows you how to get better control of your time and your activities. The chapter really is all about personal organization and self-management. You cannot manage time, but you can manage yourself and your personal activities. Administrative ability on the part of the salesperson is fundamental to success. Statistics indicate that only about 20 percent of a salesperson's time during a typical day is spent in face-to-face interviews with prospects. **Chapter 16** details the job responsibilities of the sales manager, and provides a useful introduction for classes in sales management. The chapters in this section are:

14. Service After the Sale
15. Personal, Time, and Territory Management
16. Sales Force Management

CHAPTER STRUCTURE

This seven-part structure is a guide for you to follow as you study and learn the material in the various chapters:

1. **Learning Objectives**. The bullet points at the beginning of each chapter acquaint you with the important concepts. They appear on the first page and serve as guidelines to follow as you read through the chapter.

2. **Main Chapter Body**. Chapters are organized in outline form to make it readily available for study and review. Each chapter is complemented by examples of actual sales situations that take the theory and put it into practice. The material in all 16 chapters is well documented with exhibits taken from actual sales experience.

3. **Developing Partnerships Using Technology**. Technology boxes in various chapters illustrate how sales force technology tools will impact the road warriors of the twenty-first century. They demonstrate how to increase sales efficiency in three functional areas: 1) Improved Communication; 2) Increased Productivity; and 3) Transactional Processing.

4. **Summary**. This section outlines the main points of the chapter to reinforce learning. Reading the various summaries in bullet point format gives you a feel for the content of the chapter, the key points to remember, and provides you with a tremendous resource to use when attempting to pull together concepts from several chapters.

5. **Review Questions**. Each chapter ends with a series of questions to challenge the student's understanding of the material. These questions are useful when studying for quizzes or exams.

6. **Role-Play Exercises**. These practical exercises are designed to have you do things inside and outside the classroom. Role playing exercises get you involved in active learning. The best way to learn new skills is through action. Research shows that students who just sit and listen to a teacher retain only 20 percent of what they hear. However, participants involved in active learning and doing retain a much higher percentage of the information they receive.

7. **Case Studies**. The 32 brand new case studies require you to apply the critical skills discussed in each chapter and give you training through practical learning situations.

ABOUT THE AUTHORS

David J. Lill has a combined 35 years of professional sales, sales training, and teaching experience. He taught selling and marketing classes at Baylor University, Belmont University and New Mexico State University. He earned his Ph.D. degree in Marketing from the University of Alabama. Dr. Lill is also a business consultant specializing in sales, advertising, and communications skills development. He currently conducts seminars and training courses on sales and marketing related topics. His relationship selling model is being successfully used by companies throughout the country in a wide variety of industries including insurance, telecommunications, real estate, publishing, banking, hospitality, chemical, and automotive..

Dr. Lill is the founder and president of DM Bass Publications through which he wrote, published, marketed, and sold his highly acclaimed textbook, *Selling: The Profession*, now in its 6th edition. He owned and operated an advertising firm in Louisiana where he developed and implemented advertising and marketing campaigns for a number of companies, including a local bank and department store.

Dr. Lill is the co-author of *The Handbook for Relationship Selling: Acquire Your Selling Focus* as well as *The Official Handbook for Health Club Sales: Strengthen Membership Sales in 30 Days*. In addition, Dr. Lill has published over 85 articles in various academic, trade, and professional publications. These include: *Selling Power, Journal of Advertising, Journal of the Academy of Marketing Science, Sales & Marketing Management, Business Topics, Nashville Business Journal*, and the *Journal of Pharmaceutical Marketing & Management*.

Dr. Lill has sold successfully for two large telecommunications companies, specializing in marketing information technology. In addition, Dr. Lill was the number one salesperson in Gold Unlimited, Inc and was a Shaklee distributor for over 25 years. He also worked for the *Milwaukee Journal* in their Milwaukee Advertising Laboratory Division. While there, he brought in prestigious clients such as General Mills, General Foods, and Nabisco and conducted marketing studies using Milwaukee as a test market for new product launches.

David lives in Nashville, TN with his wife, Martha. A housewife turned commercial real estate agent, she was the company's top producer. They are blessed to have two exceptional children, David, Jr. and Jennifer, and a grandson, Porter Andrew Brown. David is an engineer with TVA in Gallatin, TN and Jennifer is a published author, entrepreneur, and marketing consultant.

Jennifer K. Lill comes from a background of sales, authorship, and entrepreneurship. She has co-authored two books on professional selling, *The Official Handbook for Health Club Sales: Strengthen Membership Sales in 30 Days* and *The Handbook for Relationship Selling: Acquire Your Selling Focus*. In addition, she was the president and co-founder, along with business partner and mentor Tom Black, of the Tom Black Center for Selling Inc., located in Nashville, TN. While working with Tom, she edited and produced his widely acclaimed sales book, *The Boxcar Millionaire: Tom Black's Proven System of Sales Success*. The company was formed as a conduit for national sales training and publisher of business training products. Jennifer marketed and promoted Tom Black as a business leader, keynote speaker, and sales trainer through a personal branding strategy that she formulated. In addition, she spearheaded production of a professional website equipped with eCommerce, designed press kits for a national marketing campaign, conducted negotiations for all strategic partnerships, and oversaw advertising efforts.

While obtaining her degree in finance from the University of Alabama, Jennifer had the opportunity to sell for one of the most respected sales organizations in the country, *The Southwestern Company*. She sold educational products door-to-door by relocating and fully running the business from concept to sales, delivery, and customer service. She was the awarded

"Top First Year Dealer Award" and facilitated the recruitment and sales training of new recruits, as well as formulating and developing a system of lead finding and a unique delivery method.

Today Jennifer resides in Nashville, TN with her husband Will, their son, Porter, and their Jack Russell, Bandit. In addition to writing her own books—two with her father—Jennifer works as a free-lance ghostwriter and consultant for authors wishing to self-publish and promote themselves.

ACKNOWLEDGMENTS

Since one of our primary goals was to produce a text with real-world concepts and applications, we could not have been successful without the assistance of all those in sales who took time to share their thoughts, as well as a team of supportive friends and family. The insightful comments made by the sales professionals highlighted throughout the book add an important dimension to student learning. The success they have achieved in all areas of their lives through hard work and dedication, while upholding high standards of business ethics, should serve as a model for young, aspiring business professionals.

David Lill's Acknowledgements

Special thanks goes to four friends and business colleagues who have been true blessings to me: Deryl Bass, Jimmie Carter, Tom Hoek, and Emil Wanke—all consummate sales professionals, who each in their own way have had a profound effect on the way I think and the actions I take.

I want to thank Donald Silberstein, former Director of Business Development for the Bureau of Business Practice, Inc., for his efforts in providing the 150 cases that he made available for my use. Twenty-four of those cases were used as end-of-chapter cases in the 4th and 5th editions of this text. The 32 new cases in this 6th edition are the work of Dr. William Barnett. I cannot thank him enough for the exceptional case studies he has provided us.

My thanks and appreciation to the following professors, business associates, friends and colleagues. Their insightful suggestions, organizational ideas, and encouragement added significantly to the content of this textbook: Deborah Adams, Kingwood College (TX); Carol Anderson, United Tribes Technical College (ND); Carol Arnone, Frostburg State University; Erin Baca, University of Texas, El Paso; William Barnett, Barnett Copywriting & Consulting, Manchester, CT; Dennis Bechtol, Northwood University (FL); Vicki Befort, Arapahoe Community College (CO); Gary Benson, Southern Nazarene University; (KS); Nicholas Berning, Cincinnati State Community College (OH); L. Dean Bittick, East Central College; Dr. Kenneth Blanchard, founder of *Blanchard Training & Development*; Laurie Breakey, Pennsylvania State University; Frank Bingham, Bryant University; Bob Bricker, Pikes Peak Community College (CO); David Braun, L.A. Pierce College (CA); Miriam Burgos, Azusa Pacific University (CA); Laura Cailloux, Skagit Valley College; Glen Carwell, Kendall College (IL); Cindy Claycomb, Wichita State University; Jack Chism, Greenville College (IL); Dave Colby, Mid-State Technical College (WI); Kristi Cranwell, NCTA (NE); Dale Davis, Eastern New Mexico University; Patricia DeCorte, Delta College (MI); Bruce Dickinson, Southeast Technical Institute; Claude Dotson, Northwest College; Donna Duffy, Johnson County Community College; Kenneth DuVall, LDS Business College (UT); Terri Dwyer, Montana State University; Cinda Echard, Glenville State College (WV); Pat Ellsburg, Lower Columbia College (WA); Richard English, San Diego State University; Ken Erby, Northeastern Technical College (SC); David Fee, Utah Valley State College; Sandra Fields, University of Delaware; Bert Fisher, COO, Our Community Credit Union (WA); Olene Fuller, San Jacinto College (Pasadena, TX); Wil Goodheer, president of International University (Vienna, Austria); Shawn Green, Aurora University (IL); Carl Grunander, Weber State University (UT); Donna Gutschmidt, Lake Region State College; Dan Hall, East Central College; Michael Harstine, Grace College & Seminary (IN); Bob Hausladen, University of Louisville (KY);

Dan Heck, Kendall College (IL); Donna Heilig, Phoenix College; Tom Hoek, former president of Insurance Systems of Tennessee; Norm Humble, Kirkwood Community College; Denise Hunt, Allegany College of Maryland; Marie Johnson, Skagit Valley College; George Johnson, Marshalltown Community College; Carolyn Keck, San Jacinto College; David Kimball, Elms College (MA); Gary Kritz, Coastal Carolina University; Nancy Krumland, Southeast Community College (NE); Carsha Lapp, Northwest Technical College (MN); Desiree Cooper Larsen, Weber State University (UT); John Lavin, WCTC (WI); James Lollar, Radford University (VA); Chuck Loomis, Edmonds Community College (WA); Ruth Lumb, Concordia College at Moorhead; Shawna MaHaffey, Delta College (MI); Cyndy Mascola, Trumbull Business College (OH); Luis Martinez, Manager, Five Star Program, Chrysler Corporation; Dr. Morris L. Mayer, University of Alabama; Claudine McIntyre, Mt. San Antonio College (CA); Cheryl McCarthy, executive vice president, Surado Solutions; Becky Miles, Delaware Tech; Phillip Millage, Indiana Wesleyan University; Linda Mohr, Northwood University (FL); David Miller, Panhandle State University (TX); Dan Moore, President, The Southwestern Company; Elizabeth Murata, Edmonds Community College (WA); Gary Mucica, University of Massachusetts, Lowell; Kathleen Naasz, Centenary College (NJ); Judith Nickel, WCTC (WI); Philip Nitse, Idaho State University; Darren Olson, Bemidji State University (MN); Barbara Ollhoff, WCTC (WI); Steven Osinski, San Diego State University; Dr. Norman Vincent Peale, author of *The Power of Positive Thinking*; Nenita Perez, Guam Community College: Phillip M. Pfeffer, former president of Random House Inc.; Robin Peterson, New Mexico State University; Chris Plouffe, Florida State University; Bob Quade, Centenary College (NJ); Lyn Richardson, Ball State University; John Robbins, Winthrop University; Michael Powell, North Georgia College & State University; Tim Reese, Eastern Idaho Technical College; Les Rubenstein, St. Mary College; Luis Salas, Delta College (MI); Allen Schemmel,WSM-AM/FM Radio (Nashville); Gary Schirr, Radford University (VA); Bonnie Schultz, Northeast Community College; Holly Schrank, Purdue University; Denny Sheehan, Phoenix College (AZ); Kent Sickmeyer, Kaskaskia College (IL); Judy Signaw, Cornell University; Mary Lee Short, Santa Fe Community College; Robert Skalla, Blackhawk Technical College; Pat Swarthout, Central Lakes College (MN); Bob Tangsrud, University of North Dakota; Sandra Taylor, Athens Area Technical Institute (GA); Harry Taute, Utah Valley State College; Ray Thomas, Edith Cowan University, Perth, Australia; William Youngs, SUNY College at Cobleskill (NY); Kevin Ward, Augusta Tech College (GA); Patricia Watson, Mid-State Technical College (WI); Carolyn Waits, Cincinnati State Community College; Emma Watson, Arizona State University; Sandy Weaver, Athens Technical College (GA); Brian Williams, Southeast Tech Institute (SD); Amy Wojciechowski, West Shore Community College; Curtis Youngman, Salt Lake Community College (UT).

These individuals warrant a special thank you:

Gladys Hudson, former vice-president of Success Motivation in Waco, TX. She was my original mentor, editor and creative inspiration for many ideas in this textbook.

My family: To my wonderful wife, Martha – the love of my life! And my two remarkable children: David Jr., you have made me so proud—what a phenomenal man you have become. And Jennifer—what a daughter and precious mother to our grandson, Porter! She is my co-author and editor-in-chief of the 4th, 5th, and 6th editions! There is no way this book could have been completed without their love and support!

Jennifer Lill's Acknowledgements

To my father, Dr. Lill – Dad, thanks for giving me the opportunity to work on the various book projects with you and hone my writing and editing skills. And my deepest gratitude for your love and belief in me!

To my mother, Martha – Mom you are my best friend and sounding board for all things big and small. I love you more than you could ever know.

To my husband, Will – I love you! Thanks for giving me your unconditional support and being my biggest fan.

To my son, Porter – You are the best thing that's ever happened to me. You've made my life so full of joy. Every day is an adventure with you.

To my brother and sis-in-law, Dave and Amber – I love you guys so much!

Appreciation also goes to Dean Barry Mason, Dean of the School of Commerce and Business Administration at the University of Alabama, and to Dr. David Heggem, Dr. Lew Silver, and Dr. Kim Campbell of the University of Alabama.

Knowing is not enough; we must apply.
Willing is not enough; we must do.

-Johann Wolfgang von Goeth

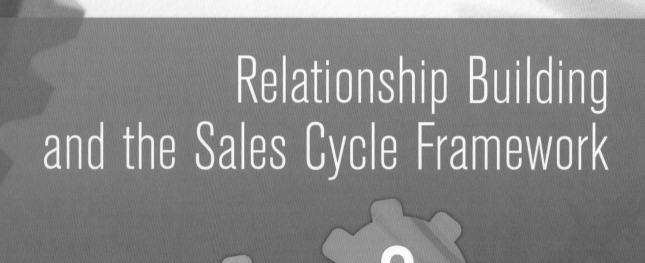

Relationship Building
and the Sales Cycle Framework

Part 1

Chapter 1 discusses the consultative nature and problem-solving approach to professional selling and details the characteristics that successful salespeople possess. Relationship selling is interactive, involves two-way communication, encourages prospect participation, employs empathy, and promotes a win-win environment. Today's style of selling favors building close and trusting long-term relationships. Positioning yourself as a consultant creates a partnership with customers. You are peers working to solve problems together.

You gain a better understanding of the complete selling situation and the problems it generates by breaking the sale into its basic tasks. There are several steps to achieving a successful sale. An eight-step sales cycle is introduced in chapter 2 and explained in detail in chapters 7 to 14. It makes sense that if you understand what the steps are in the Sales Cycle Framework for Relationship Selling, and what is required to make each step a successful endeavor, then you will become a professional in selling much quicker than those who are simply stumbling through the process trying to figure it out. The chapters included in this section are:

1. A Career in Professional Selling
2. Relationship Selling

CREATE THE SALES EDGE
Get focused, and you can...

CHANGE is often desirable, frequently necessary, and always inevitable.

REMEMBER...only you can give yourself permission to approve of you. Free your mind from negative thinking.

ENVISION yourself as a success. What you think about, you become.

ATTITUDE does determine your altitude. It is what's inside that makes you rise.

THE right angle to solve a problem is the try-angle.

ELIMINATE failure as an option, and progress naturally occurs.

THE best is yet to come. Yesterday's impossibilities are today's possibilities.

HAVE your dreams. They are the stuff great people are made of. Reach for the stars, but keep your feet on the ground.

EXTRAORDINARY desire and persistence drive ordinary people to achieve great things. Achievers are not extraordinary people.

SEVEN days without laughter makes one weak.

A smile is the shortest distance between two people.

LISTEN twice as much as you talk. You have two ears and one tongue.

ENCOURAGING feedback is a process for learning about your impact on those around you.

SUCCESS is the progressive realization of worthwhile, predetermined, personal goals.

EXCUSES are for losers. Winners have ways. May we all find the way.

DETERMINE never to give up. It's when things seem worse that you must not quit.

GOALS are dreams with a due date.

EXPECT the best of yourself. Be somebody special. The best never consider success optional.

Chapter 1

A Career in Professional Selling

Learning Objectives

- Appreciate the role of selling in our economy.

- Understand the purpose of personal selling.

- Recognize the different types of sales jobs and the requirements for success in each.

- Identify the personal characteristics that are needed for success in a selling career.

- Examine professional selling as a viable career opportunity.

Use This Page for Taking Notes

Everybody Sells

Countless daily interactions between people involve the act of selling. Some of them are universally recognized as selling: Retail salespeople sell you clothes, furniture, or cameras; an auto dealer sells you a car; and your insurance agent sells you a policy. In fact, a company is not in business until somebody makes a sale.

However, many other common transactions not typically recognized as selling involve the same skills, goals, and behavior patterns that professional salespeople use: Waiters may sell you on trying a new entrée or getting dessert; politicians try to convince constituents to vote for them or persuade other politicians to join them in promoting certain projects; celebrities sell themselves and their ideas of what is beautiful and hip through reality television and social media; and family members influence decisions such as where to live, who will use the family car on Friday night, whether to borrow money for a vacation, and even what to fix for dinner.

In other words, *you are already selling*. You are selling yourself, your ideas, and your desire for cooperation and companionship to almost everyone you engage in anything more than the most casual conversation.

Partnerships, maintaining customer relationships, strategic alliances, social networking, and global strategies are more than mere words to sales organizations today. They are the tools with which winning strategies are fashioned. Competitiveness among the world's major corporations will only continue to grow, and using yesterday's sales strategies is dangerous and increasingly ineffective as global competitors battle each other.

The latest and best marketing and sales practices are essential in gaining new markets and defending those you currently serve, whether that means checking in with customers and prospects through Facebook and Twitter or implementing an entire social media sales structure through group selling sites like Groupon.com and LivingSocial.com. A true sales professional does not succeed on the merits of basic personality traits or skills alone, but on the ability to handle change, to harness technology, and to respond to customers' evolving needs. The sales profession must rise to the challenge because, as hotel great Conrad Hilton said, "Success seems to be connected with action. Successful people keep moving."[1] Successful salespeople must keep growing and moving forward.

It is crucial to understand the business world today and know what challenges customers face, so you can truly become a *solutions provider*. Sales professionals demonstrate their value to customers by providing productive information and helping solve problems.

Understanding global strategies is essential in today's competitive marketplace.

The Value of Salespeople

New and innovative products and services are never accepted automatically. Neither individual nor business consumers can keep up with all the innovations that become available. So how do businesses expect to keep up with significant developments just in their own fields? They rely on salespeople!

A salesperson's job is to identify customer needs, determine ways those needs could be met by the products or services they offer, and then provide that information to the customer. They also work in the other direction, by identifying customer needs that cannot be satisfied by their current product line and communicating those needs to their company for consideration in the development of new products. Salespeople who consistently bring an implicit sales approach to their work build trust and loyalty with customers and become an invaluable resource to their company.[2] Therefore, they are facilitators of information that keeps them and their customers competitive. Sales is the most important job in any organization.

Compensation Potential

Because of their vital role in business, salespeople are among the best-paid employees of a company. More salespeople earn above $100,000 annually than persons in any other profession.[3] According to an annual survey of telesales representatives, the average salary falls at $65,000, with a total compensation of $119,000.[4] And according to other studies on pay for sales and marketing positions, product managers in sales positions have an average base salary of more than $98,000.[5]

These are just averages—some salespeople make less, while some make considerably more. Salespeople are the catalysts of the economy. They are responsible for keeping goods, services, and ideas flowing.

Importance of Sales Training

In today's exceedingly competitive environment, all kinds of companies provide continuing sales training on a regular basis—and many of these companies spend considerable amounts of money for training. For example, Kodak spends more than $20 million a year sending people through its courses at its Marketing Education Center. The reason is simple: Kodak sees sales training as the basis for winning all future battles.

Sales training as preparation for the future isn't an option—it is an imperative. According to Simon Bartley, CEO of UK Skills, neglecting to train today will lead to a decline in economic growth tomorrow. This means companies must see the importance of building up each individual salesperson, for the good of the entire organization. "On the ground is where skills allow an individual to achieve their goals of having a better quality of life and a real sense of personal achievement," says Bartley. In today's competitive market, companies cannot cut corners and expect to have the same results as their better-trained competitors. Training is not just a good way to stay competitive; it can serve a bigger purpose by boosting your company's bottom line.[6]

In the past, some companies viewed extensive training as an *expense*, which if not properly planned and budgeted for, may be true. However, today's corporations properly view sales training as an *investment*, and adequate training generates a desired return in the form of increased gross and net profits as well as improved cash flow.[7] Companies know that it is essential to spend money on training productive salespeople who will be long-term assets to the organization. In a recent study by the Society for HR Management, the hiring of unsuccessful salespersons is estimated to cost companies $20,000 for intermediate positions, $100,000 for senior management, and $300,000 for sales representatives, figures that include both the hard and soft costs of recruitment, training, and lost-opportunity costs.[8] As you can see, salespeople are very costly to replace. A well-trained salesperson is indispensable!

After spending large amounts of money and devoting months to training, companies have made a significant investment in each salesperson. Productive salespeople are eager to receive this training because they know that learning never stops, and their companies are equally interested in their continued growth. Sales training should not be seen as an insult. We are all simply most comfortable selling what we understand. By providing intensive hands-on training programs, companies build confidence in their sales force, enabling them to make superior product presentations. This ability also shows customers that they are dealing with a product expert who knows how to solve their problems by providing educated solutions.[9]

The Positive Nature of Selling

The difficulty with recruiting talented new salespeople is made more challenging, particularly for those firms who seek college graduates, because many college students have historically held less than positive perceptions and attitudes toward selling as a career. Surveys taken in the past have indicated that many college students see sales jobs as involving too much travel, interfering with one's home life and leisure time, a frustrating type of work, and requiring certain personality styles to be successful.

Why do these negative perceptions exist and persist? It may be due to the fact that many of us have had little opportunity to observe career salespeople at work. Our primary contact with salespeople has been with grocery store checkers, retail salespeople (many of whom have been put on the floor with too little sales training), and the telemarketing reps who call you in the middle of dinner. Unfortunately, these are the models we see when we think of sales, and consequently many tend to view sales as a job to accept if nothing better is available rather than an exciting career option.

More accurate information and education today is helping to improve attitudes toward sales as a career. Students responding to recent surveys now support the view that selling is more challenging and prestigious, requires creativity, offers career opportunities, fosters increasing integrity, and provides better financial incentives than did students in earlier studies.[10]

An increasing number of sales managers who recruit at colleges and universities are pleased with the caliber of young men and women they find. They recognize that recruiting students from college can uncover outstanding sales talent. "Get 'em while they're young" is the motto of today's college recruiters.[11] Students may not be as streetwise as someone with years of experience, but they tend to be highly technologically proficient. They also have an abundance of energy and enthusiasm, and can be hired before they develop bad habits. And because so much of today's recruiting efforts are done online, more and more young adults are attracted to careers in sales due to the convenience of online applications.

An understanding of the personal characteristics that a career in professional selling actually requires should dispel any outdated myths an individual may possess. Four areas of your personality are involved:

Personal Integrity. Continued success in sales requires the highest possible ethical standards for dealing with prospects, established customers, and your own company. A salesperson who lies or deceives customers to complete a sale is soon out of a job because customers do not place repeat orders and prospects soon get the word that this person is not to be trusted. An outstanding salesperson has high values and always operates in the most ethical manner.

Personality Structure. Sales is a demanding career, which is why you must have a positive self-image, and a persevering spirit. A person who is unable to accept the reality that not every prospect becomes a client will be devastated by failures and feel an overwhelming sense of personal rejection. The persistent myth that salespeople are arrogant, overbearing, and excessively aggressive contradicts reality. Successful salespeople are, instead, highly interested in other people and their needs and eager to be of real service to prospects and clients.

Personal Relationships. Salespeople are in an excellent position to attain status and recognition in the community. They are recognized as productive, capable professionals. You are not required to pretend, to conceal your own personality or needs, or to become a doormat for customers. Success in professional selling does not call for assuming an inferior position socially, psychologically, or financially. The most successful salespeople find that their customers become friends with whom they form lasting personal relationships. Companies can spend millions on customer relationship management systems to monitor customer retention and defection, but a vigilant salesperson can just as effectively use the personal touch to solve a problem and keep customers from leaving.[12]

Personal Abilities. Success in sales requires high levels of intellect and developed skills. You must be able to understand—sometimes quickly and almost intuitively—a customer's business needs and problems. Salespeople must interpret those needs and suggest viable solutions even if customers themselves do not have a clear picture of their own needs or cannot verbalize those needs clearly. You need a broad knowledge of the field in which you operate, and you must understand people and how to relate to them positively. The development of these skills requires not only intelligence but also continuous training, the willingness to be flexible and adapt to change, and the ability to grow beyond preconceived beliefs in an ever-changing sales world.[13]

The Basics of Personal Selling

How do you define the type of personal selling which forms the basis of this book? A comprehensive definition follows:

> **Personal Selling** is the process of ***seeking*** out people who have a particular need, ***assisting*** them to recognize and define that need, ***demonstrating*** to them how a particular service or product fills that need, and ***persuading*** them to make a decision to use that service or product.

This definition is broad enough to include any type of selling in which you may engage. It describes the commercial aspect of selling a product or service, as well as the process used to solicit funds for charitable organizations or enlist leaders for youth organizations. It also includes the activities of athletic coaches, political parties, clergy, and personnel officers in all kinds of organizations.

Because every sales situation is unique, your career in sales is an exciting and demanding one in which every day brings opportunities to develop new skills and sales strategies and ways to refine existing ones. The potential for personal and professional growth never ends. Because different prospects have varying needs, interests, ability to pay, and authority to make decisions, selling is different in every situation—and this constant change creates new possibilities and increased income potential.

Salespeople are Made, not Born

Too many people involved in selling have not attempted to learn the basic skills needed for success in the profession. They are quick to throw in the towel, claiming that they weren't born to be salespeople. They can be called "90-day wonders" because after 90 days they wonder why they ever got into the sales business. On the other hand, professional salespeople read books, take courses, ask questions, study the techniques of successful salespeople, work hard for their customers, and continually strive to outperform themselves.

"Let's close this sale before recess is over."

Selling requires a working knowledge of psychology, sociology, communication, and persuasion. It is not a natural process to close a sale. It is a skill to be learned, just like anything else. Even experienced salespeople can fail if they get to the point where they think they know it all. Success in selling is a constant learning process. You must always be a student of your profession. Successful salespeople are made, not born, and they are made with concentrated attention, repeated practice, sincere desire and goal-directed action.[14]

Exhibit 1.1 illustrates the ongoing debate—*Can selling be taught?* We are all like computers in that we are only as good as we have philosophically, emotionally, and intellectually programmed ourselves to be. Becoming a master salesperson takes time and effort. Even the best salespeople continually adapt and refine their professional skills throughout their careers.

Salespeople: Can selling be taught?

Absolutely! Josh Hinds, founder of BusinessNetworkingAdvice.com, says that while it is true that getting out of your shell and calling on prospects comes easier to some people, that doesn't mean that anyone who's willing to learn and model what other effective salespeople do can't also get similar or better results. There are countless introverted personalities who have learned to become highly effective sales professionals.[15]

Selling is definitely an art for many successful salespeople, but it is also a skill that must be honed and practiced. Someone who may not be a natural at selling can be successful with diligent and persistent study and training.[16] As the old saying goes, "you get out what you put in." The same is true for honing your sales skills. Everything for the most part can be learned. The question is if you are willing to put in the time and effort necessary to make sales a successful career.

Advantages of a Sales Career

The once-popular "Wide World of Sports" television program promised the viewer "the thrill of victory, the agony of defeat." This thrill of victory makes sales an exciting and satisfying career, but the thrill comes not just from earning the monetary rewards or beating out the competition. Those are actually minor parts of the satisfaction of successful selling.[17]

The true victory you will enjoy as a successful salesperson consists of satisfying higher personal needs.[18] Maslow's Hierarchy of Needs—as shown in Exhibit 1.2—has special significance for you as a professional salesperson.

In the beginning, salespeople concentrate on supplying their lower-order needs: earning a living, providing security for themselves and their families, and being accepted socially by their peers. As they satisfy these basic needs, salespeople can concentrate on the higher-level needs: self-acceptance (a positive self-image), making a contribution to community life, and self-actualization (becoming all one can be; knowledge and achievement for their own sake).

ΔExhibit 1.2

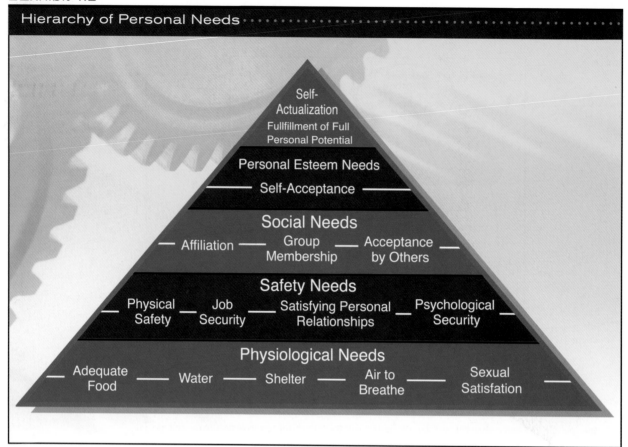

Hierarchy of Personal Needs ···

Self-Actualization
Fullfillment of Full Personal Potential

Personal Esteem Needs
Self-Acceptance

Social Needs
Affiliation — Group Membership — Acceptance by Others

Safety Needs
Physical Safety — Job Security — Satisfying Personal Relationships — Psychological Security

Physiological Needs
Adequate Food — Water — Shelter — Air to Breathe — Sexual Satisfation

A Sense of Independence and Variety

A sales career frees you from a mundane daily routine. Salespeople are likely to work in a variety of places and deal with prospects who have widely different personalities. What works with one prospect may antagonize another. Consequently, they must always be aware of every element of the environment and adjust quickly. *Selling is never boring.*

Salespeople can exercise a greater measure of control over their time and activities than many other professionals. Sales is not a nine-to-five job. The hours are quite flexible, long one day and short another. Because their day-to-day sales activities are not usually structured for them, they must also be self-starters and stay motivated.

Opportunities for Advancement

Effective salespeople are not forced into one career path. Almost any option for career advancement is open to those who are motivated to be successful and seek advancement. Exhibit 1.3 illustrates a potential career path for a highly motivated salesperson. As you move up the corporate hierarchy, the various options require a different blending of personal skills and characteristics. As a result, there is no guarantee that a successful salesperson will also make a successful manager. In fact, many talented salespeople actually refuse promotion to higher managerial positions. They simply love what they do and can often earn more money selling than they could by moving into a middle-management position.

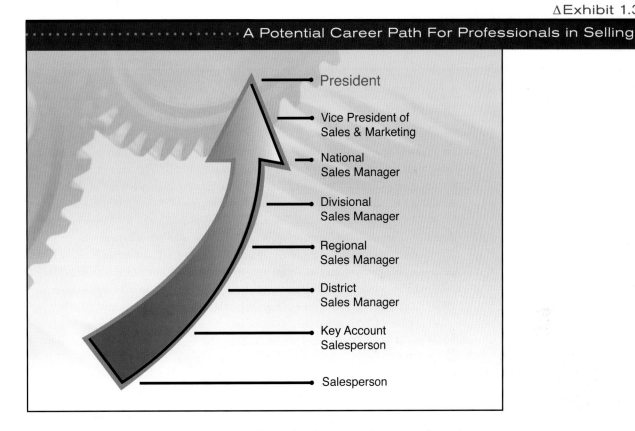

A Potential Career Path For Professionals in Selling

- President
- Vice President of Sales & Marketing
- National Sales Manager
- Divisional Sales Manager
- Regional Sales Manager
- District Sales Manager
- Key Account Salesperson
- Salesperson

Entrepreneurship. Sales is an ideal career for those who plan to one day own and run their own businesses. No business can survive without a viable marketing organization. An owner or chief executive who has been involved in sales truly understands this part of the business and is in an excellent position to launch and manage a new enterprise successfully. An entrepreneur can find people who understand manufacturing and finance, but the sales and marketing staff must share the founder's dream if the concept is to reach fruition.

Promotion to Sales Management. A sales manager may have either limited or extremely broad duties. The first step into sales management often consists of supervising two or three other salespeople— monitoring their activities, providing field training through joint sales calls, and recruiting additional sales representatives while continuing personal sales activities. More comprehensive sales management positions involve managing an entire local, regional, or nationwide sales division. Such a position might include budgeting, planning for sales training, sales promotion, and recruiting, in addition to executive duties and status in the company.

Top Management Positions. Sales experience makes an executive a valuable member of the management team. Although chief executive officers (CEOs) have traditionally come from the financial and legal ranks, companies are increasingly tapping into the sales and marketing departments to find their leaders. Organizations are looking for CEOs who are not only good leaders of people and have good strategic minds, but also have good interpersonal skills and the ability to carry out an initiative.[19] Many skills used in selling closely resemble those needed in top management. Both jobs require great people skills. It is important in both positions to maintain control under stress, to recognize opportunities and threats, and to locate, and analyze vast amounts of information. Exhibit 1.4 explains the increasing awareness of just how critical sales experience has become for the leader of a corporation.

The head of a forward thinking company simply must have intimate knowledge of specific sales methodologies to understand how to make improvements, and ultimately, increase the company's bottom line.

ΔExhibit 1.4

The CEO—A Company's Best Salesperson ·

As CEOs become more removed from the daily operations of their companies, they also become disconnected from the source of their companies' livelihood—sales and the processes used to generate them. "A CEO in a fast-growing company might not be able to disappear, if the CEO wants to keep the company on a high growth curve," says James L. Horton in his essay, "CEO Visibility in a Post-Bubble World."

A CEO can never stop being a salesperson—the best one in the company, in fact—in order to sustain profitability and secure future profits. However, it is also the CEO who sets the example for the rest of the company by focusing on what is most important.

If profitability is most important, then selling must be the CEO's focus. Since selling is the key to generating profits, the CEO must be actively engaged in the process. The CEO is the person who leads everyone by selling them—from employees to clients to stockholders.

While many CEOs have used their selling skills to build their companies into successful businesses, not every CEO is or has been a salesperson. As difficult as it is for a person in this position of power to admit, choosing to acknowledge what he or she does not know opens the door to acquiring the knowledge to become an effective salesperson. Just like anyone new to the company's sales department, the CEO may need training in the company's sales process as well.

A CEO must be intimately acquainted with how a firm's most important objective—achieving, sustaining and increasing profitability—is accomplished! By learning and utilizing an effective sales process, CEOs can lead by example, directly affect revenue growth, and ensure a secure financial future for the company, its employees, and its shareholders.[20]

Security

Companies will always need salespeople. In fact, though jobs in other sectors are still hard to come by in the current economic situation, sales personnel jobs appear to be among the first to have recovered from the poor performing years of 2008 and 2009.[21] Ambitious salespeople are eagerly sought, and most organizations provide excellent rewards and special treatment for their top sales performers. They know that quality salespeople who become dissatisfied can easily go to work for a competitor and possibly take their established customers with them.

Because salespeople are usually paid according to performance, you can directly affect your own income by deciding how much time and effort to invest in the job. Thus, your security comes from your own personal decisions about how hard and how efficiently you want to work. *Work, in many ways, is like money; if you are willing to expend enough of it, you can have almost anything you want.*[22]

Disadvantages of a Sales Career

Like any other profession, selling has some drawbacks and reasons why it is not right for everybody. The same qualities that some may see as advantages to a career in selling are in fact distinct disadvantages to others. Some people view a fixed salary as more secure than a commission-based income dependent entirely upon their direct performance in a given time period. Some see the fluctuation in the economy as a deterrent to venturing into sales and would rather their own financial well-being not be based on the stability of the global economic climate. Others dislike the irregular hours or the traveling around to meet clients that salespeople see as the variety that gives spice to their lives. Still others prefer a line of work that doesn't require as much initiative or creative energy in order to get the job done.

Probably the greatest problem faced by every salesperson is handling rejection. Not every sales presentation produces a sale. Not every prospect needs the service or product, and an ethical salesperson never presses for an order from a prospect whose needs will not be met by that product. No salesperson can ever be 100 percent successful in closing sales, even when the prospect truly needs the product or service. The best salespeople learn quickly that rejection is not directed toward them personally. Prospects who do not buy are rejecting the product or service—not the salesperson.

Not every presentation leads to a sale.

The decision seldom has anything to do with the salesperson's worth as a human being. Even the occasional prospect who reacts negatively to a salesperson does so as a result of the prospect's personal opinion—an opinion that may be colored by prejudice or completely unfounded. Rejection is not proof that the salesperson is in some way unworthy or inadequate. Salespeople who cannot separate their own personal worth from the product they sell may become too paralyzed by fear to approach another prospect because they face a renewal of rejection.

Classification of Sales Jobs

Sales jobs are so diverse that they fit a wide variety of personal needs and interests. Variety exists from industry to industry. The responsibilities of a salesperson who calls on large manufacturing companies to create awareness of computer systems for production-control are vastly different from those of the real estate salesperson who sells homes to families. Sales careers vary within industries as well. For example, the residential real estate salesperson is in a different world from that of the real estate developer who puts together multimillion-dollar projects for shopping centers, office complexes, and industrial parks. As different as sales jobs may be, they all share some basic similarities:

- The need to understand the prospect's problem.

- The need for appropriate technical and/or product knowledge.

- The need for self-discipline to relentlessly execute a sales plan.

- The ability to translate product features into benefits that resolve the prospect's problem.

There are many ways to classify different types of sales jobs: Business-to-business (B2B), business-to-consumer (B2C), direct selling, indirect selling, or personal selling, to name a few. No matter how you label the different types of selling, they can be broken down into the same basic categories. Newer tools for selling may be introduced over time, but the categories remain fundamental. The classification format developed by Derek Newton is a standard model because of his empirical research with over 1,000 sales executives from manufacturing, wholesaling, retail, and service firms. Newton's model is presented here as our basis for the four types of selling found across this variety of industries.[23]

1. Trade Selling

The trade seller's primary responsibility is to increase business from present and potential customers through merchandising and promotional assistance. They usually deal with buyers who are resellers (wholesalers and retailers). Long-term relationships are important for success. In addition to delivering orders and replenishing inventory, this salesperson's tasks involve persuading the customer to provide additional shelf space, setting up product displays in the store, rotating stock as inventory is replenished, and perhaps conducting in-store demonstrations or distributing samples to customers. Companies usually do not encourage their trade sellers to conduct vigorous sales efforts. They are expected to generate increased sales by assisting the customer move a larger volume of inventory.

2. Missionary Selling

The missionary salesperson's task is largely one of educating those who ultimately decide what product the consumer will use. The most familiar example of the missionary salesperson is the drug detail salesperson who calls on physicians to introduce and describe the pharmaceutical company's products and persuade them to prescribe their medications for patients who could benefit from them. In addition to pharmaceutical firms, food and beverage manufacturers, transportation firms, and public utility companies employ missionary salespeople.

3. Technical Selling

A fast-growing class of salespeople is the technical specialist group, the engineers, scientists, and others with the technical expertise to explain the advantages of the company's product. These salespeople sell directly to the firms that use their products.

They are very important in such industries as chemicals and machinery. They act like management consultants in that they identify, analyze, and solve their customers' problems. In the past, technical specialists have been more concerned with explaining the product than with securing the order, but many decision-makers are now more knowledgeable about technology and more likely to respond favorably to the technical specialist. Consequently, many companies are teaching these salespeople basic selling skills to help them be persuasive in making presentations and closing sales.

4. New Business Selling

This type of salesperson seeks out and persuades new customers to buy for the very first time. They are extremely vital to firms putting their focus on sales growth. New business selling includes selling new products to existing customers or existing products to new customers. The characteristics discussed later in this chapter—perseverance, empathy, ability to ask questions, initiative, and resourcefulness—are vital to sales success for this category of salesperson.

Selling for a Manufacturer. Manufacturers' sales reps sell the products produced by the company that employs them. They might sell to other manufacturers, various marketing middlemen, or directly to consumers. Exhibit 1.5 lists five specific categories of salespeople and describes the content of their jobs.

Selling at Retail. The largest numbers of salespeople are employed in the various aspects of retail selling. A retail salesperson sells products or services to customers for their own personal use. They may be residential real estate brokers, retail store clerks, insurance agents, wireless sales consultants, or direct-to-consumer salespeople who hold group meetings, sell door-to-door, or over the Internet.

Several million direct-to-consumer salespeople represent hundreds of direct-selling companies such as Amway and Mary Kay. The Longaberger Company is a direct sales company founded as a family business with just five basket makers. After researching a variety of sales methods, founder Dave Longaberger realized that the best way to sell his baskets was to demonstrate their selling points face-to-face with customers. Today, Longaberger has 70,000 consultants throughout the U.S. and annual sales approaching $1 billion.[24]

The Order Taker Versus the Order Getter. The *order taker* simply responds to requests and the *order getter* is a creative problem solver. The salesperson whose work is described as order taking reacts to customers' expressed desires. Responsive selling jobs may be either inside or outside. Inside sales jobs include retail clerks in department stores and other retail establishments. By being helpful and pleasant, retail clerks may create a few sales, but they generally just assist customers in completing the purchase of goods they have already chosen. Outside order takers are route salespeople who mainly service retail clients to deliver orders or replenish inventory.

The order taker may engage in *suggestive selling*—that is, ask you to purchase an additional item. The next time you stop at a McDonald's drive-thru and the person asks in a barely discernible

Five Types of Salespeople

Account Representative—A salesperson who calls on a large number of already established customers in, for example, the food, textiles, apparel, or wholesaling industries. Much of this selling is low-key and there is minimal pressure to develop new business.

Detail Salesperson—A salesperson who, instead of directly soliciting an order, concentrates on performing promotional activities and introducing products. The medical detail salesperson, for example, seeks to persuade doctors, the indirect customers, to specify the pharmaceutical company's trade name product for prescriptions. The company's actual sales are ultimately made through a wholesaler or direct to pharmacists who fill prescriptions.

Sales Engineer—A salesperson who sells products for which technical know-how and the ability to discuss technical aspects of the product are extremely important. The salesperson's expertise in identifying, analyzing, and solving customer problems is another critical factor. This type of selling is common in the chemical, machinery, and heavy-equipment industries.

Industrial Products Salesperson, Non-technical—This salesperson sells a tangible product to industrial or commercial purchasers; no high degree of technical knowledge is required. Industries such as packaging materials or standard office equipment use this type.

Service Salesperson—A salesperson who sells intangibles, such as insurance and advertising. Unlike the four preceding types, those who sell services must be able to sell the benefits of intangibles.

Used with permission of *Sales & Marketing Management* magazine.

voice, "Would you like a Strawberry Sundae to go with your Big Mac and fries?" You are observing suggestive selling in action. And it works!

Order getting, or creative selling, requires ingenuity and the ability to generate demand for a product or service among potential buyers. The product may be tangible such as automobiles or real estate, or the product may be intangible such as investment services or advertising. Creative personal selling generally offers the greatest opportunity for high income because it demands the highest level of personal skill, dedication, and effort.

Attributes of Successful Salespeople

There is not one list of traits that accurately describes every successful salesperson. They are as diverse as members of any other profession. They include both extroverts and introverts—and all the degrees in between: Shy and outspoken, talkative and quiet. However, certain core characteristics seem to be present to some degree in most successful salespeople, despite the numerous ways individuals express those characteristics and adapt them to their own styles and purposes.[25]

Enthusiasm

Ralph Waldo Emerson said, "Nothing great was ever achieved without enthusiasm."[26] One of the most important characteristics in new salespeople is enthusiasm—but a distinction must be made between people who are enthusiastic about their product and those who are merely eager to take the prospect's money.[27] Enthusiasm in salespeople is based on a genuine belief in the product and a conviction that it will serve the needs of the prospect.[28] Such enthusiasm is communicated both verbally and nonverbally to the prospect in terms of your own personality. Enthusiasm may be expressed as calm, quiet confidence or as excited activity. However it is demonstrated, real enthusiasm is highly attractive and reassuring to prospects.

Empathy

Empathy, the ability to understand another person's concerns, opinions, and needs, whether sharing them or not, provides salespeople with the sales edge of being able to think and understand "with" the prospect during a sales call. Empathy is the ability to pick up on the subtle clues and cues provided by others in order to accurately assess what they are feeling. Empathy is not "sympathy." Intrinsic in sympathy is loyalty, which results in a loss of objectivity. Empathic salespeople recognize how others feel while at the same time viewing them in a dispassionate and objective manner. This critical quality helps you understand a prospect while maintaining your own identity, purpose and objectives.[29]

Empathy is most useful in the sales process for handling objections and midcourse changes by the prospect. Empathetic salespeople can sense changes in prospects and adjust their presentations accordingly. By careful listening, effective salespeople absorb prospects' reactions, generate an upbeat environment, and sell themselves to prospects. The combination of sincerity and compassion enables them to tailor the presentation to mesh precisely with the prospect's stated problems.

Goal Direction

The best salespeople stay focused on their goals through the course of their daily activities. They have an understanding of how personal sales goals and organizational goals are interrelated, and they work to make both objectives happen.[30] Goal-directed salespeople often respond positively to incentives such as money, prestige, recognition, and pride of accomplishment, which they see as tools they can use to reach their overall goals. When these incentives fit into their overall plan for achieving the goals that represent self-actualization for them, salespeople go all-out to win them.

Ability to Ask Questions

Good salespeople ask questions; poor ones just keep talking. You need to remain in control of the sales interview, and the person who is asking questions is the one in control. When you learn to ask the right kinds of questions, you will gain new prospects, discover valuable qualifying information, uncover the prospects' buying motives, and be able to anticipate most objections. Questioning is your best tool for keeping the interview on track and moving toward a successful close, while also giving the prospect the feeling of remaining in control of the situation.

The person asking the questions is in control.

Resourcefulness

Top salespeople are the ones who are most resourceful. On the spur of the moment, they can think of new ways to make an old point, new applications and creative uses for products, and unique reasons for a particular prospect to make a buying decision. They can think on their feet under pressure. For these people, resourcefulness is an automatic response, like a reflex. Resourcefulness comes from an agile and analytical mind and allows you to stay on the right side of the fine line between being just right and very wrong. In a sales situation, the right word or phrase clears away the fog and reveals the solutions. The wrong word or phrase is like putting a drop of ink into a glass full of water: It obscures everything!

Resourceful salespeople always seem to have at hand a barrelful of ideas, tactics, and strategies. Exhibit 1.6 highlights the thoughts of Tanis Cornell, AT&T Global Enterprise Manager at Network Appliance, in Addison, Texas. Tanis recognizes the importance of resourcefulness and creativity in a salesperson.[31]

The Power of Resourcefulness

Is professional selling a viable career choice for an ambitious person who wants to maximize earning capacity, use unique skills and talents, and enjoy the satisfaction of being personally productive? Tanis Cornell's answer is a resounding "yes."

"In today's competitive market," Cornell says, "many products, companies, and even salespeople start to look alike to the prospect. I look for men and women with the creativity to differentiate themselves from their competition. Much more emphasis is directed at keeping current customers happy and providing long-term solutions." Salespeople must not only excel at prospecting and finding that new customer, but also excel at building long-term relationships with existing customers.

"In my years as a salesperson and as a manager, I noticed one very interesting thing," states Cornell. "There are certain individuals, regardless of gender, that excel each and every year. You can change their compensation plan; you can move them to another job or another location; you can throw any number of challenges at them that would disturb the average salesperson; but for top performers, it doesn't matter."

Administrative Ability

Efficient self-management, especially the management of time, is essential to success in selling. Your most productive time is spent face-to-face with prospects. But you are also required to attend meetings, travel, wait, prepare for interviews, read, study, attend to paperwork, and conduct after-sale follow-up and service.

Salespeople must engage in a number of non-selling and administrative tasks. This means that only a small portion of their precious time can be spent in direct contact with prospects and clients. Efficient time management can make the difference between success and failure. Time and territory management is one of the most critical issues for salespeople today. According to a survey of more than 840 salespeople among companies with large sales forces, high-performing salespeople find ways to increase time with customers and maximize the effectiveness of their time spent on administrative duties. In a comparison of high-performing companies and low-performing companies, salespeople for the high-performers spent 40 percent more time with their best potential customers and 30 percent less time on administrative duties.

Do the high-performers have fewer administrative duties than the low-performers? No—but they do know how to manage their time better. "It may seem fundamental," says John Bremen of the Watson Wyatt sales force effectiveness consulting practice who conducted the survey, "but the way sales professionals allocate their time is critical—even a couple more hours per week on these key activities can make a real difference."[32]

Initiative

All great salespeople have a powerful, unrelenting, internal drive to excel. This intrinsic motivation can be shaped and molded, but it cannot be taught. This type of motivation is what keeps great salespeople with their head above water when others are sinking during tough economic times.[33] Successful salespeople are self-motivated. They are self-starters who exercise initiative. They do not wait to be told to prospect, to be assigned calls to make, or to be urged to end the presentation with a close. They see the work that needs to be done and take personal responsibility for doing it. Creative ideas that surface during a presentation must be implemented then and there—without taking time to ask the sales manager for advice. Salespeople who have self-confidence supported by solid product knowledge and belief in their own ability to succeed feel free to exercise initiative.

Perseverance

Setbacks often outnumber triumphs, and when this happens, salespeople must have reserves of strength and resilience to fall back on. Depending upon the type of sales activity and the product or service being marketed, the number of sales closed compared to the number of presentations made usually ranges from 5 percent to 50 percent or more. Salespeople need perseverance in several areas:

- The ability to keep going to another prospect no matter how many have refused to buy.
- The ability to make repeated presentations to the same prospect over a period of time.
- The ability to continue asking for an appointment to make a presentation until one is finally granted.

Consider the story of Richard Sutton, who as a young boy met Herbert Hoover while living in Hawaii. Hoover took a liking to him and advised him to become a lawyer, and Sutton followed his advice. Hoover later urged Sutton to run for state office as a representative of the Republican party, even though Hawaii was strongly Democratic. Richard ran and lost. Disheartened, Richard wrote Hoover asking for advice. Hoover offered him sound words of wisdom: Keep running until you win. Richard followed his mentor's advice, running a staggering twelve campaigns before he finally won. The lesson from the story is this: Tell yourself you will be patient, persistent and persevere until there is tangible progress.[34]

Pleasant Personality

The way to make a friend is to be one. The salesperson with a pleasant, outgoing disposition is remembered and favored. A key to forming a pleasant personality is to like people and genuinely enjoy knowing as many different kinds of people as possible. People respond to those who like them.

Department store entrepreneur J.C. Penney said, "All great business is built on friendship."[35] How do you build friendships in today's tough competitive sales climate? Find out what the buyer needs, then make every effort to deliver it. Ask yourself: "What would I do if I really wanted to be friends with this person?" The answer will tell you how to build a long-term relationship.

When you have a pleasant personality,
prospects want to do business with you!

SUMMARY

- Selling is a basic component of all human interaction. It involves discovering needs and providing products or services that satisfy those needs.

- Salespeople are among the highest-paid professionals and make the greatest impact on profitability and success for an organization.

- Partnerships, customer relationships, strategic alliances, empowerment, and global alliances are more than mere words to sales organizations today. They are the tools with which winning strategies are fashioned.

- Professional selling offers opportunities that involve a number of different skill levels and a wide diversity of activities.

- All the personality types can be successful in sales, but certain characteristics enhance the likelihood of success: Enthusiasm, empathy, goal direction, ability to ask questions, resourcefulness, administrative ability, initiative, perseverance, and a pleasant personality.

- Selling is a demanding career that offers substantial rewards and outstanding opportunities for personal achievement.

REVIEW QUESTIONS

1. In the sense that all persuasion is a form of "selling," name the types of situations in which you most frequently "sell." In which of these are you most often successful? If persuasion is an important part of selling, is selling also a form of leadership? Explain your answer.

2. What career limits are imposed on one who chooses sales? Illustrate.

3. Are salespeople born or made? Justify your answer.

4. Why is a feeling of rejection a problem for salespeople? Is this feeling an inevitable part of a sales career?

5. Describe the four broad classes of sales jobs and give examples of each.

6. In addition to securing orders for products, in what ways do companies depend upon salespeople?

7. What responsibilities belong to the salesperson after the order is signed? How does the discharge of these responsibilities affect the entire sales process?

8. Salespeople are interdependent with other individuals in their company. Why is this true in respect to the following factors: product changes, pricing, shipping, and competition?

9. Name some qualities that seem to be shared by most successful salespeople. How do these traits contribute to success? Can they be developed, or are they innate? Does this mean that a single type of personality style is required for success in sales?

ROLE-PLAY EXERCISES

The following role-play exercises help build teams, improve communication, and emphasize the real-world side of selling. They are meant to be challenging, to help you learn how to deal with problems that have no single right answer, and to use a variety of skills beyond those employed in a typical review question. Read and complete each activity. Then in the next class, discuss and compare answers with other classmates.

Role Play 1.1 – What Do Salespersons Think?

Pair up with another student whom you do not already know. Contact a salesperson who does NOT work in retail sales (that is, AVOID department stores, electronics stores, auto dealerships, etc.; consult the types of sales positions in Chapter 1) and arrange an interview. During the interview, ask the salesperson what sort of knowledge, skills, and personal characteristics contribute most to that person's success. How is success measured or determined? Ask, further, what are the greatest challenges or obstacles to success in that person's current position. How does the person try to deal with these challenges or obstacles? Feel free to follow up with additional questions.

In class, be prepared to role-play the results of your interview; at the very least, be prepared to discuss what you learned in relation to Chapter 1.

Role Play 1.2 – Who Are You, Really?

You will work individually on this role-play. Copy the brief survey below onto a separate sheet of paper. Rate yourself on each of the personal characteristics, and put the results aside.

Enlist the help of 5 friends outside of this class who know you reasonably well. On a separate sheet of paper for each, copy the brief survey below and ask each person to complete the survey about you. Assure them that you want an honest appraisal of your personal characteristics because you are trying to determine whether you are suited for a particular profession; do not mention sales or selling.

After all 5 persons have completed and returned the survey, compare the results to your own self-rating. Are there any discrepancies between your friends' ratings and your own? If so, how do you account for or explain them? Do the results confirm or weaken your confidence in pursuing a career in sales? Which personal characteristics do you think you need to work on to become more successful? Be prepared to discuss such questions in class or online.

Please rate the person who gave you this survey according to the following personal characteristics by circling the appropriate response. Since your friend will use the results to help determine whether he/she is suited for a particular profession, it is important that you be candid. When you are finished, return the completed survey to your friend.

1. Enthusiastic

Always	Usually	Seldom	Never

2. Empathetic, Able to Understand Others

Always	Usually	Seldom	Never

3. Goal-Directed

Always	Usually	Seldom	Never

4. Able to Ask Good Questions

Always	Usually	Seldom	Never

5. Resourceful, Creative

Always   Usually   Seldom   Never

6. Well Organized, Efficient

Always   Usually   Seldom   Never

7. Self-Motivated, Responsible

Always   Usually   Seldom   Never

8. Persevering, Determined, Tenacious

Always   Usually   Seldom   Never

9. Pleasant, Personable, Outgoing

Always   Usually   Seldom   Never

CASE STUDIES

The following case studies present you with selling scenarios that require you to apply the critical skills discussed in the chapter and give you training through simulation, role-playing, and practical learning situations. They are meant to be both engaging and challenging, and like the role-play exercises, don't have one right answer.

CASE 1.1—Whom Would You Recommend?

Imagine that you work for a professional recruiting firm that has been retained by a large electrical equipment-manufacturing corporation to recommend a new salesperson for the corporation's regional sales force. Your job as a recruiter is to select and pass along the résumé of the single applicant whom you judge most likely to succeed. You conduct your search under conflicting pressures: on the one hand, you have time to interview only three candidates; on the other hand, the one you recommend must be retained by the corporation for at least three months, or your firm will be required to return its fee.

1. Greg strikes you immediately as a go-getter. Upon entering your office, he strides confidently across the room, arm outstretched to shake your hand, while he looks you in the eye and announces how pleased he is to meet you. Before you can invite him to sit, he perches on the edge of the chair in front of your desk and launches into a list of reasons about why he is qualified for this job. As he talks, you become aware that he is pleasant, well dressed, outgoing, and very enthusiastic about working for your client. He has researched the company and has marshaled all of the factors in his background that make him a good match for the position. Although you haven't said much, you really didn't need to, since Greg has done a good job of anticipating your questions and concerns. After about 20 minutes, he asks if you need anything else and stands, thanking you as he leaves for such a pleasant interview.

2. Martha presents a somewhat reserved demeanor. Although pleasant and friendly, she is obviously nervous despite her impressive résumé. As you ask about her prior experience, she reveals that her last employer terminated her because she didn't meet her sales quota. Compelled to take a direct sales job in an office supply store because of her family's relocation to New Jersey, Martha claims that she never received significant product training or positive support from management when she couldn't produce. Nevertheless,

because of her previous success as a B2B (business-to-business) representative for a hardwood importing company, she feels that she would thrive in a similar B2B environment. She exhibits pride in telling you how she cultivated potential customers for as long as two years and how she always followed up with her repeat clients to make sure that their needs were being met. Before she leaves, she briefly summarizes her selling success in a B2B situation and hopes that her lack of technical knowledge won't hamper her being considered for this position.

3. Cynthia is an older applicant who wants to change careers. There is a direct, no-nonsense air about her as she explains why. For 17 years, she worked as a mechanical engineer for a major tool and die manufacturer, rising to the level of design supervisor. When her position was outsourced to a plant overseas, she found herself at a crossroads. Frankly, she was tired of working in a design lab with the same dozen people all day, and similar jobs in her field were becoming rare. Although she admits that she has no sales training whatever, she is hoping that her technical background will gain the attention of the company's sales manager. At the conclusion of her interview, she points out that working for the same company for 17 years testifies to her perseverance, dedication, and ability to work with others. You assure her that her application will receive every consideration.

With your own firm's fee on the line, which applicant will you recommend, and why?

Which applicant most closely approximates your personality and style, and why?

Case 1.2 – The Dejected Colleague

Mike was on a rampage. Having knocked over the water cooler in the copy room, he proceeded to kick in the front of one of the copiers. Hearing the commotion, Frank, his friend and colleague, burst through the closed door, finding Mike slumped over and in tears.

"Hey, buddy, what's the matter? What's wrong?" Frank asked, putting his arm around Mike's shoulder.

"I just can't take it anymore," Mike managed to choke out between sobs. "I'm a failure. I'm going to quit. I've failed my family and myself."

"Has anything in particular happened?" Frank knew that Mike had been in a sales slump, but he didn't know exactly what Mike was coping with.

"I've lost 2 big accounts. I can't take the rejection anymore," Mike sobbed. "And the long hours and travel are killing my family life."

"I understand," said Frank softly as Mike's sobbing subsided. "Here, let me help you clean up this mess. Then, let's go get a cup of coffee somewhere so we can talk about all this."

What should Frank say to Mike in the coffee shop? Mike is clearly having some problems with aspects of the sales profession in general. Are these problems the sort of thing that salespersons can reasonably expect to encounter? What should Frank help Mike call to mind that would get Mike back on the right track? How can Frank be empathetic without allowing Mike's dejection to continue to be overwhelming?

Chapter 2
Relationship Selling

Learning Objectives

- Understand the role of relationship selling in today's market and how it differs from past stereotypes of selling.

- Learn the steps in relationship selling and the purpose of each step.

- Compare and contrast relationship selling and the traditional sales model.

- Examine the usefulness of continuous quality improvement in a sales organization.

- Recognize how to build relationships through team selling.

- Understand the importance of relationships in today's multicultural world.

Use This Page for Taking Notes

Relationships: The Heart of Selling

The profound effects of the Internet and technology on professional selling are impossible to deny. Recent reports predict that online sales will increase at a 10 percent compound annual growth rate through 2015, when online sales in the U.S. will total nearly $250 billion, and yet the e-commerce revolution is not the most important change in sales trends.[1] There is a second revolution occurring—it is in the relationship selling process where the buyer requires advice and advanced expertise. It is here that face-to-face selling has been the most effective channel to the customer. Unless you sell a product that has only a local appeal, searching for leads in the phone book or advertising in the newspaper are becoming things of the past.[2] Even Internet sales companies, such as Charles Schwab and Dell Computer, have created face-to-face sales forces to reach the segments of their markets requiring complex customized products and services. Their "clicks-and-mortar" strategies rely on sales professionals who can create significant customer value by helping clients define their problems and design unique solutions. This new selling is all about value creation: *How the selling process itself can be used to create value for the customer.*

Relationship selling, in which sales professionals demonstrate not just a product's technical features, but how it can solve a business or consumer problem and save money, isn't a novel idea. The concept has been in discussion in marketing circles since the 1980s, and with the decrease in consumer confidence in these tough economic times, it is hard to imagine companies still not adopting this style of selling.[3] Positioning yourself as consultant and partner creates a more equal relationship with prospects and customers. The willingness and ability to meet each client's needs is the cornerstone of building partnerships. Prospects and customers want *business partners,* not *tennis partners.*

Build or Break a Relationship

Partnership is a positive word that makes customers feel that you are looking out for their best interests. The partnership formed between the buyer and seller is not a *legal* partnership. Rather it is a part of the continuous quality improvement process companies are implementing. Today's sales forces take time to get to know the customer's business situation, needs, cash flow problems, decision-making process, and the competitive environment. For customers, a buying decision usually means a decision to enter into a long-term relationship with salespeople and their companies. It is much like a "business marriage." They have a variety of options and choices open to them, including not buying anything at all. But when customers make a decision to buy from a salesperson, they become dependent on that sales rep. And since they have probably had unpleasant buying experiences in the past, they are very uneasy and uncertain about getting into this kind of dependency relationship.[4]

Exhibit 2.1 illustrates the key elements that can build or break this trust-bond relationship between buyer and seller. Relationship selling allows you to grasp a company's needs by putting yourself on the customer's side of the desk. *You are first a diagnostician.*

ΔExhibit 2.1

How to Build or Break a Relationship

Relationship Builders

1. Treat customers like lifelong partners.
2. Become a solutions provider.
3. Deliver more service than you promise.
4. Schedule regular service calls.
5. Develop open and honest communication.
6. Use the "we can" approach.
7. Take responsibility for mistakes made.
8. Be an ally for the customer's business.

Relationship Breakers

1. Focus only on making the sale.
2. Simply wait for a problem to develop.
3. Over-promise and under-deliver.
4. Wait for customers to call you.
5. Lie or make exaggerated claims.
6. Use the "us versus them" approach.
7. Blame somebody else. Knock a competitor.
8. Focus on your own personal gain.

Relationship salespeople create an information transfer, a support for client goals, and enthusiasm for their success. The top salespeople have escaped the *selling mentality* and let the customer tell them their needs. In the face of increased competition in the automobile market, Volkswagen has recognized the need to more fully address and cater to customers' specific needs. Marianne Nicholas, Volkswagen's Relationship Marketing Manager, states, "Our research shows that people looking for a new car now do the majority of their research on the Internet, with visits to showrooms more than halved, down from five to two on average. The challenge for us was to respond to this change and ensure our website is equipped to give buyers and owners the information they need at the touch of a button."[5] And that is the precise mentality that will insure a company's survival. It isn't always about who has the better product or best price, but who can best provide solutions to the customer on a consistent basis, and on their terms.

> To be a consultant rather than just a salesperson you have to be a creative resource, a value provider, and a friend to clients. The relationship salesperson works hard helping others succeed—not just helping them purchase. Unless you are willing to commit to excellence, consultation will not occur. Here are some key characteristics of relationship selling:
>
> • Discover and understand the customers' problems and needs.
>
> • Partner with your customers and become a valuable resource for information.
>
> • Demonstrate to customers how they can achieve their goals with your product or service.
>
> • Have a true conviction that your company, your product, and your services are the best for your customers.
>
> • Believe in yourself because a positive attitude makes it all work.

Relationship Selling Versus Traditional Selling

If you understand what the steps are in the *Relationship Cycle of Selling*, and what it takes to make each step a successful endeavor, then you will become a professional in selling much more quickly than those individuals who are simply stumbling through the process trying to figure it out. The sales cycle model in the actual face-to-face meeting between the salesperson and the prospect includes these four steps:

1. The Approach

2. Identifying Needs

3. Making the Presentation

4. Handling Objections and Gaining Commitment

Exhibit 2.2 contrasts the amount of time the relationship salesperson and the traditional salesperson spend in each step. You can see from the figure that the old pyramid model of selling has been turned upside down.[6] The 40 percent of the equation for the traditional model that used to be closing is now *building trust* in the relationship model. Meanwhile reassuring the customer and closing has shrunk to just 10 percent in the new model.

The relationship salesperson spends the vast majority of time in the first two steps, whereas the traditional salesperson exerts most of the effort and the majority of time on presenting features and trying to close. The goal is to learn how to communicate with your business partners and establish an alliance that is extensive in scope and relevant to the customer's own vision.[7]

Relationship Selling Versus Traditional Selling

Phases	Relationship Model of Selling	time spent in each phase	Traditional Sales Model	time spent in each phase
Approach	Building Trust (Rapport)	40%	Telling	10%
Identifying Needs	Probe, Ask Questions, and Listen	30%	Qualifying	20%
Making the Presentation	Sell Benefits	20%	Presenting Features	30%
Resistance and Gaining Commitment	Reassure and Close	10%	Closing Long and Hard	40%

Customers Buy Solutions

Technology helps open new markets, speeds communications between sellers and their prospects and customers, and frankly, creates a whole new set of problems that you can help clients solve. Customers can now conduct many of their transactions online and have little need for a salesperson that doesn't add value to the transaction. This requires a much more sophisticated and complex set of skills than those possessed by the traditional salesperson.

Low-end selling—which is essentially transaction processing and order taking—continues to shift away from traditional sales forces into the more efficient, cost-effective, and faster setting provided by online sales. But this doesn't mean that the Internet will replace the professional salesperson; selling is simply becoming more strategic. It's moving up the food chain, and the need for relationship selling is increasing. Your company may sell accounting services, office equipment, or design websites. However, that's really not what customers are buying—customers are trying to increase sales and improve efficiency. By demonstrating how you can help customers achieve the goals of their organization, you distinguish yourself from competitors. Selling is still about relationships, and people buy from people they like.[8] Order-takers will vanish, but creative salespeople who know that selling is about building long-term partnerships will flourish.

The Relationship Selling Cycle

A better understanding of the complete selling situation and the problems it generates may be gained by breaking the sale into its basic tasks. These steps are presented in a logical sequence, but *they are not necessarily chronological* and the order of the steps will vary. The ebb and flow of a sales interview defies attempts to package it into nice, neat compartments.

Regardless of account size or potential, certain predictable tasks must be performed. These tasks, such as identifying prospects and determining needs, may be called the steps in a sale or the *selling cycle*. When organized into a prescribed sequence they comprise an overall structure rather than a lock-step approach to selling. The eight basics of successful selling described in Exhibit 2.3 are the focus of chapters 7 through 14, and they represent your guide to a successful sales career.

ΔExhibit 2.3

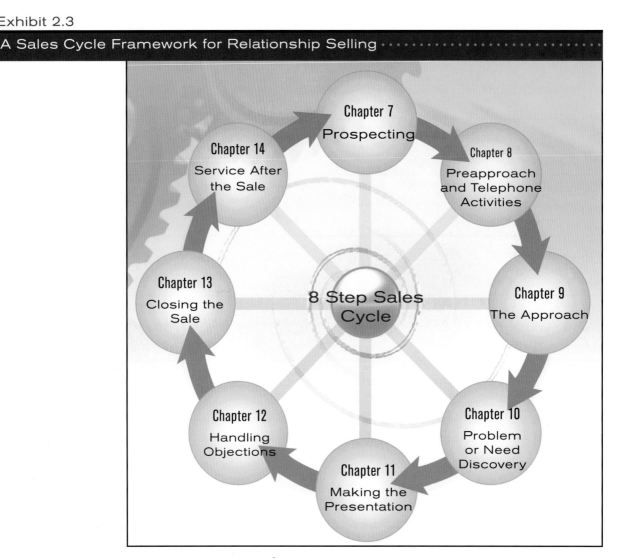

Phase One

Identifying Qualified Prospects. Prospecting is the process of searching for someone with a need for the product or service, the ability to pay for it, and the authority to make a buying decision. One of the first steps in the process of finding these qualified prospects is to review your current accounts to see who needs service, who might want to increase the quantity purchased, or who may buy new products for the first time. At the same time, survey your territory to identify new leads and find out information on the businesses in your area that might be interested in your product. The reason for this step is simple: sales professionals must study the people they want to approach.[9]

Planning Preapproach Activities. After you identify qualified prospects, establish a definite purpose for each sales call. To accomplish this, you must make an evaluation of your potential customers' needs and determine also who the decision-makers are in the companies you have studied. These activities equip you to interact with the customer and then develop an action plan and call schedule to set appointments.

Phase Two

Approaching the Prospect. Treat prospects as individuals and not as carbon copies of everyone else.[10] What happens during the opening minutes of the face-to-face encounter affects the success of the whole presentation. Some people simply do not thaw out immediately, and you must find icebreakers that help the prospect feel at ease with you. This is why you should spend time finding the prospect's comfort level. Most first-time meetings between salesperson and prospect produce an *egocentric predicament* arising from your fear of being rejected and the prospect's fear of being sold something that is not really wanted or needed. By redesigning your approach to selling, you can calm the prospect's fear of buying and reduce your own fear of selling.

Discovering Needs. During this step of the sales encounter, you and your client discover together whether the client needs or wants something that you can provide. Because the success of the whole process rests on this basic discovery, the relationship salesperson spends whatever time is necessary and asks questions to get to know the prospect's needs and problems. For this reason, one of your primary goals in every sales situation should be to create an atmosphere within which an act of trust can occur—to make a friend rather than a sale, a customer who has confidence in the integrity and ability of the salesperson, and confidence in the company and its product or service. You don't talk prospects into a sale; you listen them into a sale.[11]

Making the Presentation. Your evaluation of the prospect's situation should lead you naturally into the presentation of product benefits that fit the needs your client expressed. Every product or service has both features and benefits. A *feature* is any fact about the product or service, tangible or intangible. For example, a feature of a particular automobile is front-wheel drive. However, prospects want to know about benefits rather than features. The front-wheel drive feature is meaningless unless it satisfies some need, solves some problem, or provides some benefit to the prospective customer. The benefits of front-wheel drive might be explained in terms of ease of handling, safety, or some other performance quality that promises to satisfy the prospect's need.

Listen and take notes to discover needs.

Even better than showcasing the value of the product is to allow prospects to assess that value by discovering for themselves the benefits of owning it. The relationship salesperson is customer-oriented. A prospect does not buy without being certain that what you are saying is true. That is why you do not create sales; rather, people buy based on their own expectations. *No one likes to be sold.* They like to see the value of what is being presented, and then they make their own buying decisions based on their own assessment of whether or not your product satisfies their needs.

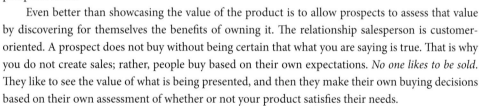

> "In professional selling, as in medicine, prescription before diagnosis is malpractice."

Exhibit 2.4 illustrates how the power of expectation works. The salesperson who holds confident, positive expectations closes far more sales than the one who expects rejection.

ΔExhibit 2.4

The Power of Expectation ···

Expectation is powerful. Three mess hall sergeants received large shipments of dried apricots. At first, they were all dismayed because they didn't see how they could ever use that many apricots. They each dealt with the problem differently. The first one "knew" no one in his outfit wanted apricots; so he cooked a large pot of stewed apricots, stuck a ladle in the pot, and set it at the end of the serving line. Sure enough, at the end of three days, his negative expectations were fulfilled; he still had most of the apricots. The second one adopted a more positive approach. He also cooked a large pot of stewed apricots; but he stood in the serving line with a big smile and a ladle in hand. "Let me serve you some apricots," he would say, as people came through the serving line. He disposed of more apricots than the first sergeant. The third sergeant decided to create a demand. He put up signs at the beginning and end of the serving line: "*Coming Tuesday: Apricots just like your Mother served. Your choice.*" On Tuesday at breakfast time, a big sign on the door announced: "*It's Tuesday! Mother's apricots are here!*" He had prepared stewed apricots and a mix of chopped dried apricots, raisins, and nuts to sprinkle on cereal. For lunch and dinner, he offered apricot fried pies, baked apricot pies, and apricot bread. His shipment of apricots disappeared quickly.

Handling Objections and Gaining Commitment. Now is the time to verbally clarify and confirm what both you and the client will do to make the solution work. This part of the overall process helps to avoid misunderstandings by bringing any that exist out into the open so they can be handled. Each clarification and confirmation adds weight to the case in favor of a positive decision. As shown in Exhibit 2.5, when the scale of decision tips far enough toward the positive side, the prospect can, and does, say yes. When that happens, everyone wins—the client, you, and your company. Relationship selling is a matter of presenting positive benefits that respond to a need, use, and value. Selling in this manner reduces your need to deal with resistance, answer objections, or haggle over price. Since the client has been an active participant throughout, the commitment and close should be the natural conclusion to a successful sales interview.

ΔExhibit 2.5

The Scale of Decision ···

Selling positive benefits tips the scale of decision...

Objections
Excuses
Resistance

Need
Use
Value

Phase Three

Service After the Sale. The final phase of relationship selling is service after the sale. "Whether you call it customer retention, account management, relationship management, or just staying in touch, developing a strategy so that you don't lose the customers or clients you have is vital to the success of any business—especially now," says Rhonda Abrams, president of The Planning Shop, publisher of books for entrepreneurs.[12] Service, service, and more service is what counts and gives you a competitive edge. Plenty of satisfied customers do not come back unless you create some kind of trust-bond relationship. Ultimately, you should look at customer satisfaction as an economic asset just like any other asset of the company. Service after the sale must be viewed as another essential step within the sales cycle.[13] Creating customer satisfaction is an income-producing endeavor. Too many salespeople perform service mechanically, without thinking of the impact their actions have on customers. Clients must sense that you truly care about them. Service after the sale is your way of expressing appreciation for their business. Service makes the difference and is as important as the quality of the product.

Continuous Quality Improvement

There has been so much written on Total Quality Management that some have dismissed it as merely a theory that is discussed because it sounds good. But to ignore the underlying principles of TQM would not be sensible. The scope of a typical TQM program covers three main areas: 1. The quality system, 2. The process of continuous improvement, and 3. The development of the staff involved.[14] TQM is an essential building block for relationship selling, and the principles have practical implications for salespeople.[15]

How does TQM fit into relationship selling? Most organizations have a strong strategic plan in place to achieve excellence and make sales. Where they struggle is in the *execution*. Organizations get the outcomes they seek only when they successfully hardwire excellence across all operational areas, and one way to achieve this is through implementation of Total Quality Management.[16] TQM has a customer orientation, and it is an outside-in approach to business. The center of all discussions is the customer; every one inside and outside the company is a customer. Continuous quality improvement is a philosophy, an overall style of management that focuses on customer satisfaction. Federal Express CEO Fred Smith states that, "We aim for 100 percent customer satisfaction and all FedEx employees must have an 'above and beyond' attitude when doing their jobs. The attitude of doing whatever it takes to serve the customers is reflected from top to bottom in the organization's structure; this kind of spirit is integral to the FedEx work culture."[17] But even before the customers can be serviced, Smith states that, "Employee satisfaction is a prerequisite to customer satisfaction."[18] Therefore, TQM not only focuses on fostering healthy relationships with customers, but also on building connections within organizations.

The list below highlights the main points of TQM that deal directly with fostering relationships and building lasting associations. While there are variations in the language and scope of TQM programs, it is possible to target these five principles that are especially relevant in the practice of relationship selling:

1. *Listen and learn* from your customers and your employees.

2. *Continuously improve* the partnership.

3. *Build teamwork* by establishing trust and mutual respect.

4. *Do it right the first time* to ensure customer satisfaction.

5. *Improve communication* in your own company to broaden the utilization of your company's resources. Everybody is involved in the relationship.

Service Quality

What does an organization have to do to provide exceptional service quality and how does the salesperson fit into the process? First, in order for everyone in your company to become customer-oriented, they must think in terms of the whole process rather than just their own tasks. The goal is to develop a customer, and that's a process in which the salesperson is only one player. The process includes production people, finance and marketing people, as well as customer service reps. So it's not left to you to solve a customer's problem; the whole organization gets behind the effort. Building customer relationships is everybody's responsibility.[19]

It is important to focus on how you relate to plant and office employees, because this can make a difference in the way they treat your customers. It pays to be liked and appreciated by staff people, especially those in sales support, credit, billing, and shipping. Take a lesson from Mark Twain, who said, "I can live for two months on a good compliment." Take a moment from time to time to compliment and thank the support people in your company for the great job they are doing.

TQM is established today thanks to the pioneering work of W. Edwards Deming. One of Deming's most important lessons is his "85-15" rule.[20] When things go wrong in the field, there is an 85 percent chance the system is at fault. Only about 15 percent of the time can the individual salesperson be blamed. TQM means the organization's culture is defined by and supports the constant attainment of customer satisfaction, through an integrated system of tools, techniques, and training. Prospects and customers notice and think about everyone they come in contact with during the sales encounter. The relationship between perceived effort and customer service is a powerful one. When you and the customer interact, the quality of the interaction itself is an important part of the relationship. If the customer sees that the salesperson is focused on empathy during their interaction, it translates more naturally to customer happiness.[21] Exhibit 2.6 shows the dynamics of this interaction. Service quality has two dimensions: 1.The process of delivering the service, and 2. The actual outcome.

ΔExhibit 2.6

The Service Quality Interaction

Most business success stories involve taking an old idea or product and doing a better job with it than the next company. Amazon.com didn't invent book selling; they just did it better, giving customers the ability to have convenience, speed, and a wide selection at their fingertips. And the executives who now run Amazon are blazing new trails with the Kindle e-reader and the Cloud Player for music. Then there is Southwest Airlines! They aren't the oldest airline around, but no one before Southwest had figured out how to offer passengers a simple and consistent service without extra fees in a way that has kept it a profitable business while other airlines struggle to survive. The overall point is this: You can get a lot out of a current product or service if you change the processes around it, or change the process by which it is delivered. The objective is to change those processes enough that you are delivering more value to your customers or, at the very least, hold on to those customers by offering a fair price.

Managing Customer Relationships

When maintaining relationships with prospects and customers no longer falls to one individual in your company, a need arises for a Customer Relationship Management (CRM) system to reinforce the TQM mindset throughout the company. Technology tools are critical for organizing information on contacts and for communicating with prospects and customers throughout the sales cycle. With such a wide array of communication methods currently available, the salesperson needs to be sensitive to the customer's preferences and willing to adapt to meet their communication needs. Does the customer prefer phone communication, email, or online forms? Are they more likely to get information and make choices about purchases via Facebook, Twitter, or a company blog? Knowing the inclinations of each customer is key to getting the most out of your CRM system.

A word of caution is warranted, however, in any discussion of technology and social media. When so much of the work day is spent looking at a laptop screen or tapping out messages on a smartphone, it can be easy to forget that the goal of using technology is relating to customers, and customers are people.[22] If the end goal changes to having the newest technology and flashiest website, purely for the sake of being the newest and flashiest, you've missed the point. Technology is useful only so far as it helps develop and maintain good customer relationships. The comfort and familiarity of a salesperson who cares can never be replaced by gadgets or media.[23]

The $332,000 Customer

Tom Peters, author of *A Passion for Excellence*, says, "A customer is not a transaction; a customer is a relationship."[24] The missing link in service often is intense awareness of the customer's point of view. The process of handling the problem is as important to customers as the solution of the problem itself. The logical inference is that every company better organize its service delivery system to answer every customer's implied question: "What are you going to do for me today?"

Peters uses the example of Dallas car dealer Carl Sewell, who has written a book called *The $332,000 Customer* because a loyal lifetime Cadillac customer buys that much from him. Peters goes on to suggest that happy lifetime customers generate four or five happy lifetime customers for you. So in fact, one Cadillac customer is roughly a $1,500,000 customer. Two investments Sewell has made illustrate his understanding of the value he places on customer satisfaction. Number one, he bought a street sweeper to keep the front of his dealership extra clean. First impressions count for everything, and people judge his dealership by the cleanliness of everything including the road in front of it. Secondly, he convinced an upscale local restaurant to open a branch in his service bay. When it's a simple repair, a lot of his customers come in and enjoy a hot meal while the work is being done.

Loyal, lifetime customers put more money in your pocket.

Exhibit 2.7 illustrates the kind of behavior wanted in a quality-driven sales organization and the kind that exists in the typical organization.[25] To move from left to right, use the twelve essential elements of TQM and your commitment to customer satisfaction to guide you. Some salespeople will read this and say, "This is nothing new; it is simply common sense." They are right, of course, but it has taken many years for men such as W. Edwards Deming, Joseph Juran, and Genichi Taguchi to refine and teach this philosophy.[26]

ΔExhibit 2.7

Culture Changes in a Sales Organization

Traditional Management Model	Total Quality Management Model
Focus on product	Focus on service
Company knows best	Customer knows best
Transactions	Relationships
Individual performance	Team performance
Firefighting management	Continuous improvement
Blame/punishment	Support/reward
Short-term (year or less)	Long-term (years)
Intolerant of errors	Allows mistakes
Autocratic leadership	Participative leadership
Bureaucratic	Entrepreneurial
Top-down decisions	Consensus decisions
Inward-focused	Outward (customer)-focused

Team Selling

Companies facing the dual problem of increasingly fierce competition and the need to increase the efficiency of sales functions are learning from the example of industries like telecommunications and pharmaceuticals. These industries have mastered the art of "bundled sales." *Bundled selling* is a strategy wherein companies sell a number of their products or services "packaged" together. By successfully reconfiguring their sales organizations to allow representatives to sell across many sectors, they've increased their market share and, as a result, their profitability.[27] But with this bundling of products comes a need for a larger sales team who can efficiently handle the growing packages of goods and services; and that is where team selling comes in as an indispensable force in today's aggressive market.

Team Selling is a cooperative action by two or more professionals directed to selling a product or service. The sales team often consists of at least one salesperson, supported by technical specialists, a combination that utilizes the relationship expertise of the salesperson as well as the technical competency of other personnel throughout the organization.[28] Team selling involves not only several people from the seller's company but also a purchasing team from the prospect's company. The concept of team selling balances perfectly with the principles behind TQM because team sales builds lasting relationships, breaks down walls, and opens communication through teamwork. That's why two heads really are better than one.

The team approach gains an advantage over one-on-one selling, because it utilizes the strengths of each individual on the team. Some professional salespeople may lack the patience and attention to detail that is required to eventually guide the prospect to commit. Yet, technical support people involved on the team may possess these very characteristics, as they tend to be detail-oriented by nature. Similarly, a personality that appears too abrupt in the eyes of a client may be offset by a conservative personality who can energize the client with a sense of confidence. Team selling greatly increases the chances for chemistry with the decision makers of the purchasing company.[29]

Benefits of Team Selling

A healthy team attitude begins with a solid commitment to help team members win. There is no room for prima donnas within the team. The only person who is allowed to be the prima donna is the customer.[30] One of the primary benefits of team selling is that it enables a company to improve its relationship with customers, by allowing direct communication between the buyer and product specialists before the sale is made. Thus, the seller can more accurately define the customer's needs, and the buyer can have questions answered by an individual who has an intimate knowledge of the product. This creates an aura of authority and trustworthiness for the company and the salesperson.

Imagine the technical expertise required to sell satellite time to the telecommunications industry, a service of Satellite Corporation. The needs of each client are unique, and once the sale is made, the relationship has just begun. Buyers not only want to know what the service can do for their company, but also who will be working with them after the sale is made. For these reasons, Satellite Corporation requires that all employees act as informal partners of the sales department and are expected to contribute their expertise in making all sales. Technical people, for instance, frequently accompany salespeople on calls, and the salespeople work closely with their marketing colleagues to produce the brochures, technical guides, and other materials used in setting up and closing a sale.

Team Member Roles

The sales manager should appoint the account's salesperson as the team leader, and the technical and creative experts assume supportive roles. The leader may begin, coordinate, and close the presentation, calling on specific personnel to use their expertise in amplifying certain points. Appoint a strong leader to enhance team development. The leader must have the authority to ensure that all members of the team participate and perform their assigned team duties.[31] During the presentation, technical experts must know when to contribute and when to remain silent. Team members should reinforce the leader's presentation with body language and affirmation.

Teamwork Closed a $575,000 Sale

Bill King, sales manager of Laerdal Medical Corporation in Illinois, has seen first hand the value of a well-built sales team. King had been pursuing a client, a local community college, for over a year. Rather than give up on the school and return home after a sales trip to Chicago, King made one more stop. An administrator at the college called him and said the school was still interested in looking at Laerdal's mannequins, on which the school's nursing students could practice medical procedures. During King's last contact with the prospect, he was unable to work through the college's budget limitations. So for over a year, King had his inside sales team maintain a relationship with the client via email and phone calls. For months, salespeople called to persuade college officials that buying the mannequins, who start at $50,000, would place the college in the ranks of the University of Chicago for medical training. To appear sharp for each call, the sales team maintained precise conversation notes through an electronic sales tracking system. The payoff was remarkable. King returned to the school for one final demonstration—and then closed the $575,000 deal. "The most important thing was that everyone on the team worked together," he says.[32]

> Teamwork is the ability to work together toward a common vision. The ability to direct individual accomplishments toward organizational objectives. It is the fuel that allows common people to attain uncommon results.
>
> -Andrew Carnegie

Find a Combination That Works For You

While some companies do have extensive teams, one very common sort of teamwork is the two-person sales call team, often made up of a sales rep and a sales manager or a sales rep and a technical expert. It is so common that many companies don't think of this as team selling.[33] There is much to gain by pairing salespeople. Such partnerships can be productive both for the individual sales reps and their companies. To illustrate how this partnering could prove beneficial, consider this illustration:

Openers and Closers. For some salespeople, their greatest skill is the ability to capture the attention and interest of prospects. This is analogous to the carnival barker whose job it is to get you inside the circus tent. We know that making a good first impression is critical to future sales success. The problem is, some salespeople lack substance and depth in subsequent meetings with a prospect, and hence can benefit by being teamed with a detail-oriented sales rep who knows how to close. Together, the opener and closer produce a winning performance.

Major-league baseball managers have a similar situation to the one just described. A manager has starting pitchers (openers) and relief pitchers (closers) on his ball club. Many of baseball's best starting pitchers average six or seven strong innings each time out. The relief pitchers then come in and shut down the opposing team and save the game for the starter. Neither player is complete on his own. Together, however, they produce a winning performance.

Selling in a Multicultural World

With all of the recent talk about the globalization of markets, it can be easy to forget to look within our own companies for examples of the increase in cultural diversification. The sad truth is that while other professions have seen jumps in their numbers of workers from diverse ethnic backgrounds, the sales profession has been slow to follow.[34] But with minority-background business people now totaling 17.8 percent of owners of U.S. firms, you should expect to see advances in the numbers of multicultural sales professionals to follow.[35]

Today's Diverse Workforce

These changes are exciting! Think of the benefits your company has to gain from the knowledge and experience of salespeople from diverse cultures. The multicultural background of your own sales staff is the bridge to developing more meaningful relationships with customers from around the world.[36] Though it is important to remember that each customer is an individual who shouldn't be stereotyped, understanding the broad characteristics of the different cultures represented in the business world can lead to better relationships, both within your company and with all customers.[37]

An Emphasis on Diversity. Understanding the multicultural perspectives of your sales force and your customers does not come without effort. For this shift in understanding to take place, companies will need to focus on ways to make improved relationships with multicultural partners a priority. As with other aspects of communication coming from your company, this shift needs to happen in a way that reminds customers and employees alike that they are valued as individuals. No one likes to feel that they are simply being used.

One such company that has made a successful commitment to ethnic diversity is Lehman Brothers. The financial services titan began a program in 2005 that led to doubling its annual direct expenditures with minority-owned and woman-owned suppliers. As a result, by 2006 the firm had already seen a 29 percent increase in tier-one diversity spending. Their focus, however, isn't merely on the dollars gained in revenue because of their diversity initiative. Lehman's diversity manager Aaron Blumenthal says, "Regardless of contract size, the establishment of the business relationship is just as important to us." Relationships remain at the heart of developing trust and partnerships in a multicultural sales setting.[38]

Equipped for Understanding

Once companies have made multicultural relationships a priority, they must take active steps to make it happen. Employee education is essential! Depending on the level of interaction with people from varied backgrounds, the training may involve only a small component of new employee orientation. For others, it may mean the need for ongoing training. For Telvista Company, with headquarters in Dallas and operations in Mexico, managers are required to be enrolled in continuing lessons in Spanish or English. "This will help us achieve more comfort in doing business with each other," says Paulo Silva, president of Latin American client engagements for Telvista.[39]

A key principle behind TQM is that customer satisfaction begins inside your company with employee satisfaction. Only when you understand, respect, and support salespeople from all backgrounds can you understand and relate well to your customers.

The evidence of improved relationships is in the sales figures. A study published in *Personnel Psychology* shows that minority salespeople working in pro-diversity companies increase their annual sales by $21,000 to $27,000 per individual. Patrick F. McKay of the School of Management and Labor Relations at Rutgers University, says, "A pro-diversity climate is important to mitigate discrimination among African-American and Hispanic employees because they are most likely to experience discrimination." The employees' confidence in their company is seen in their confidence as salespeople, which in turn is reflected in their increased sales.[40]

SUMMARY

- The traditional role of selling has evolved from the art of persuasion to the psychology of relationship selling.

- The relationship cycle of selling begins with approaching the prospect, discovering needs, presenting your product or service as the solution, overcoming objections, and gaining commitment. Service after the sale completes the cycle.

- The purpose of the relationship approach to selling is to discover the needs or problems of the prospect. You become a solutions provider! It is customer-oriented and requires extensive knowledge of the prospect.

- Build relationships through customer-oriented continuous quality improvement. This is an outside -in approach, encouraging the mindset that every one inside and outside the company is a customer.

- Team selling fosters relationships by encouraging a sharing of ideas, resources, capabilities, and responsibilities.

- Understanding the perspectives and needs of your multicultural sales personnel leads to improved relationships with all types of customers.

REVIEW QUESTIONS

1. Compare and contrast the stereotype of traditional selling and professional relationship selling.

2. What questions must a salesperson answer 'yes' to before it is possible to make a recommendation to buy?

3. What is the difference between the features of the product and its benefits? Which is most useful in the selling situation? Why? Should the other, then, be mentioned at all? How?

4. Name at least three reasons why a prospect may resist making a buying decision. For each reason, tell how the salesperson could have prevented this particular type of resistance.

5. If sales resistance is encountered, how can the salesperson close the sale in spite of the resistance? Is this always synonymous with what is regarded as "hard sell"?

6. What is the purpose of service after the sale? What does it include? Whose responsibility is such service?

7. Who needs to be conversant with the organization's basic philosophy of business? If that philosophy is not understood by all members of the organization, what types of problems might result? Why?

8. To what extent must a sales rep agree with the company's commitment to continuous quality improvement?

9. What are the key principles of the Total Quality Management philosophy?

10. What is Team Selling? Describe the benefits and specific guidelines for successful team selling.

11. Why is multicultural diversity within companies important for businesses today? What impact does increased diversity have on the customer?

ROLE-PLAY EXERCISES

The following role-play exercises help build teams, improve communication, and emphasize the real-world side of selling. They are meant to be challenging, to help you learn how to deal with problems that have no single right answer, and to use a variety of skills beyond those employed in a typical review question. Read and complete each activity. Then in the next class, discuss and compare answers with other classmates.

Role Play 2.1 – Can You Spot "Relationship Selling?"

Divide into 4-person teams for this exercise. Working individually, conduct an online search to find 2 sales training videos that reflect traditional selling techniques and 2 sales training videos that present relationship selling techniques. Exchange your results with your other team members (this can be done online as well). Discuss everyone's results and, as a team, decide which single example of each approach is best or most obvious, and why.

Be careful that your team's final selection includes 2 videos that focus on the same part of the sales cycle (e.g., closing vs. closing, approach vs. approach, presentation vs. presentation). Otherwise, when you present your videos to the rest of the class, they would have no logically compelling reason to decide between them; they would be comparing apples with oranges, as it were.

In class (utilizing available technology), present your team's two selections and invite discussion of each by the class. Prod the class to consider each example in light of the two approaches to selling described in Chapter 2. *Without presuming that one approach is superior to the other*, ask the class which approach they find most effective, and why. No matter which video a majority of the class seems to prefer, see if you can convince them otherwise!

Role Play 2.2 – Enjoyable Selling

For this exercise, pair up with another student whom you do not already know. Agree between you that for this exercise one of you will adopt the role of traditional seller, and the other the role of relationship seller. Outside of class, develop a complete sales script from approach through closing for selling your counterpart a new home entertainment system. Your script should be developed according to traditional sales methods or relationship sales methods as outlined in Chapter 2.

In class, alternate making your respective sales pitches to one another. Regardless of whether a sale was closed successfully in either case, jot down a brief response to each of the following questions. Think about the reasons for your responses, and be prepared to discuss them in class or online.

- What difficulties arose as you employed your script to sell the home entertainment system to your counterpart?
- Can you attribute any of these difficulties to the method of selling—traditional or relationship—that you used?
- *As a customer*, what did you find annoying, if anything, about your partner's approach to selling?
- *As a seller*, what did you find most annoying about your approach to selling?
- Given your total experience in this exercise, which approach to selling do you prefer, and why?

CASE STUDIES

The following case studies present you with selling scenarios that require you to apply the critical skills discussed in the chapter and give you training through simulation, role-playing, and practical learning situations. They are meant to be both engaging and challenging, and like the role-play exercises, don't have one right answer.

Case 2.1—The Nervous VP for Sales

As vice president for marketing & sales for Netwerx, Inc., a firm specializing in videoconferencing equipment and software systems, Tom Nelson was nervous. He had just left a meeting with the company's chief financial officer, Brad Poindexter, that had not gone well. Tom had passed along the news from one of his sales managers that a major account was on the verge of going sour. The sales manager had reported that Secure Title, a title search and insurance company with offices in 50 major metropolitan areas, had not responded to communications regarding renewal of their annual contract. The account was worth $450,000 per year to Netwerx; and in the current business climate, they could not afford to lose it. Worse, word on the street was that Secure Title was aggressively shopping for a lower price, since its own business had fallen off due to the commercial real estate collapse. Brad, the CFO, had pushed Tom hard: "What in blazes is the matter with your people? Tell 'em to get on the horn and find out what's going on. If we lose this account, heads will roll, starting with yours, Tom!"

Tom had been worried for quite a while before this crisis. From a friend in R&D, he knew that Netwerx was about to roll out an improved, more efficient software package that would run on their existing videoconferencing hardware, but no meetings with marketing and sales had been held.

Moreover, other vendors with inferior products were touting their lower price with some success. Netwerx had already seen a 17% decline in annual revenues. With no Christmas bonus last year, some of his salespeople were getting restless.

Ever since the annual meeting of the National Marketing and Sales Association last fall, Tom had been mulling over the desirability of shifting strategies for Netwerx. At the meeting, he had been exposed to a series of presentations on "relationship selling" and TQM. Netwerx had never entertained such an approach. Up to this point, the company had focused on touting the superior features of their system, giving their clients tickets to sporting events and golf outings, and aggressively closing sales. But Tom feared that such a traditional approach might not be effective in a sluggish economy. A meeting of Netwerx's executive committee was scheduled for next week. The CFO had made it clear that he expected a positive report from Tom.

What should Tom say to the executive committee? Which factors should Tom consider as he decides what to do?

Case 2.2 – 4-Leaf-Clover's Transition

The "boiler room" at 4-Leaf-Clover, a 66-year-old financial planning firm, was aptly named. Hour by hour, day in and day out, the phones never stopped. Using automatic dialers connected to a high-end CRM (customer relationship management) system, the sales force continually called random prospects to elicit new business. Typically, after a few perfunctory questions, attention would turn quickly to a presentation of the features and advantages of new financial instruments structured for wealthy individuals who were not averse to risk. The psychological temperature of the stress-filled room was high. Most staff members quit after less than a year; those who stayed more than 2 years were called "veterans." What worked in the past, however, was no longer as effective, especially in a volatile economy plagued by recent financial scandals.

Jasper Harrington, vice president for sales at 4-Leaf, has just convinced his superiors that something different, called "relationship selling," should be tried. Harrington wants to begin with a select group of 6 high-producing salespersons to see if they can outperform their colleagues regarding total revenue acquired over a period of 6 months. If the project is successful, the new program will be rolled out company-wide. The only catch? Harrington must train his trial group himself.

How should Harrington structure his training? What points should be emphasized for the sales group? Where do you think Harrington will encounter the strongest resistance from this group? What can Harrington say that might convince the trial group to make the switch to becoming consultants, rather than just salespersons, for their clients?

As the project goes forward, how should Harrington measure the performance of the trial group in terms somewhat more meaningful than total revenue produced? What other criteria of performance are important for assessing the success of relationship selling?

"Individual commitment to a group effort—that is what makes a team work, a company work, a society work, a civilization work."

–Vince Lombardi

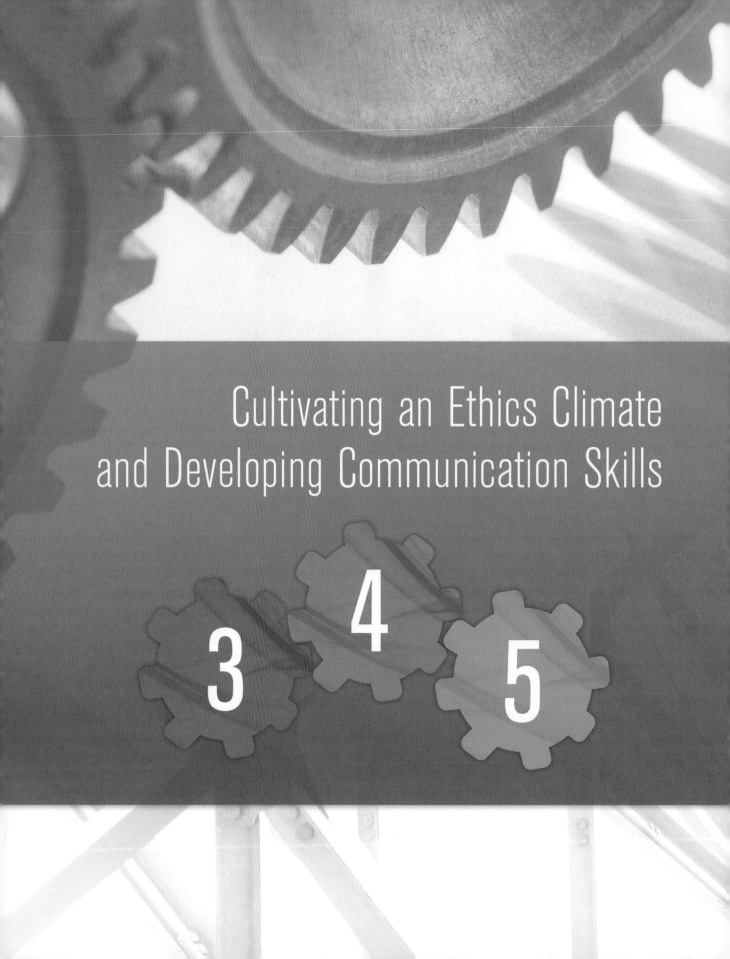

Cultivating an Ethics Climate
and Developing Communication Skills

3 4 5

Part 2

Few professions give you more opportunities for rejection on a daily basis than does the field of sales. Because of the often-cutthroat nature of selling, some salespeople do whatever it takes to stay ahead and edge out the competition. Chapter 3 discusses the need for a strong ethical and moral character to sustain a sales career. Honest and caring service brings customers back and assures success. Success in professional selling also depends upon your ability to have a productive exchange of information with prospects and customers.

The more you understand about prospects and their decision-making process, the more readily you can discover what they need and want, and this is covered in more detail in chapter 4. Because success in relationship selling depends on accurately getting your message across to prospects, chapter 4 also describes how to break through communication barriers.

An especially useful tool for gaining insight into how the prospect is thinking is knowledge of the social styles model, which is discussed in chapter 5. A social style is the way a person sends and receives information. It is a method for finding the best way to approach a prospect and to set up a working relationship with that person. The chapters included in this section are:

3. Ethical and Legal Issues in Selling
4. Purchase Behavior and Communication
5. Finding Your Selling Style

"It's OK, Kid, Everybody Does It"
by Jack Griffin

When Johnny was 6 years old, he was with his father when they were caught speeding. His father handed the officer a twenty-dollar bill with his driver's license. "It's OK, son," his father said as they drove off. "Everybody does it."

When he was 8, he was present at a family council presided over by Uncle George, on some dubious ways to save money on their income tax return. "It's OK, kid," his uncle said. "Everybody does it."

When he was 9, his mother took him to his first theater production. The box office man couldn't find any seats until his mother discovered an extra $5 in her purse. "It's OK, son," she said. "Everybody does it."

When he was 12, he broke his glasses on the way to school. His Aunt Francine persuaded the insurance company that they had been stolen and they collected $75. "It's OK, son," she said. "Everybody does it."

When he was 15, he made right guard on the high school football team. His coach showed him how to block and at the same time grab the opposing end by the shirt so the official couldn't see it. "It's OK, son," the coach said. "Everybody does it."

When he was 16, he took his first summer job at the supermarket. His assignment was to put the overripe strawberries in the bottom of the boxes and the good ones on top where they would show. "It's OK, son," the manager said. "Everybody does it."

When he was 18, Johnny and a neighbor applied for a college scholarship. Johnny was a marginal student. His neighbor was in the top 3 percent of his class, but couldn't play right guard. Johnny got the scholarship. "It's OK, son," his parents said. "Everybody does it."

When he was 19, he was approached by an upperclassman who offered the test answers for $50. "It's OK, kid," he said. "Everybody does it."

Johnny was caught and sent home in disgrace. "How could you do this to your mother and me?" his father said. "You never learned anything like this at home." His aunt and uncle were also shocked.

If there's one thing the adult world can't stand, it's a kid who cheats.

Chapter 3

Ethical and Legal Issues In Selling

Learning Objectives

- Develop principles upon which to base ethical behavior.

- Identify the sources of influence on ethics and ethical behavior.

- Understand your role in maintaining the ethical position of the organization and simultaneously behaving in an ethical manner toward customers.

- Discover what loyalty to the company requires in the event that your employers may be involved in questionable ethical behavior.

- Recognize the implications of federal and local laws regarding ethical standards.

Ken Blanchard and Norman Vincent Peale

One of most the significant books published in the area of business ethics is *The Power of Ethical Management*. Written by Dr. Kenneth Blanchard and Dr. Norman Vincent Peale, this book is of special significance for salespeople who are on the firing line between their customers and their employers.

Few individuals have had as great an impact on successful company management as has Kenneth Blanchard, co-author of *The One Minute Manager* and *The One Minute Manager Library*. Dr. Blanchard is the founder of a management consulting firm, Blanchard Training and Development Inc., in Escondido, California.

Dr. Norman Vincent Peale was the author of thirty-four books. *The Power of Positive Thinking* is one of the most widely circulated books ever published. It has been translated into forty languages and has enjoyed sales of over twenty million copies. He was also the founder of the monthly magazine *Guideposts*, which has a circulation of sixteen million.

The basic message of *The Power of Ethical Management* is simple: You don't have to cheat to win! Blanchard and Peale tell us that many people demand immediate tangible evidence that ethical conduct works, but such evidence is often not available. In fact, you may actually get farther in the short run by cheating. But in the long run, where it really counts, you never gain by unethical conduct. The authors remind us that "nice guys may appear to finish last, but usually they're running in a different race." Unethical behavior occurs in sales because people forget the real purpose of professional selling—to fill the needs of others.

Salespeople sometimes say near the end of the day, "I ought to make one more sales call before I go home. I wonder who I might be able to see this late?" Blanchard and Peale suggest that the better question might be, "I wonder if there is someone else I can help before I go home?" When salespeople focus on their purpose—solving the problems of clients and helping customers be more successful and more profitable—they understand the need for ethical behavior. Cheating, lying, and short-changing the customer on service may bring a satisfactory profit today, but is a sure way to court failure for the future.

A Question of Ethics

Erin Hood feels as though she is being torn apart. The pharmaceutical company she works for is pressuring her to meet a sales quota twenty percent higher than last year's. She is a single parent with two children to support, and she sees an opportunity to meet her sales quota if she can beat out a competitor for a large order from a drugstore chain. She is tempted to plant some carefully worded negative comments about the competitor in the ear of the store chain's purchasing agent. What should she do? What would you do?

Erin is facing a situation that falls in the category of ethical considerations. Because salespeople are relatively free and independent operators, they may encounter more ethical dilemmas than many other business people. For this reason, you must be clear on your own ethical standards before getting caught up in something that escalates beyond your control.

Ethics is an old subject, but it is certainly not worn out. The Greek philosophers, for example, suggested that, "A merchant does better to take a loss than to make a dishonest profit." And as Rob Roy once said, "Honor is a gift man gives himself."[1] A loss may be momentarily painful, but dishonesty does irreparable damage. America is reeling from the shocking, unethical, and immoral activities of a variety of business and government leaders and other public figures. It is not companies, institutions and political organizations, however, that are unethical; individual people are unethical. Ethics is a personal matter. The ethics of a business, government, or other organizations is merely a reflection of the combined value systems of its members.

Business ethics is an aspect of societal ethics. Traditional values seem to have given way to a widespread sense of *anything goes*; and "Sell at any Cost!" seemed the mantra the early salesperson in the U.S. learned.[2] Look at what we parade in front of people, implying approval, in the media and society: sexual allure, constant violence, conspicuous consumption, the soft life, "reach for all the gusto you can," and enjoy life now. As a result, many Americans want immediate personal gratification and will act in whatever manner seems to promise it. People have been questioning that businesses can even have and act in accordance with ethical standards—and for good reason. Given recent scandals in investment banking, subprime mortgages and insider trading, it's widely assumed that corruption is common within the global marketplace.[3]

Some say that business ethics is an *oxymoron*, a contradiction in terms. They suggest that business and ethics are incompatible because "ethics is values-ridden and grounded in philosophy and religion" while businesses need to be ruthless and dishonest in order to finish first.[4] This thinking is ludicrous! The notion that honest businesses and salespeople finish last is poisonous, and it is untrue. Unethical behavior is self-destructive; it generates more unethical conduct until a business or person hits rock bottom financially, spiritually, and morally.

"MY COMPANY AND I DISAGREED ON WHAT ETHICS ARE EXACTLY."

Used with permission from The Boxcar Millionaire[5]

The Origin of Ethics

A *legal standard* is enforced by laws and statutes, but an *ethical standard* is an outgrowth of the customs and attitudes of a society. Most of us have a shared idea of what we mean by ethics, but defining it in a way that everyone would accept is hard. Essentially, ethics is a systematic effort to judge human behavior as right or wrong in terms of two major criteria: Truth and Justice.

The root of the word ethics derives from the Greek word *ethos*, which means the character or sentiment of the community. A society cannot exist unless people agree fundamentally on what is right and wrong, just and unjust. Without shared norms of behavior, we would have anarchy in our political system and chaos in our daily lives. If we consider the United States to be our larger community, our ethical standards have been influenced philosophically by a combination of Greco-Roman and Judeo-Christian thought, Enlightenment philosophy and industrial advances made available by the scientific revolution. The three most important value-forming institutions in America are family, church, and school. Many people believe that the decreasing strength and changing roles of these three institutions have produced a society with lower ethical standards than those of its earlier history.

The Bases for Ethical Systems

Philosophers and ethicists point to two systems to describe ethical thinking. The first of these is the *deontological* base, the use of specifically stated rules, for example, the Ten Commandments or the Golden Rule. Some believe these rules come from a higher power, some think the rules are intuitive, and still others hold that the rules are discovered by using reason.

The second system of describing ethical systems is the *teleological* approach. This system defines right and wrong in terms of end results. Though research suggests that organizational follow-through and individual moral approaches to ethical problems also influence decision making at the management level, a foundational study reported by Dr. Thomas Wotruba found that marketing executives' response to ethical problems is predominantly utilitarian.[6,7] The utilitarian model falls under this approach and is illustrated by the idea proposed in the nineteenth century by Jeremy Benthem that society's goal is to produce "the greatest good for the greatest number."[8] This approach says that in trying to determine a course of action in an ethical dilemma, the individual should assess what good or harm would come to the parties involved and follow the course of action that would have the most positive results for the most people. In fact, several studies have found that if employees perform actions that violate their company's stated rules—their managers would react more harshly if the outcome of the acts were negative rather than positive. In other words, punishment was less severe if management saw the outcome as "good."[9]

With these two bases consciously or unconsciously affecting us, we can expect to experience ambivalent attitudes when faced with making ethical decisions. In the bestseller, *The Closing of the American Mind*, Allan Bloom theorized that much of our moral and ethical ambivalence comes from family and educational system teachings in which almost everything is relative and in which there are no moral absolutes."[10] Though Bloom's theory inspired some heated debate in academic circles, more recent studies of Bloom's work agree "teaching that values are subjective becomes a problem" because it limits the successful and ethical implementation of any value system. This kind of critique on "the value of values" can lead to more relativism and apathy.[11]

The paths you choose will reveal your true character.

Guidelines for Ethical Behavior

Today, no matter which specific method of ethical decision-making is followed, most Americans embrace three basic guidelines: Universal nature, truth telling, and responsibility for one's actions. Without them, the free enterprise system itself would be threatened and any kind of business exchange would be difficult. Our society would disintegrate into a "dog-eat-dog" environment.

Universal Nature. The universal nature guideline is a derivation of the Golden Rule. We want others to play by the same basic rules by which we would play in a similar situation. This guideline sets up a basic level of trust between people and makes life predictable.

Truth Telling. A salesperson needs to believe that what others say is true. The idea of honesty may originate in a set of rules we have been taught, but truth telling makes sense on purely logical grounds as well. Trust facilitates cooperation, buyer commitment, and the development and maintenance of long-term, client-salesperson relationships.[12]

It's not always simple to be truthful with prospects. At times, it is easier to tell a little white lie if it means setting up the all-important face-to-face interview or getting a commitment over the phone. For that reason, some salespeople's "techniques" when cold calling have become entrenched in lies. Have you ever received a call from a telemarketer who told you he was calling to take a survey, only to discover moments later that this was his way of keeping you on the phone long enough to explain why he was really calling and what he was selling?[13] Some might say this technique is acceptable; but the truth is, that salesperson lied to you. Would you trust someone who lies in his or her first conversation with you? Of course not—and neither will your prospects.

Responsibility for Your Actions. President Harry S. Truman kept a sign on his desk stating, "The buck stops here." He reminded himself that he had no one to blame when things went wrong. Individuals may choose to live by this attitude and accept personal responsibility for their actions, or they may attempt to follow the impulse of the moment and blame someone else for the consequences. If we and society demonstrated a higher level of trust and credibility based on a willingness to accept responsibility for personal actions, our system would work more efficiently and in a less suspicious atmosphere.

Influences on a Salesperson's Ethics

Although individual salespeople each have a basic value system and may know what is right and wrong, they encounter many new influences and experience many new pressures on the job. Nothing creates more direction for employee's decision-making or a better balance for judgment than ethical guidelines.[14] Knowing in advance what can be expected and having a feel for how to balance and integrate them into a personal code of ethics make handling ethical decisions easier for any individual.

Company Code of Ethics

Many companies have codes of ethics; some companies adhere strictly to the code as part of corporate culture and may have ethics training for new employees and an ethics committee to rule on ethical dilemmas. A recent study examined the relationships among ethics code awareness, perceived corporate ethical values, and organizational commitment. Two key findings emerged. First, those aware of the existence of an ethics code in their organizations viewed their organizations as having more ethical values than those not aware of an ethics code. Second, respondents showed higher levels of commitment when they were aware of an ethics code in their companies. The results suggest that ethics codes may lead to higher levels of commitment by increasing the belief that their organizations have strong ethical values, as long as the existence of these codes are adequately communicated.[15]

Exhibit 3.1 is a brief overview of the United Professional Sales Association's Ethical Code of Conduct.[16] The UPSA is an organization of member-based sales professionals whose overall mission is "advancing the profession of sales." They have designed an entire Ethics Selling Framework upon which its members must abide; it reflects best practices and points out what is not permissible in today's business climate. The fundamental principles of the Framework are of a general nature and provide excellent guidelines for the buying-selling experience. Members agree to uphold the intent of the Code of Conduct, Ethical Code and a Professional Buyer's Bill of Rights. These types of ethical practices and codes are becoming more commonplace as organizations with large sales forces see the need to improve and build on mutual trust between their prospects and their salespeople.

ΔExhibit 3.1

The UPSA Ethical Code of Conduct

- I will maintain high standards of integrity and professional conduct.
- I will accept responsibility for my actions.
- I will continually seek to enhance my professional capabilities.
- I will sell with fairness and honesty.
- I will encourage others in the profession to act in an ethical and professional manner.

Federal sentencing guidelines have been established that reduce punitive damages based in part on what a company has done to prevent ethical problems.[17] Driven by these government actions and fear of retribution and by the competitive advantage clear ethical standards may gain, companies are paying more attention than ever to the behavior of their employees. Ethics is a monetary issue as well! For example, a study conducted by researchers at the University of Central Missouri found that ethical behavior in business to business selling had positive economic impacts; when salespeople acted with strong moral judgment, they helped build better, customer-oriented relationships that resulted in long term sales.[18]

Some companies are thorough and exacting in implementing a code of ethics, but others keep their codes buried in filing cabinets; still others have no formal code of any kind. Implementing a code of conduct statement communicates to salespeople—and their customers—that companies have high moral standards. In addition, organizations can gain several benefits when they adhere to a core set of ethical values embodied in a code of conduct:[19]

Greater Motivation Among Co-Workers. Although many employers have yet to fully recognize the significance of staff morale, in a recent U.S. survey, 94 percent of responding employees declared company ethics to be an important, if not critical, aspect to their working lives.

A Demonstrated Respect for the Law. When top management makes a formal commitment to endorse an ethical company culture, the subject becomes of greater significance and, consequently, the company's personnel pay more attention to compliance with the laws and regulations affecting the organization.

Protection of the Company's Reputation. In the eyes of the consumer and the general public, companies are responsible for the activities undertaken by all of the partners with whom they deal, including customers and suppliers. A company culture based on solid ethical standards contributes to preserving and improving the company's reputation.

Improved Business Relationships. Due to pressures exerted by investors, consumers, and human rights groups, advertising campaigns have been launched to boycott the products of certain companies that were accused of not adopting ethical standards. From this perspective, a clearly defined ethical culture is a useful way to choose business partners with which long-term ties are desired.

As one research study suggests, most companies and multi-national corporations have extensive ethics codes, many of which can be found in shortened form on their websites. These web-based ethics codes share a common language, which includes words like *trust, responsibility, governance, safety, disclosure* and *caring*. The frequency with which these words are used across websites suggests companies and corporations are beginning to create an informal, generally accepted global ethics code. The study is also quick to point out, however, that a company may not always act ethically even if they develop this kind of ethics code.[20] As a salesperson, you need to know where the company stands and whether its stand is consistent with your own. And the time to do this is before you're hired, not after.

Ethics codes fit into the larger, increasingly more popular framework "Corporate Social Responsibility" (CSR). CSR focuses not only on the managerial processes needed to monitor, meet, and even exceed ethical norms within the company, but also on the development of products and policies that reflect good corporate citizenship to the client or consumer. Though this can mean sponsoring a fundraising event like a major run, a local team, or a charity, it can also mean choosing products or developing procedures that reflect the company's environmental good will. This is often called "going green." As bestselling author J. Walker Smith writes, a growing number of companies are making CSR a major component of their product pitches. Because products must have key benefits to the consumer, companies are hoping to tap into the consumer's personal concern for the environment. In other words, especially in green marketing, "doing well by doing good is the new mantra of the socially responsible bottom line."[21]

Starbucks, for instance, strives to combine consumer driven demands with environmentally and socially responsible production methods. Starbucks CEO Howard Shultz writes to the heart of this method in his recent book *Onward: How Starbucks Fought for Its Life without Losing Its Soul*:

> "Valuing personal connections at a time when so many people sit alone in front of screens; aspiring to build human relationships in an age when so many issues polarize so many; and acting ethically, even if it costs more, when corners are routinely cut—these are honorable pursuits, at the core of what we set out to be."[22]

Executives as Role Models

The likelihood that unacceptable selling practices will occur has more to do with how executives behave. If a sales manager gives the impression that you must do anything possible to make more sales, salespeople infer that dealing unethically is acceptable in order to succeed. More than anything, an organization's culture influences sales reps' behavior with clients. Dr. Eli Jones, co-director of the *Program for Excellence in Selling* at the University of Houston, says, "Sales managers must emphasize ethical selling behavior in words and actions."[23]

The company's top executives must keep in check the pressure the managers put on their salespeople. If the CEO comes around once a year with a pep talk on moral behavior but proceeds the rest of the year to use underhanded methods of doing business, salespeople get a mixed message. When individuals are confronted with ethical dilemmas, they draw on some various sources for guidance in making decisions. Salespeople's decisions are guided by organizational policies, codes, rules and norms, as well as interactions with other people in the organization.

> "As a manager the important thing is not what happens when you are there, but what happens when you are not there."
>
> -Dr. Kenneth Blanchard

Ethical conflict may arise when salespeople's ethical values differ from those perceived to be held by their immediate supervisors or top management. Here are some ideas to consider that may foster ethical behavior within an organization:[24]

- Codes of ethics that are effectively communicated are likely to result in greater ethical behavior.

- The presence and enforcement of codes of ethics have been found to be associated with higher levels of ethical behavior.

- Corporate goals and stated policies strongly influence managers' decisions on whether to act ethically or unethically.

- When a climate is created where ethical values and behaviors are fostered, supported, and rewarded, more ethical behavior will exist.

Examples Set by Colleagues and Competitors

A salesperson sometimes discovers that colleagues and/or competitors are acting unethically. Imagine that you are riding in a cab one day, and a colleague asks the driver to provide a receipt for expense account purposes and to indicate a figure higher than the actual fare. As an observer, do you join in the activity, rebuke the colleague, report the colleague (commonly called *blowing the whistle*), or ignore it? A customer reports that a competitor has said you have an alcohol problem and are therefore undependable. Do you simply deny the charge, or do you retaliate by making detrimental remarks about your competitor?

The whistle-blower who quits or is fired may find another good job. A number of employers are happy to hire workers who demonstrate such a strong commitment to high ethical standards and will protect them when necessary. Nevertheless, there is no guarantee of employment, especially in a slow market. One study on whistle-blowing found that two thirds of whistle-blowers lost or were forced to retire from their jobs and were blacklisted in their field.[25] The whistle-blower may lose seniority and retirement benefits and must often move to another city. The needs of family members must be considered. Moreover, rightly or wrongly, the whistle-blower can frequently be seen as lacking the team spirit that many employers prize, and instead comes across as a complainer or fanatic.[26]

The Bottom Line

One of the most powerful influences on salespeople is profits—their own and those of the company. However, as business author Arie de Geus writes, the most sustainable companies put more emphasis on their awareness of the world around them and their capacity for positive change than they do on profit. To live long, de Geus writes, companies must "take care to develop a community. Processes are put in place to define membership, establish common values, recruit people, develop employees, assess individual potential, [and] live up to a human contract."[27]

Focus on the REAL bottom line—your customers.

A company's survival will surely be compromised if common values are not established and acted upon and if salespeople take casual views of the legal and ethical implications of their behavior. Short-term profits may be maximized by unethical behavior, but the company's very existence could be threatened if it were hit with huge fines or an unwanted exposure in the media. Although short-term profits are important for both the company and its salespeople, the long-term success and good name of the company must always be the first priority.

Groupthink and Gamesmanship

Groupthink refers to the pressure exerted on salespeople to be part of the group and not to buck the system—to be team players, no matter what. Being a team player is good if the team has ethical goals and plays by ethical rules, but if the group's thinking runs afoul of your own personal code of ethics, you must weigh your options carefully. Psychologist Irving L. Janis warns against "groupthink," which he suggests can cause flawed judgment.[28]

Unfortunately, there are examples of groupthink in every profession, and the pharmaceutical industry has not been spared its share of such activity. Two salespeople and three pharmacists pleaded guilty to their roles in a scheme involving the illegal sales of drug samples to pharmacies in New Jersey and New York. The operation generated more than a $1 million in illicit profits for all the parties involved. The salespeople, former Procter & Gamble reps, stole samples from doctors' offices and sold them to the pharmacists.[29] They also paid doctors and office personnel to obtain supplies. Here, a number of people conspired to cheat others and somehow convinced themselves that what they were doing was all right. After all, if others in the industry were engaging in similar activity, making money at it, and not getting caught, then why shouldn't they?

Gamesmanship is becoming totally caught up in winning simply for the sheer joy of victory and a dislike of losing. Much of our culture nurtures this type of competitive spirit—from winning the high school football game to beating a friend at chess or golf. The typical gamesman in selling looks for shortcuts and is willing to use any technique to sell a product or service. To the gamesman, winning means doing whatever is necessary to make the sale.

One case study demonstrated that, in numerous circumstances, salespeople and staff in a hostile workplace full of a gamesmanship mentality simply used their feelings in order to survive. The study showed irrational emotions being used as strategic tools of defense against a vindictive, aggressive, and hostile work place.[30] The dangers of gamesmanship are quite clear—the temptation to cross over the line into unethical or illegal behavior.

Developing a Personal Code of Ethics

Clearly many competing forces that influence a salesperson's decisions have an ethical dimension. Situations often arise in which a clear right or wrong is not easily apparent and discretion in behavior is up to the individual. Because the influences that come to bear upon a salesperson do not always agree and because conflicting demands are numerous, each salesperson must develop a personal code of ethics that supersedes all other claims.

Responsibility to Self

In the final analysis, the still, small voice of conscience is the arbiter of conflicting ethical claims. It provides the ability to say that you have made the best decision under the circumstances and take full responsibility for it. If you have personal integrity, then you cannot be dishonest with others—company, competitors, or customers.

Responsibility to the Company

Salespeople sometimes rationalize that cheating here or there in dealing with the company would not hurt. After all, the company makes lots of money and what you do would never be noticed. Several areas particularly lend themselves to temptations to be less than ethical

Accuracy in Expense Accounts. Often padding expense accounts is relatively easy. A salesperson can add extra mileage, submit charges for a meal that was actually eaten at a friend's house, or take friends out to dinner and report the charge as entertaining customers. Abuse of expense accounts is prevalent in both government and business circles. Volkswagen, for example, fired a number of managers and employees after it was discovered employees used their expense accounts to pay for lavish vacations.[31]

Falsification of expense accounts is not only unethical, but it can also lead to dismissal if it is detected. As a practical matter, it unnecessarily increases the costs of the company and may put it at a competitive disadvantage.

Honesty in Using Time and Resources. The temptation to do some shopping between sales calls, to linger over a third cup of coffee in a restaurant, and to sleep late in a hotel room are examples of ways a salesperson may misuse time. No time card is punched, and slipping in personal time may be relatively easy. This ultimately hurts both the salesperson and the company because fewer sales calls are made. Dishonesty in expense accounts and in time and resources can be considered as theft. As one business journal reports, "according to the FBI, internal theft is the fastest growing business crime" and is responsible for the failure of one third of businesses.[32] Misusing resources such as automobiles and selling samples for one's own profit hurt the company.

Accuracy in Filling Out Order Forms. Certain kinds of compensation plans, particularly contests, may cause salespeople to withhold or delay orders or to oversell some items. This practice ultimately hurts the company because it results in unhappy customers. It also takes unfair advantage of co-workers who compete fairly to win contests.

Representing the Company. The salesperson is the spokesperson for the company and for that reason must accurately represent products and services and deliver the kind of follow-up service that the company promises. Exaggerating the capabilities of a product or failing to point out any problems that might be associated with its use is unethical and can be disastrous to a long-term relationship with a customer. In some instances, it is also illegal, with the potential for causing both the salesperson and the company serious legal consequences. In addition, a company that prides itself on service to customers will be sorely disappointed with a salesperson who makes a sale and neglects to check with the customer about any additional service needs.

Responsibility to Competitors

Being honest and refraining from taking unfair advantage are the basic guidelines when dealing with competitors. Making untrue, derogatory comments about competitors or their products is poor business. At the very least, the legal implications of this behavior simply make the risks too great. In the same sense, pumping a competitor's salesperson for information at a trade show in order to steal their customers is not ethical. Some salespeople go so far as to use sabotage, espionage, and dirty tricks to gain unfair advantage over a competitor. These tactics include hiding the competitor's products on a display shelf and planting "spies" in a business to hear their sales presentation. Persuading a customer to put out a fake request for bids to see what bids competitors would submit is another unfair tactic sometimes practiced. The basic theme in this area is to gain customers fairly and squarely by providing quality products and superior service.

Responsibility to Customers

Behaving honestly and providing quality information and services are the primary ingredients for establishing mutually satisfying relationships with customers. Fortunately, the stereotype of the silver-tongued, flattering, deceptive, door-to-door salesperson of the past is disappearing. Still, many opportunities for unethical tactics exist.

Overselling or Misrepresenting Products or Services. Some salespeople persuade customers to buy more than they need because the salesperson needs to meet a quota or wants to win a trip to the Caribbean. Overselling eventually catches up with the salesperson because customers realize that they have more than they need. In addition, repeat sales probably won't be possible for a very long time.

Lying about the capabilities of a product, the date the company can make delivery, or the nature of the warranty are all unethical ways to win a quick sale while running the risk of legal action or a permanent loss of the customer in the long run.

Keeping Confidences. Because of the relationship between the salesperson and the customer, the salesperson may be privy to valuable information. That information could be very useful to some other customer, and providing it might ingratiate the salesperson with the new customer. Failing to keep confidences is, of course, unethical, and eventually it results in a reputation for the salesperson as an untrustworthy gossip. The word "salesperson" has, for a lot of people, come to suggest a less-than-honest person, and many consumers have been burned by the unethical behavior of a salesperson. To break through this stigma and have an open, honest dialogue requires that salespeople pass two tests shortly after they walk in the door. First, they must make the prospect comfortable. Second, salespeople must pass the "credibility" test. One of the best tools for creating credibility is a story—an example of how the salesperson helped someone like the prospect solve a similar problem.[33]

Gift Giving. Although giving a customer a token gift as a thank-you or as a reminder of the salesperson and the company is customary, the intent with which a gift is given usually reveals its ethical or unethical nature. If a gift is a way to get business or a bribe, then it is unethical and may well be illegal. Sometimes a salesperson may even give an "under-the-table" gift in order to secure an order.[34] The value of the gift in comparison to the sale is also something to consider. In America, it is generally understood that no gift should exceed a monetary value of between $25-50. That being said, one study has suggested that in the pharmaceutical industry even small gifts like pens can influence the recipient's decision making processes without the person being aware of this influence.[35] It may be wise for the salesperson to explore the ethics behind giving even small gifts.

Hope this "speeds" things along.

Entertaining Clients. Policies regarding entertainment are similar to those that cover gift giving. In some industries, entertaining a client with a meal, an excursion, or tickets to the theater or a football game is customary. If the intent is as a means of saying thank-you to a customer or of developing a more personal relationship, entertainment may be acceptable and even expected. Finding out the rules of behavior in a particular industry and within an individual company is important. For instance, Lockheed Martin, known for its strict enforcement of its ethics code, has a policy that no employee should accept nor provide a meal that is lavish or excessive. Lockheed further restricts gift giving to United States governmental officials to under $10, a policy more stringent than the government's own.[36] In fact, the United States Office of Government Ethics states that no executive branch can accept a gift over $20 at once or of a total of $50 in a calendar year, or a meal beyond light refreshment inside the United States.[37]

Operating in a Global Environment

Salespeople today may operate not only in the United States but also in a foreign country where norms of behavior may be different. Which morality should salespeople follow, their own or that of the country in which they find themselves? In some countries, "grease" or "speed" money makes the wheels of a government agency or a company move faster. In Japan, there is much gift giving in business relationships, and it is viewed as a time-honored tradition rather than a bribe. A company usually has guidelines for an employee to follow in a foreign country, but bribery is universally condemned and is in fact illegal whether it is practiced at home or abroad. Today, from high tech to toy companies and from automobile to aerospace companies, most codes of conduct now include instructions on how their representatives should behave in foreign settings. Tyco International, with 250,000 employees and $40 billion in annual revenue, makes electronics and medical supplies and also owns ADT Security Systems. This once ethically beleaguered company is now recognized as a leader in ethical business practices with a clear gift and entertainment policy, which is included in the following insert:[38]

Tyco International Gift and Entertainment Policy

While customs and practices can vary among cultures, sharing modest gifts and entertainment is often an important way of creating goodwill and establishing trust in business relationships. All of us have a responsibility to make sure that our business gifts and entertainment practices are reasonable and consistent with Tyco policies, industry codes and local laws.

A. Giving and Accepting Gifts

Lavish spending on business gifts is unacceptable. It can create the perception that we are trying to obtain, or give, favorable business decisions by providing individuals with personal benefits. Whether we are the giver or recipient, to ensure we do not create a perception of impropriety, gifts and entertainment must be:

- Infrequent and not excessive in value
- Directly related to building customer or supplier relationships
- Never in cash
- Never tied to a potential contract or business tender
- Logo items whenever possible
- Reported in accordance with our Conflicts of Interest, Gifts and Business Entertainment policy

B. Business Entertainment

Modest and appropriate meals and entertainment may be accepted or provided by Tyco employees where the primary purpose of the meal or entertainment is business-related. The employee, as well as the customer, supplier contractor or partner, must be present.

Americans selling overseas must abide by both United States law and the laws of the countries in which they sell. Patronage or payments to people in exchange for favors that would be considered bribes in America are the accepted way of doing business in many countries. Operating as a free and independent agent in a foreign country can be extremely difficult. To ease operations in countries with customs much different from the United States, most companies align themselves with a local company or agent who can deal with ethical and cultural issues and cut a path through foreign laws and bureaucracy.

Ethics and Job Tenure

When is it time to look for a new job? Of course, you want to be affiliated with a company of which you as a salesperson can be proud. Disagreements or issues of unethical behavior on the part of the company may, however, emerge during your employment. Deciding how to handle conflicts involving ethics can be stressful because your decision may mean either your termination or resignation. Weigh the options carefully and determine who is being helped and who is being hurt. Are there any alternative, creative options that minimize risk and allow career and conscience to be reconciled?

Whistle-Blowing

According to Nancy R. Hauserman, "In the pursuit of the goals of productivity and consumption, we have failed to preserve individual and community values. The individual has been reduced to a cog in the corporate wheel, a capital investment, a corporate property."[39] This attitude can make salespeople feel unimportant and fear that their ideas, suggestions, or revelations are not valid. This reaction is particularly true if they attempt to pass on valuable information to superiors and are rebuffed.

Consider the following situation:

Sandra Baker landed a great job as an educational software company sales rep. She is required to go on frequent business trips with her manager to colleges across the country. On the second trip, her manager books a dinner with a potential client at a very posh restaurant. Sandra is startled to realize that each main course is at least $50 and the wine purchased with the meal is the best of the best. She does a quick tally of the additional appetizers, desserts and drinks in her mind—the potential client's meal adds up to over $150. She's just familiarized herself with the company code of conduct policy, which states client meals should be under $50. She decides this must be an exception, but also decides to watch her manager more carefully. On her next trip, the manager engages in the same kind of behavior. This time, Sandra questions him; he responds by saying he'll just report there were more people at the meal. He also implies, as a junior, she should be careful with her own reputation and job security.

What should someone like Sandra do?

In Sandra's situation, a number of options could be considered:
- Make discreet inquiries into how common this type of expense is in the company and then decide how to proceed.
- Talk to her manager about the gift giving and see if they can implement a more ethical way of entertaining clients.
- Blow the whistle on the manager by reporting him to his superior.
- Ignore the whole situation and continue selling.
- Look for another job.

As careful as a salesperson may be when joining a company, an ethical dilemma such as this may arise eventually. In the best of all possible worlds, the violation should be exposed and those responsible punished, but what if pointing a finger at someone would cause the whistle-blower to be fired and put self and family in financial difficulties?

On the surface, the wiser course appears to be to keep quiet and let the problem resolve itself. Sometimes the best policy is to keep quiet until solid evidence can be accumulated or until the co-conspirators are identified, but silence as a long-term strategy is indefensible. The violation is likely to be exposed at some point, and being part of a cover-up is not a desirable position. Inaction can even be grounds for legal action.

We all naturally desire a positive work environment, and most people do not like to have disagreements with their bosses or co-workers. Nor do people want to be branded as a "rat" or somehow disloyal to the company by revealing unethical practices. So, when should you blow the whistle, and when should you "keep quiet?" Here are some basic guidelines to use when deciding if a situation merits whistle-blowing.[40] These guidelines may not be applicable to every situation you encounter, but they are a good place to start:

Probability of Effect. The probability that the action will actually take place and will cause harm to many people must be considered. An employee should be sure that the action in question will actually happen. The employee must then have absolute proof that the event will occur and that harm will be done.

Temporal Immediacy. An employee must consider the length of time between the present and the possibly harmful event. In addition, an employee must also consider the urgency of the problem in question: The more immediate the consequences of the potentially unethical practice, the stronger the case for whistle-blowing.

Concentration of Effort. A person must determine the intensity of the unethical practice or behavior. The question is how much intensity does the specific infraction carry. For example, according to this principle, stealing $1,000 from one person is more unethical than stealing $1 from 1,000 people.

How the Company Treats the Salesperson

The company may treat its salespeople as partners joined with it in a common mission or simply regard them as cannon fodder out in the field. Salespeople are an extremely valuable resource to a company and deserve to be treated fairly, informed of decisions affecting them, and protected from situations in which they might be under pressure to make unethical decisions. Glenn Wilson discusses what companies can do to prevent unethical behavior among salespeople:

- Avoid setting up management-incentive systems in a way that makes fudging the data tempting.

- Be accessible to salespeople in order to get early warnings on troublesome developments.

- Set up appropriate controls not only on financial accounts but also in customer complaints, salesperson dissatisfaction, and expense accounts.

- Set sales goals that are motivating but not impossible to achieve.[41]

If salespeople know their ideas are important and their judgment valued, they feel ownership in the organization and want to do a better job overall. According to a 2010 employee-based survey, Facebook ranked as the world's number one employer in terms of employee satisfaction. Employees suggested Facebook treated them with openness in communication and offered employees paid vacation days, parental top-ups and a range of other benefits. In the same survey, Southwest Airlines ranked number two. An employee wrote, "The company was founded on the principle that in order to succeed you need to treat your co-workers as well as you do your customers. This has led to industry-leading salaries, benefits and a fabulous place to work."[42] Companies like Facebook and Southwest Airlines have adapted to this new reality that workers need to feel valuable, so they are treating their employees not as forces to be controlled but as individuals to be empowered, in order to unshackle their skills, talents and potential.

Managing the Sales Territory

One of the most excruciating decisions that salespeople face is that concerning territories. A salesperson may have spent years cultivating customers in a territory only to have it divided by management or even taken away. A key account that is the salesperson's bread and butter may be made a house account so that the salesperson no longer gets those commissions. One of the common e-commerce blunders is that companies do not consider the impact of their Web strategies on sales force compensation.

The most important thing is to involve your sales reps in the decision and treat them in a straightforward manner. That's exactly what Tupperware Corporation did when it began selling its household products on its website. According to Christine Hanneman, "Our salespeople are involved in all of our channels, including our website."[43] Customers who purchase the Tupperware products on the company's website are asked who referred them, and the referring salesperson gets the normal commission.

Other aspects of fair treatment are involved in firing, demotion, and payment. When salespeople must be fired or demoted, they should be told the real reason. Decisions concerning compensation for salespeople should be handled with kid gloves, especially if reductions are forthcoming. In addition, decreasing compensation calls for careful, ethical decision making; such action is, moreover, extremely demoralizing and may lead to losing salespeople who will cost the company money to replace and retrain.

Be careful of gender power plays in the workplace.

Workplace Harassment and Discrimination

Another part of building and participating in an ethical business is the development and adherence to workplace harassment and discrimination guidelines. The United States Government's Equal Employment Opportunity Commission defines workplace discrimination as engaging in acts that prevent people from being hired, from keeping a job, or from receiving an equitable wage based on their age, gender, disability, national origin, pregnancy, race/color, or religion. Workplace harassment can be defined as any act, including offensive remarks, unfavorable treatment, or creating a hostile work environment, that may also eventually lead to the employee leaving or being fired from the job. The EEOC further defines sexual harassment, which violates Title VII of the Civil Rights Act of 1964, even more extensively:

"Sexual harassment can include unwelcome sexual advances, requests for sexual favors, and other verbal or physical harassment of a sexual nature.

Harassment does not have to be of a sexual nature, however, and can include offensive remarks about a person's sex. For example, it is illegal to harass a woman by making offensive comments about women in general.

Both victim and the harasser can be either a woman or a man, and the victim and harasser can be the same sex.

Although the law doesn't prohibit simple teasing, offhand comments, or isolated incidents that are not very serious, harassment is illegal when it is so frequent or severe that it creates a hostile or offensive work environment or when it results in an adverse employment decision (such as the victim being fired or demoted).

The harasser can be the victim's supervisor, a supervisor in another area, a co-worker, or someone who is not an employee of the employer, such as a client or customer."

In today's legal environment, any institution's failure to recognize the consequences of workplace sexual harassment can be a capital blunder. For employees in organizations lacking sound policy practices, the negative impact from sexual harassment—including liability, embarrassment and lost productivity—can be extensive.[44]

Sexual Harassment in Action

Read the following true-life situation and imagine what you would do if you were in Joseph's position.

Joseph was a male oilrig worker on a platform in the Gulf of Mexico. He was repeatedly sexually assaulted and "harassed, threatened and humiliated by members of his crew. He reported the incidents, but no action was taken against the offenders, and [he] "eventually quit—asking that his pink slip reflect that he 'voluntarily left due to sexual harassment and verbal abuse.'"

The situation just described is one of 20 groundbreaking sexual harassment cases as retold by *HR World*. In this case, "Joseph Oncale filed a sexual-harassment suit against his crew, but the District Court of Eastern Louisiana held that as a male, Oncale was not protected against the 1964 legislation that prohibits sexual harassment. After the decision was appealed to the U.S. Supreme Court, however, it was reversed by a 1998 ruling that declared that sexual harassment also "applied to harassment in the workplace between members of the same sex.'"[45]

On the surface, sexual harassment in the workplace appears to be on the decline. Complaints made to the Equal Employment Opportunity Commission dipped below 12,000 last year for the first time in 13 years. Interestingly, at the same time overall reporting rates have fallen, the number of men reporting a sexual harassment complaint has increased by 5 percent.[46] That's likely because companies are being more aggressive in encouraging people to report problems and then investigating them, thereby catching complaints before they reach the levels that prompt lawsuits. "By the time a lawsuit has been filed, it's too late," said Daniel A. Rizzi, deputy practice group leader of Nixon Peabody's national labor and employment law group in Jericho, New York. "An employer and HR professional should be looking to engage in preventative measures. An ounce of prevention is worth a pound of cure."[47]

Great gains have been made in the understanding and reduction of sexual harassment incidents in the workplace, particularly as the EEOC encourages employers to provide sexual harassment training. In fact, such training is now required by law in California for companies with over 50 employees. This training must be repeated every two years, and must be completed by new-hire managers within 6 months. As one trainer says, the focus in not on creating a culture of fear, but of creating "a respectful workplace that's productive and safe for everyone."[48] When considering employment with a particular company, make sure that there is a clearly defined sexual harassment policy firmly in place.

Ethics As Good Business

Ethical behavior may sometimes appear to be an unattractive alternative. After all, for every inside trader, fraudulent salesperson, or immoral politician who gets caught, perhaps hundreds get away with unethical behaviors. However, the recent bumper crop of ethical scandals in corporate America has brought with it a renewed concern for ethics. Some of the newfound conscience in corporations has filtered down to business people and individuals in every walk of life.

Gary Edwards of the nonprofit Ethics Resource Center in Washington, D.C., says that ethics is receiving more attention partially because of awareness on the part of businesses of "the enormous costs of unethical activity, in fines and penalties, in increased government regulation, and in damage to their public image."[49] In short, companies are paying attention to ethics because it happens to be good business strategy.

Professional salespeople who are honest and aboveboard in relationships with employers, customers, and competitors alike become trusted and valued individuals. The key to making repeat sales is to build up these kinds of relationships and maintain them. A well-defined personal code of ethics as part of one's character and as a basis for behavior is an invaluable asset.

Checkpoints in Ethical Decision Making

When faced with an ethical conflict, a standard set of questions to ask yourself is helpful. Use the five questions suggested below to guide your thinking.

A Five-Question Ethics Checklist:

1. Is it legal? Look at the law and other standards.

2. Is it fair to all concerned?

3. Would I want someone else to act this way toward me?

4. How would I explain my actions to someone else?

5. How will it make me feel about myself?

These questions first require careful evaluation regarding existing standards and personal liability. Next, the questions are designed to activate your sense of fairness and rationality. Last, realize that your personal feelings are important because negative feelings adversely affect positive performance. Ultimately, if your truthful answer to any one of these questions damages your self-image or causes you to be troubled by your conscience, then you should probably avoid the action in question.[50]

The ethics checklist can also be applied to the actions of a salesperson's company. An issue many sales professionals face today is how to sell products and services for a company that condones unethical practices. Salespeople who conduct business properly despite other ethical breaches within their companies aren't safe from trouble. Salespeople would be wise to report the problems through multiple channels within the organization to ensure that their concerns are heard.[51]

Legal Issues Facing the Salesperson

A serious problem faced by company sales forces today is a combination of antitrust law complexity and inadequate preventive legal guidance. Selling can sometimes be a mine field for salespeople who lack the legal expertise required to avoid violating various antitrust laws. Often without realizing it, sales representatives violate legal regulations through various actions every day, and they can be held personally liable. Fines can be imposed up to $1 million for individuals and $100 million for companies; criminal sanctions may also be imposed. Exhibit 3.2 illustrates some of the legal traps for unwary salespeople.[52]

∆Exhibit 3.2

Legal Traps for the Unwary Salesperson

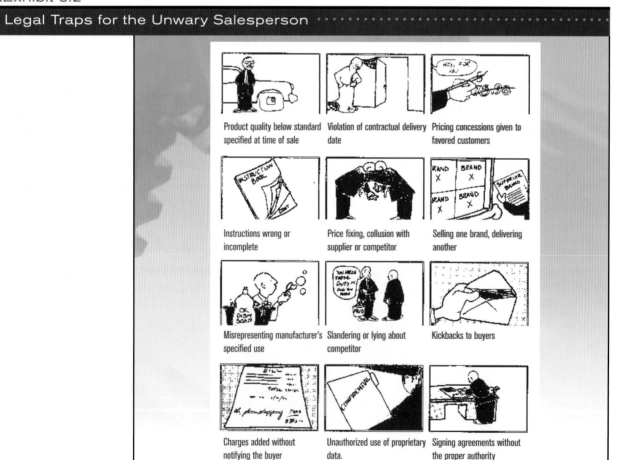

Product quality below standard specified at time of sale

Violation of contractual delivery date

Pricing concessions given to favored customers

Instructions wrong or incomplete

Price fixing, collusion with supplier or competitor

Selling one brand, delivering another

Misrepresenting manufacturer's specified use

Slandering or lying about competitor

Kickbacks to buyers

Charges added without notifying the buyer

Unauthorized use of proprietary data.

Signing agreements without the proper authority

Companies must properly train salespeople about required legal compliance to keep violations to a minimum. Actually, we would have practically no need for laws if all businesses played by the same ethical rules of the game. However, too many firms and individuals find the temptation to violate rules irresistible. Their violations, basically, fall into two broad categories:

1. Monopolistic actions, such as price-fixing or the acquisition of competitors.
2. Deceptive actions, such as false claims about products or services; or disparaging remarks about competitors.

A number of laws have been passed to preserve fair competition. You might consider these government regulations to be your rules of the game. They serve to protect two groups: The consumer by preventing monopolies and eliminating practices that tend to be deceptive; and business competitors by establishing rules that prevent powerful rivals from depriving smaller firms free access to the market and by protecting competitors from those who would engage in deceptive practices.

Exhibit 3.3 outlines the antitrust legislation that most profoundly affects salespeople. Whenever you aggressively pursue an account, you can face temptations. In the heat of the battle, you may exaggerate or perhaps actually think you have said something clearly to the prospect. For example, the sales representative must completely and in the clearest language possible warn the prospect of any potential hazard connected with use of the product. Saying, "Use of this equipment at improper voltage levels will result in damage to the product and concomitant operator hazard" may not be good enough.

A better statement would be: It must be plugged into 115 volts only. If used at a higher voltage, it can fly apart and injure or kill you." The courts may rule that the vague wording in the first statement is analogous to a sign in your yard that reads, *"Please keep off the grass,"* which is an insufficient warning if you know that the grass conceals rattlesnakes.

ΔExhibit 3.3

Key Antitrust Legislation Affecting Salespeople

Sherman Antitrust Act (1890). Section 1 deals with competition. It prohibits contracts, combinations, or conspiracies in restraint of trade. Section 2 deals with market control. It prohibits monopolies or attempts to monopolize.

Federal Trade Commission Act (1914). Established the Federal Trade Commission, a 5-member board of specialists with broad powers to investigate and to issue cease-and-desist orders. Section 5 of the act declares that "unfair methods of competition in commerce are unlawful" along with "unfair or deceptive acts or practices." (this latter phrase was added by the Wheeler Lea Act of 1938, which amended the FTC Act.)

Clayton Act (1914). Supplements the vagueness of the Sherman Act of 1890 by prohibiting certain practices. For instance, Section 2 of the act deals with price discrimination; Section 3 deals with tying clauses and exclusive dealings; Section 7 with intercorporate stockholdings; and Section 8 with interlocking directories. The key phrase stated in the law is, "where the effect may be to substantially lessen competition or tend to create a monopoly in any line of commerce." It provides that company personnel who violate the act can be held individually responsible.

Robinson-Patman Act (1936). Specifically amends Section 2 of the Clayton Act. It adds the phrase "to injure, destroy, or prevent competition." The law: (1) defines price discrimination as illegal (subject to certain defenses), (2) provides the Federal Trade Commission with the right to establish limits on quantity discounts, (3) prohibits promotional allowances except where made available to all "on proportionately equal terms," and (4) forbids brokerage allowances except to independent brokers.

Oh, and watch out for the rattlesnakes!

The pharmaceutical and high-tech industries have had some recent struggles over anti-trust legislation. A case filed on behalf of 14 independent California pharmacists targets not only the price differences between the United States and other countries, but also recent efforts by some American drug makers to prevent cheaper drugs from coming into the U.S.

The Microsoft anti-trust case is perhaps the biggest and best known in American history; here, Microsoft was accused of abusing monopoly power by bundling Internet Explorer into Microsoft Windows packages, which made it impossible for other browsers to compete. Interestingly, Microsoft settled the case by agreeing to some special conditions that ended up giving it antitrust immunity in licensing Windows with other platform software.

In view of all the laws affecting business, obviously sales representatives can say or do many things to get themselves, as well as their companies, into quite a bit of trouble. Since jail time for those who break antitrust laws has doubled, and the fines they face are much higher, it's safe to say crime doesn't pay. Exhibit 3.4 points out six tactics for salespeople to consider following as protection for themselves and for their companies when out in the field selling.[53]

ΔExhibit 3.4

How Salespeople Can Protect Against Violating Antitrust Laws

1. Know the difference between "sales puffery" and specific statements of fact made during the sales presentation and avoid using unwarranted exaggeration to make your story sound good.

2. Thoroughly educate each customer on all aspects of the product before completing the sale.

3. Know the technical specifications, capabilities, design peculiarities, and special characteristics of the products you sell.

4. Read carefully any and all promotional literature published by your company on the products being sold. Challenge what you consider to be untrue or exaggerated claims.

5. Study the company's terms of sale policies. Overstating your authority to establish prices can legally bind the company.

6. Stay current on all federal as well as state laws which affect warranties and guarantees.

The Uniform Commercial Code (UCC)

In addition to the federal antitrust laws, many other laws in all fifty states deal directly or indirectly with personal selling. Because of the diversity of these state laws, an attempt to cover them here is impractical. However, one set of regulations is consistent among the forty-nine states that have adopted it (Louisiana is the lone exception). The Uniform Commercial Code is a set of guidelines that spell out in some detail the conditions under which a sale may be consummated. It is a law that covers virtually all business transactions. The following aspects are governed by the UCC:

1. An offer to sell may be legally binding if it is made in writing, conveyed electronically or simply stated orally by the salesperson. A distinction is made between a legitimate offer to sell and an invitation to negotiate or deal.

2. The financing of the product or service must be explained clearly and completely. Salespeople must know the legal ramifications of any credit arrangements made with customers. Truth in lending also requires full disclosure of finance charges prior to closing the sale.

3. The salesperson must know the legal responsibilities if either party fails to live up to respective contractual obligations. For example, if the buyer is not able to pay the monthly finance charge, when can the seller take back the merchandise? If the goods are damaged or destroyed in transit, who is responsible for them?

4. Warranties and guarantees offered by the seller are basically the same and are governed by the UCC. The code defines both express warranties and implied warranties. *Express warranties* are statements and promises found in the advertising, sales literature, and labeling and in oral statements made by the salesperson. *Implied warranties* are a result of state law and the assumption that the product complies with those laws. Implied warranties are also in effect unless a disclaimer is made.[54] To be on the safe side, the salesperson should state what is promised as well as what is not promised. The warranty statement should also set time or use limits and clearly specify who is providing the warranty. For example, if you are a distributor representing a manufacturer's product, make certain the customer knows that the manufacturer, not you, is providing the warranty.

Cooling-Off Law

In addition to the regulations provided by the UCC, nearly all states have additional laws regulating door-to-door selling. Much in-home selling has been characterized as high-pressure selling. The cooling-off law gives buyers three days to think over their decision without a salesperson present. If buyers feel the decision is really not in their best interest, they may void the contract. This law applies to purchases for $25 or more. Firms selling door-to-door must typically provide potential buyers with information concerning these factors:

1. The number of days before the contract is binding.

2. How to cancel the agreement legally.

3. Any penalties involved in cancellation.

Despite any short terms gains you may make by behaving unethically in dealing with companies or individuals, doing the right thing is the only way to conduct yourself in the long run. Unethical behavior is selfish behavior, but when you abide by honest practices, you can rest easy knowing that you have other's best interests at heart and not simply your own.

There is no pillow as soft as a clear conscience.

SUMMARY

- It is essential that you develop your own personal code of ethics, but you should also be aware of the ethical obligations your company sets forth.

- Salespeople who find themselves in situations in which company violations are evident must make difficult choices about whether to blow the whistle on the company or settle on another strategy that could include finding another job.

- Ethics is a very smart business decision because salespeople who are honest in relationships with employers, customers, and competitors become trusted and respected business professionals.

- When faced with an ethical conflict, use a standard checklist of principled questions to guide your thinking.

- A series of federal laws was passed beginning in 1890 with the Sherman Antitrust Act, followed by the Federal Trade Commission Act, the Clayton Act, and the Robinson-Patman Act. These make engaging in practices that inhibit fair competition or deceive the customer illegal.

- Forty-nine states have adopted the Uniform Commercial Code, which defines in some detail the conditions under which a sale may be consummated. It defines exactly what is meant by a sale, sets out required information for financing and truth in lending, and states a salesperson's legal responsibilities.

- Because door-to-door selling has had the reputation of being high-pressure, special cooling-off laws have been passed in most states. These laws give the buyer a three-day period to break a sales agreement.

REVIEW QUESTIONS

1. We have heard much about questionable corporate activities, insider trading scandals, defense contract fraud, health risk cover-ups, and so on. Does this mean that corporations are not interested in ethics—that the bottom line is that corporate greed takes precedence over moral responsibility?

2. What kinds of management tactics make salespeople more likely to exhibit unethical behavior?

3. Should there be any focus on morality in institutions? After all, you cannot have institutional integrity without first having individual integrity, and isn't that the domain of home, church, and school?

4. Does having a corporate code of ethics for salespeople really do any good? Out in the real world where salespeople compete for sales, is a code of ethics practical? Do salespeople need channels of communication and support structures along with an ethics code?

5. Some years ago a Fordham University priest attended the Friday luncheon meeting of the Sales Executives Club of New York where he talked much about honesty in day-to-day business dealings. Asked why he did this, he replied, "What sales executives have to do puts them, among all business people, at the greatest risk of losing their souls." Do you agree with his statement?

6. A half century ago the medical department at Johns Manville Corporation began to receive information implicating asbestos inhalation as a cause of asbestosis. Manville's managers suppressed the research and concealed the information from employees. The entire company

was eventually brought to its knees by questions of corporate ethics. How can we explain this behavior? Were more than fifty years' worth of Manville executives immoral?

7. Name the major pieces of legislation and their basic requirements that govern the ethical behavior of companies and salespeople.

8. Explain the operation of the cooling-off law.

9. When some specific safety precautions are needed in connection with using a product, what are the responsibilities of the salesperson in giving this information to the customer?

10. For your personal reflection: Do you believe you would ever be at risk of succumbing to groupthink or gamesmanship and participating in unethical or illegal activities? Have you ever been persuaded by peer pressure to do something for which you were later sorry? What can you do to lessen the possibility of compromising your own personal ethics?

ROLE-PLAY EXERCISES

The following role-play exercises help build teams, improve communication, and emphasize the real-world side of selling. They are meant to be challenging, to help you learn how to deal with problems that have no single right answer, and to use a variety of skills beyond those employed in a typical review question. Read and complete each activity. Then in the next class, discuss and compare answers with other classmates.

Role Play 3.1 – What is the Effect of Company Codes of Ethics?

Pair off with another student with whom you have worked previously in this class. After briefly conducting online research to locate some major companies in your area that have codes of ethics (you might have to contact their human resources office to obtain a copy), identify one company for further scrutiny. Interview a sales manager at that company and ask the following questions:

1. Does your company have a code of ethics for employees in sales? Do you have a copy?

2. Is the content of the code included in sales training for new employees? Are they tested on their understanding of it? Are they required to indicate their acceptance of the code?

3. Do you use or refer to the code when deciding whether a particular sales practice should be adopted or followed? If so, does the code actually influence your decision? If you don't use or refer to the code, why not?

4. In your opinion, does the code of ethics actually help or impede the company's ability to succeed?

After the above interview, proceed to interview a salesperson for the same company, *but without the knowledge of the sales manager*. Ask the same four questions and later jot down a record of the responses. In class, for each question, role-play the response of the sales manager and of the salesperson. See if the class can account for any differences between them.

Role Play 3.2 – Crossing the Line?

You will work independently on this exercise. As a class, in groups, or independently, view the film, Disclosure (1994), starring Michael Douglas and Demi Moore. Take notes, and be prepared to discuss the following questions:

1. Was Tom Sanders (Michael Douglas's character) a victim of sexual harassment according to law, or was Meredith Johnson (Demi Moore's character) merely aggressive in pursuing what was otherwise a consensual relationship?

2. At what point might Meredith have crossed an ethical or legal line?

3. What actions might Tom have taken to prevent any inappropriate behavior, and when?

4. Given Tom and Meredith's previous relationship and their current positions, was there anything that Tom could have done to preserve his dignity while still retaining his job?

5. To what extent was the company liable for protecting Tom against Meredith's predatory behavior?

6. By reversing stereotypical gender roles, has this film created a distorted picture of sexual harassment that amounts to an injustice against female employees?

7. If *you* were in Tom's shoes, what would you do?

Role Play 3.3 – Ask an Attorney

Invite an attorney to class that works with sales contracts and a sales representative he or she is acquainted with. Ask the attorney and sales rep to present several real-life mini scenarios of borderline sales activities from their personal experiences. Let the students decide (in writing and orally) if those involved acted ethically and legally and explain why.

CASE STUDIES

The following case studies present you with selling scenarios that require you to apply the critical skills discussed in the chapter and give you training through simulation, role-playing, and practical learning situations. They are meant to be both engaging and challenging, and like the role-play exercises, don't have one right answer.

Case 3.1 – Selling Off-Label

In the pharmacy industry, off-label marketing involves selling prescription drugs for purposes and conditions that are not identified on the FDA-approved label and accompanying specifications. This means that a drug that has been approved and tested for efficacy and safety for very specific uses is marketed and prescribed by physicians for uses for which such testing has not been performed or concluded. Accordingly, selling drugs off-label violates important ethical codes for the industry and is considered a criminal offense.

Over the past several decades, pharmaceutical companies have been found in violation of such laws and codes. In recent years, several major companies—Johnson & Johnson, AstraZeneca, Eli Lilly & Co., and Pfizer—have paid enormous fines and been subjected to other penalties for such violations.[1] Since 2004, Lilly, Bristol-Meyers Squibb, and 4 other companies have paid $7 billion in fines and penalties. Most spectacularly, Pfizer alone paid $2.9 billion in fines and settlements in 2009 for this practice.[2] Despite the fines, billions more were retained as revenue from off-label sales. With such sums at stake, the pressures on company representatives are immense.

Gwen Olsen was a sales representative selling Haldol (Haloperidol) for McNeil Laboratories. Haloperidol is an antipsychotic drug that is also used to treat verbal and motor tics as in Tourette's disorder as well as explosive behavior in children. When Gwen found that her sales quota for this drug

---

1 "Drugmakers Continue Off-Label Marketing Despite Large Fines," NJ.com, 6/6/2010, http://www.nj.com/business/index.ssf/2010/06/drugmakers_continue_off-label.html, accessed 4/4/11.

2 "Pfizer Broke the Law by Promoting Drugs for Unapproved Uses," Bloomberg.com, 11/09/09, http://www.bloomberg.com/apps/news?pid=newsarchive&sid=a4yV1nYxCGoA, accessed 4/4/11.

was going to fall short, thereby disqualifying her for an important bonus, she asked her manager what to do. He recommended marketing the drug to nursing homes and physicians who cared for their patients. The suggestion worked, and Gwen increased her sales by 25%. Nevertheless, she noticed that the drug was being used for off-label reasons, mainly to control the behavior of elderly patients who were difficult to manage. The extreme decline of one patient whom Gwen had befriended caused Gwen to undergo a crisis of conscience for her role in the unapproved use of the drug. For the full account, watch Gwen's description of the situation that she faced: http://www.youtube.com/watch?v=v5jYU20dH4A&feature=player_embedded.

After watching the video, come to class prepared to discuss the following questions:

1. Was what Gwen did unethical or illegal? Citing principles discussed in Chapter 3, explain your answer.

2. Should Gwen really be upset at her own behavior? Doesn't most of the responsibility fall on her manager and the company?

3. Knowing how difficult it is to find high-paying sales positions, do you think Gwen did the right thing by leaving pharmaceutical sales? Would you? Explain.

4. Leaving questions of legality aside for a moment, should selling drugs off-label really be considered unethical? If a society's ethics is simply the sum-total of individual decisions, and if selling off-label continues to be widespread in the pharmaceutical industry, how can anyone say that a strategy that is routinely adopted by so many is unethical?

Case 3.2 – Boxed In

As the smoke curled up from the small fire in his boss's ashtray, Nick Roberts realized that he was in a tough spot. Having just graduated from college, he had recently moved to Dallas, Texas, with his wife and infant son. He had majored in economics and history as an undergraduate and, through connections provided by his wealthy father-in-law, had landed a lucrative position as corporate salesperson with Southwestern Container Corporation. The company manufactured and sold corrugated containers to businesses throughout the southwest. He and his wife were thrilled about his new job and their prospects for the future. But now, Nick wasn't so sure.

You see, the fire in the ashtray served a very real purpose and was no accident. Nick's boss had just concluded a phone call in his office with his counterparts at two other companies. As the 20-minute conversation among the three competitors proceeded, Nick and the other sales staff were allowed to listen via speakerphone. The sole topic discussed was the price structure for various grades and sizes of corrugated containers for the region. The three companies thrived on competing for business accounts based on service, but they had come to realize over time that competing on price or price plus quality reduced their profits. If they could agree on price, they could sell boxes more cheaply to larger customers and more expensively to smaller customers. And overall, they could keep prices elevated without having to worry about being undercut by a competitor. Life was easier, simpler, and more lucrative that way. At the conclusion of the conference call, Nick's boss touched a match to his notes and dropped the burning paper into his ashtray.

As the meeting broke up, Nick was sweating. What should he do? If he sold containers according to the agreed price structure, was he acting unethically? Could he even go to jail? After all his father-in-law had done to get him this job, how could he just walk away? How would his young family survive? Should he blow the whistle on the entire company? Nick's mind was swirling. What would you advise him to do, and why?

"Communication—the human connection—is the key to personal and career success."

– Paul J. Meyer

Chapter 4

Purchase Behavior and Communication

Learning Objectives

- Determine the differences between individual and organizational buyers.

- Learn the environmental influences on the purchase decision process.

- Find out what goes into the successful sending and receiving of a message.

- Examine methods for overcoming communication barriers.

- Understand the importance of using the voice as a communication tool.

- Explore the effects of body language and proxemics in selling.

ΔExhibit 4.1

Lincoln's Gettysburg Address

"Four score and seven years ago our fathers brought forth on this continent, a new nation, conceived in Liberty, and dedicated to the proposition that all men are created equal.

Now we are engaged in a great civil war, testing whether that nation, or any nation so conceived and so dedicated, can long endure. We are met on a great battlefield of that war. We have come to dedicate a portion of that field, as a final resting place for those who here gave their lives that that nation might live. It is altogether fitting and proper that we should do this.

But, in a larger sense, we cannot dedicate—we cannot consecrate—we cannot hallow—this ground. The brave men, living and dead, who struggled here, have consecrated it, far above our poor power to add or detract. The world will little note, nor long remember what we say here, but it can never forget what they did here. It is for us the living, rather, to be dedicated here to the unfinished work which they who fought here have thus far so nobly advanced. It is rather for us to be here dedicated to the great task remaining before us—that from these honored dead we take increased devotion to that cause for which they gave the last full measure of devotion—that we here highly resolve that these dead shall not have died in vain—that this nation, under God, shall have a new birth of freedom—and that government of the people, by the people, for the people, shall not perish from the earth."

The famous speech delivered by President Abraham Lincoln at the dedication of the Gettysburg National Cemetery on November 19, 1863

Exhibit 4.1 is the famous Gettysburg Address given by President Abraham Lincoln. The entire speech lasted about two minutes with a total of 268 words: 198 are one-syllable words, 50 are two-syllable words, and only 20 are words of more than two syllables. Despite the lack of eloquent or complicated verbiage, the Gettysburg Address is recognized as a classic model of the noblest kind of oratory.

When asked to explain Britain's wartime policy to Parliament, Prime Minister Winston Churchill said, "It is to wage war, by sea, land and air, with all our might and with all the strength that God can give us." As Neil Armstrong first set foot on the moon he said simply, "That's one small step for man, one giant leap for mankind." These leaders demonstrate that you don't have to use big words to make a *big* impact.

Not only are small words more understandable and exact than large words, they also add elegance to your speaking and writing. Realize and appreciate the persuasive power of a well-written sales proposal. Just think how much more you could sell if you could talk and write equally well. If you must choose between a large word and a small word, pick the small word every time. Take a lesson from your local highway department. Place a sign at the boundaries of your speech that reads: *Caution—Small Words at Work.*

CAUTION:
SMALL
WORDS
AT WORK

Consumer Behavior: Why People Buy

- A retail salesperson working at a furniture store in Las Cruces, New Mexico convinces a middle aged couple to purchase a Memory Foam mattress set by emphasizing her own back problems and experiences with the product.

- Students from a rural school corporation in Union City, Indiana, convince members of their community to donate funds for their renewable energy source program that is designed to generate revenue to help benefit the school's budget by offsetting utility costs. The students receive the necessary funds from the community members to successfully launch the program and are able to install a wind turbine from the Nordic Windpower company.

- The Kellogg Company in Battlecreek, Michigan, has decided to make and market a new cookie with a toffee embedded shortbread cookie center coated in a hard chocolate shell in their Keebler division. Three competing salespeople who are offering a machine that will make this product begin calling on Kellogg. This major capital investment requires consideration by top executives, tax specialists, production personnel, and marketing personnel. The three salespeople will have direct, frequent contact with all of these Kellogg personnel and will call in technical experts to assist. The purchase decision will take many months to complete.

These three situations involve consumer behavior and illustrate some diverse aspects of the purchase decision process. *Consumer behavior* is the set of actions that make up an individual's consideration, purchase, and use of products and services.[1] The term consumer behavior includes both the purchase and the consumption of products or services. Your role is vital in this process of matching the company's product offerings to the needs of the prospective buyer.

Countless factors determine whether or not a prospect will purchase any given product. One major determinant of a brand's competitiveness is how a product's package is perceived. The difficulty lies in measuring or projecting the marketplace impact of a particular design system for your product or service. For years, it has been accepted that consumer research should take place to test potential packaging changes for well-established brands. Certainly, fundamental changes to the appearance of Cheerios, Tide, or Kraft products would not happen without consumer research to assess new design systems. However, relatively few companies take a disciplined approach to evaluating the performance of their current packaging. As a result, major decisions to change a brand's appearance are often made on the basis of intuition or in response to competitive activity. As a result, many packaging changes come years too late, after the brand has gone into decline. In other cases, unnecessary redesigns may waste resources and risk confusing or alienating its users. Brand usage and familiarity are powerful forces, and it is vital that your product appeal to the senses of your prospect, especially for higher priced items.[2]

However, the process does not end with the sale of a product or service neatly presented in a well-designed package. Salespeople must be equally concerned with consumer satisfaction after the sale. This chapter introduces a model of the consumer's decision-making process, considers a number of environmental factors that influence this process, and then examines both the verbal and nonverbal elements of the communication process, with special emphasis on body *language and proxemics* (the use of space).

The Purchase Decision Process

Consumers make multiple product decisions every day, and each decision they make depends on how they process information.[3] The model shown in Exhibit 4.2 provides a useful tool for examining the buying process. It presents a view of the buyer as someone observed not in a single act, but in a complex problem-solving process. Obviously, this model cannot provide all the answers for salespeople, but it does provide knowledge that can be used in individual sales situations as a guide for understanding what the prospect faces and deciding how you can best assist in the decision-making process.[4]

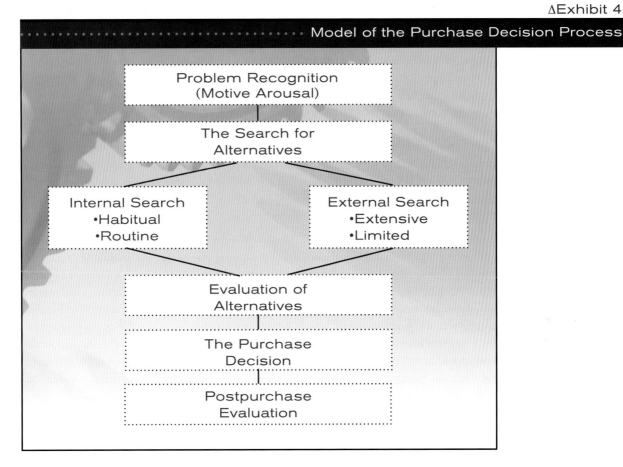

Model of the Purchase Decision Process

To understand why an individual makes a certain purchase decision, you must look at events leading up to and then following the purchase act itself. A buyer passes through five stages:

1. Problem recognition
2. Search for alternatives
3. Evaluation of alternatives
4. The purchase decision
5. Post-purchase evaluation

Problem Recognition. The purchase process begins with conscious recognition that a problem or need exists and must be satisfied. A need may be something regarded as necessary, or something that the individual wants or desires and therefore perceives as a need. No one takes action until motivated to do so, and this motivation arises from the awareness of a need. Therefore, salespeople must recognize needs that are already active or to find a way to create or stimulate recognition of a need of which the prospective buyer has not yet become aware. *All kinds of needs affect buying decisions.* Abraham Maslow defined the five levels of needs as physiological, safety, social, esteem, and self-actualization. Regardless of the kind of need, some buyers will not be aware of the nature of their needs until a salesperson brings them out into the open.

Search for Alternatives. After recognizing an unsatisfied need, the buyer begins to search for information concerning the available alternatives. The search may involve both internal and external sources. The internal search makes use of the buyer's previous experiences, learning, and attitudes, and often occurs without conscious effort. Even in the organizational markets, much purchasing is routine. A great deal of it can be done through catalogs or simply a phone call to a regular supplier. However, the external search process adds dynamics. It may require an extensive information search or a more limited search for alternatives.

The Internet provides consumers with faster, more advanced ways to search for alternatives. Companies that want to survive in this information-rich marketplace must demonstrate that they can effectively communicate with customers and prospects through the latest methods of technology.[5] To successfully compete in the online marketplace, companies are looking for ways to implement social media in their marketing campaigns in order to reach online customers.[6] Online buying provides more options because customers can research and compare competing products. In fact, the popularity of *comparison shopping websites* such as Shopzilla.com and NexTag.com have seen substantial growth in the last several years because they allow purchasers to read reviews and compare products side-by-side in every area, from appearance to performance.

Evaluation of Alternatives. The search process provides the buyer with knowledge of several alternative products. All individual consumers have specific criteria they use for making a decision—personal mental rules for matching alternatives with motives. These criteria are learned by actual experience with the product or derived from information obtained from commercial or social sources.

If you can determine the buyer's *choice criteria*, you can tailor the presentation to focus on specific product or service benefits that differentiate your product from those of the competition. Once you have matched the prospect's buying motives with what you have to offer, the *determinant* attributes come into play: Price, reputation, service capabilities, and design components. Identifying the dominant buying motives that determine a particular buyer's behavior in the actual decision-making process is vital to closing the sale.

Purchase Decision. After evaluating all the alternatives discovered during the search process, the buyer is ready to make the purchase decision—actually, a whole set of decisions. Buyers want to minimize their risk and simplify the decision-making process as much as possible. The professional salesperson knows this and assists the buyer in making decisions. The salesperson finds out how the product or service fits into the buyer's system by asking questions: *Who else will use it? How is it to be used? Where? When? With what other products will it be used?* Your role in assisting prospects to reach a satisfactory purchasing decision is what makes relationship selling such a rewarding and fulfilling career.

Post-purchase Evaluation. The purchase decision process continues after the product or service choice has been made. The buyer evaluates the purchase in terms of pre-purchase expectations and decides whether it has been satisfactory. Sometimes the buyer experiences post-purchase anxiety or *cognitive dissonance*, also commonly known as buyer's remorse. The magnitude of the anxiety or tension depends on the importance of the decision and the attractiveness of the rejected alternatives. You can help lessen this feeling by providing exceptional customer service and follow-up after the sale (as discussed in Chapter 14).

Influences on the Purchase Decision Process

Buying motives cannot be observed directly, but can be inferred from observed behavior. Exhibit 4.3 illustrates some of the many *psychological* and *sociocultural* factors that influence a buyer's purchase decision process. You must understand the significance and impact of these factors at the various stages of the decision-making process:

1. Behavioral concepts, such as perception and self-image, affect problem recognition.

2. Sociocultural factors, such as culture, physical environment, and social class, all influence the nature and scope of the information search.

3. Psychological factors, such as the mood of the moment, attitudes, and perception of oneself, combine with sociocultural factors to influence purchase decisions.

You can make positive use of these factors by becoming proficient in the art of communication—the sending and receiving of messages in a manner that results in understanding, productive discussion, and fulfillment of a want or a need.

∆Exhibit 4.3

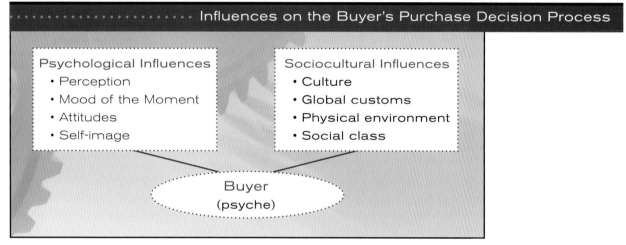

Influences on the Buyer's Purchase Decision Process

Psychological Influences
• Perception
• Mood of the Moment
• Attitudes
• Self-image

Sociocultural Influences
• Culture
• Global customs
• Physical environment
• Social class

Buyer
(psyche)

Psychological Influences: It's All in Your Head

Several psychological factors affect a prospect's buying decision. You must be aware of these factors and understand the role they play in the process. Once you learn how these factors influence the sales process, you can use them to your advantage in future selling situations as they enable you to more accurately read the prospect's overall disposition.

Perception. Individual behavior is an organized and meaningful response to the world as that particular person sees it. We perceive situations according to our own personal needs, values, expectations, past experience, and training. Exhibit 4.4 illustrates the difference in individual perceptions. How many squares do you see? Can you find them? Check the answer given in the chapter endnotes.[7] If you didn't see that many, you may be exercising selective perception. What prospects perceive as important to themselves is often not what you think is most important. It's not good enough to just say "hello" when you call on someone. While recognition is a good thing, it doesn't take the place of meeting the customer's expectations. Clients, as well as prospective customers, now have significantly higher service expectations today than ever before.

∆Exhibit 4.4

How Many Squares Do You See?

The sophisticated market and high levels of competition have educated the business world and the individual consumer to expect more.[8] You must work to build the right perception in the minds of your customers and prospects.

Mood of the Moment. Perception is also influenced by an individual's psychological state or the mood of the moment. On some days a minor mishap may be laughed off, but if nothing has gone right all day, the same situation may make your blood boil.

Attitude. Attitudes are merely habits of thought and habitual patterns of response to stimuli and experiences. Because they have been used so often, they have become automatic and are used to save the time that would be required to think about a situation and make a decision. For example, some prospects operate from the concept that what has been done in the past is the best way to do things in the future. In other words, their attitude is that change is bad. Any attitude that makes the purchase decision more difficult creates a barrier that must be overcome before a sale can be made.

Negative attitudes are a problem because they are often unconscious. Because they are often habitual responses based on past experience, the individual involved no longer thinks about them and is unaware that they exist. In contrast, prospects who adopt attitudes of open-mindedness, enthusiasm, innovativeness, and willingness to explore new ideas are a joy for the relationship salesperson to find.

Self-Image. Self-image is an individual's unique and personal self-appraisal at a given moment in time. It affects what is perceived as reality and, as a result, how communication proceeds. In choosing how to communicate, even more important than what is true is what the person believes is true.[9] Self-image often has a great deal of influence on a prospect's tendency to be a conspicuous consumer. *Conspicuous consumption* is a relatively new trend in which consumers spend money on unnecessary

Self-image affects how we see and react to circumstances.

and unproductive leisure expenditures and big-ticket items that are considered more "flashy" than practical. Perhaps it is a way purchasers can compensate for a less than positive self-image, or perhaps they practice conspicuous consumption for other reasons. Regardless of the motive, be aware of the power of this buying motive.[10]

Most psychologists suggest that by age seven or eight we have decided what kind of person we are, the kind of person we will become, how our world will respond or react to us, with what kind of people we want to deal, and what our environment will be like.[11] The self-image includes dimensions that are not technically "self," but they are so closely identified with the self that they operate as though they are real. For example, people routinely talk about "my" company or "my" school, and some parents see their children as extensions of themselves. We as humans have a tendency to attach ownership to anything we can.

Every behavior can be explained if the individual's self-image is understood. In one sense we are all self-centered, and we act in keeping with what we consider best for us at the moment. If you wish to communicate effectively, you must learn to recognize these important dimensions of the prospect's self-image:

1. **Physical.** People picture themselves as tall or short, weak or strong, attractive or unattractive, lean or overweight. They buy products that fit their self-image or promise to change it to fit a desired goal.
2. **Social.** Individuals see themselves as liked or disliked, accepted or rejected, loved or unwanted, successful or failures.
3. **Moral.** Internalized values give people a picture of themselves as loyal or disloyal, honest or dishonest, straightforward or devious.

Sociocultural Influences

In addition to psychological influences, it is essential to understand how sociocultural influences operate to determine people's communication.

Culture. Culture is a way of looking at life that is handed down from one generation to another. Arguably, it is almost completely learned. The effects of culture can be observed in what people do, see, and use, and in how they reach judgments about people, events, and experiences. Individuals' values develop as a result of their reactions to the environment in which they live. Our cultural environment exerts a powerful influence on how messages are both sent and received. A large percentage of Americans attach a positive connotation to concepts such as success, competition, efficiency, freedom, and material wealth. However, the positive reception to these words is not universal. Even within the United States, subcultures of many kinds exist, each with its own set of values, priorities, and concepts. Even more pronounced are cultural differences that affect communication among people from different parts of the world, a fact that has broad implications for salespeople in the global marketplace of today.[12] Exhibit 4.5 illustrates that selling to and dealing with prospects from overseas demands cultural sensitivity. For example, in Japan that means showing a business card the same respect you would show a person.[13]

ΔExhibit 4.5

Treat a Business Card with Respect

Steve Waterhouse faced the moment he had been waiting for. His firm had been courting a big Tokyo meeting planning company for the past six months. At a National Speakers Association convention in San Antonio, Texas, Waterhouse had the good fortune (or so it seemed) to meet with the firm's representative to discuss services his company might buy. "He handed his business card to me in the traditional Japanese way," Waterhouse recalls—extending the card while holding onto both corners. "I took the card and scribbled a note on the back of it." Much to his dismay, Waterhouse looked up to find the man appalled at what he had just done. "I quickly put it away and then apologized profusely, but the damage was already done." Steve Waterhouse lost a sale worth $100,000 to his company!

A Global Perspective. Foreign cultures adhere to business customs, protocols, and body language used in basic communication that differ greatly from those used in America. If you want to sell to international customers, whether here or overseas, you must first establish rapport. Insensitivity to other people's customs and ways of communicating may derail your best selling efforts. With major companies moving large portions of their operations overseas, American business people, and specifically those in sales, must be aware of the differences they will encounter when dealing with others outside the U.S. and learn how to best use those differences to their advantage.[14]

Those who sell to international customers may get by with a wink and a "see ya later," but only if they know how their language and gestures will be interpreted; body talk does not have a universal language. According to Diane Ackerman's book, *A Natural History of the Senses*, "Members of a tribe in New Guinea say good-bye by putting a hand in each other's armpit, withdrawing it, and stroking it over themselves, thus becoming coated with the friend's scent." Thank goodness that when we say goodbye to a client, we can just shake hands—or can we?

In France, the traditional American handshake is considered much too rough; a quick handshake with slight pressure is preferred. Throughout Latin America, however, the greeting is often more exuberant. A hearty embrace is common among both men and women. They often follow it with a slap on the back. In Ecuador, greeting a person without shaking hands is a sign of special respect. Throughout India, it is considered rude to touch women, so never offer to shake their hands. Exhibit 4.6 illustrates several cross-cultural considerations when conducting business globally.

ΔExhibit 4.6

Cultural Differences From a Global Perspective ·

1. Avoid slang or sports metaphors such as, "That proposal is way out in left field!" or "Are we in the ballpark on price?" They may mean nothing to other cultures.

2. Always use your last name when answering the telephone in Germany such as, "Schultz speaking." When you call a customer say your last name first: "This is Schultz, Thomas Schultz."

3. Americans and Canadians typically take a business card and pocket it without reviewing the information. In France, Italy, Switzerland, and Japan, the business card is an extension of the person who gives it so cards need to be treated with much respect.

4. After introductions, Americans and Canadians will tend to move quickly into business. However, in Latin America and China business can only proceed after a relationship has been built.

5. In Japan, you can never be too polite, too humble, or too apologetic. Make apologizing routine. This is one of the greatest areas of cultural difference between our two countries.

6. Always appear to be less informed and less skilled in the negotiation process than you really are. To the Japanese there is no such thing as a quick deal.

7. The British and Russians are masters at using the pressure of silence. Don't speak until your prospect has responded to your last comment.

Physical Environment. Americans usually keep their houses and offices at a cozy 72 to 78 degrees; the British prefer an indoor setting of 60 to 65 degrees. Other elements of the environment, such as sound level, are also important. Most people of middle age and older enjoy a quiet, restful environment; younger people tend to be stimulated by loud music and object less strenuously to machine noise. Don't attempt to make a presentation to a 60-year-old prospect over dinner in a restaurant that features live rock music, unless of course that prospect is Steven Tyler. The physical environment must be conducive to communication.

Social Class. From the beginning of civilization, social classes have existed to some degree. In the United States, social structure is less rigid than in some other nations, in which it may be tied to religion, kinship, or inherited ownership of land. Americans often climb into new social classes by earning higher educations and filling prestigious jobs. Social class groupings are based largely on source of wealth, occupation, education, type of housing, and location. It is important to be aware that people tend to adopt buying behaviors, tastes, and ways of communicating that are in keeping with the social class to which they consider themselves members.

Organizational Versus Consumer Buying

Business-to-business buyers include all organizations—both profit and nonprofit—that buy products or services for their own use, resell to other organizations, or sell to the ultimate consumer. Individual consumers, with a comparatively small number of transactions, are not considered in this category. The five-stage purchase decision process fits the ultimate consumer buyer adequately, and the two processes are generally similar, but the organizational buyer follows a more complex purchase decision process. The following are the four main areas where fundamental differences exist between consumer purchasing and organizational buying:

Decision Maker. The ultimate consumer is the decision maker in a purchase. In an organizational setting, decisions are often made by a team, commonly referred to as a buying center. The *buying center* is an ad hoc, cross-departmental, decision-making unit consisting of all individuals who play a role in formulating the purchasing recommendation.

Buying Criteria. Individual consumers have a limited set of factors to weigh in making a buying decision, whereas business markets often require products that are complex, expensive, and purchased in larger quantities.

Length of Relationship. Organizational buyers desire to stay with suppliers longer, to reduce the need for frequent negotiation. This interdependence underlies the need to build a long-term relationship. As a result, many business buyers and sellers have formed what are referred to as *strategic business alliances*.

Buying Motives. Every buying decision made—consumer or organizational—is based on a dominant motive. Buying motives may be either rational or emotional. Your selling skills are not nearly as important as the customer's reasons for buying. In fact, your reasons for selling are useless if they don't match the customer's reasons for buying.[15] Individual consumers often buy based on emotion and later attempt to rationalize their decisions. For organizational buyers, however, rational motives are usually dominant, though they must take emotional motives into account as well. Exhibit 4.7 lists the basic motives that lead to both consumer and organizational purchases.

ΔExhibit 4.7

Consumer and Organizational Buying Motives

Consumer Buying Motives	Organizational Buying Motives
• Alleviate fear	• Economy
• Secure social approval	• Flexibility
• Satisfy bodily needs	• Uniformity of output
• Experience happiness or pleasure	• Salability
• Gain an advantage	• Protection
• Imitate	• Utility
• Dominate others	• Guarantees
• Enjoy recreation	• Delivery
• Improve health	• Quality

Multiple Buying Influences

The responsibility for organizational buying decisions may lie with more than a single individual. Organizations often set dollar limits beyond which purchase decisions must involve additional executives, more red tape, and more paperwork. Buying committees or teams drawn from the various departments become involved in decision making. The members of this team, called a *buying center*, share common goals and knowledge relevant to the purchase decision. A major reason for working with the buying center is to discover the key person or persons who actually make or strongly influence the final decision. Researchers have identified five specific roles played by the people who constitute a buying center:[16]

1. **Users**. These individuals are those who will actually use the product or service purchased; for example, a telemarketing sales force whose members will be the primary users of a proposed new telephone system.
2. **Buyers**. Buyers have formal authority to make the purchase, such as the purchasing agent.
3. **Influencers**. Influencers are the individuals who provide information, directly or indirectly, throughout the buying process to members of the buying center. For example, the supervisor for the telemarketing division may suggest certain features needed in a telephone system to make the calling process more efficient.
4. **Deciders**. This role is played by those who have the power and authority to choose from among the various suppliers. They make the final decision.
5. **Gatekeepers**. Within any typical organization, the information needed in the decision making process is influenced by the gatekeepers—those who control the flow of information into the buying center.[17] Gatekeepers are invaluable to the group's decision-making process.

The Communication Agenda

Relationship selling thrives on good communication. Communication can be viewed as the verbal and nonverbal passing of information between you, the *sender*, and your prospect, the *receiver*. However, for effective communication to take place, each person must understand the intended message. Thus, the goal of communication is a *mutual understanding*.[18]

Exhibit 4.8 shows the channel through which communication must flow in a selling situation. At each intersection the potential exists for both roadblocks and opportunities. Although the model considers communication from the salesperson's perspective, in any successful relationship both parties participate meaningfully in an active two-way process.[19]

ΔExhibit 4.8

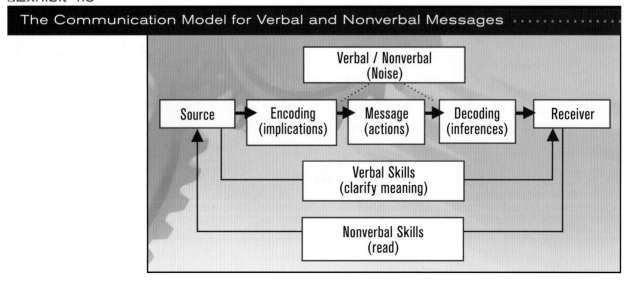

The Communication Model for Verbal and Nonverbal Messages

Encoding the Message

Encoding is the process in which the salesperson converts an idea or concept into *symbols* the buyer can clearly understand. You know what you are trying to say; the real challenge is getting your point across.[20] This requires the proper mix of symbols to express your meaning correctly. The most common symbols used in delivering a message are words, pictures, numbers, sounds, physical touch, smell, body movement, and taste. You must encode the message, organize it, and put it into a presentation format the prospect will understand, accept, and believe. Effective encoding of your message is based on a thorough knowledge of the prospect's needs.

Communication is successful if the symbols chosen make it possible for the prospect to understand. The ultimate challenge in communication is to transfer your thoughts, ideas, and intentions without distortion or omission. Because communication is affected by the assumptions and needs of both parties—as well as by outside factors such as time constraints, interruptions, and the environment—communication is often far from perfect.

There are three basic purposes for encoding your message:

1. To influence the attitudes and behavior of the prospect.

2. To move the buyer through a sequence of mind changes until a buying decision is made.

3. To obtain affirmative action upon the five fundamental buying decisions: need, product, source, price, and time.

The Message Itself: More Than Words

The actual message is a blend of symbols that are used to influence a change in a prospect's attitude or behavior, and it involves both verbal and nonverbal elements. In his book, *Silent Messages*, Albert Mehrabian points out that words convey only 7 percent of feelings and emotions, tone of voice conveys 38 percent, and visual communication conveys the remaining 55 percent.[21] Nonverbal elements in the presentation make up the majority of the total impact. In essence, *it's not what you say, but how you say it.*

If verbal and nonverbal messages conflict, the listener generally relies on the nonverbal message. Exhibit 4.9 illustrates the contribution of various factors to the messages we deliver to others and the amount of control we maintain over each one. The factors most easily controlled are those that have the least effect, and those with the biggest impact are the most difficult to control because they happen automatically.

ΔExhibit 4.9

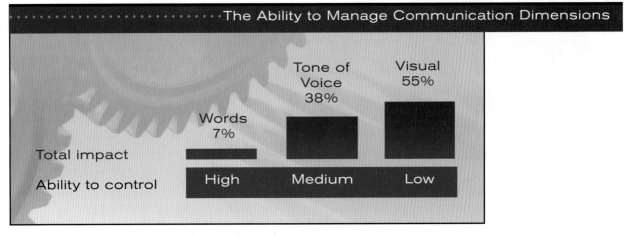

The Ability to Manage Communication Dimensions

The process of delivering the message begins with visual impressions because they happen first. If a salesperson walks hesitantly into a prospect's office wearing a listless or worried expression, the prospect is immediately wary. That provides an instantly unappealing visual message. If the salesperson then extends a clammy palm with a "dead-fish" handshake, an unpleasant touch is added; and if an unenthusiastic message is delivered in a monotone, the sound itself drowns out the words. In this scenario, the cluster of negative nonverbal cues completely masks the real message.

Research suggests that if the first thirty seconds of a communication result in a negative impression, you must spend the next four minutes just to overcome that impression before any communication can truly begin.[22] Unfortunately, the prospect may decide not to buy before the situation can be reversed.

Decoding the Message

Decoding is the mental process by which prospects figure out the meaning of a message. It is the way in which your prospect attempts to translate the symbols used in your presentation into something that relates to their needs. If the message was obviously both understood as intended and also accepted, there is no problem. At this step in the process, either real communication or misunderstanding will occur. Your prospects listen to your message, and then make their own inferences or conclusions. If the prospect fails to understand the message, the result is called *noise*, which means that a breakdown in communication has occurred. This happens when there are barriers to effective communication, as discussed in the following section.

Common Communication Barriers

Seldom does the buyer interpret exactly the same meaning that you perhaps intended, and when the result of decoding is different from what you encoded, noise exists. Anything that interferes with or distorts understanding of the intended message is called *noise*, and it can take many forms that may affect any or all parts of the communication process. There are logical reasons why your sales message may not be understood or accepted. Here are some reasons for such miscommunication:

Words. All language is a code. Even if you and your prospect use the same words, you are likely putting out different meanings. This is especially true when it comes to electronic forms of communication where it is difficult for the reader to interpret the true meaning of the words.[23] Noise is created when words are inappropriate or are written in a confusing manner. For example, casual profanity that may offend the listener, language implying that the listener is poorly informed, language that assumes too much knowledge on the listener's part, language that obscures the real meaning, or formatting of written words that may seem offensive to the reader.

Distractions. Any element that may focus the prospect's attention on something other than the message is a distraction. The effectiveness of marketing programs is tied to the level of distraction of the consumer.[24] Some typical distractions are inappropriate dress, uncomfortable room temperature, loud noise that makes concentration difficult, confusing language in marketing materials, or a nagging personal problem occupying the prospect's mind.

Timing. If a prospect has some reason for not wanting to listen, no amount of communication skill on your part is enough. The prospect may be feeling under the weather, may be preoccupied with an unpleasant disciplinary task, or may be facing a pressing deadline. Some prospects need time to warm up before getting down to business; others want to get right to your proposal and skip the small talk.

Some prospects will interrupt your presentation by answering a phone call.

Interruptions. Telephone calls, people walking in to you ask questions, and emergencies represent the kinds of interruptions that reduce or distort the impact of the message.

Technical Erudition. Information overload often complicates a message. Prospects need time to process information from different sources. An unconscious desire to appear personally knowledgeable often results in the salesperson talking too much, poorly organizing the presentation of features and benefits, or wrongly assuming that the prospect has adequate knowledge. As a result, the prospect fails to see a need for the product or service. Avoid using technical terms or jargon without clarification.[25]

Listening Habits. If the prospect is a poor listener, the salesperson is faced with a monumental challenge in designing a message and delivering it in an effective and successful manner. The other end of the spectrum is the salesperson who is a poor listener, who never picks up the prospect's cues that are the keys to molding the message for quick acceptance.

The buyer will draw conclusions from the messages received and react accordingly. Recognizing this feedback is crucial to a salesperson's success. During face-to-face communication, verbal and nonverbal feedback is immediate and very revealing. Become skilled in receiving feedback so that you can adapt your sales presentation to fit each individual buyer's requirements. Use the feedback loop from the prospect to you to bring you closer to an exact understanding of what is being said by each participant. This filters out the noise and results in clear communication.[26]

Using Your Voice As a Sales Tool

The first impression you make is often based on your voice. When you call for an appointment, your voice is all you have for communicating. A voice that is pleasing and confident is a great asset. Your voice and how you use it play an important part in your success in selling. Several basic components of verbal communication deserve your attention.[27]

Articulation. Do you recall the device Professor Higgins used in *My Fair Lady* to help Eliza Doolittle improve her speech? He had her talk with marbles in her mouth. To be understood at all, she was forced to form her words with extreme care. As a result, her articulation improved. When you speak, do people hear separate words and syllables, or *doyourwordsallruntogether*? A salesperson with poor articulation leaves prospects confused and bewildered.

Volume. The normal volume of the speaking voice varies during conversation. The same is true of a sales presentation. Stressing a benefit may call for increased volume. Lowering your voice, sometimes almost to a whisper, may produce quite a dramatic effect; it causes the prospect to lean forward (a body position that signals agreement or approval) to avoid missing your words. Variation in volume enhances the message if it is not overdone.

Silence. Silence is a powerful selling tool. Use it to give the prospect time to absorb the full impact of what you have said. Slight pauses between major points in the presentation suggest that you are thoughtful, intelligent, and analytical. Pauses also give the prospect an opportunity to comment, ask a question, or think about how the idea you have presented can be applied to an existing need or problem. Avoid becoming so enamored with the sound of your own voice that you talk all the time.

Rhythm. The rhythmic pattern of your speech comes from your basic personality style and your emotions of the moment. Some voices seem to flow in long, continuous sentences, whereas others come in short, choppy chunks. Just as the rhythm in music changes to indicate that something new is happening, the same thing happens in speech patterns. Be alert to any changes in your own or the prospect's speech patterns. Changes are even more revealing than initial patterns. If the prospect suddenly shifts to a more drawn-out rhythm, for example, the message may be "Let me think more about that" or "I don't believe what you're saying."

Rate. The tempo of your delivery should be comfortable for you as a speaker and for your listener. Speaking too rapidly may cause you to lose a prospect who customarily speaks more slowly and feels that your fast pace is pushing for a decision without allowing time for thought. Speaking too slowly may make the prospect want to push your fast-forward button. A moderate pace allows you to enunciate clearly, establish natural rhythmic patterns, and speed up or slow down for proper emphasis of some point.

Selling Without Words

Although people have the option not to speak, they are, nevertheless, always communicating. Nonverbal signals are a rich source of information, and one's own nonverbal behavior can be useful in responding to others, making stronger connections with clients and colleagues, and conveying certain impressions about oneself.[28] Different people have different levels of competence in nonverbal communication skills, and some professions require more skill than others. The success of a professional gambler depends on the ability to exercise strict control over nonverbal messages to disguise a bluff. A mime depends exclusively on nonverbal skills to deliver a message. However, to achieve excellence in the sales profession, you must be skilled in both verbal and nonverbal communication. Two particularly important components of nonverbal communication are *body language* and *proxemics*.

Body Language

Body language can be conceived of as messages sent without using words. The essential elements of body language include shifts in posture or stance (body angle), facial expressions, eye movements, and arm, hand, and leg movements. It includes every movement and gesture, from the subtle raising of an eyebrow to the obvious leaning forward of an interested listener. Through body language, prospects express their emotions, desires, and attitudes. As a result, body language is a valuable tool for discovering what the prospect is really saying. When you can read the prospect's body language and, in addition, control your own body signals to add impact to your words, you are likely to be understood.

The Language of Gestures. Important signals involve body angle; position of hands, arms, legs, and the face—especially the eyes and lips.[29] All of these should be observed as a cluster of gestures that together state a message. A prospect sitting with arms crossed may be communicating doubt or rejection or may simply be sitting comfortably. In this case, you must also observe whether the legs are crossed, the body withdrawn, the eyes glancing sideways, and an eyebrow raised. All these signs, taken together, surely suggest doubt or rejection, but one of them in isolation is inconclusive.

Body Signals. A hunched figure, rigid posture, restless stance, or nervous pacing may contradict what a person says verbally. Prospects allow you to sit closer if they feel comfortable and lean toward you if they like what you are saying and are intent on listening. John Molloy used videotape to study the behavior of successful and unsuccessful salespeople. One mannerism difference noted was the relative calmness of professional salespeople in comparison to those who were less successful. Their body movements were smooth and unhurried; there were no jerky motions, particularly when handing a contract or a pen across the table. Every movement was gradual. Less successful salespeople exhibited jumpy, nervous movements that were picked up—perhaps unconsciously—by prospects.

Look for changes in the prospect's body posture and gestures. For example, one who is ready to buy shows signs of relaxation: Nodding in agreement, mirroring your movements, moving to the front of the chair, extending the palm of the hand outward toward you, and uncrossing legs. Your posture and gestures also communicate your feelings to the prospect. If you sit in an open, relaxed position, you are likely to be more persuasive and better accepted than if you sit in a tight, closed posture.

Hand Movements. Rubbing the back of the neck may indicate frustration, but it can also indicate that the prospect has a sore or stiff neck from painting the bathroom ceiling over the weekend. Next time you are speaking with a client, notice his hand movements and read his hands as indicators of what he is really feeling. People can say so much with simple, unthinking hand motions. If you begin to notice that you are also making involuntary hand gestures during a meeting, focus your hand gestures toward your presentation or notes rather than letting them give away what you are feeling! Evaluate the following hand gestures in the context of other nonverbal clues.

Hand gestures may reveal a prospect's true feelings.

1. **Hand and head gestures**. Tugging at the ear suggests the desire to interrupt. Pinching the bridge of the nose and closing the eyes says that a matter is being given serious thought.
2. **Posture**. Leaning back in the chair with both hands behind the head communicates a sense of superiority.
3. **Involuntary gestures**. Involuntary hand gestures that contradict a facial expression are likely to reveal the true feelings. Tightly clasped hands or fists indicate tenseness.
4. **Steepling of the hands**. Fingertips together, forming what looks like a church steeple, often indicate smugness, self-confidence, or feelings of superiority.

Facial Expressions. Eyebrows, eyelids, eyes, lips, jaw, mouth, and facial muscles all work together to communicate feelings and emotions. Research attributes as much as 70 percent of nonverbal message sending to the muscles of the face.[30]

The face is a highly reliable indicator of attitude. A person may avoid eye contact when trying to cover up true feelings. Increased eye contact signals honesty and interest. Be sure to maintain eye contact at critical moments of the presentation. For example, when describing technical characteristics of the product, direct the prospect's eyes to the product itself, the brochure, or the specification sheet. In contrast, when stressing the benefits of using the product, maintain direct eye contact. Lack of eye contact sends a negative message that neutralizes the impact of the intended benefit. Proper eye contact makes a positive statement that words alone cannot.[31] In a survey by Incomm Research, 80 percent of trade show attendees said they were more likely to perceive a company or product positively if its sales reps were smiling. Kevin Hogan, author of *The Secret Language of Business*, conducts seminars that demonstrate how factors like voice tone, proximity, or eye contact affect customers.[32]

Suspicion and anger are shown by tightness around the cheeks or along the jaw line. Muscle movement at the back of the jaw line just below the ears indicates an angry gritting of the teeth. A sudden flush of facial redness may warn that the situation has taken a bad turn; embarrassment or hostility may be radiating under an apparently calm exterior.

An isolated gesture or posture is seldom a reliable indicator of attitude or feelings. Obviously, you have to take a look at the buyer in the context of the whole situation. The buyer may fold her arms just to be more comfortable. Generally, if there is an objection, the whole body will become more rigid. You will see other signals as well: Skin texture will tighten up; voice tone will change. The prospect may even have a frustrated look on her face. When a cluster of gestures is consistent with the verbal messages, it is relatively safe to accept their validity.[33]

The Science of Proxemics

Proxemics is the distance individuals prefer to maintain between themselves and others. Most people seem to consider the observation of desired distance a matter of courtesy. Violations of distance comfort risk closing down the communication process. Highly successful salespeople tend to move closer to clients when closing a sale. Their skill in reading the individual prospect allows them to move as close as possible without causing discomfort for the prospect. The difference between how successful and unsuccessful salespeople use physical closeness can be observed in the prospect's reaction. Carefully test for the existence of comfort barriers; then place yourself just outside those barriers.

Exhibit 4.10 shows the four basic zones or ranges that apply in the typical sales situation. Generally speaking, the intimate zone is about two feet (hence the expression, "Keeping someone at arm's length"). Enter this range only if invited. Moving inside the intimate zone, except for a handshake, is not a good idea. Beyond that, we all have a personal zone, which is an envelope around us extending from two to four feet. Move into the buyer's personal zone only after invitation, which typically occurs after you establish a satisfying professional relationship. The outer shell is the social zone, which extends up to 12 feet.[34]

ΔExhibit 4.10

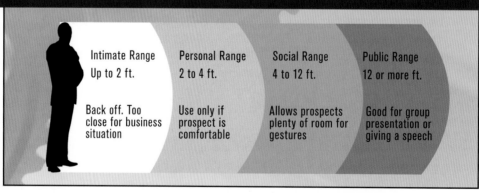

How to Use Space

Intimate Range Up to 2 ft.	Personal Range 2 to 4 ft.	Social Range 4 to 12 ft.	Public Range 12 or more ft.
Back off. Too close for business situation	Use only if prospect is comfortable	Allows prospects plenty of room for gestures	Good for group presentation or giving a speech

A number of factors enter into the amount of space various individuals need. Cultural differences, age, gender, and personality are important, as is the type of relationship that exists between salesperson and client. Peers tolerate a closer range of contact than people with a wide gap in age or status. Conversations between two women occur at closer range that those between two men or between a man and a woman. People with outgoing, open personalities are willing to be closer than those who are shy or withdrawn. Salespeople can move closer to long-term clients than to new prospects.

SUMMARY

- The consumer's purchase decision process involves five stages:
    1. Problem recognition
    2. Search for alternatives
    3. Evaluation of alternatives
    4. The purchase decision
    5. Post-purchase evaluation

- Organizational buyers must abide by specific restrictions and buying procedures, often consult with other executives, and must deal with budget constraints. Purchases of this nature often involve a purchasing team, sometimes referred to as a buying center.

- Salespeople are successful in closing sales when they discover the buying motives of the prospect, present benefits of the product that relate to those motives, and are sensitive to both psychological and sociocultural influences.

- Communication is the vehicle for delivering your message in a manner that the buyer comprehends, accepts, and believes.

- Understanding body language and how prospects use their space adds to your ability to communicate with the prospect.

- We send the majority of our messages in daily communication through nonverbal means. We *are* *always* communicating!

REVIEW QUESTIONS

1. Formulate a brief definition of consumer behavior.

2. Why must salespeople understand consumer behavior?

3. What are the five stages of the buying-decision process? What is a salesperson's function in each of these stages?

4. What is cognitive dissonance? How can a salesperson prevent it?

5. What differences exist between individual and organizational buyers?

6. What is a buying center?

7. What are the three main purposes a salesperson may have in encoding a message to be presented to a prospect?

8. How can you be sure someone has received, understood, and accepted your message?

9. What is the role of perception in the buying-decision process?

10. What are some of the psychological influences on the purchase decision process?

ROLE-PLAY EXERCISES

The following role-play exercises help build teams, improve communication, and emphasize the real-world side of selling. They are meant to be challenging, to help you learn how to deal with problems that have no single right answer, and to use a variety of skills beyond those employed in a typical review question. Read and complete each activity. Then in the next class, discuss and compare answers with other classmates.

Role Play 4.1 – Learning from Advertising

For this role-play, divide into teams of 4 persons each. Outside of class, conduct an online search for two videos of TV advertisements, one of which reflects having considered the psychological, behavioral, and socio-cultural influences on customers' purchase decisions as outlined in Chapter 4, and the other of which does not. As a team, discuss and analyze the two videos that your team has selected in terms of why each ad is or is not effective vis-à-vis the purchase decision process.

Be prepared to show and discuss your videos in class, pointing out precisely those features of each video that your team found to be effective or ineffective, and why.

Role Play 4.2 – Brief Selling Situations

Appoint 3 students to participate in an active role-play in front of the class. Divide the class into teams and give each group a brief selling situation. Give each group fifteen minutes to prepare a presentation and invite the 3 students in the role play to present their situation to the class. Allow each team to critique the presentation in terms of their own ideas and the following:
- The model of the purchase decision process
- The ultimate consumer or organizational buying motives
- Any psychological or sociocultural influences present
- The communication process in general
- Barriers to effective communication

Role Play 4.3 – Choose Your Words

Does word choice affect understanding? What common saying has been reworded in each of the statements below?
- A single in-and-out movement of a small cylindrical object with an oblong opening in one end through which an elongated fiber is passed produces the fortuitous circumstance of precluding the necessity of performing nine such procedures at some future date.
- A wildly gyrating fragment of consolidated solid mineral matter is never encapsulated in a cutaneous layer of bryophytic living organisms that do not possess locomotive qualities in themselves.
- You may succeed in conducting a large, solid hoofed herbivorous mammal of the family Equidae to the brink of a reservoir of liquid oxide of hydrogen, but there is no surety that you will succeed in coercing said mammal to imbibe a potation.
- Members of the populace who sojourn in habitations of an amorphous inorganic transparent material made largely of silicates are well advised to eschew propelling concretions of earthy or mineral matter.

CASE STUDIES

The following case studies present you with selling scenarios that require you to apply the critical skills discussed in the chapter and give you training through simulation, role-playing, and practical learning situations. They are meant to be both engaging and challenging, and like the role-play exercises, don't have one right answer.

Case 4.1 – The Return

Ben's manager was not happy. "Do you realize what you just cost this company?" he growled at Ben. "We just took back a $1,600 home entertainment system from some guy named John Stafford. He was hot. Said that Ben Walker had just pressured his wife into buying this piece of crap and that he'd never do business here again. What happened, Ben?"

"I don't know," Ben replied. "Mrs. Stafford seemed very content with the purchase. Said her husband had been wanting something like this and that she wanted to surprise him. She signed the contract and paid with her credit card. No problem as far as I could tell."

"Well, there was a problem all right!" Ben's manager hissed. "Mr. Stafford didn't like the features on this system, especially the audio. It wasn't like anything he'd been looking for. So now we have to eat the restocking costs, and you're out the commission. This had better not happen again. I want you to go think about it and tell me what went wrong and how you're going to avoid this kind of mess in the future." With that, the manager stormed back into his office.

Ben was perplexed. For the eleven months that he'd worked at Ocean Front Appliances, he had come to enjoy selling the three major product lines they carried. Sure, there was pressure, but the commission structure was high enough to make it worth enduring. In the case of Mrs. Stafford, he thought he'd done his job, at least well enough to get the sale. Over lunch, he confided in Marcia, another salesperson who was very successful, that he didn't understand what had happened.

"I remember her," Marcia replied. "I was just on the other side of the display while you were working with her, and I thought at the time that this one could go sour."

"What do you mean?" Ben asked.

"Well, Mrs. Stafford was obviously nervous. She kept saying, 'I just don't know.' And then, you'd explain some other feature, and she would respond, "Do you think my husband will like this?"

"I remember. I kept having to reassure her," Ben said. "So I thought I'd just move on and show her how terrific this system really is."

"I know, Ben, but when she kept backing up, you should have recognized the clue that she really wasn't ready. You closed her, but I think she appeased you to get out of the store."

That stung. Ben was going to have to really think about this some more.

Given the above scene, what do you think, in light of what you've read in Chapter 4, that Ben should consider? Specifically, where did Ben go wrong with regard to the customer's decision process, the customer's motivation for buying, and communication?

Case 4.2 – X-Ray Vision

Carla was furious. As a representative of MediTech, she had just spent the better part of 3 months cultivating the purchasing agent for a regional medical firm in her territory to buy the latest upgrade of MediTech's fMRI (functional MRI) machine, only to be told when she tried to close the sale that he would have to "consult others." Todd, the purchasing agent, had never mentioned consulting anyone before now. For him to brush her off like that, Carla fumed, was insulting. When she stormed into her sales manager's office with her tale of rejection, however, he remained unperturbed.

"What do you mean, 'I should have known better?'" Carla exclaimed. "How could I have known that Todd would resort to such a transparently cheap dodge?"

"Look. I know you just came over to us recently from pharmaceutical sales," replied her manager, "but that experience should have taught you something."

"What?"

"Well, for starters, think about what you're selling. It's expensive, and the time before it becomes obsolete isn't all that long."

"But Todd knew all that some time ago. I never hid anything from him. He didn't bat an eye when I told him what their 5-year projected cost would be," said Carla.

"Maybe not. But he's not the one who is most impacted by increased cost. Think about who will use the new fMRI. Physicians, that's who. And you know even better than I how much physicians like to be in control," the sales manager pointed out.

He continued, "Unless they're convinced directly that there's a huge medical benefit that will justify the higher fees they must charge, they'll revolt. Those issues are outside Todd's responsibility."

Even though Carla's manager was accurate in pointing out the details that he mentioned, what was Carla missing in her general approach to Todd? What should she have done differently? Why should the points that her manager raised with her have caused her to change her approach? What can she do not to remedy the situation and get the sale?

Chapter 5
Finding Your Selling Style

Learning Objectives

- Recognize the different behavioral styles.

- Identify your own dominant social style.

- Learn how to deal with people who operate from each of the various styles.

- Understand the concept of versatility and how it affects your ability to relate to all social styles.

- Become familiar with gender issues in selling.

- Discover how neurolinguistic programming can be useful to salespeople.

Several weeks into her job as a sales and marketing coordinator for a non-profit organization aimed at the early intervention of special needs for infants and toddlers, Sue Wagner realized that something was very wrong. The problem was not with the work itself. Sue loved her job of maintaining public awareness programs, arranging timetables for promotional activities, and charting the recruitment of new referral sources. It was her boss that concerned her. Sue approached her boss with a new public awareness campaign plan. She had everything completely organized and detailed complete with charts and graphs indicating potential areas of expansion. Halfway through her presentation, the boss interrupted her and began presenting his own ideas in a chaotic and disorganized manner. Each of his ideas were irrelevant to the situation and would complicate the carefully laid out plans made by Sue. When Sue tried to point this out, her boss got upset and demanded that Sue make the changes that he presented and would not accept anything less. Sue was very confused because the 'ideas' that her boss presented were not feasible in her opinion.

Some call such an incident a personality conflict. Others would say they are simply not on the same wavelength, or perhaps they're not seeing eye-to-eye. Let's call it what it really is—a difference in social styles. Conflict or miscommunication will exist not simply because of work pressures, but because of social style differences. Sue, as you will learn in this chapter, has an *analytical* social style, while her boss has an *expressive style*. Unknowingly, they communicate disrespect to one another. This lack of understanding and knowledge concerning behavioral styles can cause lost sales, frustration, resentment, or resignation.

Proper communication ceased in the situation because Sue did not recognize that her ideas got her boss thinking, and he did not stick around to clarify his suggestions. Sue stopped listening and took her boss's brainstorming personally, seeing it as criticism rather than as development of her original thoughts. They were like the two old-timers who sat on the front porch in their rocking chairs reminiscing about days gone by. Both were so hard of hearing that neither ever knew for sure what the other was saying. They just took turns talking, each lost in his own memories, but content that there was someone nearby. If you want to close more sales, however, "being nearby" isn't enough.

Success and Behavioral Styles

Because of the importance of communication in the selling process, successful salespeople constantly search for new ways to make their communication more effective. They are eager to learn how they may better anticipate and avoid conflict situations. Gauging your client's personality will help you close the sale and succeed in business.[1] A selling transaction, whether it involves products, services, or ideas, is a communication exchange in which two individuals develop a mutually desirable solution to a problem about which both are concerned. The best sales relationships are long-term ones based on mutual trust and credibility. The pertinent question then becomes, "How can I sell so that I demonstrate respect for the customer, build credibility for myself and my product, and set up a win-win situation for both of us?"

The concept of behavioral styles is of tremendous importance for salespeople; and it is an idea formally developed by the Swiss psychologist Carl Jung.[2] Jung built upon and extended the knowledge of the adult ego state developed by Sigmund Freud, who first introduced the idea. Jung's work on behavioral functions resulted in a theory of personality that included four functions: *Intuition, thinking, feeling*, and *sensing*. Since his death in 1961, his work has become increasingly popular through the publication of his writings and the work of others who interpret and continue to apply his principles.

Several behavioral style models of special interest to salespeople have been developed and introduced by various authors. David Merrill and Roger Reid began the development of their Social

Styles Model in the early 1960s. Dr. Paul Mok, working independently of Merrill and Reid, developed what he referred to as the Communicating Styles Technology Model. The Wilson Learning Corporation and Dr. Tony Alessandra and Associates Inc. expanded and added their own research to these original models. The material presented in this chapter has been gleaned from these four related approaches.[3]

The Social Styles Model

Everyone learns as a child that family members and friends have different personalities. Perhaps you could always elicit sympathy from your mother but found that your father considered each situation and evaluated the circumstances prior to sympathizing or reprimanding you. You may have had a sibling who had a totally different personality from everyone else in the household. In your family, you had time to learn the ways you can best persuade or get along with various relatives. In a business or social situation, you have less time to evaluate and adjust your persuasive skills. The prospect's manner and social style are often deceptive and you may miss what is happening. The most common mistake is not understanding how prospects think and make decisions.[4] The social styles model provides a useful tool for making such an evaluation in the shortest possible time. The better you understand personality types, the more successful you will be in communicating with the various people you meet.

Each person has a primary communicating style that is blended or fine-tuned by a secondary style. These primary and secondary styles shape others' perceptions of you and filter your perceptions of other people. A second dimension to this model comes into play when you are under stress. At such times, you may shift to a different style of behavior. You may be aware of the shift yet feel unable to prevent it. People use four basic styles to deal with the world. Each is based upon one of four basic functions of human personality:

1. The driver or sensing function of taking in here-and-now sensory information and reacting to it.

2. The expressive or intuitive function of imagination and abstract thought.

3. The amiable or feeling function of personal and emotional reactions to experience.

4. The analytical or thinking function of organizing and analyzing information in a logical fashion.

The Four Communicating Styles:

Driver

Expressive

Amiable

Analytical

Everyone uses each of the four functions, but the frequency of use differs among individuals.[5] These styles can even be observed in young children. Behavioral patterns, Jung claimed, are genetically determined and are seen in infants during their first days of life. Like adults, young children process experience according to their own individual styles. It is important to recognize that on occasion, people will have the tendency to switch from one pattern to another as their mood, nature or purpose of the purchase changes.[6]

Basic Communication Concepts

Four basic concepts underlie the behavioral styles communication model presented in this chapter:

1. A style is an overall approach used to receive and send messages. It consists of verbal, nonverbal, and behavioral elements. Everyone uses a blend of the driver, expressive, amiable, and analytical styles, although each person has a favorite style that is used more often than others.
2. Every person operates the majority of the time from a favorite style. This is the primary style. Everyone also has a secondary or backup style that may replace or modify the primary style.
3. Because style is reflected in behavior, you can identify someone else's primary style by observing behavioral clues. These clues include use of time, manner of speech, typical reaction to others, and approach to job performance.
4. People respond favorably to a style that is similar or complementary to their own primary and backup styles. When a salesperson's style is too different from that of the prospect, the resulting style conflict can be disastrous to the outcome of the transaction. What is said is often much less important than how it is said.[7]

Behavioral Styles in Selling

In selling, most of us tend to use one or two predominant styles, and your choice of style affects what you do and say. It also affects what prospects hear and believe during your presentation. Understanding the strengths and liabilities of your primary communicating style and learning to be versatile in your style can help you sell to more prospects more often.[8] The objective of this chapter then is to help you learn how to manage your daily interactions with customers and prospects more productively.

Exhibit 5.1 illustrates that your most damaging weaknesses (-) are merely exaggerations or over-extensions of your strengths (+). Your behavior responds to circumstances like the volume dial of a radio. When the volume is just right, the music is pleasing.

ΔExhibit 5.1

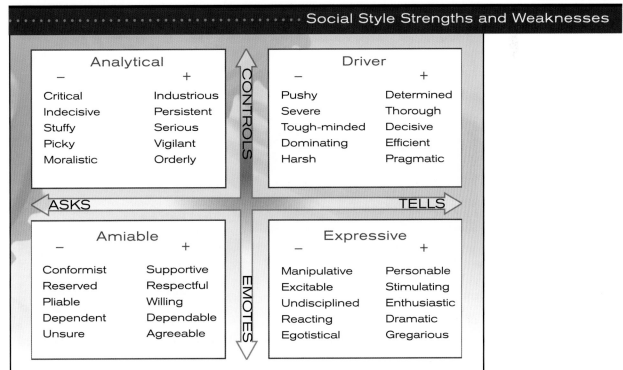

Social Style Strengths and Weaknesses

Analytical		Driver	
−	+	−	+
Critical	Industrious	Pushy	Determined
Indecisive	Persistent	Severe	Thorough
Stuffy	Serious	Tough-minded	Decisive
Picky	Vigilant	Dominating	Efficient
Moralistic	Orderly	Harsh	Pragmatic

CONTROLS

ASKS   TELLS

EMOTES

Amiable		Expressive	
−	+	−	+
Conformist	Supportive	Manipulative	Personable
Reserved	Respectful	Excitable	Stimulating
Pliable	Willing	Undisciplined	Enthusiastic
Dependent	Dependable	Reacting	Dramatic
Unsure	Agreeable	Egotistical	Gregarious

Similarly, when a behavioral style is used in moderation it is a strength; when overused (that is, when the volume is too high), it becomes a weakness and leads to ineffective communication. Professional selling is all about managing relationships. Remember that a customer is not a transaction—a customer is a relationship! Most people don't even think about working on relationships in their daily lives. On the other hand, relationship salespeople take time to think about and understand the people around them. The relationship selling approach will strengthen and enhance your selling style by turning you into a relationship-oriented helper. The relationship style of selling is the 21st-century approach to helping clients and prospects buy.

When you go for your next job interview, you will likely be asked to take a personality test. The use of personality inventories in personnel selection has grown in popularity over the past decade. A recent study that summarized the results of fifteen prior studies that investigated the relationship between personality traits and job performance has found convincing evidence of the effectiveness of the use of personality inventories in applicant selection.[9] Although your personality style is not a true predictor of overall work performance, it can predict success in specific occupations or relate to specific criteria, which is why is it vital that you determine where you fall in the behavioral styles model and the descriptions found in this chapter.

Remember that the emphasis in studying behavioral style characteristics is on surface behavior, not on an in-depth personality analysis. Human behavior is predictable because ninety percent of our actions are controlled by habits and attitudes.[10] The social styles model does not describe a person's complete personality because it omits reference to the individual's beliefs, ethics, abilities, and intelligence. What it does is describe the basic attributes or characteristics of behavior: *assertiveness* and *responsiveness.*

Attributes of Behavior

When you meet someone for the first time, your mind subconsciously reacts to two main characteristics: assertiveness and responsiveness. *Assertiveness* represents the effort a person makes to influence or control the thoughts and actions of others. *Responsiveness* is the willingness with which a person outwardly shares feelings or emotions and develops relationships.[11]

Assertiveness and responsiveness levels vary from one individual to another, and anyone may be high or low in either dimension or in both dimensions or anywhere in between. Several basic terms provide a thumbnail sketch of the characteristics of each dimension:

Low in Responsiveness	High in Responsiveness
• formal and proper • fact-oriented • guarded, cool, and aloof • disciplined about time • seldom makes gestures • controlled body language	• relaxed and warm • open and approachable • dramatic and animated • flexible about time • oriented toward relationships and feelings

Low in Assertiveness	High in Assertiveness
• introverted • supportive, a team player • easygoing • avoids taking risks • good listener • reserved in their opinions	• risk-taker • swift in decision-making • willing to confront others • very competitive • take-charge attitude • expresses opinions

Recognizing Social Styles

Combining the assertiveness and responsiveness characteristics makes it possible to develop a map of what others are doing or saying. Exhibit 5.2 shows the relationships among the four social styles. The horizontal axis is the range from the least to most assertive. Assertive people take a stand and make their position clear to others. Because they are ambitious, competitive, and quick to take action and express strong opinions, they are located on the telling end of the social style axis. Nonassertive individuals are seen as cooperative, silent, and slow to act, and they are located at the asking end of the axis. The least assertive individuals are in quartile D, and the most assertive in quartile A, with quartiles B and C representing intermediate levels of assertiveness.

The vertical axis indicates the range from least to most responsive. Non-responsive individuals, those in quartile 1, are largely indifferent to the feelings of others, reserved, and no-nonsense in attitude. The responsive individuals found in quartile 4 are strongly people-oriented, concerned about relationships, and subjective. Those in quartiles 2 and 3 display intermediate levels of responsiveness.

ΔExhibit 5.2

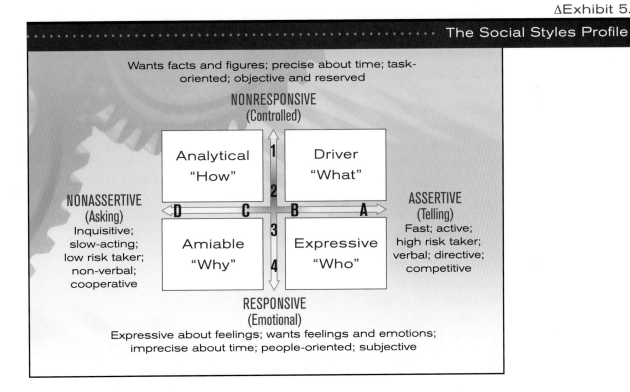

The Social Styles Profile

Identifying the Four Behavioral Styles

Identifying the levels of assertiveness and responsiveness a person demonstrates is not a precise method of complete personality evaluation. With study and practice, however, Dr. Mok suggests that you can become 70 to 80 percent effective in using your observations to predict habitual behavioral patterns and be prepared to use your knowledge to improve the communication environment. Each possible combination of the two traits suggests one of the basic social styles. The four styles are linked to distinctive and unique habits of interactive behavior. The name given to each style reflects general characteristics rather than full, specific details. Keep in mind that no one style is preferred over another. Each has its own strengths and weaknesses, and successful people as well as failures are found in each style group, as are people of both sexes and all ethnic groups, ages, and other segments of the population.[12]

Drivers tell and control, are high in assertiveness, and low in responsiveness. They control others by telling them what to do and control themselves by remaining objective. They are task-oriented and combine personal power and emotional control in relationships with others. They are *control specialists*.

Expressives tell and emote. Like drivers, they are highly assertive, but they are also high in emotional responsiveness. They attempt to tell people what to do, but place more emphasis on their relationships with people than they do on the task itself. They are *social specialists*.

Amiables ask and emote, are low in assertiveness, and high in responsiveness. They rely on a personal feeling approach to get things done. They are *support specialists*, combining personal reserve and emotional expression.

Analyticals ask and control, and they are low in assertiveness and responsiveness. They are highly task-oriented but soften that style with low assertiveness. They ask rather than direct. They are *technical specialists*, combining personal reserve and emotional control.

The Professor of Human Behavior

Tom Hoek has earned what could be called a Ph.B—he is a *Professor of Human Behavior*. He says that we are all in the people business. As salespeople we observe and verify behavior and have a constant need to become expert at interpreting what we see. Tom is the former president of Insurance Systems of Tennessee, Inc., a training firm in Nashville, TN, specializing in insurance and investment training courses.

In any personal relationship that you have, Tom suggests everybody has their own particular point of view. Ultimately, in every situation, the most persuasive person wins. When you understand behavioral styles technology and what motivates each of the styles you can adapt your own style to meet the needs of others. Just exercise a bit of applied psychology. All of us have a way we like to be treated.

Tom uses the phrase *Psychological Reciprocity* to describe what should happen in a sales situation. You make the initial attempt to adapt to the prospect's social style. The prospect is then motivated to move toward you—to reciprocate. Real communication and understanding occur much quicker than if each person stays firmly entrenched in their own particular style.

Behavioral styles technology helps you present the right product in the right way. Tom suggests that styles are fixed early in life—it's what you do with your style that makes a difference. Tom uses style flexing to complement the other person's style. He says this is truly win-win selling. Tom's motto is: "He who trims himself to suit everybody will soon whittle himself away."

Versatility as a Communication Tool

When people of different styles meet and behave strictly according to the characteristics of their own personal styles, conflict often results. A salesperson who is an *amiable* and a prospect who is a *driver* can quickly arrive at cross-purposes. A driver client wants to get facts and to accomplish the task at hand; the amiable salesperson wants to cultivate a personal relationship.

When such a situation occurs, the only way to avoid an escalation in miscommunication or a conflict is for one of the two people involved to engage in some style flexibility. In an ideal situation, both are willing to move part way, but the salesperson must be capable of making most of any necessary temporary adjustments. This willingness to try behaviors not necessarily characteristic of your style is called behavioral flexibility or versatility.[13]

Versatility is a person's willingness to control personal behavior patterns and adapt to other people as a means of reducing the possibility of ineffective communication. The salesperson's own personal style does not change, but rather techniques are applied that work in that particular situation.[14] For example, when meeting with an analytical, the expressive salesperson can incorporate versatility by talking less, listening more, and focusing on facts. Versatility should never be equated with either insincerity or mere imitation of the prospect's style. Versatile salespeople seek a reasonable compromise. They do not become so highly changeable that their pace and priority needs are constantly set aside for those of clients.

Being versatile helps you see things from your prospect's point of view.

The more versatility you have, the better your chances are for success. If you understand that each individual has a unique behavioral style you will be better able to adapt your approach to match. This means that you will need to learn how to 'read' the behavior patterns of each prospect. By doing so, you will be able to respond to your prospect's style in a way that makes it easy for you to communicate, exchange information, and close a sale.[15]

Some salespeople are far more successful than others. Why do these people always seem to be able to close the sale? The truth is that certain natural-born salespeople have learned how to adapt their sales presentation to each unique client while serving everyone equally. They are at ease with both the demanding and the easygoing client. Sometimes their communication is loud and forceful. Other times, it's quiet and reassuring. What these successful salespeople know is that selling is personal. Determining each client's unique personality style helps them predict and influence behavior.[16]

Strive for *Psychological Reciprocity*. That is, as the salesperson, you make the initial attempt to get into the client's world. The person is then challenged to move toward you; to reciprocate. *And you connect!* Rapport is established with the client much quicker than if each of you had stayed firmly entrenched in your own particular social style.[17]

Be aware of the multitude of areas in a sales situation that make versatility one of the greatest tools you have to get a yes from your prospects. The following aspects of a face-to-face interview often require the need for you to stay versatile, responsive, and ultimately, willing to adapt and change to fit each situation:[18]

Comfort. Does the prospect seem nervous or edgy?

Tension. Is there an air of tension or general discomfort?

Prospect assertiveness in asking questions. Does the prospect provide you with more sales ammo by asking questions that may reveal a way to sell them?

Prospect responsiveness to your presentation. Is the prospect with you, or do they seem to be preoccupied.

Level of openness. Is the prospect sharing pertinent information that will help you better discover how to serve his needs?

The Interaction of Styles

The dimensions of assertiveness and responsiveness operate in people's pace and their priorities. *Pace* is the speed at which a person prefers to move. Those who are low in assertiveness (analyticals and amiables) prefer a slow pace; those high in assertiveness (drivers and expressives) prefer a fast pace in conversation, deliberation, and problem solving.[19]

Priorities concern what a person considers important and tend to be related to the dimension of responsiveness. Those who are low in responsiveness put tasks at the top of their priority list, and those who are high in responsiveness put relationships in first place. These conflicts may be summarized as follows:

Styles Shared	Dimension	Source of Conflict	Area of Agreement
Analytical/Amiable	Low assertiveness	Priorities	Pace
Driver/Expressive	High assertiveness	Priorities	Pace
Analytical/Driver	Low responsiveness	Pace	Priorities
Amiable/Expressive	High responsiveness	Pace	Priorities
Analytical/Expressive	None	Both	None
Amiable/Driver	None	Both	None

Conflicts that involve only priorities or only pace can be handled with relative ease; real trouble results when the styles of two people conflict in both pace and priorities.

Fortunately, few people are locked into a single style. Between the extremes of each dimension are many degrees of responsiveness and assertiveness. The descriptions of the four styles, then, do not represent absolutes. If you deal with every customer in the same way, you will close a small percentage of all your contacts, because you will only close one personality style. But if you learn how to effectively work with all four personality styles, you can significantly increase your closing ratio.[20]

Salespeople who do not adjust their behavior to meet the style needs of clients face deteriorating situations. For example, an expressive salesperson's questions may be interpreted as a personal challenge or attack by an analytical prospect. If the analytical prospect responds to the questions merely to save face, the expressive salesperson then tends to talk more, move faster, and push the analytical into still greater conflict.

In any situation, conflict is finally relieved in a manner typical of the individual style. The expressive usually attacks verbally. The driver tends to become overbearing, pushy, and dictatorial. The amiable generally submits in order to avoid conflict at all costs but experiences resentment and distrust. The analytical withdraws—flight rather than fight. *In a conflict situation, most people tend to move to the extreme dimensions of their favorite style.*

To avoid distrust and ultimately a breakdown in communication, you must meet the needs of your prospects, especially their behavioral style needs. Treat them as they want to be treated, and move according to the pace and priority they desire. The most successful salespeople are be able to help customers verbalize problems, and to create a solution that customers would not have developed alone by letting them set the pace.[21]

Identifying Pace and Priority

How do you go about determining someone's pace and priorities? Ask yourself these three questions and observe the answers:

1. How *fast* does the person make decisions and get things done?

2. How *competitive* is the person? Not primarily in sports, but:
   • Is the person competitive in a conversation?
   • Does the person fight for air time in a meeting?

3. How much *feeling* is displayed in a verbal and nonverbal communication?
   • How often does the person smile?
   • Do they gesture broadly?

Your goal is to identify pace and priorities accurately and respond in an appropriate manner. How can you find out your prospect's information preferences? Use one of these statements to assist you:[22]

> 1. "Ordinarily I have an organized presentation and get right to it, but today maybe I should get to know you better. What would you like me to do?"
>
> 2. "I am prepared to get right into my presentation or if you prefer we can chat a bit so that I can learn about you and your organization. Which do you prefer?"
>
> 3. "There are a lot of ways I can start explaining exactly how this process would work based on the concerns you were kind enough to share with me at our meeting last week. Would you prefer I start with the end in mind and then work backwards, or would you like to hear the step-by-step details first?"

The expressive and amiable styles would respond to these statements indicating a desire to chat and get to know one another. The driver and analytical styles would want you to begin your presentation.

Gender Style Differences

While it is essential to recognize and adjust to different social styles, it is also necessary to recognize the contribution that gender makes to our communication in the business world. The issue of proxemics, the distance that individuals prefer to keep between themselves and others, also becomes more recognizable when speaking to someone of the opposite sex.[23] That is why we must be sensitive to gender issues and adjust to them just as we do for social style differences. If not handled correctly, these seemingly insignificant differences can break down communication lines and damage relationships, and this ultimately hurts your company and your income!

One way to ensure effective cross-gender communication is to emphasize and encourage male and female distinctions in management processes and interpersonal relationships. By emphasizing the differences in a positive manner, the different viewpoints can be highly productive. Both men and women bring to the selling table different perspectives, experiences, and communication skills, and they interpret language in very distinct ways. Ultimately, however, they use these distinctly different styles and patterns of speech to deliver roughly the same message.

Use the strengths unique to your gender and style.

There is no proven significant differences between men and women in how smart they work, in how hard they work or in how well they perform.[24] Although there have been numerous studies conducted over the past several years regarding sex-related differences, the results are often contradictory. The plethora of research does, however, provide some new perspectives to consider concerning the growing role of women in corporate America. In various studies, women demonstrated higher levels of contingent reward, or behaviors in which a leader rewards followers for the completion of tasks. Contingent reward behavior has been identified as a predictor of effectiveness, which would suggest that women may actually possess a leadership advantage in some cases.[25]

Relating to the Opposite Sex

Whether or not you have experienced how gender differences hinder relationships in selling when handled improperly, it is clear that the unequal treatment of employees by management hinders the success of any business. A research study by Russ & McNeilly concluded that managers who treat male and female sales reps the same miss the potential benefits that different gender styles provide.[26]

A key question to ask is whether or not gender differences, in and of themselves, create diverse ways of thinking or different behavioral relationships. If so, what are some things to be aware of when you're selling to someone of the opposite sex? Research by Siguaw & Honeycutt found that women were engaged more frequently in customer-oriented selling than were their male counterparts.[27]

Despite significant advances in gender relations, inequalities still exist in the business world that sometimes make it difficult for men and women to fully relate to each other. Mary Blair-Loy, Founding Director of the Center for Research on Gender in the Professions at the University of California, San Diego along with Erin Cech, studied gender inequalities through a survey of successful women professionals. Their research examined two possible ideologies that could explain gender inequalities. The first asserts that the inequalities are a result of differences in training, experience, and personal motivation, and suggests that women who fall behind have only themselves to blame. The second ideology states that the inequalities are a result of various structural factors such as discrimination, stereotyping, and exclusion from social networks.[28] Which ideology is more accurate—or a combination of both—remains to be seen. Either way, we must work to overcome ingrained stereotypical ideas of gender roles and recognize the importance of both sexes at the negotiation table.

When men and women find themselves sitting across from one another at the bargaining table, they must learn to adjust their styles. During the sales interview they should use the strengths unique to their gender.

Our society is changing, and one of the key ways it is changing, at least in the business world, is that men and women are becoming more alike in their dealings with clients and customers. Just because something is written about the differences between men and women, it does not mean that it has value in every selling encounter between men and women. For example, when a woman nods her head, that doesn't necessarily mean she agrees with what a man is saying. When a woman crosses her arms, she is not automatically indicating she is closed to the idea being presented. She just may be tired or cold. Likewise, if a man doesn't look you in the eye when he is speaking, that does not necessarily mean he's hiding something—it may be his style. Acting on generalities, regardless of gender, can kill a sale more quickly than anything else.[29]

Exhibit 5.3 provides some suggestions for dealing with gender differences. You must be prepared to communicate effectively with your male and female sales managers, fellow sales reps, as well as the men and women decision-makers you call on. No one can make a sweeping statement about how all women or all men like to sell or be sold. In any selling situation it's vital to communicate in a way that substantiates what's meaningful to that individual, and gender may help determine what a client feels is important. Subtle, gender-based changes may give you the edge you're looking for to boost sales.[30]

Δ**Exhibit 5.3**

How Can Men and Women Better Understand Each Other? • • • • • • • • • •

Salesmen:

- *Report talk vs. rapport talk*. Male bonding through storytelling and anecdotes is fine; however, women are more interested in your product than your latest fishing trip.
- *Stop interrupting*. Men interrupt women more often than other men. This is a good way to lose a sale. Learn to listen.
- *Feel the sale*. There is more to selling than numbers. Women are interested in emotional satisfaction as well as the bottom line.
- *Control your language*. Never again in a professional situation use the words "honey," "dear," or "sweetie." This is simply intolerable and might be offensive to some people.

Saleswomen:

- *Speak confidently and clearly*. It has been established that men will interrupt women, especially if they sound tentative or unsure.
- *Feed them data*. Men love facts and the illusion of being cool and rational. Let them know you have also done your homework. Remain enthusiastic; just rein it in a bit.
- *Practice your humor*. Women tend to use humor less than men. Being funny at the right moment is very important.
- *Watch your language*. Avoid "girl talk" when presenting to men. Words like "lovely," "charming," or "adorable" should be excluded from your sales vocabulary.

While there are some fundamental differences in how men and women interact, there are no absolute truths and, in sales, we must be careful about making assumptions based on gender alone. So rather than focus on your prospect's gender, you should cater to your prospect's character and personality first and foremost.

Everyone is unique with her or her own unique personality style, and everyone makes buying decisions in a different way. In any selling situation it's important to communicate in a way that highlights what's important to the individual customer, and in some cases, gender may help determine what that customer feels is important. Subtle, gender-based changes to your interactions with prospects may give you the edge and boost your sales.

Culture Style Differences

Along with gender differences between men and women, it is important to recognize the cultural differences. To succeed in the global market, sales managers and teams need to understand how these cultural differences affect behavior and business. According to Sinan Caykoylu, author of *Cross-Cultural and Gender Differences in Leadership Style Perspectives*, sales managers and sales teams cannot adopt a "one size fits all" approach to their leadership style. They need to be able to diversify their approach in a way that allows them to understand how different cultures and genders react to certain behaviors.[31] For example; in Arab countries it is critical to follow the customs of the area to avoid offending those with whom you are dealing. A salesperson should not inquire about a man's wife or any other female relationships. It is important to learn the customs and personal cultural background of your prospect before your presentation or even your first introduction. Without this knowledge, your words, actions, and body language may inadvertently offend your prospect, costing you the sale.

Reading the Prospect's Environment

Important clues to a client's style are in the environment as well as in verbal and nonverbal actions. Observe how the office is decorated and arranged, how objects are displayed, and what seating arrangements are available. Suppose that upon entering a prospect's office, you notice family pictures on the desk, nature posters, a round desk, and a separate seating area with four comfortable chairs. What would be your first impression of that client's behavioral style? Did you say *amiable*? If so, you are right. Next, you can confirm or adjust your initial impression by observing the prospect's actions and speech. If the prospect rises to greet you personally and sits in an easy chair your impression of amiable would tend to be confirmed.

Let's try another example. You enter the prospect's office and notice a diploma, an achievement plaque, and a poster on the wall that says "Why not?" The desk presents several jumbled stacks of paper and a generally chaotic appearance. Two overstuffed chairs by the open side of the desk provide seating. A bookcase with stacks of books and folders intermixed and a plant on the file cabinet, complete the furnishings. The disorganization, the wall decorations emphasizing achievement, and the comfortable and accessible seating suggest that this office houses an *expressive*.

What does your prospect's office say about him or her?

However, a word of caution is needed. Roger Reid tells of a Texas company that mandated that all of its top executives display pictures of their families on top of their desks. He also notes that in some companies the top executives do not select or arrange anything in their offices. The pictures on the wall, chairs and desks, and office layout are selected and done for the executives by staff or consultants. Thus, you must confirm any initial environmental impression by noting the prospect's actions, tone of voice, speech patterns, and interpersonal behavior.[32]

Verbal, Nonverbal, and Behavioral Characteristics

You can use knowledge of these styles to characterize the observable behavior of most prospects. Although we all possess traits from each of the styles, one style ordinarily dominates. Of course, identifying a social style does not provide a crystal ball that unerringly predicts a person's future actions and decisions, but it does provide a basis for forming reasonably accurate expectations about recurring behavior and for being prepared to respond appropriately. Both verbal and nonverbal clues are useful in identifying social style. Exhibit 5.4 summarizes the behavior typical of each of the four styles.[33]

ΔExhibit 5.4

Typical Behavior Associated With Each of the Four Social Styles ················

Analytical

- Cautious in decisions and action
- Likes organization and structure
- Asks specific questions
- Prefers objective, task-oriented, intellectual work
- Wants to be right, so collects much data
- Works slowly, precisely, and alone
- Has good problem-solving skills

Driver

- Decisive in action and decision making
- Likes control; dislikes inaction
- Prefers maximum freedom to manage self and others
- Cool, independent, and competitive with others
- Low tolerance for feelings, attitudes, and advice of others
- Works quickly and impressively alone
- Has good administrative skills

Amiable

- Slow in making decisions or taking actions
- Likes close, personal relationships
- Dislikes interpersonal conflict
- Supports and actively listens to others
- Weak in goal setting and self-direction
- Seeks security and identification with a group
- Has good counseling and listening skills

Expressive

- Spontaneous actions and decisions
- Exaggerates and generalizes
- Tends to dream and get others caught up in those dreams
- Jumps from one activity to another
- Works quickly and excitedly with others
- Seeks esteem and group identification
- Has good persuasive skills

Drivers

Drivers exhibit minimum concern for the feelings of others. A vice-president of marketing for a major theme park in Ohio was heard to say, "My secretary used to drive me to distraction. I'd ask her how her weekend went and she'd actually tell me. In detail! All I wanted to hear was fine or not so hot." Now those are the words of a true driver. If you say something harsh, they don't even seem to notice. They consider yes-people to be weak. Stand up to drivers. Sell to them by showing them what your product can do. Drivers' feelings are not easily hurt because they do not take things personally.

Drivers tend to be intense, competitive, fast-paced, and goal-oriented. They pride themselves on the ability to get things done. They like to make things happen. They are willing to accept risks and want to know the estimated outcome of each option. Convince them that your proposed action works and that it will provide all the benefits you promise. They are more impressed by what they see and hear than by what others say about you or your offering.

Drivers are action driven, resourceful, organized, and pragmatic. They also tend to impose high standards on themselves and others. As a result, they may be seen as impatient or tireless. They push to perfect their own skills but also invest time and effort in coaching other people in skill development. At their worst, they appear to give inadequate consideration to the long-range consequences of their actions. They draw criticism for seeking to impose on others their expectations for drive, speed and zeal. Under stress, drivers can seem anti-intellectual and may defensively overreact to any opinions differing from their own, especially to those that seem to resist action. Drivers are likely to feel that any failure is evidence that others were not loyal enough or willing to work hard enough to make the project a success.

Customize Your Selling Style to Hit A Hole In One With The Driver

Drivers do not care about developing a personal relationship with you. They are impatient and need to be in control. Therefore:

1. Spend little time attempting to relate to them on a personal level.

2. Move fast and isolate the most dollar-related product benefits that can be verified by producing concrete evidence.

3. Do not make a lengthy presentation citing all the benefits. Be brief and stress the bottom line.

4. The fewer visual aids you use, the better. Any visuals you choose to show must be absolutely relevant to the major points.

5. Ask questions to involve them, get them to talk, and allow them to lead. Depend on your choice of subject matter in asking questions to maintain control of the interview.

6. They will test you to see what you are made of; so be willing to joust with them. If you challenge them, challenge the concepts rather than the person.

7. Answer objections immediately, and never try to bluff.

8. Present several alternatives from which they may select their own solution. Avoid telling them what is best.

9. An action close stressing an immediate opportunity works well.

Expressives

Expressives temper assertiveness with concern for the feelings of others. They are motivated by recognition, approval, and success. You must compliment them. They desire success, but are recognition motivated. Show them how to win. Let them talk and they often sell themselves. Tell them who else uses your product. Testimonials from well-known people or people they respect are important.

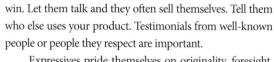

Expressives pride themselves on originality, foresight, and the ability to see the big picture. Reinforce their self-image as visionaries and idea people, and they will be receptive to your ideas. At their best, expressives often see new possibilities and present fresh ideas and approaches to problems. At their worst, they seem to base decisions on opinions, hunches, or intuition rather than on facts. They want to delegate the details to someone who has time for it while they are free to dream. They may be impatient when others demand some documentation before accepting the vision or ideas they offer. Under stress, expressives run the risk of seeming detached. They appear indifferent to problems and seem to be living in an ivory tower. They may spend time defending their ideas instead of trying to make them work in practical manner.

Expressives thrive on spontaneity. The expressive's love of risk-taking makes it easier for them to take a chance on your product. Refer to the product as a "sure bet" or guarantee that you will "make this risk pay off big." To reach them, you must emphasize the importance of risk-taking to making progress and meeting goals, and show the expressive your product's payoff potential by sharing exactly what it can do and what that means to them. When you have a qualified expressive whose needs match your product's benefits, you should not have to do much persuading. Remember, expressives are intuition-driven.[34]

A Presentation Strategy For The Expressive

Expressives are visionaries and dreamers. Therefore:

1. Plan to show them how they can personally win and how their company can benefit.

2. Open with innovative ideas for them to grow and win with through your offering.

3. Ask open-end questions that allow them to talk at length about "their" plans for growth. Then relate your product's benefits to their plans.

4. Present proposals and seek feedback, using them as sounding boards. Convey respect for their intelligence, foresight, and prominence. Be careful, however, to avoid patronizing them.

5. Use some showmanship. They like to see the yellow binder, but are not necessarily interested in the details of what it contains.

6. Never argue or back them into a corner.

7. Ask if they want you to respond to their stated concerns. Often they respond, "No, I just wanted you to know how I am thinking."

8. Use testimonials, especially from well-known people because they identify with who else uses the product.

9. Allow them to carry out their own game plan, not yours.

Amiables

Amiables are submissive, people-oriented, and willing to go along with the crowd. They need time to get to know you personally, so allow plenty of warm up time. They are undisciplined in the use of time. Agreeable in nature, they are also easily hurt. They want to be liked.

Amiables tend to be perceptive and observant individuals who are concerned with whether they like you, trust you, and can picture a positive long-term relationship with you. They are highly people-oriented in their management style and resent doing business with anyone who makes them uncomfortable or is unresponsive to their feelings. Their business decisions are markedly influenced by how their various options might impact the people in the organization. Before they accept your proposal or idea, they must be convinced that you personally believe in it. They must also know what risks are involved—especially risks to personal relationships.

Amiables at their best are truly perceptive and aware, skilled in communication, and empathetic listeners. Their insight enables them to assess organizational politics accurately. At their worst, they seem more concerned with the process of interaction than with the content of the matter at hand. They appear to be flying by the seat of their pants instead of relying in any measure on logic and thought. They seem to regard their own emotions as facts and act on the basis of their feelings. They may be criticized for being defensive, over-reactive, and too subjective.

Belonging to a group is important to amiables. To sell effectively to them, you have to show them that you are a team player. Position yourself as their newest team member by first building rapport, then work side-by-side with them to accomplish the goals they've set. To minimize the amiable's insecurities, talk about the problems your product can solve and how solving them will help improve control and performance in the workplace, which will enhance management's image of them. It is the amiable's job to nurture the team, so don't forget to outline what your product will do for the people in the company.

A Presentation Strategy For The Amiable

Amiables must be convinced that you are authentic and have their best interests at heart. They have a difficult time saying yes. Therefore:

1. Plan to approach with as much personal information as possible.

2. Avoid a rigid or canned approach and presentation.

3. Make an informal presentation with visuals and testimonial information integrated.

4. Use empathy and show that you understand and accept their feelings.

5. Spend some time relating. Move to a first-name basis quickly.

6. Be open and candid. Develop a personal relationship with them.

7. Offer them money-back guarantees and personal assurances.

8. Avoid asking directly for their business. Instead, assume that they are favorably disposed to your proposition and suggest an easy next step.

9. Be prepared to use third-party references and case histories that link them to others.

Analyticals

Analyticals are thinkers. They need time to assess and assimilate what they hear and see. They want to know just how things work and often say they want time to think things over. Product information is crucial. Know everything possible about your product, and don't expect to hear them say much.

Analyticals tend to be highly logical, organized, and unsentimental. They tend to be fact-oriented and value accuracy. Their contribution to the management team is their ability to solve difficult problems and make sound, rational business decisions based on evidence and intelligent inferences rather than on imagination or gut feelings. They take a logical approach to responsibilities. The more supporting data you can provide for your ideas, the more likely you are to sell to them. They have little interest in your opinions and more in your ability to assemble and organize supportive data for use in weighing options and arriving at a systematic, well-thought-out solution to problems.

At their best, analyticals appear to be a consistent force for progress. They are top-flight planners and doers. They can cut through untested ideas and emotional fervor to find the core truth. They are effective organizers for research and planning. They are valuable in executing logical, painstaking, and profitable projects. At their worst, they are overly cautious and conservative.

They emphasize deliberation over action. They may become so involved in evaluating all the various details of a situation that others may regard them as indecisive stumbling blocks to innovative action. Under stress, analyticals can become rigid and insecure. They may fear taking risks. They seem more concerned with being right than with seizing opportunities.

In sales interviews with analyticals, be well prepared and equipped to answer all questions. Be cordial, but move quickly to the task. Study their needs logically. Ask lots of questions that show a clear direction and pay close attention to their answers. Support your logical proposal with full documentation.

Customize Your Sales Presentation For The Analytical

Analyticals are data-oriented and slow to make decisions. They are naturally suspicious and extremely cautious. They read and study everything. Therefore:

1. Know their business thoroughly. Go in with facts and the evidence to back them up.

2. Use a logic-based, low-key style of relating.

3. Be sure prospects understand the structure of how you will present the information and solicit feedback.

4. Emphasize tested, proven, well-documented aspects of your product's benefits.

5. Make use of visual aids—charts, graphs, written "leave-behind" documents— in the presentation.

6. Present information in a controlled, professional, highly organized fashion.

7. Point out the pros and cons of your offering. They will be thinking about them.

8. Present a detailed summary of major points and use the summary as a close.

9. Avoid saying, "Well, in my opinion. . ." They don't care about your opinions, just facts that you can document.

Neurolinguistic Programming

An entirely different approach to communicating effectively and understanding more about prospects is offered by neurolinguistic programming (NLP). It looks at how people create the results they want. In your career, this understanding can be the difference between success and a lost sale.[35] The primary focus of NLP is to pinpoint styles by eye-movement exercises designed to ascertain whether one is visual, auditory, or kinesthetic.[36] When it first began to attract attention, many people considered NLP to be just another pop-psychology craze similar to the various communication approaches that have been offered as the ultimate answer for managers who wanted increased personal power and influence, for lawyers who wanted to sway judges and juries, and for salespeople who wanted to sell anything to anyone. Instead, however, NLP offers one more way to observe people and understand their needs. It is entirely different from the behavioral styles theory, but in no way contradicts it. Neurolinguistic programming is the brainchild of linguist John Grinder and psychotherapist Richard Bandler.[37]

Identifying Modes of Perception

NLP is based on recognizing and then appealing to the dominant modes of perception used by another person. We all use these modes to map reality and build a model of what the world is like that can guide us through our environment. NLP is the science of how the brain learns. All of us have a basic learning mode: visual, auditory or kinesthetic. Each is used in various situations, yet most of us will favor one mode.[38]

Auditory. Some people perceive the world largely by hearing. They learn more quickly by listening than by reading or seeing. Experiences presented through other senses are mentally translated into an auditory mode. These are the people who test ideas by how they sound. They often use responses like, "I hear what you're saying," "It sounds good to me," and "I'm hearing a lot of complaints about that situation." Ways to reach this style of learner are to use webcasts, podcasts, and discussion groups.

Visual. Other people perceive the world largely through sight. They learn and form opinions from what they see. They are the ones who originated the saying, "Seeing is believing." They form mental pictures of their experiences as a means of interpretation. They frequently use sentences like, "I see what you mean," "I'm in a fog about the whole concept," and "Do you get the picture?" This visual style responds best through videos, graphs, pictures, diagrams, and illustrations. Other ways to reach this style of learner is through the use of video webcasts or in-person demonstrations where they can see facial expressions and body language.

Kinesthetic. A smaller number of people perceive the world through the sense of touch. They feel life. Everything has a texture that either attracts or repels them. Subsets of the kinesthetic mode are the gustatory (taste) and the olfactory (smell) modes that sometimes come into play for kinesthetic people. Those operating in the kinesthetic mode say things like, "This deal just feels right (or wrong)," "That was a smooth presentation," "That transaction left a bad taste in my mouth," and "I smell something rotten about this deal." Tactile or kinesthetic learners respond best when they can interact with the information being presented. Some ways to do this is to have interactive surveys, demonstrations, websites, or games.

Bandler and Grinder first used this information to teach therapists how to recognize these representational modes and use them to build rapport with their patients, to establish a climate of trust, and to improve communication. They soon realized that this powerful communication tool would work for people other than therapists. They began to train a number of people to teach these techniques.

NLP has been used by people who have turned it into a powerful manipulative tool for their own benefit to the detriment of others. When used ethically, however, it is a helpful method for cutting down the time needed to build trust and rapport—a necessary process in relationship selling.[39] Its misuse does not discount its effectiveness; many kinds of knowledge can be twisted into tools for satisfying personal greed by those whose value systems allow such unethical action. If you look at NLP as an additional tool for interpreting the behavior, needs, and motivation of people, you can use it just as ethically and helpfully as you can use the information about behavioral styles and body language.

Some salespeople seem to have a natural or intuitive ability to identify a prospect's behavior and personality traits and to adapt to them. They seem to possess an automatic radar system that instantly and unobtrusively sends out test signals, interprets the feedback, and then chooses the best tactics for establishing rapport. Developing such skills is one of the most difficult parts of sales training. NLP is one technique you can use to develop this ability.

You may recall the final episode of the *Celebrity Apprentice* the year John Rich won over Marlee Matlin—two very impressive celebrities who raised millions of dollars for their respective charities during the show. In fact, their fund raising efforts set an all-time record! Well this is a favorite show of the authors. One of the other celebrities was Gary Busey, who was more than a little "eccentric" throughout the season. During the final episode, Gary—true to form—wanted to express himself, but what he said surprised and thrilled us at the same time. He went on and on about the value of NLP! He said that, because of his NLP training, he could look into the eyes of people and tell what they were thinking. I am sure everyone in the live audience and the vast majority of the television viewers thought, "That is one crazy guy," but we didn't think so. He was and is absolutely correct. Who would have thought? Remember 'crazy' old Gary Busey as you digest and learn this useful technique. You just never know where an endorsement will come from.

Learning Eye Cues

Our eyes are seldom still. The direction they move during a conversation reveals the system of perception that is active at the moment. Exhibit 5.5 illustrates the various eye cues that help to identify the operative system. Eye movements in most people are similar and can usually be expected to show these processes:[40]

ΔExhibit 5.5

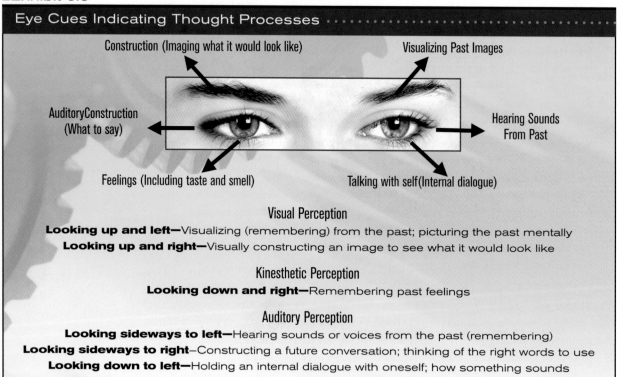

Eye Cues Indicating Thought Processes · · · · · · · · · · · · · · · ·

Construction (Imaging what it would look like)

Visualizing Past Images

AuditoryConstruction (What to say)

Hearing Sounds From Past

Feelings (Including taste and smell)

Talking with self(Internal dialogue)

Visual Perception

Looking up and left—Visualizing (remembering) from the past; picturing the past mentally

Looking up and right—Visually constructing an image to see what it would look like

Kinesthetic Perception

Looking down and right—Remembering past feelings

Auditory Perception

Looking sideways to left—Hearing sounds or voices from the past (remembering)

Looking sideways to right—Constructing a future conversation; thinking of the right words to use

Looking down to left—Holding an internal dialogue with oneself; how something sounds

Some left-handed people reverse the normal right and left eye cues; therefore, eye cues can be used only as clues to be confirmed by further observation.

Interpreting Predicate Words

Most people are fairly consistent in eye movements, body language, behavior style, and all the other ways anyone has devised to help salespeople tune in on their prospects. NLP teaches us to look at eye cues and test them against predicate words, that is, how people talk. Exhibit 5.6 provides a list of predicate words that provide important information to confirm what is observed from eye cues. These words tell you how the other person is processing information. When these words match eye cues, you are on fairly safe ground in deciding which mode of perception is operating for the prospect at that moment.[41]

ΔExhibit 5.6

Predicate Words: A Guide to the Modes of Perception					
Visual		**Auditory**		**Kinesthetic**	
analyze	look	announce	noise	active	intuition
angle	notice	articulate	proclaim	affected	lukewarm
appear	obscure	audible	pronounce	bearable	motion
cognizant	observe	discuss	remark	concrete	panicky
conspicuous	perception	dissonant	report	emotional	pressure
dream	perspective	divulge	roar	feel	sensitive
examine	picture	earshot	rumor	firm	shallow
focus	scene	enunciate	shrill	flow	softly
foresee	sight	gossip	silence	foundation	solid
glance	sketchy	hear	sound	grasp	structured
hindsight	survey	hush	squeal	grip	tension
horizon	vague	inquire	talk	hanging	tied
idea	view	interview	tell	hassle	touch

Salespeople who are good builders of rapport use a few initial questions to get the prospect to talk so they can discover which type of system is in use. Salespeople do not have to memorize a long list of specific questions to evoke the crucial responses needed to determine a prospect's system. The usual opening dialogue a salesperson uses to get acquainted and put the prospect at ease serves admirably. For example, compare the two responses given to the question below and determine which system the answers seem to indicate:

QUESTION: That's an impressive trophy. Do you play a lot of golf?

ANSWER A: I play in a club foursome every Saturday. I enjoy keeping active. It wards off some of the pressure. Sometimes when things get into an unbearable hassle, golf relieves some of the tension. Gripping the club, feeling the impact as I hit the ball, and getting into the swing of the physical motion seems to put me back on a concrete foundation and makes me ready to get back in touch with reality instead of lapsing into panicky emotions.

ANSWER B: I play on Wednesday afternoons and see it as an opportunity to get away from the work scene when the picture gets too crowded or blurred. On the golf course I have time to lose myself in a new perspective. I look down the fairway all the way to the horizon and dream of seeing my ball fly all the way to the hole in one shot. Of course, I've actually never done that, but the dream lets me focus on what is most important, observe the obstacles, and picture a way to avoid them. Then when I get back to work, the whole view seems to have more clarity and the path around the obstacles becomes conspicuous where before it had been obscured because I was too close to the trees to see the forest.

How did you identify the systems used by these two different people? The first was *kinesthetic*. Did you note some of the key words such as:

active	feeling	panicky	pressure	motion	emotions
hassle	foundation	concrete	tension	touch	

The second answer was *visual*. Note the key words in this response:

see	look	picture	scene	horizon	view
picture	conspicuous	dream	clarity	blurred	focus

Be sure to take into account the eye cues, body language, and any other information you have about the prospect as you attempt to decide which system the prospect is using. Remember that we all use the different perceptual fields, often in quick succession, but most of us have one we use more often than the others. When eye cues fit the predicate words used, the salesperson has a fairly sound basis for deciding what is going on in the prospect's mind. Once you know the prospect's favorite system, you know how that person usually maps out the environment and plans a route to the solution of a problem or to the reaching of a goal. Then you can speak a language the auditory prospect can *hear*, draw a picture the visual prospect can *see*, or structure something concrete the kinesthetic prospect can *grasp*.

The following chart summarizes some of the key features of the four social styles. Salespeople are only as good as their reflex actions allow them to be. Rather than a Ph.D., perhaps a salesperson should have a Ph.B.—Professor of Human Behavior. Study the chart below; learn how to read behavioral styles. There's an old saying—if you want to get better at something, learn more about it.

Social Styles Summary	Driver	Expressive	Amiable	Analytical
Backup Style...	Autocratic	Attacker	Acquiescer	Avoider
Measures personal value by...	Results	Applause or approval	Security	Accuracy, "being right"
For growth needs to...	Listen	Check	Initiate	Decide
Needs climate that...	Allows to build own structure	Inspires to reach goals	Suggests	Provides details
Takes time to be...	Efficient	Stimulating	Agreeable	Accurate
Support their...	Conclusions and actions	Dreams and Intuitions	Relationships and feelings	Principles and thinking
Present benefits that tell...	What	Who	Why	How
For decisions, give them...	Options and probabilities	Testimonials and incentives	Guarantees and assurances	Evidence and Service
Their specialty is...	Controlling	Socializing	Supporting	Technical

SUMMARY

- Knowledge of behavioral styles is a useful tool for gaining insight into the thinking of buyers. The model uses the assertiveness and responsiveness dimensions of behavior to assess an individual's social style.

- Versatility is your ability to adjust your own personal pace and priorities to facilitate interaction with a person of another style.

- Recognizing typical behavioral cues makes it possible to classify people quickly into one of four basic personality styles: Driver, expressive, amiable, or analytical.

- Gender differences require diverse ways of thinking and using our behavioral relationships. Adjust to different gender styles to enhance communication.

- A related tool for communication is neurolinguistic programming (NLP), which uses observation of eye cues and typical predicate words to discover the particular perceptual field a person is using at a given time.

- Never attempt to adopt a style that is an insincere imitation of the prospect. Take the lead in finding common ground with the prospect. Practice and use psychological reciprocity.

REVIEW QUESTIONS

1. What is meant by assertiveness and responsiveness as dimensions of behavioral style?

2. Which style is characterized by each of these pairs of dimensions?

    a. Low assertiveness and high responsiveness

    b. Low assertiveness and low responsiveness

    c. High assertiveness and high responsiveness

    d. High assertiveness and low responsiveness

3. What is a backup style and what is its importance to the salesperson?

4. Explain this statement: The strengths of a particular behavioral style are the source of that style's typical weaknesses.

5. Point out some strengths of each of the four behavioral styles and show how they can be used as assets in selling. Identify some of the weaknesses of each and tell how they can damage sales effectiveness.

6. What is a perceptual field? How is it observed in a person's behavior?

7. Read the statements below and determine what perceptual field the speaker is probably using:

    a. There is so much noise in here, I can't hear myself think.

    b. The atmosphere was heavy and damp; there was an oppressive stillness, thick with apprehension.

    c. I am watching developments in that particular stock; before I buy, I want to see the progress it makes this quarter and get a picture of what to expect in the future.

d. The rookie quarterback was calling the first play of his career. He repeated the coach's instructions in his head, and the murmur of the crowd filled his ears. He could hear his heart pounding with excitement.

e. The rookie quarterback was calling the first play of his career. He could still see the coach's face in his mind, imposed on the vision of the great sea of faces in the stands, with all eyes focused on him—a tiny speck on the playing field.

8. What kind of sales aids would you use in making a presentation to a person with a visual perceptual field? What changes would you make when talking to a prospect with an auditory field? How would you deal with a prospect with a kinesthetic field?

9. Is it ethical for a salesperson, by employing behavioral flexibility or versatility, to alter personal behavioral style or to match perceptual fields with a prospect? Are there limits to which such adaptation should adhere? Explain.

ROLE-PLAY EXERCISES

The following role-play exercises help build teams, improve communication, and emphasize the real-world side of selling. They are meant to be challenging, to help you learn how to deal with problems that have no single right answer, and to use a variety of skills beyond those employed in a typical review question. Read and complete each activity. Then in the next class, discuss and compare answers with other classmates.

Role Play 5.1 – Reading Your Sales Staff

Because of this course and what you have learned from this book, many of you will eventually become sales managers or leaders in your organization. How well you succeed will largely depend on how well you are able to "read" other people, to determine their basic personality orientation and to respond appropriately. You might as well begin to practice that skill now when there is relatively little risk.

Using the chart in Exhibit 5.2, write down where your dominant social style falls on the chart. Briefly describe why you characterize yourself in the way that you do.

Next, pair up with another class member whom you do not know. It is essential for this exercise that you not know the other person in any significant way. As your instructor directs, in class or before, the two of you should chat for 10 minutes about any topic(s) whatever. At the conclusion of the chat, jot down where your conversation partner falls on the chart in terms of social style. Briefly add the most important reasons for your decision. Do gender differences play any role in your analysis? Your partner should do the same for you.

Finally, based on what you've learned from Chapter 5, each of you should describe what you think the greatest challenge will be for the other person in relating to other people. Why? What suggestions would you offer to help your conversation partner in becoming more versatile in relating to others? Be insightful and constructive in your comments.

Role Play 5.2 – Learning Styles vs. Presentation Styles

For this exercise, the class should be divided into teams of 4 persons each.

Each team should break out for a 20-minute discussion of the learning styles of each team member. Do some team members respond better to auditory means of communication rather than visual? Are there primarily visual learners represented on the team? What about kinesthetic aspects of communication and learning? During the discussion, team members should share anecdotes about the most memorable presentations they have witnessed, and why.

Following the initial discussion, the team should then spend 10 minutes critiquing modes of communication in this course. Do the class presentations in this course favor auditory learners, visual learners, kinesthetic learners? Based on the principles of neurolinguistic programming (NLP), briefly list constructive suggestions for improving communication and learning in this course.

Finally, for the remainder of the class, the teams should come together to discuss their findings, especially their suggestions for improving communication in the course.

CASE STUDIES

The following case studies present you with selling scenarios that require you to apply the critical skills discussed in the chapter and give you training through simulation, role-playing, and practical learning situations. They are meant to be both engaging and challenging, and like the role-play exercises, don't have one right answer.

Case 5.1 – The Client Who Wouldn't Say Anything

Jimmie Carter was frustrated. He had just returned to his office after meeting with Marjorie Styles, owner of a local jewelry store. After visiting his company's website, Marjorie had phoned to request an appointment at her office to discuss creating a new website for her store. Jimmie was a web designer and one of the founding partners, along with Alice Stallings, of the firm that had now grown to bill over $750,000 per year. Clearly, they knew what they were doing.

As Jimmie barged into Alice's office, slamming the door behind him, Alice looked up. "I take it that the meeting didn't go well," she said calmly.

"Boy, that's an understatement!" Jimmie declared. "Marjorie Styles is really exasperating. I don't know whether we can work with her."

"Why? What happened?"

"Well, when I walked into her office, I noticed that she had pictures of her family—you know, husband, kids, the family dog—on her desk. So I remarked, as I usually do, on how nice her family looked and asked about where they like to go on vacation. Marjorie said, 'Oh, anywhere,' and sat down. I tried a little more informal chit-chat, but she sort of stared over my shoulder. The entire meeting went downhill from there."

"What do you mean?" Alice asked.

"What I mean is that the woman wouldn't say anything! At least not anything helpful. For instance, when I asked her why she wanted to change her website, she said, 'Because the one I have now stinks.' I followed up and asked if she could be more specific, and she said, 'No, this website just doesn't work for me anymore.' 'What, exactly, don't you like about it?' I asked. 'Everything,' came the response. What am I supposed to do with that?"

"Well," Alice prodded, "what did you do with that?"

"I couldn't think of anything else. So I launched into a description of what we could do. You know, that we could change the color palette, insert some video on the home page, make the navigation more intuitive, improve email management, yada, yada, yada. I then handed her a copy of our fee schedule."

"And her response to all that was what?"

"Virtually no response. All she said was that she would have to think it over and that she would get back to me. I asked if she minded if I followed up in a few days, and she said, 'No, that would be ok.' And that was it."

Based on what you have read in Chapter 5, where did Jimmie go wrong? Specifically, what cues did Jimmie pick up on with Marjorie, and why do you think he misread them? Based on the admittedly sketchy information in Jimmie's report to Alice, how would you characterize Marjorie's basic social style? What is Jimmie's style? Why might their respective differences in style have resulted in miscommunication?

What should Alice do in response to this situation? Should she try to help Jimmie understand why Marjorie might have responded to him as she did? Should she have Jimmie contact Marjorie to meet with her again in a few days in order to try a different approach? If so, what should that approach be, and why? Or should Alice contact Marjorie herself, taking Jimmie out of the loop, and try to repair the situation. How might Alice's approach differ from Jimmie's. What could Alice do to obtain Marjorie's business?

Case 5.2 – Another Boring Meeting

Human beings have probably been complaining about boring meetings ever since sitting around the fire in front of their cave. Today's sales meetings are no exception. Derek Johnson's last sales meeting turned out to be a model for inducing lassitude among his sales force. The meeting lasted for 90 minutes, and despite the assistance of a steaming vat of coffee, a couple of people in the front row were actually dozing by the time the meeting ended. On the way down the hall back to his office, Derek overheard comments such as, "Boy, that sure was a waste of time!" and "I hate meetings when we're told to be enthusiastic while the meeting itself is dead." Rather than endure more disrespect, Derek was tempted to cancel sales meetings altogether and just let everybody sink or swim on their own.

Nevertheless, as a mere sales manager, Derek knew that his vice president would never tolerate his running a sales team without meetings. Besides, the office supply company for which Derek worked was taking delivery on Blackberry's PlayBook™, Research in Motion's answer to Apple's iPad™. Since Derek's company didn't carry the iPad because of licensing restrictions, he knew that PlayBook sales would be crucial to this year's success. To make sure that his team understood the PlayBook's features and would promote it vigorously, Derek concluded that he needed to have yet another sales meeting.

This time, however, he determined that things would be different. In the first place, he invited a regional representative from Research in Motion to help explain the PlayBook's features. In fact, the RIM rep promised to bring a 30-minute video that would thoroughly present the PlayBook in the most favorable light. Derek had previewed the video online and knew that the music and visuals were terrific. No one would be sleeping through that! He also had a stack of promotional literature to hand out to everyone. This meeting would indeed be different!

From what you have learned from Chapter 5, would you say that Derek is on the right track? What theoretical principles underlie Derek's new approach to the PlayBook sales meeting? If you were attending the meeting, what more should Derek do to keep you from falling asleep? What could Derek do to make the meeting even more effective in generating enthusiasm and improving learning?

"**Your professionalism** is defined not by the business you are in, but by the way you are in business."

— Dr. Tony Alessandra

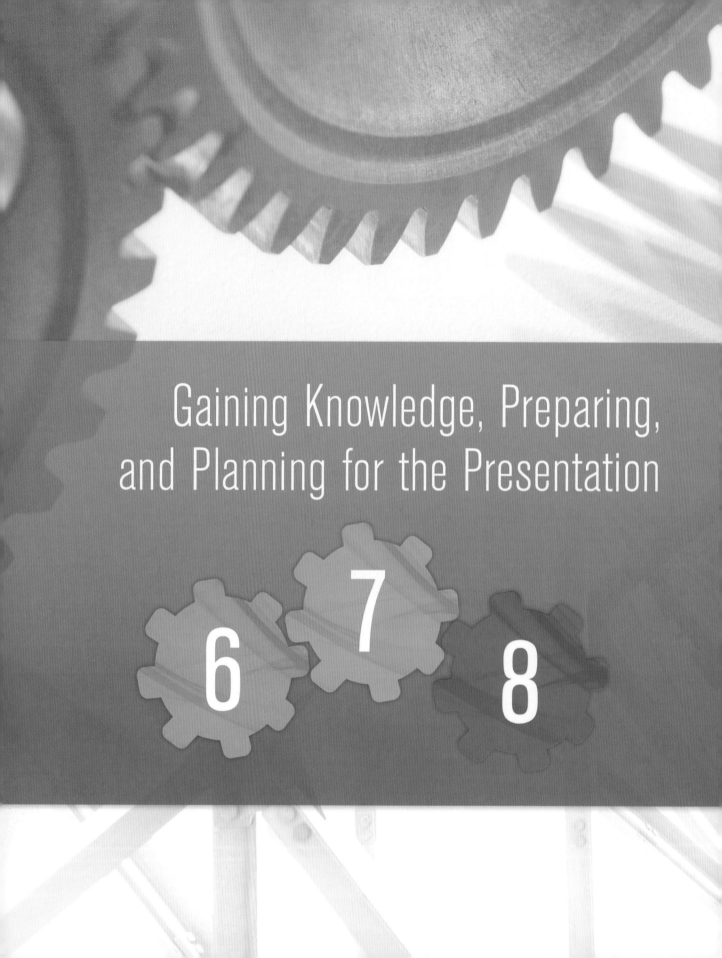

Gaining Knowledge, Preparing, and Planning for the Presentation

6 7 8

Part 3

Part three is comprised of the all-important processes that must occur before the first sales call is ever made. Chapter 6 prepares you for success in a sales career by focusing on gaining product knowledge, developing a specific plan for self-motivation and goal setting, and introducing the use of sales force technology.

Chapters 7 and 8 discuss the procedures for locating and qualifying prospects and identifying the information needed to prepare for an effective presentation. Chapter 7 is a thorough look at prospecting. As the saying goes, "I'd rather be a master prospector than a wizard of speech and have no one to tell my story to." Chapter 8 discusses the process of gathering preapproach information and presents a six-step telephone track for scheduling that critical first appointment with a prospect. The chapters in this section are:

6. Preparation For Success in Selling

7. Becoming a Master Prospector

8. Preapproach and Telephone Techniques

Goal Setting
is the strongest
human force
for self-motivation.

Chapter 6

Preparation for Success In Selling

Learning Objectives

- Study what type of information makes up the product knowledge needed for success in selling.

- See how sales technology tools impact salespeople and how to use them to your advantage.

- Examine the various types of social media available and know which ones to focus on as a salesperson.

- Understand the concept of product positioning.

- Identify the three types of motivation and how they operate in affecting human behavior.

- Learn how to accept personal responsibility for maintaining self-motivation and exercising initiative in selling.

- Recognize the importance of setting and achieving goals for personal success.

Use This Page for Taking Notes

Preparing to Sell

Success in sales involves more than simply getting a person to say yes. If it were that simple, every salesperson would be successful. Rather, a lucrative, long term selling career involves a combination of the training provided by your company with your own active preparation in learning as well as personal commitment. Because the company's bottom line ultimately depends upon your efforts, your preparation is a significant mutual concern; and the more help your company gives, the easier your job becomes. Adequate preparation for success in selling involves at least three areas that are discussed in this chapter.

Successful salespeople prepare themselves with the right tools.

- Product knowledge
- Sales force automation
- Motivation and goal setting

Certain elements in each of these three areas are the primary responsibility of the company; some are primarily your responsibility. No matter who bears the responsibility, both you and your company are active participants. Too much is at stake for either party to take a passive approach to preparation.

Product Knowledge

Newly hired salespeople may have some general knowledge of the company's field or industry and may even have some knowledge of the specific product they will be marketing. However, salespeople are often hired with little or no knowledge of the company and its products, or even of the industry. Obtaining product knowledge is one of the first prerequisites to success. A study conducted among buyers about their perceptions and attitudes toward the salespeople they interact with indicated that buyers' greatest dislike is an unprepared salesperson.[1] Ultimately, two things must take place to achieve the preparedness buyers are looking for: first, your company must provide you with adequate product information to make you feel comfortable representing the product, and more importantly, it is up to you to study and learn about your product.

What do you need to know about the product? One answer to that question is everything! Nevertheless, you cannot delay beginning sales activity until you have learned everything. In fact, in most cases it is impossible to learn everything due to changes in product lines and advances in technology. And once you do begin making calls and closing sales, you can never cease to learn about the product or service. Gaining product knowledge is an ongoing process.

The Product Itself

Product knowledge begins with the product itself: its specific features, its benefits, and its acceptance in the marketplace. Product knowledge includes knowing all available options—how it can be adapted to the particular customer's needs and how it performs under varying conditions. Detailed product knowledge prepares you to answer any question a customer might have and to offer whatever reassurance is necessary in the process that helps the customer reach a decision.

When you are thoroughly educated on the product, you can answer detailed, technical questions from expert buyers or explain it in simple terms to someone who is considering such a purchase for the first time. You seldom tell a prospect all the information you have, but having all the information gives you an entire library from which you can choose the best items for the current situation. Exhibit 6.1 shows how two salespeople used specific product knowledge with varying results.

ΔExhibit 6.1

Using Product Knowledge To Close The Sale ·····························

A software salesman called on the owner of a small business who was looking for a solution to the mountain of paperwork that was burying his accounting department in red tape and slowing up shipping of orders. The salesman had been well trained in product knowledge and was eager to demonstrate his expertise. He overwhelmed the prospect with computer jargon—dual-core and quad-core, webhosts, and firewalls—and he peppered his sales talk with terms like mbps, OS, and OEM software. He left without an order.

Later, another technical salesperson called. She told the prospect how quickly the product she represented would process orders so they could be shipped, and how time and paper handling could be reduced in preparing and sending invoices. She then explained that daily reports could be produced to summarize orders received and shipped, cash received, and other transactions that would provide solid information upon which good business decisions could be made in a timely manner. She got the order!

Product Performance

Performance information is another vital area of product knowledge. How long will your product last? What kind of wear and stress does it tolerate? How fast does it run? How easy is it to upgrade? How much training is necessary for an employee to operate or use this product? How fuel efficient is it? Can it be repaired? How much maintenance is required? Who performs needed maintenance? Are spare parts readily available? These are all questions relating to specific performance issues, and if your customer doesn't voice them, rest assured that he is thinking them.

In the more technical industries, salespeople have access to company engineers and advisors who furnish engineering and technical information when it is required; sales knowledge in this case means knowing who to call on and when to ask for back up. If a product is too technical for a person to understand, be sure you can explain the benefits in a way that your customer will understand.

Manufacturing

Product knowledge also includes knowledge of the manufacturing methods and processes that affect the performance or durability of the product; and these vital ingredients of quality affect buying decisions. An understanding of the manufacturing process may help enable you to explain why a price that seems high to the prospect is actually quite reasonable, or why delivery takes longer than the buyer had expected.

Distribution Channels

The company's distribution methods are another important area of product knowledge. What delivery channels are used? Why? Are exclusive dealerships granted in certain areas? Is selective distribution used? Do discount houses and chains sell the product in competition with other types of retail outlets? Another important element of distribution concerns pricing policies. Such policies include dealers' costs, availability of quantity discounts, applicable credit terms, and whether the company will consider negotiating special deals.[2] Not every customer will be interested in such details and merely want to know they will receive the product as promised. However, for your more thorough prospects, these particulars must not be omitted.

Company Information

Product knowledge also involves gaining as much information as possible about the company you represent. You need to know something about the history of the company: who founded it and when, how the present product line evolved, the company's position in the marketplace, its past and present performance and growth, its primary customers or clients, and any other information that may be of interest to prospects are a few examples of the types of facts that help you sell more effectively.[3] It is important to be aware that your prospects may be almost as knowledgeable about your company and its products and performance as you are.

In the world of investment sales, customers now perceive themselves as more sophisticated and knowledgeable about various companies and their investments than ever before. A recent survey showed that 79 percent of prospective investors are either somewhat or very confident about making their own investment decisions. When asked where they turn for information and advice, a significant majority of these prospects said they are using the cable news channels. Whether they watch MSNBC, Fox News, or CNN, these individuals believe they're becoming increasingly aware of differences in investment companies, types of investments, and financial products.[4] Viewers now have the ability to choose whether to watch content from cable news outlets online, through social media, or through smartphone apps.[5] With the amount of up-to-the-minute news and sources of information available to today's consumer, it is essential that you stay current on your company, your product, and the market.

Service Available

Once the product is sold, your responsibilities have just begun. It is outstanding service after the sale that will cement the client-salesperson relationship and ensure repeat orders for years to come— and repeat commissions! You must know the company's service policy in regard to repairs, updates, and replacements. Which of these is the company's responsibility, if any? What charges are made for service? Who performs the service? On what kind of time schedule? What kind of consulting service is available to adapt or adjust the product to the customer's needs? Your customers will inevitably ask some or all of these questions, so it is imperative that you know the answers.

Product Knowledge Application

Product knowledge is ineffective unless you can apply it to the specific problems or needs of a particular client. When you know the exact materials and specifications used in manufacturing, you can successfully advise a prospect to order your product and expect it to perform as desired. This knowledge also helps you suggest what custom changes might be made in the product to fit the specific needs of a client.

It is likely that the products or services you sell are readily available commodities. However, exemplary service is not a readily available commodity. Therefore, if you have outstanding product knowledge and deliver it through an exceptional service model, you can differentiate yourself, attract clients, and build long-lasting professional relationships.[6] Product knowledge can either be a help or a hindrance, depending on how it is used. Exhibit 6.2 illustrates how salespeople can use their special knowledge to close—or lose—a sale.

ΔExhibit 6.2

Using Product Knowledge To Fit The Need ···

An automobile salesman was showing a new car to a husband and wife. They informed him that the wife would be primarily driving the car for neighborhood errands. The salesman spent a lot of time explaining that the car had front-wheel drive and that the motor was mounted at a ninety-degree angle to the traditional position. He loaded his sales talk with terms like engine ratios, rpm's, and torque; and he bragged about the car's ability to accelerate from zero to sixty faster than any of the competition. The woman's questions about what purpose those features served for her needs produced even more complicated explanations that did not interest her or her husband. Ultimately, the couple bought a car demonstrated by a salesperson from another dealer. He stressed styling, keyless entry, the in-dash navigation system, and the comfort of seat warmers; and then he invited the wife to test-drive the car. You may know the intricate details of your product, but unless you first listen to the prospect, you may as well know nothing.

Knowledge of the Competition

Another overlooked area of product knowledge is information about the competition. Learn about your major competitors' product lines; know their credit terms, their prices, their delivery schedules, and their reputations for service. Most buyers—either personal consumers or company purchasing agents—are not weighing the advantages of buying a product against those of not buying; rather, they are trying to decide which product to buy, yours or the competition's. The following story is an example of how one salesperson used his knowledge of the competition's product to make the sale:

Ken Andrews was involved in a highly competitive bidding situation for his company, a manufacturer of GPS systems for automobiles. He was facing a representative of a Japanese competitor who Ken knew had a lesser-quality product but offered it at a lower price. Ken's product had superior attributes and was easier to use, therefore giving him the edge in technology and quality. The selling opportunity presented for him was to show how the prospect's company could save money by buying a more expensive, but higher-quality product. The end result of his sale was that he won at a higher price through a better product offering.[7]

One of the advantages of studying your competition is that you are reminded of the good points of your own product and what makes it unique. This will help refresh your presentations, especially if you have been selling the same product or service for a long period of time. Once you are reminded of what makes your product different from the competition, you can stress those areas where your product excels and effectively gain a lasting advantage over your competition. Exhibit 6.3 provides an overview of the four areas of competitive advantage.

ΔExhibit 6.3

Differential Competitive Advantage

Product Superiority

Versatility	Appearance
Efficiency	Design
Storage	Mobility
Handling Time	Packaging
Safety	Life Expectancy
Adaptability	

Service Superiority

Delivery	Installation
Inventory	Maintenance
Credit	
Training	
Merchandising	

Source Superiority

Time Established
Competitive Standing
Community Image
Location
Size
Financial Soundness
Policies and Practices

People Superiority

Personal Knowledge and Skill
Skill of Support Personnel
Integrity and Character
Standing in Community
Flexibility of Call Schedule
Interpersonal Skills
Mutual Friends
Cooperation

Sales Force Automation

Paper calendars and Rolodexes are long gone, and the electronic information age is well under way! Today's professional salespeople are not simply computer-savvy; they use every outlet available to them to do their jobs. Email, the Internet, integrated marketing, and database marketing are just a few of the tools that salespeople use every day to communicate with their customers and companies. Computers and smartphones have become instrumental and indispensable tools to foster and build relationships with customers and to manage information and key accounts with greater efficiency.

With the automation of today's sales industry, salespeople can have clear direction and the right incentives, but if they don't have the right tools, their numbers will suffer despite their best intentions. Sales force and sales task automation is unavoidable, but there is one danger to such mechanization. It goes back to the old adage of "garbage in, garbage out." Mark Engelberg, president of TimeLinx Software said this: "Companies always want to put in the latest technology, thinking it is the answer to their problems. But if you automate a mess, you just have an automated mess."[8] The fact is that many companies simply don't take the time to understand the underlying processes before adding the technology. For example, your company could add an expense reporting system for salespeople to submit to accounting, but then forget to buy a license for the accounting department to allow them to use the system. For this reason, proper steps must be taken to ensure that you and your company are ready to automate!

To keep up with the increasing demands of the continually changing, increasingly competitive marketplace, salespeople are expected to become more productive at everything they do. They must see more prospects, provide more value, and do a better job with each customer on which they call. The good news is that technology relieves salespeople of many administrative duties that would normally rob them of time that could be spent planning and selling. Through the use of technology, salespeople can quickly analyze facts and figures and transmit information efficiently to both their customers and companies. Exhibit 6.4 illustrates the impact technology has on product training.[9]

ΔExhibit 6.4

Aflac: Embracing The Way Of The Future In Sales Training · · · · · · · · · · · · · · · ·

When it comes to sales training, the top priority for Aflac, the $25 billion insurance powerhouse, is to match the type of training to the salesperson and the content. "We look at what format worked best in the past, as well as the learner's individual preference," says Dena Wilson, talent manager for Aflac in Columbus, Georgia. Aflac takes advantage of all training formats, including webcasts, instructor-led classroom training, internally developed courses, web-based courses, and anything else that might work and fit the content, Wilson says.

Until recently, when a company like Aflac brought in a trainer to teach its sales force, business as usual would grind to a halt as the company's entire sales team sat trapped in a room for often days at a time. But the Internet has changed the old way of doing things. Today, through the use of webcasts and online training, salespeople can receive real-time training from experts from all over the world, and the company can choose when they want to participate. Ultimately, a blend of webcasts, books, and classroom training may be the best option.

Web-Based Sales Training

Gone are the days when the only method of sales training was to either rotate people through a long and arduous program or close down once a year for an annual sales seminar. Web-based technology makes training easier and more affordable by maximizing flexibility and effectiveness for both the sales force and sales managers. Web-based training can range from simple text-based product information to intricate simulations that mirror a real-life sales interview.[10] The benefits of web-based training include:

- 24-hour access to training programs—allows for fast and convenient training.

- Increased interactivity among large and spread out sales teams.

- Instant access to new product information and current product updates—allows sales force to have up-to-the-minute accuracy of information.

- Direct performance measurements with immediate feedback.

- Reduces costs of airfare, hotel stays, and convention expenses.

- Sales reps can focus their attention on the specific training they need.

One such web-based training system is Cisco WebEx. The WebEx Training Center allows companies to utilize the value and reach of all three major forms of training: online, in-person and self-paced training. WebEx supports up to 1,000 participants per session with real-time sharing of files and applications, on-demand presentation delivery, breakout sessions, virtual hands-on labs, and chat with threaded Q&A. It is one of the most comprehensive training platforms on the market today. WebEx Training Center is an open service platform, which means it allows partners and users to have access to content management, training management, and self-paced training so that the users and their company have an integral say in the content and pace of learning.[11]

Another online training system, ePath Learning, is one of the proven providers of affordable online eLearning solutions. The company's strategy is to deliver the "technology platform of convergence" resulting in a solution that delivers the best of both technologies via its browser-based, easy-to-use delivery model. Dudley Molina, President and CEO of ePath Learning states that, "Considering our extensive product portfolio and continuing development of new products and services, ePath Learning provides sales managers with the capability to dynamically train and certify their sales team to meet the changing needs of the market while ensuring consistency in the message being communicated. This indeed is a strategic competitive advantage."[12]

Thanks to eLearning, sales training is at your fingertips.

E-learning is the way of the future in sales training, but even the best Internet training cannot replace live sales training, role plays, and simulation exercises. The industry is ultimately headed toward blended training. It is not wise to totally eradicate face-to-face training, but when combined with online training, they form a mutually beneficial relationship.[13]

The Impact of Sales Technology Tools

The companies that find ways to respond quickly to customer needs and make information readily available to their business partners will gain the all-important competitive edge. The implementation of an effective sales force automation program provides numerous company benefits which relate directly to improving the bottom-line—your company's profit.[14] Sales force automation can help increase your sales efficiency in three functional areas:

I. Improved Communication

Laptops. Laptops provide you with desktop power wherever you go and have gained immensely in popularity over the desktop, especially since their prices have become very affordable. With Wi-Fi connections now almost ubiquitous, laptops are indispensable for salespeople to maintain constant access to important contact information, sales scripts, and emails. They enable greater time management during flights or commutes, where the busy salesperson can type away at important documents or stay caught up on reading reports.

Smartphones. Smartphones have it all. They are a computer, the Internet, your email, phone, address book, notepad, road map, and entertainment all in one. One popular smartphone on the market today is Apple's iPhone™, but the Android™ and BlackBerry™ also have large contingents of loyal users.[15]

Tablets. Between a laptop and smartphone in size, tablet computers are the next wave of technology to sweep across both the business and the personal entertainment landscape. With similar features to the iPhone, the iPad™ is the first tablet to make a breakthrough into everyday use. It remains to be seen which other tablets will take off.

For each of these three types of devices, vast improvements to Wi-Fi access and 3G, and 4G networks have translated to vast improvements in the efficiency of communication. Never again will you miss an important email while on a sales call or at lunch. Face-to-face interaction with global clients without travel costs is a way of life for business today. Many salespeople are conducting the majority of their sales calls through videoconferencing with Cisco or Skype. Live-feed video conferencing is a great alternative for proposals and presentations.

Telecommuting is also widespread because of the advances in communication technology. No more fighting rush-hour traffic! Not only can you stay on top of your email, but you can also update databases, product information, and appointments from the comfort of your home. Many companies still encourage their salespeople to conduct business from the office, but for more disciplined salespeople, this is an excellent option.

II. Increased Productivity

Contact Management Software. When it comes to your prospect list, there will be no more paper mess and scribbled notes that are easily lost. Contact Managers are programs that enable salespeople to keep track of their leads, appointments, and tasks. They are related to calendars, but integrate email and personal file information such as phone numbers and addresses with task lists and histories of interactions. In addition to providing the functionality of an electronic listing all your customer contacts, contact management software offers you powerful tools for tracking detailed customer information; scheduling appointments, activities, and to-dos; and integrating a number of Internet resources into a single sales force automation solution.[16]

Some of the better-known software programs available today include Goldmine™, Infusion™ and ACT!™. With the number of quality programs available, the key is to find one with which you feel comfortable working and can easily understand. Websites such as CompareCRM.com have reviews and comparisons of the latest Contact Managers on the market to assist in making the best decision for your needs. Apps are also available for managing contacts on-the-go and for coordinating sales information among members of a team. FileMaker for the iPad or iPhone allows businesses to manage contacts, documents, and assets, all from the convenience of a smartphone or tablet.[17]

Customer Relationship Management (CRM) Software. In the world of professional selling, customer relationship management (CRM) is a broad term that covers concepts used by companies to manage their relationships with customers, including the capture, storage, and analysis of customer information. CRM is more than just contact management software; it is a tool that can move companies to a higher level with customers. Well-integrated CRM systems are used daily as the central point of customer contact.[18] Microsoft Dynamics™, Brainsell™, and LeadMaster™ are just a few of the CRM products available today. One of the leading CRM products on the market is salesforce.com™, who is moving beyond software on your computer to cloud-based computing systems.

Another company offering a cloud-based, hosted system is Surado CRM Solutions™. Unlike CRM software that resides on a salesperson's computer hard drive, hosted CRM is a web-based application, allowing users to access their sales data from any computer or device with Internet access. With products in all 50 U.S. states and over 64 countries worldwide, Surado is well positioned to become a dominant player in the CRM industry.[19] For more on this company, refer to the *Developing Partnerships Using Technology* box on the following page.

Sales Apps. Another way that salespeople can maximize the use of their smartphones and tablets is through the use of apps designed for mobile sales. One such app available for the iPad is FatStax, developed by Red Funnel Consulting. The app includes features such as a product cart, address book integration, and offline product search capabilities, giving sales professionals access to their product information without requiring a Wi-Fi connection. FatStax also allows a single user to manage multiple product catalogs.[20] As tablet technology develops, the availability of apps for selling will develop as well.

Mapping Programs and GPS Technology. With the level of sophisticated mapping technology available today, no salesperson will ever be lost or late to an appointment. Real-time location finders and interactive mapping systems are widely available on smartphones and come standard in many new car models. With the information clearly plotted on a map and a friendly voice guiding you, effectively navigating your territory has become immeasurably more accurate.

III. Transactional Processing

Electronic Data Interchange (EDI) Technology. With EDI technology, your entire company has up-to-date order, processing, and fulfillment information. When customers place an order they have instant access to product information, sent to them in an email or a link to an informational website. The selling chain is automated to include customers, distributors, and suppliers.

Corporate Contact Management and Custom Reporting Programs. These programs and software provide shared contact information that is modified and updated by everyone in the sales office. You can customize reports to the specific needs for each of your individual customers and prospects. Examples of these types of programs are eSalesTrack and Fuse5.

Developing Partnerships Using Technology describes how Surado CRM Solutions can enhance a salesperson's effectiveness and productivity. Surado provides a number of product options including Online SaaS (Software-as-a-Service) and On-Premise (in-house based CRM). With this software, the entire life-cycle of the sales process is covered, from the way you generate leads, qualify an opportunity, review competition, develop and present a value proposition, secure agreement support, order fulfillment, and maintain existing relationships while you seek new ones.

Developing Partnerships Using Technology

Leveraging Technology to Improve Performance

In an increasingly competitive environment, sales teams must manage a range of competencies and toolsets faster and more effectively than ever before. Presentations, revenue forecasting, sales follow-up, lead generation, cross selling, and scheduling appointments are all part of a day's work. To achieve peak performance, **Surado CRM Solutions**™ provide easy-to-master tools, which create consistent and effective results that translate into increased revenues and profitability.

The company empowers sales teams by providing an intuitive system that presents a comprehensive, single view of the customer across the entire organization. Combine this with a powerful Knowledge Base and Automated Business Rules to create a consistent sales methodology throughout your entire team. With these tools, your sales team is able to manage the complete prospect-to-customer life cycle with efficiency and effectiveness.

Benefits of Surado CRM Solutions:

1. Provide a consistent and coordinated sales process across the entire team.

2. Target resources toward highly qualified opportunities and the real decision makers.

3. Maintain contact with your customers, even when on the road.

4. Help you know your competition and structure your presentation to emphasize your strengths.

5. Empower sales teams with powerful research and reporting tools.

6. Increase efficiency by integrating with third-party applications.

For more information visit: www.SuradoCRM.com

Social Networking

Now more than ever, salespeople have increasing opportunities to relate to customers and prospects on a daily basis through social media. Within the past few years, the phenomenon of social media has skyrocketed in the daily life of consumers. In 2010, the amount of time per person spent on social media sites increased by 67 percent. The two biggest social media sites, Facebook and Twitter, saw traffic increases of 200 percent and 1,500 percent, respectively, during that year.[21] The field is wide open for savvy salespeople and innovative companies to use the social media phenomenon to their advantage. As with other technology tools, the question isn't, "Should I use social media to help me sell?" but "*How* will I use it?" What will be the impact of social media on sales forces in the next few years? We are certainly entering an exciting time in the life cycle of this phenomenon.

Social Media Sites

Social media is a web-based tool that gives users a way of connecting with each other online. Connections made through social media sites can be based on prior personal relationship, whether family, friend, or business, or they may be made with complete strangers whose profile indicates a common interest or area of background. If the power of selling is in the strength of relationships, social media provides a way for salespeople to relate to more people than ever and in less time than ever.

Every individual has preferences and styles that determine their personality and what makes them unique. Some people prefer quiet one-on-one conversation, while others are most comfortable in a rowdy group discussion. The same goes for social media preferences: Each customer has likes and dislikes about the various sites available today, and companies must be willing to meet the needs of their customers on this issue as on others. Salespeople, too, must pay attention to customers' communication preferences and work to communicate in the way that is most comfortable for the one who is most important in the sales relationship: the customer.[22]

The following are a list of social media sites that are beneficial for salespeople today:

Facebook. When Facebook was created in 2004, its original purpose was to provide a way for students on college campuses to network with one another. Today, however, there are 500 million users in 70 language translations, and 37 percent of them are over the age of 35.[23] Companies and individual salespeople alike utilize Facebook fan pages to build profiles of their products and services and to keep their brand prominent in the daily newsfeed of Facebook users. Targeted ads are another way that salespeople can use Facebook to make contact with prospects.

Twitter. In 140 characters or less, 200 million users are sending out an average of 140 million "tweets" per day.[24] With less room to build a robust profile than on Facebook, Twitter users primarily tweet links to useful information or news, whether it be about upcoming events, fantastic deals, or informative reviews.

LinkedIn. LinkedIn is the business side of social media. On LinkedIn, you won't find photos from your college roommate's recent vacation or inane status updates about what's for dinner. As the world's largest online professional network, LinkedIn has 100 million users, including executives from all Fortune 500 companies. CEO Jeff Weiner notes that the success of LinkedIn is about connecting talent with opportunity in a way that impacts lives and careers.[25]

Specialized Sites. Aside from the powerhouse sites listed above, smaller social networking sites cater to more specialized interests. Depending on the field, a salesperson may need to be involved in a niche site as well as the major ones like Facebook and Twitter. For those of us in the book publishing world, relating to potential readers on Goodreads.com is a must, while some in the music industry have found sites like Noisetrade.com to be an effective way of relating to listeners and potential music buyers. Whatever the product is that you sell, it is imperative to find out the latest ways to network with other salespeople and customers.

Product Positioning

The level of competition today is astounding. There are so many brands, and for every brand there are salespeople trying to get the sale before the next guy. It's a fast-paced, cutthroat race, and the competition is coming from all over the world. That makes positioning—the marketing strategy of differentiating a product or company in the mind of a prospect—more important than ever. Once a business identifies what makes it unique in the eyes of the consumer, that element should become the focus of its entire marketing and sales strategy. What makes your company and your product line different? Exhibit 6.5 gives sales professionals five points that will enable them to go into an organization and say, "Allow me to explain to you how and why my company and its products are different."

ΔExhibit 6.5

Key Points for Developing a Powerful Market Position

FIND OUT what qualities of your products and services are most important to your customers. Use that information to custom-design a unique niche for yourself.

PUT TOGETHER a marketing strategy built around several features that are important to your customers and will set you apart from the competition. And then develop an integrated marketing communication message that reinforces those attributes in the customer's mind.

REMEMBER the way you service your customers or sell to them can be a powerful difference. For example, if you are in an industry where the prevailing culture stresses face-to-face selling, the ability to buy directly online can be very attractive.

RECOGNIZE that focusing on the few attributes that really set you apart means you can't be all things to all people. When you shout, "Hey, everybody," you end up satisfying nobody. Focus on those customers that are a part of your specific target market.

KEEP an eye on how your competitors are positioning themselves. Be ready to respond to their claims and make sure you maintain a differential competitive advantage.

Positioning refers to developing a specific marketing mix to influence potential customers' overall perception of a brand, product line, or organization. The term was popularized by Jack Trout and Al Ries in their book, *Positioning: The Battle for Your Mind*. Positioning is the place a product occupies in potential customers' minds relative to competing offerings. Once a position is selected, product, price, place, and promotion strategies and tactics are designed to reinforce the sought-after position. These marketing mix components represent a bundle of individual dimensions that are designed to work together to create a competitive advantage.

Apple is a company that has become known for consistently positioning itself as an innovator that offers unique benefits for its customers. When Apple launched the iPod, within a couple of years it cornered 65 percent of portable MP3 player sales, due in large part to the iPod capitalizing on newer technology and holding a vast number more songs than their flash-memory player competitors.[26] Apple's Mac computers sell even better than the iPod: In the "premium" computer price range over $1000, Apple's revenue share is 91 percent. Their strategy is to offer high-quality computers that are highly customizable and more stable and secure than their PC competitors. As such, they do not sell low-end, low-price computers, focusing instead on the high-end where they have achieved such great success. Apple COO Tim Cook says, "Our goal is not to build the most computers. It's to build the best." The strategy works, and Apple has positioned themselves to great advantage.[27]

Integrated Marketing Communication

Setting in motion all the pieces in a sales and marketing program takes coordination. Integrated marketing communication uses computerized databases to orchestrate the conception, timing, and execution of all the marketing elements. Each of the seven modules shown in Exhibit 6.6 has a specific function, and they should be designed to work together as a company-wide, interactive, closed-loop communication system. Integrated marketing provides management with the ability to quantitatively measure the impact a specific action has on sales and customer perceptions and determine the optimal level of sales stimuli—price, advertising, sales promotion, direct mail, and personal selling—needed to bring a specific reaction in the market. The logical solution is to create a marketing database accessible to all parties. The salespeople who go through this process will know more about their prospect and customers than anyone else in the company.

ΔExhibit 6.6

A Closed Loop, Integrated Marketing Communication System

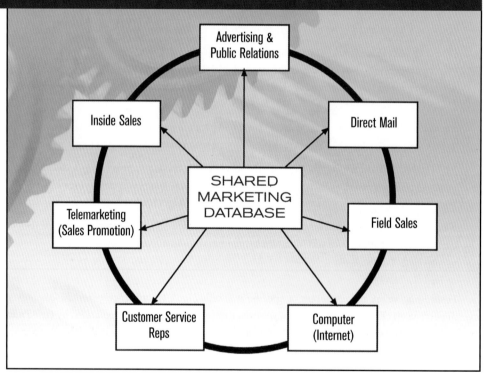

The goal is to deliver marketing communications tailored to the unique needs of a target audience. In the retail clothing market, for example, Gap Inc. delivers a series of coordinated messages by using a combination of communication vehicles: online advertising, email newsletters and updates, and a return to TV advertising. As a result of this multi-pronged approach, Gap Inc. is able to have daily interaction with the millions of people in its database.[28] This is a truly integrated approach to sales and marketing.

Integrated marketing is a communication campaign in which all the elements come together to form one comprehensive, consistent positioning strategy. Depending on the situation, an organization selects what kinds of communication should be used and when. This may include direct mail, email newsletters, telephone selling, customer service, public relations, trade shows, or face-to-face selling. One way that companies have capitalized on the highly automated capabilities of software and the Internet is through email newsletters, updates, and specials. When customers log-on to a company's website to make an online purchase, the company is then able to send targeted emails to each customer. Many customers consider this method of marketing less intrusive than telemarketing and more environmentally friendly than direct mail.

The advent of selling sites such as Groupon has also given companies a way to develop new and exciting methods of using an integrated marketing strategy. General Mills recently launched an experiment using Groupon's social coupons to offer a sampler pack of their consumer packaged goods, including baking mix, dinner kits, and snack items. Customers purchased the sampler pack worth $40 at a reduced price of $20. General Mills then sent out emails requesting more information from customers in exchange for free home delivery and a booklet of coupons for in-store redemption. The strategy, says General Mills, is to use Groupon's online site to increase in-store sales, making it a truly integrated approach to reaching customers through a variety of communication methods.[29]

Motivation And Goal Setting

Salespeople often find that they have the needed product knowledge and sales and computer skills but have trouble getting around to using them, or else they work hard and long but find that what they accomplish fails to bring them lasting satisfaction. The missing ingredient is motivation.

Numerous definitions have been given for motivation. Perhaps the simplest is that *motivation is the reason for taking action.* This definition can be expanded slightly to say that motivation is the *impetus* to begin a task, the *incentive* to expend an amount of effort in accomplishing the task, and the *willingness* to sustain the effort until the task is completed.

The question most asked of business consultants is, "How can we motivate our sales force?" The answer most given by consultants is, "You can't." The reason for this answer is that the question typically implies that somewhere there are strategies, techniques, or gimmicks that, once discovered and implemented, will double or triple sales motivation and productivity. Consultants realize that genuine and lasting motivation is not something management does, but rather a process that management fosters and allows to happen.[30]

The primary responsibility for developing and sustaining motivation rests with you; the company's role is to provide a supportive climate in which the development and sustaining of motivation is encouraged. Bob Nelson, author of *1001 Ways to Reward Employees*, says, "What motivates people the most takes just a little time and thoughtfulness." Recognize them as individuals and you're giving them what they most crave. Read *The Lighthouse Story* for an inspirational idea that cost just a few dollars but paid enormous dividends.[31]

The Lighthouse Story

Jonathan Berger, director of strategic accounts for Square D/Schneider Electric, had a salesperson on his team close a very important account that put a fairly large bonus in the sales rep's pocket. So Berger decided to take the extra step that made this sale a truly memorable triumph. He knew the sales rep's wife had a passion for photographing lighthouses, so he sent her a small crystal lighthouse with a note that recognized her husband's achievements and thanked her for her support and the time she had invested. The wife wrote Berger back and said, "Never has anyone in any company ever acknowledged my existence or the contribution I make to my husband's career." This story is good enough to pass on.

Practical Motivation for Salespeople

All motivation theories agree that motivation arises as a response to either an external or internal stimulus. Recognizing those stimuli that operate in your own experience can help you discover ways to control either the stimuli or your responses to them in a way that produces a positive, sustained motivational power and the success you desire. Motivation may arise in fear—the fear of punishment or withholding of acceptance if behavior does not conform to expectations. It may come from incentive— the promise of reward for desired behavior. But the most effective type of motivation is that arising in attitude—behavior chosen because it fits the values and standards chosen by the individual as guiding principles for living and performing.[32]

Fear Motivation. Fear as a motivating force has some value. Fear is a natural emotion designed as protection from danger. Fear motivation has some advantages.

- It protects the individual from self-destruction or harm.
- It protects society from undesirable behavior.
- It is sometimes the quickest way to accomplish a desired reaction.

In spite of these advantages, fear motivation has serious disadvantages that more than offset its benefits.

- *Fear is external.* It is effective only as long as the enforcing power is stable. When the parent, teacher, or sales manager is out of sight, fear motivation is materially weakened.

- *Fear is temporary.* Threats or punishment may control behavior for a time, but people tune out warnings if they discover that threats are not always carried out.

- *Fear is negative.* It is directed largely toward not doing something or toward doing something unpleasant merely because it is an imposed duty rather than a chosen activity. A warning not to do something creates a void that may be filled by another equally undesirable behavior.

Incentive Motivation. The use of incentives for motivation is generally considered more enlightened than the use of fear. The attempt to produce motivated activity by offering incentives is common in sales organizations. Some common incentives used include the appeal to work harder to earn increased commissions; contests, certificates, and plaques for quotas reached; bonuses; the promise of an enlarged or better sales territory; and perks such as a reserved parking place, a private office, a personal secretary, or a company car. You have to understand what motivates each individual on your team and use that information.[33] Like fear motivation, incentive motivation has advantages.

- *Incentive motivation calls for extra effort.* When a promised reward is highly desirable, salespeople put forth almost superhuman effort to win it.
- *Incentive motivation is positive* and promises something desirable. Salespeople are not frozen into inaction by fear of being punished or deprived.

It's All a Matter of Perspective

Two salesmen fell on hard times and ended up broke in a small town in Montana. They needed money to move on and learned that the town paid $20 each for wolf pelts. They sensed the opportunity. That night they set out with a couple of clubs and some borrowed supplies and made camp in the distant hills. They were no sooner asleep than one was startled by an eerie howl. He crawled outside the tent to find himself surrounded by hundreds of snarling wolves. Back into the tent he crawled and shook his buddy. "Wake up!" he cried. "Wake up! We're rich! " It's really all a matter of perspective!

Like fear motivation, however, incentive motivation carries built-in disadvantages.

- *Incentive motivation is external.* Behavior depends upon the initiative of the person who offers the reward rather than upon the salesperson who will earn it.
- *Incentive motivation is temporary.* A salesperson may put forth a great deal of effort to win a sales contest or to earn some desired reward but not continue that level of activity or effort once the contest is over.
- A promised reward that is *not perceived as desirable* provides no motivation for action.
- Incentives once earned often come to be *regarded as rights* instead of a special privilege for outstanding performance. For example, salespeople who qualify for a company car by high productivity and enjoy this reward for several years feel incensed if the requirements for having a company car are raised and they fail to meet the new quota, even though they improve their sales for the year.

Attitude Motivation. Attitude motivation operates on the concept that the only lasting and uniformly effective motivation is the personal motivation that comes from the internal structure of the individual. It is based on a strong self-image and a belief in the possibility of success. Attitude motivation is self-motivation. All great salespeople inherently possess this powerful, internal drive. Self-motivation can be shaped and molded, but it cannot be taught.[34]

Self-motivation is the result of the choices made by individuals in response to conditioning influences. Fear and self-doubt are the habitual attitudes of some people, but others choose, instead, to respond to life positively. For example, some salespeople who are told they're too inexperienced decide that they are and always will be. Then they wait for someone to tell them what to do. However, others respond to the statement by choosing to believe that their condition is temporary. As a result, they are willing and eager to try different activities, stretch their imaginations, and attempt new goals.

They do not wait for someone else to motivate them; they are always reaching out for new experiences. These salespeople are self-motivated. What you are, then, is not entirely a result of what happens to you. What you are is a result of how you react to what happens to you, and your reactions are a matter of choice.[35]

The advantages of attitude motivation are the opposites of the disadvantages of fear and incentive motivation:

- *Attitude motivation is internal.* Because attitudes come from within, you do not need to wait for an outside stimulus to make appropriate choices and take action.
- *Attitude motivation is permanent.* An attitude, once thoroughly established, continues to operate on an automatic basis until you do something to alter it. Self-motivation is the only kind of motivation that can be sustained over a long period of time.

Attitude Motivation Through Goal Setting

The single most important tool for developing self-motivation is a program of personal goals. A personal goals program creates desire—one of the most powerful emotions operating in human experience. If you want to be able to choose where you will go with your sales effort, and how you will get there, you need clear goals and strategies. Only then will you have the power to direct your efforts.[36]

Exhibit 6.7 on the following page is the Million Dollar Personal Success Plan that Paul J. Meyer, founder and chairman of the board of SMI International, developed for his own use at the age of nineteen. It provides a workable plan for achieving success in selling.

ΔExhibit 6.7

The Million Dollar Personal Success Plan ·

The Million Dollar Personal Success Plan
By Paul J Meyer
Founder of SMI International Inc.
www.success-motivation.com

I. Crystallize Your Thinking
Determine what specific goal you want to achieve. Then dedicate yourself to its attainment with unswerving singleness of purpose, the trenchant zeal of a crusader.

II. Develop a Plan for Achieving Your Goal, and a Deadline for its Attainment
Plan your progress carefully: hour-by-hour, day-by-day, month-by-month. Organized activity and maintained enthusiasm are the wellsprings of your power.

III. Develop a Sincere Desire for the Things You Want in Life
A burning desire is the greatest motivator of every human action. The desire for success implants "success consciousness" which, in turn, creates a vigorous and ever-increasing "habit of success."

IV. Develop Supreme Confidence in Yourself and Your Own Abilities
Enter every activity without giving mental recognition to the possibility of defeat. Concentrate on your strengths, instead of your weaknesses… on your powers, instead of your problems.

V. Develop a Dogged Determination to Follow Through on Your Plan, Regardless of Obstacles, Criticism or Circumstances or What People Say, Think or Do
Construct your Determination with Sustained Effort, Controlled Attention, and Concentrated Energy. OPPORTUNITIES never come to those who wait… they are captured by those who dare to ATTACK.

Crystallized Thinking. You must know what you want to achieve. If your goals are hazy and poorly defined, you cannot plan concrete action steps for their achievement. You must write down and date your goals. Monitoring your status keeps you focused.[37] Without specific action plans, much of your time and effort is wasted. Chapter 15 will address action plans and effective time management techniques in much greater detail.

A Plan of Action with Deadlines. A written plan of action keeps you on track and headed toward the achievement of your goals. You know exactly what to do next. A written plan also reveals conflicts between various goals so that you can plan ahead and make a reasonable schedule for the time and resources needed to reach all your goals. Deadlines provide you with the needed time frame for achieving your goals. They give you something to aim for.[38] Because most of us now use such a small percentage of our real potential, target dates serve the purpose of drawing out more potential and using it to bring desired goals into being. Deadlines help you maintain a positive attitude of expectancy toward goals achievement. They eliminate distractions and help you to think creatively.

Sincere Desire. A burning desire to achieve the goals you want often makes the difference between a wish and a goal. A *wish* is something you would like to have but are not willing to invest enough time or effort in order to achieve it; a *goal* is something you want so intensely that you will exert whatever effort is needed to reach it. The more goals you achieve, the more desire you develop. The greater your desire, the more you can achieve. Desire is an ascending spiral of success.

Supreme Confidence. Success demands supreme confidence in yourself and your ability. Self-confidence enables you to undertake challenging goals and believe you can succeed. Self-confidence lets you see problems as opportunities and obstacles as stepping-stones to success. Self-confidence builds your credibility so that the buyer is open to considering the solutions suggested. Self-confidence makes it easy to ask for the order—not once, but again and again until the sale is closed successfully.

The secret to developing this kind of confidence is a growing list of goals accomplished. Each time you succeed in reaching a goal you have set and worked toward, you gain added belief in your own capability to achieve. Confidence in your own personal ability is the greatest source of security you can possess.

Dogged Determination. Determination to stick to your plan of action until your goal is achieved is an outgrowth of desire and confidence. When you have a burning desire to achieve your goals, you are not easily swayed by others' thoughtless comments, by the disapproval of someone who does not understand your goals, or the active opposition of those who fear to be compared with you in either effort or

Stay determined to reach your goals.

results. Determination is the quality that enables you to continue calling on a difficult prospect until you close the sale. Determination gives you the creative freedom to discover new tactics for achieving your goal when your first effort fails and to think up more ideas until you discover a way that works.

All of these success elements are interdependent. Use of each increases your power to use the others. Success in any one intensifies your belief in the others. Self-motivation is the only real and lasting motivation. Its development is your responsibility. The company and sales manager can provide a climate in which self-motivation is easier, but even the most negative climate cannot de-motivate you without your permission.

Success and the Total Person

Organizations emphasize that sales forces are essential to corporate success. However, organizations seldom pay much attention to what constitutes success for an individual. Too often success for salespeople is measured only in terms of the amount of sales generated. This narrow view of success has been responsible for destroying the self-confidence of untold numbers of salespeople. An understanding of what success really means frees you to become all that your potential allows.

One of the most comprehensive definitions of success is this: "Success is the progressive realization of worthwhile, predetermined, personal goals."[39] This definition is especially applicable to salespeople, who can begin their careers with relatively little training compared to that required of other professionals. Because success is progressive, you can be successful immediately just by choosing to pursue goals that are personally fulfilling and then beginning to work toward them. Obviously, such a beginning is not made at the level expected of a master salesperson with long experience but at a level consistent with present reality. When you learn this truth, you have the patience to study, learn the art of selling, and practice your skills.

Too many people fall into the same erroneous thinking that organizations often follow in measuring success. Those "worthwhile, predetermined goals" must involve more than money and position or the success that is achieved is likely to be hollow. Mike Singletary, former head coach for the San Francisco 49ers and pro bowl linebacker for the Chicago Bears, has spoken to Christian youth groups all over the country. As a member of the NFL Hall of Fame and devoted father and husband to a wonderful wife and seven children, he is someone who should be heard. In his motivational and inspirational talks, Mike encourages his young audiences to develop their potential in all areas of life, not just their athletic skills. Likewise, salespeople who concentrate only on career success and neglect other areas of life find their lives less than happy.

Money and position are fairly low on the hierarchy of needs that all people experience. For this reason, goals must be set in every area of life: physical and health, mental and educational, family and home, spiritual and ethical, social and cultural, financial and career. Total personal growth in these areas is effectively pictured in Exhibit 6.8 as spokes on a wheel. If some spokes are uneven, the wheel that represents total life achievement is not round. The ride is very bumpy, and the passenger feels dissatisfaction and a vague sense of uneasiness or unhappiness. Unmet needs prevent the enjoyment of achievements in other areas. Monetary success means little to the salesperson whose family life is shattered, health ruined, or the respect of friends lost. All areas of life must be included in a plan for becoming a "total person."

∆Exhibit 6.8

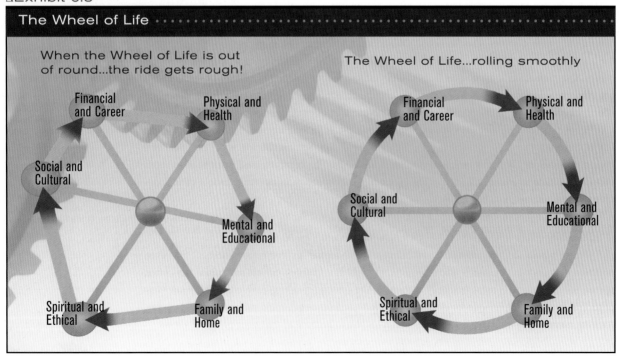

The Wheel of Life

When the Wheel of Life is out of round...the ride gets rough!

The Wheel of Life...rolling smoothly

This definition of success also implies that success has different meanings for different people and that not every salesperson belongs in a particular organization selling a specific product or service. To succeed, salespeople must market a product or service in which they personally believe. Once salespeople know what they want from a selling career and dedicate themselves to achieving those goals, the responsibility for reaching success is largely in their own hands. *Too many people confuse action with progress and effort with results.* Trying hard does not guarantee success. Success comes as a result of determining the desired goals, finding out what activity is required to reach those goals, and then completing those actions based on a personal commitment to oneself. Real success never comes by accident.

SUMMARY

- Preparing for success in a sales career includes three areas of special importance: Product knowledge, sales force automation, and motivation and goal setting.

- Product knowledge includes knowledge of the entire industry or field and specific knowledge about your product or service.

- Sales force automation and technology tools increase your personal productivity, communications capabilities, and transaction-processing efficiency.

- Social media is a way for salespeople and companies to connect with others in their business, as well as customers and prospects. Relating through social media is another aspect of the overall sales relationship between salesperson and customer.

- Positioning refers to the place a product occupies in customers' minds relative to competing offerings. Once you select a position, design product, price, and promotion strategies to reinforce the desired position.

- All motivation comes primarily from one of three sources: Fear, incentive, and attitude. Fear and incentives used as motivating forces are limited in effectiveness because they depend on someone else as the source. Attitude motivation is internal and permanent.

- Successful goal setting begins with crystallized thinking about what is important to you, then developing a plan of action with deadlines for achievement.

REVIEW QUESTIONS

1. What contribution can business school courses make to success in selling? How much academic work in sales or marketing is necessary to guarantee success in professional selling?

2. Does the company that hires you have any responsibility for preparing you for sales success? If so, what specific types of knowledge, information, or other input is the company's responsibility?

3. Name at least four areas of product knowledge that are important for salespeople.

4. What advantage does knowledge of the competition's offerings provide for the salesperson?

5. What would you do about product knowledge if you were hired to sell a highly technical product for which you have little background or understanding?

6. Sales force automation can help increase a salesperson's effectiveness in at least three distinct ways. Discuss each one and give an example to illustrate.

7. Name at least four social media sites that are popular today. What are the main uses of each site?

8. Explain how fear and incentives are used as sources of motivation. Can you give an example from your own experience of how both of these were used by someone else in an attempt to motivate you?

9. What limits the effectiveness of fear and incentives as motivating forces?

10. What are the advantages of using attitude as a basis of motivation?

11. Explain how goal setting affects self-motivation.

12. How does a personal goals program produce self-confidence? What is the value of self-confidence to salespeople?

ROLE-PLAY EXERCISES

The following role-play exercises help build teams, improve communication, and emphasize the real-world side of selling. They are meant to be challenging, to help you learn how to deal with problems that have no single right answer, and to use a variety of skills beyond those employed in a typical review question. Read and complete each activity. Then in the next class, discuss and compare answers with other classmates.

Role Play 6.1 – Positioning Your College

Every organization—businesses both small and large, not-for-profit organizations, professional societies, etc.—must differentiate itself from its peers and competitors. Your college or university is no exception. The competition for students among higher education institutions is keen. After all, without the revenue supplied by a sufficient number of students through tuition and financial aid programs, many colleges and universities would have to close their doors. To appeal successfully to enough students, colleges and universities must position themselves vis-à-vis their competitors, i.e., they must communicate to prospective students how they are different from and superior to other schools in meeting student needs. Salespersons (and, yes, admissions officers for colleges and universities are salespersons) often overlook the importance of positioning in their quest for product knowledge.

Imagine that you are the Director of Admissions at the college or university through whose good auspices you are taking this course. The Vice President for Enrollment Management has just asked for your professional estimate of the school's current positioning strategy and your recommendation for any changes that you think are warranted. What do you say in your one-page report? In thinking about your report, take another look at Exhibit 6.5 (p. 137) in Chapter 6.

Be sure that your report draws upon your analysis of your college's website and other marketing materials and that you have at least looked at the websites of some of your college's closest competitors. How is your college presenting itself as distinctive? Does it work? Is there anything that you think should be changed in your college's current strategy? Bring your findings to class and be prepared to discuss them.

Role Play 6.2 – How Much Product Knowledge is Enough?

For this exercise, you should pair up with another student in the class.

Most people are aware that B2B sales, especially for highly technical products, require a great deal of product knowledge and knowledge of the business in general. But many assume that retail sales—where many salespersons get their start—is easy in that regard. After all, how much is there to learn about most retail products?

Select a retail product line and, with your partner, interview at least 2 salespersons who handle that line. Please try to conduct your interviews when the stores are not busy or outside regular business hours, since nearly all retail salespersons work on commission. When they are talking with you, they can't make any money. The products might be mobile phones, household appliances, furniture, upscale clothing, sports equipment—nearly anything at all. Keeping in mind the various types of product knowledge presented in Chapter 6, ask the salespersons what sort of training their company provided to acquaint them with their products. Ask them how long it took until they felt comfortable presenting features and answering customers' questions about their products. Find out how much they need to know about their company's procedures, methods of getting their products into customers' hands, their company's history, financing or payment policies, etc. And finally, ask how often they have to update their product knowledge in order to remain on top of their game.

Summarize your findings in one or two pages and be prepared to discuss what you learned in class or online.

CASE STUDIES

The following case studies present you with selling scenarios that require you to apply the critical skills discussed in the chapter and give you training through simulation, role-playing, and practical learning situations. They are meant to be both engaging and challenging, and like the role-play exercises, don't have one right answer.

Case 6.1 – Motivation through Compensation

Dwayne Connors, Regional Vice President for Sales at DirtCheap Corporation (an agricultural equipment manufacturer), didn't know where to turn next. Because of declining sales, his predecessor had been fired. The company had tried a policy of management by fear that was approved at the highest levels. During that 3-year period, the company had reduced the base pay of all salespersons whenever they failed to meet the month's quota. The rationale was, "If they don't sell, why should we pay them [their full base pay]?" As the company president put it, "Confronted with the fear of disaster, they'll perform." Well, they didn't. Some salespersons resigned outright. Others failed to make quota month after month. As district sales manager, Dwayne noticed the plunging morale and declining sales figures. He had promised a different approach that, he thought, would get better results.

So, for the past 9 months, Dwayne had instituted a system of positive incentives. First on the list was a compensation structure that awarded salespersons a higher percentage commission the more they sold. For example, if a salesperson made quota, a 10% commission on total sales would be added. If a salesperson sold 150% of quota, a 25% commission would be paid, and so forth. Increased productivity would therefore be rewarded directly and immediately; and some salespersons had the potential of earning large sums, even surpassing Dwayne's fixed salary. In addition, Dwayne initiated a series of sales contests for lines of equipment that were overstocked. For a period of 4 months, sales improved and morale began to improve. Dwayne thought he had licked the problem by using carrots rather than sticks.

But now, after the last 5 months of stagnating results, Dwayne was stymied. Sales had slumped once again, although not alarmingly. He was beginning to receive caustically worded emails from his superiors at headquarters wondering when his "new approach" would pay off. What to do?

Given what you have learned in Chapter 6 about attitude motivation or self-motivation, how would you advise Dwayne? What steps might he and his sales managers take to help the sales force to improve their motivation to succeed? If graduated commissions and sales contests didn't turn the tide permanently, what might?

Case 6.2 – Rescuing Greyhounds

After 35 years of a very successful career in technical sales, Walt decided to give something back to his community during his retirement. He and his wife had rescued a couple of retired racing greyhounds in recent years and found them to be adorable, loving companions. So it seemed natural as a result for Walt to volunteer his services to the local greyhound adoption organization. Little did Walt know what he had gotten himself into!

Because of his background in sales, the organization's executive director decided that Walt should become the group's chief fundraiser. The job called for Walt to write grant proposals, visit philanthropic foundations to solicit financial support, and to make presentations on the organization's behalf to various community groups. In short, his job was to "sell" the organization and its needs to those who could provide financial and other resources.

From his experience selling air quality monitoring systems, Walt appreciated the value of product knowledge. Without it, a sales representative could not respond to a client's questions and concerns, could not position the product vis-à-vis the competition's offerings, and could never gain sufficient confidence to convince a client to buy. In fact, Walt put so much emphasis upon product knowledge that he assembled a team to keep him abreast of new developments. But what was the "product" in the case of the greyhound rescue organization? What did Walt need to know in order to sell this product effectively?

Based on the principles and categories of product knowledge presented in Chapter 6, describe the "product" of Walt's greyhound adoption agency and outline in a page or two what Walt needs to know about it in order to represent the agency effectively. This might require some research regarding retired racing greyhounds and the agencies that try to help them.

Chapter 7

Becoming a Master Prospector

Learning Objectives

- Understand the importance of prospecting.

- Find out who your prospects are.

- Learn the characteristics of a qualified prospect.

- Become familiar with a variety of prospecting methods.

- Understand how to manage prospect information accurately and consistently.

- See the value of technology in the management of prospect information.

The Concept of Prospecting

A salesperson without prospects is as useful as a doctor without patients. Great salespeople ask smart questions, know how to close a deal, and have excellent follow-up techniques; the one trait they demonstrate more consistently than any other is constant prospecting, enhanced by creative approaches that build value and lasting relationships. They see opportunities everywhere and they know it's not just the numbers—but the numbers are what count.[1] After all, you have to see more to sell more.

If your closing ratio is lower than you'd like, the problem may be that you don't have enough qualified prospects and not that you are a poor closer. If you see enough people, sooner or later you will sell to someone. Confucius said, "Dig the well before you thirst." To succeed in selling, locate qualified prospects in advance—before you need them. Develop multiple sources from which names of prospects flow constantly.

Prospects are everywhere—all you have to do is look!

As competition in many fields grows, it is increasingly difficult to turn prospects into customers. For example, a survey of trade show exhibitors found that while 80 percent of leads receive follow up, less than 70 percent of exhibitors had any formalized plan in place to conduct this follow up.[2] In other words, salespeople aren't handling the leads they do get correctly, thus throwing away potential customers—and commission! Paul Peterson, Senior Director for FrontRange Solutions' CRM Business Unit, said, "That is a startling statistic, and I think a lot of executives don't even know they have this problem in their company. Leads that fall by the wayside are off the radar and it can be an invisible problem." The bottom line is that both the marketing and sales departments need access to a central storehouse of all prospects and customers—a "corporate memory"—where employees can track responses to marketing campaigns and look at the history of sales efforts. As the company interacts with that prospect or customer, every piece of communication and history needs to be in one spot. Call it a CRM system or a sales force automation (SFA) system, but the key is to get marketing, sales and, if possible, other departments to work from the same contact record.[3] Here are three other basic principles to help you hold onto leads in a highly competitive market:

1. **Qualify Leads**. Pay attention to lead qualification. Have a process in place and the resources and skills to qualify those leads. Generating leads is akin to building the Alaskan pipeline. Figure out how to build the pipeline and get the oil flowing.[4]

2. **Nurture Leads**. There will likely be some leads that aren't ready for sales. A nurturing process that includes phone calls, email, and postal mail is necessary to keep in touch with those prospects until they're ready to see a salesperson.

3. **Add Value**. The worst thing you can say is, "I'm just calling to find out if you've gotten that budget yet." Send case studies, newsletters, or e-magazines with editorial content. That way, you are not only checking in, you are contributing to their productivity.

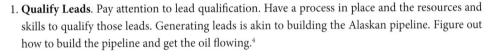

I would rather be a master prospector than a wizard of speech and have no one to tell my story to.

- Paul J. Meyer

Qualifying the Prospect

Establish a pattern for prospecting to avoid wasting a monumental amount of time calling on leads that are not prospects. When all you have is a name and address, you have only the possibility of developing a prospect. Exhibit 7.1 illustrates the process of moving a name from the status of lead to that of a qualified prospect. Truly qualified prospects are those who are a fit for you because they possess the necessary characteristics that make them logical buyers for your product or service. Apply a detailed screening process to each lead to increase your chances of successfully completing a sale.[5] The best prospect can be defined this way:

> **A Class "A" qualified prospect** is one to whom you have been referred by a person the prospect respects, one who has the ability to make a buying decision and to pay for the product or service, and one about whom you have all the personal information you need to make a good presentation.[6]

ΔExhibit 7.1

Action of the Salesperson in Developing Leads into Qualified Prospects · · · · · · ·

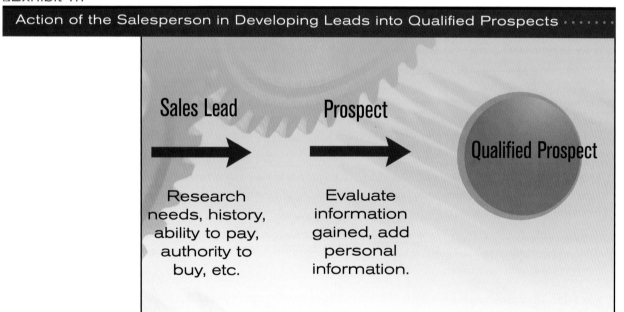

Sales Lead → Prospect → Qualified Prospect

Research needs, history, ability to pay, authority to buy, etc.

Evaluate information gained, add personal information.

There are few things as disheartening as going through the entire sales process only to discover that the person with whom you are speaking was never a real prospect to begin with. So, in order to avoid this, you must ensure that you have found a class "A," qualified prospect before you spend your valuable time trying to sell something to someone who cannot or would not ever buy from you.

The best way to determine if you have a qualified Class "A" prospect is to use the MADDEN Test. When you use The MADDEN Test to qualify prospects, it will help you ensure that they have MONEY, are APPROACHABLE, have DESIRE, have DECISION-MAKING ability, are ELIGIBLE, and have a NEED you can satisfy.

So, the next time you think you might have a Class "A" prospect, use the MADDEN Test, which is detailed on the following page.

MONEY

Separate the talkers from those who actually have the means to purchase. You will save yourself and your company many headaches by determining a prospect's ability to pay before spending your time and energy gaining a client who may quickly become more of a liability than an asset.

APPROACHABLE

Can you get an appointment? The president or CEO of a large company may grant an initial interview only to a senior level executive in your company. Do not hesitate to ask for such help when there is real possibility of gaining an important client. Individual prospects are often approachable only if you are willing to fit your time schedule into the unique time needs of their business or profession.

DESIRE

The prospect may be satisfied with a present supplier and have no desire to change. You can sell to such a prospect only if you create or discover a desire that will motivate the prospect to move from their present supplier to you. The prospect may desire to save money, enjoy a wider variety of services, receive more dependable service or quicker deliveries—all of which may have been the basis for selecting the present supplier in the first place.

DECISION MAKER

Be sure the person you visit is the decision maker. If you are unsure, then start with the head of the company. If you reach the CEO or COO, conducting business may be easier than you think. They earned the top spot by making tough calls and appreciate the tough call you've just made. A survey of business to business sales companies revealed that 63 percent of respondents found reaching the right decision maker was the key to improved sales.[7] Salespeople spend a great deal of time talking to people who are not in a position to make a buying decision. When you first contact a prospect, ask who else will be involved in making the decision and set up an appointment with all individuals at one time if possible.

ELIGIBLE

Determine whether the prospect is eligible to buy from you. Some prospects are already committed to a competitor and cannot buy. Others need a product with greater or smaller capacity than you can offer, or are in need of a service that is more or less extensive than yours.

NEED

Determine the need level for your product or service. To accomplish this you must ask questions and listen carefully to determine what the prospects' buying motives are in order to uncover their specific needs. Then decide if your company has the products that effectively satisfy those needs. Ask yourself—will the business your company gains be worth the amount of time you must invest to get it?

Methods Of Prospecting

While it may be true that *practice makes perfect*, this is only applicable to prospecting when you practice the correct methods. Incorrect practice on a musical instrument only produces an increased ability to make errors. This idea applies to prospecting—aimless, hit-or-miss prospecting, no matter how much of it is done, generally leads to failure. To streamline the job of prospecting and produce better results, master a number of different methods and use the ones that work best. The following is a list of eleven prospecting techniques discussed in this chapter.

1. Referrals—The use of referrals is one of the most powerful prospecting techniques available to sales professionals.

2. Center of Influence—A person who believes in what you are selling, influences others, and is willing to give you names and help to qualify them.

3. Group Prospecting—Bringing a number of people together at the same time and place and capturing their names and other information about them.

4. Planned Cold Calling—Calling on a lead without first making an appointment and knowing little or perhaps nothing about the person.

5. Direct Email and Direct Mail—Choosing or creating a mailing list of individuals, businesses, or professional people who appear to be at least partially qualified and sending them a communication that requests a reply.

6. Observation—Prospects are everywhere, so keep your eyes and ears open. Scan local newspapers, trade publications, and the financial pages of major news magazines and papers.

7. Business Associations and Civic Groups—Membership in various civic groups such as the Chamber of Commerce gives you opportunities to meet people who can become prospects for a product or service.

8. Networking Groups and Events—In networking groups, salespeople from different businesses share information about the sales climate and exchange prospect information. At networking events, a number of businesses may come together to target specific prospect demographic groups.

9. Directories—Directories help identify possible prospects and provide information to determine whether they actually have the potential to become customers.

10. Company-initiated Prospecting—A company may provide initial prospecting for salespeople. This frees them to have more face-to-face interviews with qualified prospects.

11. Websites—A company can market its services and find customers utilizing the power of the Internet. A subcategory of websites is called hypersites, where prospects can access your website and see only products and information useful to them.

Referrals

The use of referrals is one of the most powerful prospecting techniques in sales. Level 3 Communications, a major telecommunications company, suggests that as much as 50 percent of its sales come from referrals. A *referral* is a name given to you as a lead by a customer, a friend, or even a prospect who did not buy, but felt good about you and your product. The factor that makes this prospecting method valuable is its leverage. Until the proper time to use that leverage arrives, a referral is just a lead like any other.

Once you qualify a referred lead by securing all the information needed to show that this person fits the pattern of prospects upon which you call, you are then ready to use the valuable leverage that is yours by reason of the referral. Those who provide referrals should be willing either to make an initial contact for you or to allow you to use their names. Referrals work because people are naturally fearful or skeptical of strangers, especially those who try to persuade them to make some kind of decision. People accept you and your product more readily if someone they know and respect has sent you.

Gain More Referred Leads. Salespeople do not have more referrals because they don't ask, or perhaps because they don't know how to ask. There are two reasons why people do not immediately provide referrals. The first is that they find it difficult to think of names. Basically, they simply do not want to exert the mental effort to decide who might be interested. The second reason is they consider themselves to be "conscientious objectors"—they claim they just do not give referrals. Sales professionals estimate that 20 percent of clients won't give referrals no matter how you ask. Another 20 percent of clients will always give referrals. It's the other 60 percent where a plan of action is essential.[8]

Exhibit 7.2 illustrates a step-by-step approach to use when you ask for referrals. Practice and rehearse it with your favorite clients or those who have given you referrals in the past.[9] Customers think of themselves as professionals, and they like to buy from professionals. Asking for referrals should become an automatic part of every presentation you make.

ΔExhibit 7.2

A Seven-Step Approach for Gaining More Referred Leads

1. **Ask for referrals with respect**
   Open the dialogue with something like this, "I have an important question I want to ask you." This will capture your prospect's attention and indicate to them just how significant this is to you.

2. **Ask for their help**
   Soften them up by saying, "I'm trying to build my business and I would value and appreciate your help."

3. **Explain the course of action you propose**
   Tell them what will happen if they give you a referral, and also let them know that you will remain professional and report back to them.

4. **Gain their permission to explore**
   You might give them another softening statement: "I understand how you feel." Then you can go on to say, "I was wondering if we could agree on who you know who might also benefit from the products I have to offer. Are you comfortable with that?"

5. **Narrow their focus by describing your ideal prospects**
   Once you have been given names, make a first step toward qualifying them. Ask your client, "If you were in my place, who would you see first?" Ask why. Then find out which one to contact next.

6. **Report back to them**
   Whenever you receive referrals, be sure to report back to them the result of your interviews with leads.

7. **Thank them**
   Always offer thanks for giving you referrals regardless of whether they bought from you.

What to Ask. The principal thing you ask for in a referral is for your client to make it easy for you to contact a new prospect. The variable in each situation is how this contact should be made. What to ask for depends upon your client's need for control of the situation:

- Some customers want to handle the communication themselves.

- Others want minimal involvement. They prefer that you initiate the contact for them.

- Still others may have very specific instructions on what they want you to do or say with their referrals.

The best way to find out how much control your client wishes to have is to simply ask by using an alternate of choice type question: "Would you prefer that I call Mr. Evans, or would you want to personally call and talk to him on my behalf?" Here is a sample statement that can be used to make the client feel comfortable about giving you names:

"I'm not asking you to recommend me or my product. I am merely asking you to give me an introduction to some people you know. I will talk to them, as I have with you, in a professional manner and give them an opportunity to learn about me and my company."

The Million-Dollar Referral

Michael Twining, sales rep for a large distributor of agricultural products, has a clever way to secure more referrals. Whenever he gets a referral by an existing customer he quickly mails a handwritten thank-you note and includes a lottery ticket with the message—*Thanks a million for the referral. I hope you win a million!*

It costs very little and always creates a lot of good will and laughs on his next visit with that customer. Michael says, "It almost always gets me at least one more referral."[10]

When to Ask. Make asking for referrals a part of the selling cycle. A logical time to ask for referrals is right after the close. A customer who buys is sold on you and likely to feel good about giving you names. Sometimes, however, a customer wants to use the product or service before giving referrals. Often, salespeople go after referrals at the wrong time. They start asking for referrals before the ink on the contract is dry. You can't ask for referrals; you must earn them. The best referrals come from satisfaction, not a signature.

Centers of Influence

This method of prospecting is a specific application of the referral method. In both methods, you begin with a satisfied customer or with a person whose interest in you or your product has developed to the point of desiring to help you. The important distinction between the two is that a center of influence can give you far more prospects and is both willing and able to provide new names on a continuing basis.

The best sales tool you have is a person who believes in what you are selling, is influential with a number of people who are potential customers, and is willing to give you the names of these people and help you qualify them—that is the essence of a *center of influence*. When you have several centers of influence, you always have plenty of prospects. People respect the center of influence to the extent that an introduction from this source virtually assures you of an audience. Cultivate their friendship, sell yourself, and ask centers of influence to help. Getting that person on your team can open doors that would otherwise remain closed. Think how you would react if such a person called you and said:

I had lunch this past week with Dwight Wagner, a business associate of mine. I think he is person you would like to meet, and I told him about you. He will be calling you this week; I hope you will meet him.

Centers of influence are one of the most valuable assets you can have as a salesperson. Follow up every lead they provide, and then report your results to them and thank them. Find a way to show your gratitude by being of service to them. After all, a mutually beneficial relationship is rewarding to both parties.

Group Prospecting

Many companies use group prospecting with great success. The idea is to bring together a number of people, from eight to twenty or more. The group may meet in a home, a conference room in a hotel, or in an office. Your purpose is to inform prospects about your product or service.

Some direct sales companies use this method to find prospective distributors or salespeople. Among the well-known organizations that use this approach are Tupperware, Pampered Chef, Amway, Shaklee, and PartyLite Inc. Companies that use party-plan selling not only expect to make sales at the parties, but hope to find prospects who will agree to host parties at which new prospective customers and party holders are likely present.

A variation of this method is to attend or set up an exhibit at a networking meeting that targets a specific demographic. Mom Café, a networking organization that targets professional women, holds monthly events and invites service-based businesses and vendors to market to specific clientele.

Yet another variation is to look for groups of potential prospects and offer to be a guest speaker. Members of civic clubs may be ideal prospects for you, and they are always looking for speakers who have beneficial information for their members. If you establish your credibility, you may be able to close your speech with a brief presentation. Meet as many members of the audience as possible before and after the meeting, ask for business cards, and give them yours. If they were impressed enough to want you to call, you know you have a qualified prospect.

Planned Cold Calling

Some may say that prospecting is nearly a lost art. As a salesperson, you will stand above the crowd if you are not afraid to do a little cold calling.[11] Cold calling can be an enjoyable part of your day if you accept the reality of the situation. As Dr. James Oldroyd, an expert on the measurement of cold calling says, "Most growth in the sales industry is in this area. Companies are adding new inside sales departments at a rate of 7.5 percent annual growth. By the end of 2012 thousands of companies are expected to add inside sales departments."[12] It's clear that cold calling serves as an excellent supplement to other prospecting efforts if it is carefully planned. Here are some guidelines for cold calling:

Knock, knock... Don't be afraid of cold calling.

Supplement Your Existing List. Because cold calling is designed to supplement your current prospect list, be careful that cold calls never take so much of your time that you neglect calling on qualified prospects and existing clients. Set aside a specific amount of time each week for cold calling, but never at the expense of more profitable activity.

Preplan Cold Calls. Develop several effective door openers and experiment until you find which ones work best for you. Give the prospect something related to your product or service, such as a newsletter, brochure, calendar, or share an idea that may save the prospect time or money. Your door opener should be something that causes the prospect to remember you when you later call for an appointment to make your presentation.

Stay Enthusiastic. Set a goal to turn every cold call into a warm call. When you make cold calls, the person you want to see is almost certainly not in or too busy to receive you. If you remain enthusiastic in spite of such responses, you make a positive impression on the receptionist. You may even get enough information to qualify prospects without meeting them. When you call again, you will be remembered; and receptionists exert a great deal of influence on who sees the boss. Impress them with your professionalism and you will find those doors to the buyers open more easily.

Golden Opportunities

Most salespeople would agree that cold calling is the toughest part of selling. But, at the same time, the rewards can be great. "When I started making cold calls I decided to call them warm calls because most prospects want to be treated with friendliness and spoken to in a positive manner," says Irby Stewart with Positive Communications in Thunder Bay, Ontario. Because he took this positive approach, Irby became the top salesperson across Canada selling Brian Tracy's two-day video seminars. Recently he developed another point of view toward cold calls. It struck him that he should be calling them *opportunity calls*. That's what they really are. Viewing cold calls as golden opportunities gives him even greater incentive for selling to clients and prospects. Now go out and create some golden opportunities for yourself![13]

Email and Direct Mail

The success of direct mail prospecting depends upon the management of mailing lists. Some lists are better than others, and the best investment of your time and budget demands careful planning and analysis. The product or service you sell has a great deal to do with what kind of list you use.[14] The goal is a list of people or businesses that are already at least partially qualified prospects. Exhibit 7.3 has some suggestions for sources of email and direct mail lists.

Suggested Sources for Building Direct-Mail Lists

Membership rosters

- Professional societies and trade associations (medical, accountancy, manufacturers, air conditioning, electricians)
- College Alumni lists
- Civic clubs (Kiwanis, Lions, Civitan, Optimist)
- Religious Groups
- Women's organizations (Altrusa, AAUW, Junior League)
- Special-interest groups (Audubon Society, garden clubs, environmental protection groups)
- Community business groups (Chamber of Commerce, Jaycees, Business and Professional Women)

Directories and Databases

- Professional online directories or purchased database lists

People you have done business with in the past

- E-newsletter subscription field from your own website
- Examples include home builders, bankers, accountants, and auto service and repair companies

People you have networked with in person and through Social Media

- You can gain targeted prospects through public LinkedIn, Facebook, and Twitter accounts.

Develop a coding system to show which types of lists produce the highest percentage of responses. Code the names of people who actually respond. Even if you do not sell to them immediately, they have some interest in your product or service and might become active prospects at a later date. Much of today's direct marketing happens through the use of social media tools like Facebook fan pages and Twitter. Dell, for example, uses a Twitter feed to communicate special sales to followers, who in turn communicate the same deals to their followers. This approach alone generated Dell a 2 million dollar profit last year.[15] It's important to stay on top of ever-changing trends, and to realize that the best social media sales happen if you pay careful attention to the ease of consumer movement between media platforms, including email.

Power of Observation

No matter what methods of prospecting you elect to use, your own powers of observation provide many of your best prospects. Social media tools make observation more powerful and accessible than ever. By following Facebook pages and Twitter users, you'll be able to keep connected to your current clients at the same time that you can track prospects who "follow" them. Keep an eye on feeds for event notifications, announcements, birthday notices and even changes in relationship status. Send a congratulatory note to a client on a new marriage or baby; send a personal message to a prospect who is launching a new store. If you are connected in LinkedIn,

join a relevant group and follow conversations on hot topics. Explore the public profiles of connected groups and individuals—you never know how or when a valuable connection could present itself.

Joining Civic Groups

Membership in civic groups can give you opportunities to meet people who are prospects for your product or service. Their meetings provide you with regular times to meet more people and build relationships. Exhibit 7.4 lists tips for using membership in civic clubs as prospecting opportunities.

ΔExhibit 7.4

Tips for Using Membership in Civic Clubs for Prospecting

- Carefully select the groups you join.
- Assume leadership responsibilities to work for positive visibility.
- Set contact goals for each organization meeting.
- Follow up with contacts.
- Maintain an information file on the contacts made in each organization.
- Use "remeet" goals to help you develop closer relationships with people.
- Reach out to new members.

In selecting groups to join, consider the kinds of prospects you need to meet. It is also beneficial to choose organizations to which decision makers belong. Set goals to meet a certain number of new people at each meeting and to reconnect, or establish stronger relationships, with a certain number of others. Keep an updated file of the organization's members as you meet and learn about them. Avoid actively selling at the meetings, but you may ask someone to tell you the best time to call to set up an appointment. Building relationships through these contacts lays the groundwork for active selling in the future.

Networking

Networking refers to the active cooperation between business people to share information about the business climate, specific happenings in the business community, and prospects. It involves the 3 C's: *connecting, communicating, and cooperating*. It's believed that 70 to 80 percent of all employment is found through networking.[16]

Sharing information and names of prospects just makes sense. For instance, if you are a realtor involved in a pending real estate development, it could be to your advantage to alert a banker who may prove helpful to your client in arranging financing. You benefit, your client benefits, and so does the banker. When you regularly serve clients with your product or services, you have opportunities to learn about additional needs you cannot fill. Sharing your customers' names and information with other salespeople who can help is a tangible service to your customers.

Using Directories

Don't overlook directories as a source of prospects. Though once a commonly accessible directory, the phonebook is becoming replaced by online directory resources like the ones displayed in Exhibit 7.5. Directories cannot replace other means of prospecting, but they are excellent supplements. Some directories are useful in identifying possible prospects; others are helpful in learning more about prospects to determine whether they have the potential to become customers.

Use Directories to Identify Prospects

1. **Moodys.com** and **standardandpoors.com** both offer analytics, data gathering and social media directories for a fee.

2. **ThomasNet.com** provides information about who makes what and where almost anything may be purchased. Information is also provided about the corporate structure of the manufacturer and about its executives.

3. **Citydirectory.com** supplies detailed information on individuals living in specific communities throughout the United States and Canada. Here, you can subscribe to a free industry specific trial before signing up for the product.

4. **Biztradeshows.com** and other online directories list names, dates and location of trade shows for many industries internationally.

5. **Salesgenie.com** (previously directoriesUSA.com) also offers a free trial of industry specific list creation tools.

Company-Initiated Prospecting

Company-initiated prospecting frees up time for salespeople to concentrate on the top priority of all sales activity—face-to-face interviews with qualified prospects. This is where results are generated. Everything else is merely preparation for the sales arena.

Make the Most of Telemarketing. Telemarketing is an industry that has experienced incredible growth.[17] Some firms rely almost completely on telemarketing for leads; others use it as a supplement to other lead generation methods. However, one issue with telemarketing is its high cost. For smaller companies, the equipment, software, implementation, and training necessary to run a telemarketing center is simply too high. The good news is that more affordable solutions are becoming available. TeleMarketingKey, a provider of telemarketing solutions, develops solutions for all sizes of call centers, catering primarily to small and medium-sized organizations that require technology that both enables their agents to perform their duties and allows management to monitor and supervise the organization.[18] Additionally, more companies are outsourcing their telemarketing functions. When you think of outsourcing, you probably think overseas. There is a great deal of that, especially in India, Canada, Mexico and the Philippines. But, there is also a growing number of distributors and part-time agents domestically, even stay-at-home parents making calls during their free time. No matter the size or scope of operation, it is important that callers have the tools necessary to be productive, especially in remote locations, and that management can monitor their efforts and progress.

Personalization Through Internet Marketing. Companies both large and small have embraced the power of selling through personalization on the Internet. Facebook, for example, mines users' information and updates to generate user-specific ads. Other companies embrace the hypersite model, where several similarly targeted companies share user interface and data between them and produce content targeted to a specific consumer. Other companies, such as the Body Shop, utilize an e-rewards newsletter program. Even the products through which we access the Internet are customizable. Consider, for instance, the introduction of smartphones, where users can download a multitude of apps to suit specific needs.

Make the Most of Current Customers. A study of 183 company executives conducted by the Patrick Marketing Group (PMG) of Calabasas, California, found that 70 percent of them felt that expanding relationships with existing customers is the biggest factor challenging the success of their sales teams.

These numbers suggest the importance of existing customers as sources of new revenue, says Craig Shields, senior marketing consultant at PMG. Firms realize that it is easier and less expensive to penetrate existing accounts and flush out their potential than to only prospect for new clients. It is estimated that *it costs 5 to 10 times more to go out and get a new customer* than to keep your existing customer base. Some companies take the initiative in furnishing salespeople with the names of past customers who are no longer active.[19]

Websites: Harness the Power of the Internet

All companies and salespeople alike should now run a well-designed, user-friendly website, especially as consumers continue to shift from the telephone to online tools as their primary means of contact. Don't forget a website acts as the company's representative, so you want it to reflect your professionalism in terms of design and content quality. Exhibit 7.6 outlines the reasons you need a website working for you.[20]

ΔExhibit 7.6

8 Big Reasons A Well-Designed Website Is Essential for Any Professional · · · · ·

1. **Sales sites offer 24/7 support**—Even when your business is closed, your website stays open, offering product and service information to your potential clients.

2. **Websites cater to introverts and extroverts alike**—Websites help people make decisions by arming them with knowledge and information. Introverts are quiet by design; they aren't likely to pick up the phone or walk in to talk with you until they have done as much online fact-finding as possible. For these people, the Internet is a very valuable tool, and your virtual sales assistant/website will be your most valuable 'employee.' And don't forget the extroverts; they too will appreciate the information you share on your site.

3. **Your website can effectively prospect for new clients**—A search engine optimized site can attract customers who may not have otherwise phoned or come to your place of business.

4. **Your website can be professional and knowledgeable**—Like a great salesperson, your website can be appealing, charismatic, equipped with in-depth product knowledge and up to date information, and can make a great pitch. You have complete control over the information your sales assistant presents, and you can change and rework that information until you get it just right.

5. **Your site can convince customers to return**—Like a great sales assistant, your website can convince people to come back. Keep your site content dynamic and fresh, giving visitors a reason to return and see what's new.

6. **Your sales assistant should get to know people on a personal level**—Getting to know people isn't easy to do in the virtual world, but it's certainly not impossible. A carefully designed site can gather visitor information. Your site might offer newsletter subscription, product sales, friend referrals or marketing surveys. A visitor who interacts with your site can give you a name and contact details. In other words, a visitor who interacts with your site becomes a lead.

7. **Your sales assistant should be able to close a deal or get you one step closer to closing**—Your site design should mimic your real life strategy when it comes to closing a sale. If you are selling products, an online shopping cart might be in order. If you are selling services, you might need an online signup or contact form.

8. **Follow up**—The actual sale should not be the end of the sales process. Satisfied customers can lead to repeat business and referrals. Your sales assistant should ask your customers what they thought of their experience. In the online world, customer satisfaction surveys or short post-sales polls (built into your site) can give great feedback and can help you to improve your sales strategy.

Components Every Sales Website Should Have. An endless array of sales websites and blogs exists on the Internet today, so yours or your company's site really needs to stand out from the crowd. The most professional looking sites remain relatively clean and simply designed; in other words, they know who they are marketing to and design the site for that audience. The best sites are also user friendly, with easily navigable pages and links to key content. According to some experts, the sites with the most value, however, are often linked to blogs with more user interaction and high-quality content that is *not* a recycled product pitch; continuous updates and marketing efforts here are key.[21]

Another key component for any sales website is an easily accessible and time-conscious payment portal. Customers must be able to purchase your product at the most convenient time and the most convenient place for them with the least work possible.[22] There are a number of invoicing and payment systems on the market today; Paypal is the most well-known system.

Use Affiliate Program Marketing. You may want to offer ad space on your website, or even place ads on other affiliated sites. Google Adsense is the most well known affiliate marketing program and can even earn your website some revenue. Google Adsense targets and customizes ads based on your website's content. You can choose how you would like your site to be paid for these ads, whether through user visits, earnings by user location, browser type, and referring source or by Adsense impressions, clicks and revenue.[23] Alternately, if you are the advertiser, you can bid on premium ad space available on other websites. Of course, you should research other affiliate marketing programs, decide if you want to broker your own ads, or opt for a no ad website based on your ideal prospect's profile.

Take advantage of the Internet to quickly find more qualified leads.

Managing Prospect Information

Diligent prospecting is useless if you do not have a system for managing and using the information you find. Many contact management systems on the market today will help you organize your contacts and priorities, but be aware of how to classify and prioritize contacts so you can make the most of your prospecting time.

Initial Recording of Leads

The initial information you need about prospects depends a great deal upon the product or service you sell, but it will, in all likelihood, include these items:

1. Prospect's full name and nickname (if you know it)

2. Email address and regular address

3. Phone number (including cell phone if possible)

4. Name of company he or she works for

5. Position in company

6. Family information (spouse, number of children, etc)

7. Personal information (club memberships, college attended, hobbies)

8. Approximate income (if your product or service is to be sold to the individual rather than to the company)

9. Source of prospect (Did you get his or her name from a referral or otherwise?)

Classification of Prospects

When you first find the name of an individual or company prospect, assign a classification to the name. One classification system uses the letters A, B, and C.

- **Class A** prospects are those about whom you have adequate information to make a presentation. You know they have the money to buy and the authority to make a decision. Ideally, you also have a referral from someone they respect.

- **Class B** prospects are those about whom you have inadequate information to make the best possible presentation. You may not know enough to be sure they need your product or service. You may not know whether they have the authority to make a decision or whether they can afford to buy. You may not have a referral to help open the door. When one or more of these items is missing, the proper action is research rather than approach.

- **Class C** prospects are people whose names you have found in some way, but about whom you have little or no information other than a name. They are leads, not prospects.

Prospecting activity involves not only finding new leads but also qualifying existing leads by adding information that allows you to move them up to Class A status.

Scheduling Contacts

When you have classified a prospect as Class A, determine when you will initiate contact, either by telephone, email, personal visit, or direct mail, according to the method of approach you choose. Set up your electronic calendar or contact management system to send reminders, or download a tickler app to ensure you take the proper action on the date assigned. The same tickler file will help you schedule later contacts if your first attempt to schedule an interview is not successful. Once a prospect's name enters your file, it stays there permanently until you close a sale or determine that the person is not a prospect for your product or service. If you make a presentation and do not close, choose a time for a new attempt and schedule an appropriate time for contacting the prospect again.

When you discover that a person is not a viable prospect for you and will probably not become one in the foreseeable future, then that person can still be an important contact. The impression you have given by your professionalism may cause that person to recommend you to someone who will prove to be an excellent prospect.

Automating Prospect Information

Professionals need to make sure their prospect files are organized from the moment of input, especially as the client base grows and accessing contact information needs to be as efficient as possible. This is why the most widely used software in selling is contact management programs. These programs were developed to help you collect, organize, classify, and keep track of prospect information. *Developing Partnerships Using Technology* describes some of the common features found in contact management programs.

Developing Partnerships Using Technology

It's time to throw out your Rolodex and invest in a Contact Management Program.

Sales is one of the most mobile professions. Whether you are a realtor or an educational software rep, chances are your iPad, smartphone, or laptop travel with you and are always just a reach away. Most companies now use contact management programs to help you track your prospects, leads, and clients. As technology gets smarter, so do these programs. All good contact management programs have key features like pre-defined fields where you can enter basic information like name, company, phone, website, email, etc. Some of the newer, more advanced systems also have fields for social media tracking through programs like Facebook and Twitter.

Other features include advanced search options, journals and histories tracking, and email and Internet integration. Most programs also have direct marketing campaign capability, finance and task tracking, and two-way calendar synching. Each individual program also comes with its own unique assets, like cloud-based solutions, analytics and forecasting, instant messaging and smart sales applications.

The kind of program you or your company purchases will depend largely on the size of the company, how easy you find the software to use, budget, and personal preference.

Check out these websites for additional information:

www.smartcontactmanager.com
www.act.com
www.goldmine.com
www.maximizer.com
www.salesforce.com

Using all the web tools available to you—whether through social media, e-newsletter campaigns, researching company websites or purchasing data sets from data mining companies—there is simply no excuse for making a truly "cold" call anymore. *Data mining* is the process of electronically searching through stacks of records to find useful information so that you can go into a call knowing about the prospect before ever meeting him. Being as thorough as possible in your approach to prospecting goes a long way in securing new accounts and allows you to achieve the treasured personalized approach to selling. Put yourself in your clients' shoes and you can offer your clients a real solution. This accomplishes more than merely establishing a solid rapport with prospects; it builds a relationship that will inevitably yield more success in the future.[24]

If you fail to plan, you plan to fail.

SUMMARY

- Prospecting is the skill that keeps salespeople in business. Once you have leads, qualify them to determine whether they are true prospects that have a need for your product and are in a position to make a buying decision.

- Make sure prospects pass the MADDEN test.

- Two of the most effective prospecting methods are referrals and centers of influence. When someone they respect makes the introduction, you have a built-in sales assistant— the influence of the person who provided the lead and the initial contact.

- Group prospecting is securing names of possible prospects at trade shows, through speaking engagements, or in any situation where you have the opportunity to meet a number of people. Cold calling also provides a supplemental source of new prospects.

- Networking is a valuable source of new prospects for salespeople who are willing to share information about their customers or clients. It's all about connecting, communicating and cooperating.

- Efficient management of information means that needed data is always at your fingertips. Utilize a contact management system to keep track of prospects as you record initial information, upgrade prospects, and schedule the time you want to contact each one.

REVIEW QUESTIONS

1. How does your skill in prospecting exert a direct effect on your ability to close a sale?

2. What characteristics make a qualified prospect?

3. What is a referral? How do you get referrals?

4. What is the advantage of having referrals from your clients?

5. What is a center of influence?

6. Name several directories that might be helpful sources of prospects. Where would you look for these directories?

7. What is observation prospecting? Name several places a salesperson might find prospects through observation.

8. How does networking work for salespeople? Why were women active in organizing formal networking groups? Is this an important activity for men as well as women?

9. What methods do companies use to provide leads for salespeople? Why would the company be interested in providing leads instead of having individual salespeople do all the prospecting?

10. What kind of records are needed for keeping track of prospects?

11. How long should a prospect's name remain in your prospecting system?

ROLE-PLAY EXERCISES

The following role-play exercises help build teams, improve communication, and emphasize the real-world side of selling. They are meant to be challenging, to help you learn how to deal with problems that have no single right answer, and to use a variety of skills beyond those employed in a typical review question. Read and complete each activity. Then in the next class, discuss and compare answers with other classmates.

Role Play 7.1 – Finding the Right CMP

For this assignment, you will work individually. Imagine that your company's vice president for sales and marketing has concluded that the company is dropping too many good sales leads because there is no good way to track contacts or continuing developments. At a major sales meeting, the vice president asks the entire sales force to recommend a good contact management program (CMP) that will allow anyone in the company to access contact information. The vice president emphasizes that the program should be robust, well tested, and relatively inexpensive. The salesperson who compiles the most complete and persuasive recommendation and whose choice is actually adopted by the company will receive a nice bonus and a chance for promotion. You want the bonus and the promotion.

After conducting research online, select three acceptable CMPs and recommend one as superior. Which criteria do you use in making your final recommendation? How do you respond to the recommendations of others in your class?

Role Play 7.2 – Qualifying the Prospect

For this exercise, the class should be divided into teams of 4 persons each.

One of the most important, yet most difficult, tasks of any salesperson is to qualify the prospect. Chapter 7 recommends the MADDEN approach to qualifying prospects. This approach identifies the information that salespersons need in order to consider a prospect or lead "qualified."

Nevertheless, asking for the necessary information (or finding it by other means) is often difficult. For example, it would be tactless and counterproductive to ask, "Do you have the money or authorized budget to pay for this product?" Or again, imagine the response to the direct question, "Do you have the required authority to purchase this product?"

The MADDEN approach specifies *what* you need to know. The task for your team in this exercise is to think of *how* to obtain this information, to devise clever, inoffensive ways of soliciting needed information from prospects. In the first instance, confine your methods to what you might say or ask in a personal interview. If you have time, develop other research methods that might help you obtain the needed information.

Jot down your recommendations and the reasons for them, and be prepared to present and discuss them in class or online.

CASE STUDIES

The following case studies present you with selling scenarios that require you to apply the critical skills discussed in the chapter and give you training through simulation, role-playing, and practical learning situations. They are meant to be both engaging and challenging, and like the role-play exercises, don't have one right answer.

Case 7.1 – The Trade Show

Judy had just accepted a position as sales representative with NewLine Papers, a manufacturer of high-quality specialty papers for businesses that use direct mail to promote their products and services. Typically, such businesses must use papers that are attractive to look at and hold, that absorb inks quickly because of high-speed printing, and that can stand up to the rigors of automatic folding equipment. In order for Judy to learn more about the business and to acquire good leads, her sales manager has sent her to the U.S. Postal Forum (USPF) annual meeting in Las Vegas.

Judy decided that for this trip to pay off in terms of generating solid leads she needed to engage in careful planning. A quick check of USPF's website allowed her to compile a short list of attendees who might be interested in NewLine's latest product. About a week before the trade show, she phoned a couple of them to arrange an appointment. They willingly agreed; so she flew to Las Vegas in the hope that she could snag an order, not just a couple of good leads. This would surely impress her manager!

After checking in at the convention hotel, Judy called Ned Harris, her first appointment for the next morning. Ned wasn't in, but she left a message indicating that she could meet him just off the lobby at 10:00 a.m. Her second appointment, Anita Scoby, answered on the second ring. She and Judy agreed to meet tomorrow afternoon at 2:30 following a major speech by the head of the U.S. Environmental Protection Agency. So everything was all set.

Ned arrived for their meeting the next morning a couple of minutes late, explaining that he was not a morning person and needed a second cup of coffee. They moved to the hotel's coffee bar and settled at a small table. Judy brightened when Ned reported that his company had actually done business with NewLine some years before. Immediately, Judy pulled out a couple of samples from her briefcase and launched into her presentation of the outstanding features of the new product. Ned listened attentively, sipping his coffee and sitting with arms folded. When Judy finished her spiel, she asked if he had any questions. He didn't. She then asked whether Ned's company would be interested in placing a trial order. He replied, rather curtly, that he didn't know, that he would have to get back to her on that, and that he was late for another meeting. With that, he picked up his newspaper and left, leaving Judy reflecting on what had happened.

Her meeting that afternoon with Anita Scoby was even more brief. Before Judy could begin to describe the samples that she had placed before Anita, Anita cut her off, explaining that she had no authority to engage in any such discussion, that while she was interested in Judy's product, her own role was in sales for her company, and that she was attending the trade show merely to network with other clients. She wished Judy luck and promised to pass along Judy's information to more appropriate people at her firm.

As Judy flew home the next morning, she wondered what she had done wrong. She had researched attendees of the trade show and had obtained appointments, but she was returning home with no orders and, worse, no real leads.

Where do you think Judy went wrong? What would she need to do in order to become a "master prospector?"

If you were sent to the trade show by your manager, what would you have done? What would have been your objectives? Which tactics would you have employed to fulfill those objectives?

Case 7.2 – The Over-Eager Realtor

Sherry Huffman had just moved with her husband to San Diego from upstate New York where she had lived for her entire life. At age 30 and having worked in real estate for 7 years, Sherry had no intention of giving up her career. She therefore joined a real estate company in San Diego and began searching for prospects. She realized that being a realtor in San Diego was going to be more challenging than in small-town New York where she was already known by nearly everyone in the area. In her new, larger city, she would have to cultivate a new sphere of influence in order to build up a web of former, satisfied clients who could subsequently help generate new business. In other words, Sherry realized, she would have to network aggressively (among other tactics) in order to succeed.

There was only one problem: networking, in the sense of meeting and cultivating new acquaintances, was new to Sherry. In New York, she was already networked; she didn't have to work at it or meet new people. Now, however, she would have to get to know new people to the point where they could begin to trust her.

Sherry's first foray into networking was to join the local Chamber of Commerce. What better source of new prospects, she thought, than successful, established businesspersons from a variety of fields? In typical fashion, she approached the task enthusiastically.

At the first meeting of the Chamber that Sherry attended, she introduced herself to the president and proceeded to work the room. As small groups of people carried on sometimes animated conversation during the cocktail hour, Sherry went from one group to another, introducing herself, distributing her business cards to all, and saying something like, "Hi! I'm Sherry Huffman. I just joined Golden Bear Real Estate. Here's my card. If any of you are in the market to buy or sell real estate, please give me a call." Generally, people looked at her a little quizzically, politely took her card, and returned to their conversation. Sherry began to get the feeling that something was wrong. This wasn't going to be easy.

After dinner, the Chamber president approached Sherry. "I couldn't help noticing how you managed to introduce yourself to everyone before dinner. Very impressive! But I think it would be wise for you to slow down a little. This isn't a real estate open house, you know."

The president's words stung. On the way home, Sherry's eyes welled up and she pounded the steering wheel in frustration. What had she done wrong? How could she rectify the situation? What changes would you recommend to Sherry to turn her into a master prospector through networking?

Qualities of High Sales Performers...

1. **Exchange information** rather than present products. They tend to ask a variety of questions that force the customer to analyze, evaluate, speculate, or express feelings.

2. **Know when to close.** They advocate their products only after they have identified or created an important need and involved the customer in developing the solution.

3. **Sell to people, not organizations**, and demonstrate a strong commitment to meeting customer needs.

4. **Are perceived by prospects as genuine advocates** of prospects' needs, even while actively promoting the company and its products or services.

5. **Provide value added** to the customer. They act as a resource able to directly provide expertise to the customer.

6. **Regularly establish trust** within their own organizations by sharing information, encouraging participation in decisions, and recognizing the contributions of the internal staff to their success.

7. **Engage in behavior** such as maintaining eye contact, showing enthusiasm, asking questions about customers' needs, restating accurately and being prepared with effective responses to buyers' objections.

Chapter 8

Preapproach and Telephone Techniques

Learning Objectives

- Recognize the importance of the preapproach in the sales cycle.

- Learn the objectives of the preapproach and the planning needed to make it effective.

- Study how to prepare for an effective preapproach.

- Understand how the preapproach fits into the sales cycle as an extension of prospecting, including the power of social media in the preapproach phase.

- Discover effective methods for making telephone calls that are successful in leading to presentations.

- Understand the six-step telephone track and how to use it to make appointments.

Preapproach and the Sales Cycle

See enough people. See the right people. See them at the right time.[1] That sounds logical enough! The pivotal part of this advice however, is the "right people." How can you be sure that you are investing your time in calling on qualified prospects? The answer lies in your diligence in collecting information about the leads you record in your prospecting system.

When someone gives you a referral, ask questions to learn what you need to know about that prospect. Research the prospect's business or industry and the company itself. Discover personal information that will help you know what kind of personality to expect. The various activities that provide this necessary personal and business information are called *presale planning* or the *preapproach*. The preapproach is the planning and preparation done prior to actual contact with the prospect.

In gathering such information, you learn who to call, why, when, and where. Seemingly insignificant details might be the key to the approach that spells the difference between a sale and a no-sale. Leave nothing to chance. For example, details such as the correct pronunciation of the prospect's name can be secured in advance. Roger Capps, an industrial salesperson, thought he was well prepared to call on an important new prospect, only to find himself sent on his way after less than a minute. The prospect, Mr. Hajovsky, had no time for Capps, who made the fatal error of mispronouncing Hajovsky's name. Capps could have avoided the lost opportunity by taking a few seconds to ask the receptionist for the correct pronunciation.

The sales cycle is a continuous process with no clear break between one phase and the next. In practice, you cannot separate the prospecting, preapproach, approach, and need discovery elements into different segments; rather, they blend together and become one. They are discussed separately for convenience, but the exact point where one phase ends and the next begins will likely never be the same. Exhibit 8.1 illustrates the absence of clear dividing lines between these steps in the relationship selling process.

ΔExhibit 8.1

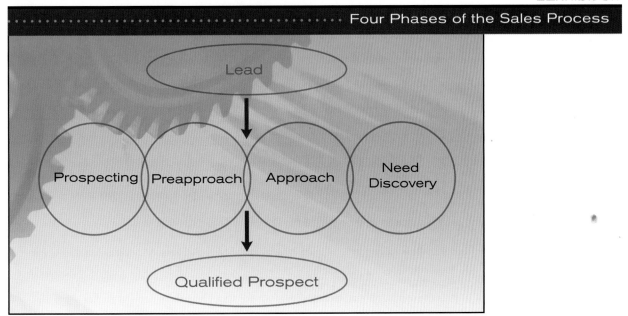

Four Phases of the Sales Process

The numerous types of selling vary so widely that few broad generalizations can be made about the amount of preapproach information to gather. Depending on the type of selling in which you engage and the product or services being sold, the preapproach differs considerably. At times, qualifying prospects can only be accomplished during the approach and need discovery process by asking questions, observing, listening, and interpreting verbal and nonverbal signals.

Preparation and Preapproach

Before engaging in the actual presentation process, sales professionals must analyze all the information they have available to them about a prospect to understand as much about them as possible. During the preapproach phase, sales professionals try to understand the prospect's current needs, current use of brands, and feelings about available brands.

In addition, they must identify decision makers, review account histories, assess product needs, plan a sales presentation to address the identified concerns of the prospect, and set call objectives. Salespeople also develop a preliminary strategy for the sales process during this phase, keeping in mind that the strategy may have to be refined as they learn more about each prospect.[2]

The type and quality of information uncovered during the preapproach is vital. Just as students dislike doing homework after school, many adults have a similar aversion to the groundwork and prefer to skip ahead to the "real work." However, the preliminary steps are a must. Successful sales professionals rarely even make a cold call without some sort of preparation.[3] When they are ready for a formal sales call, professional salespeople have studied and analyzed the prospect's personality, company, operations, needs, and financial position.

One of the most thorough ways to prepare is to develop a checklist of questions to answer before you make a sales call. Exhibit 8.2 presents a helpful checklist designed to help gather the essential sales information you need before you are face-to-face with a prospect.

ΔExhibit 8.2

Checklist of Sales Essentials for Collecting Preapproach Information · · · · · · · · · ·

✓ What business is the company in? What are its products and markets? Who are its primary customers?

✓ How big is the company? Where does it rank within its industry? Can this company give me enough business to make this call worthwhile?

✓ Who is the ultimate decision maker in buying my product?

✓ Who else influences the buying decision?

✓ How often does this company buy my type of product or service?

✓ How well is the company satisfied with its present supplier of similar products?

✓ What plans does the company have that could affect its future need for my product?

✓ What are the background and personal interests of each person concerned in the buying decision?

✓ Is the company's staff technically informed? Can I help them develop greater expertise?

✓ Do we (or can we) use their products or services in our company?

✓ Do any of our top executives know any of their executives personally?

Preparing for sales calls is time well spent; and most buyers are not receptive to those who skip this step. "If buyers perceive you as unprepared, you won't get that chance to call on them again," said Adrian Miller, owner of Port Washington-based Adrian Miller Sales Training. According to a Sales Industry Trends Report, 61 percent of executives expect salespeople to spend about 30 minutes preparing, and nearly 63 percent expect them to spend less than 20 minutes in preparation. The study included a survey of 141 sales managers and vice presidents at companies with sales of between $5 million and $50 million around the United States.[4]

According to their findings, the most important information a salesperson can gather is competitive insight, understanding who influences the buyer and industry trends. Other important factors include new and upcoming product and service launches, corporate directives, and share of the market. Leaders say the best way to get salespeople to invest in preparation time is through example, and by discussing strategies. It pays to do your homework.

Prepare for the Presentation

Do your research to find out about the prospect and develop a purpose for the call, linked to a potential client benefit.[5] Set a goal for each contact with a prospect, know what you want to accomplish, and how you plan to do it. There is much more to preparation than simply gathering and reviewing information. Rehearsal eliminates the stammering, nervous speech habits, and repetition that can result from lack of preparation.

Allow time in your daily schedule to prepare the sales approach and presentation you will use in each call. Decide how you can make the best possible use of sales literature and other tools provided by your company in this specific call. Review company websites and the personal profiles of your contacts on LinkedIn or other social media sites. Plan how to incorporate visual aids into your approach and presentation for maximum effectiveness.

When preparing for a presentation, making a video of your sales talk allows you to see how you really look. "That's the best way to coach people," says Ken Taylor president of Decker Communication Inc. Digital webcams on computers and smartphones make self-video easier than ever. Video also allows you to hear your use of "non-words" such as *um, uh,* and *you know.* Here are some rehearsal tips:[6]

- Practice your presentation with specific customers in mind.
- Video presentations to show sales reps their strengths and weaknesses.
- Make large, exaggerated motions until you feel comfortable making more natural-looking gestures.

Visualize Successful Selling

Salespeople can learn a great deal from the training habits of world-class athletes. Many track stars use visualization techniques to help them focus on a specific event. An integral part of their training consists of what are called "mental toughening sessions." They run the race over and over in their minds. Over a ten-year period, Edwin Moses won 122 consecutive races in the 400-meter hurdles. His power of visualization became so acute that when he mentally visualized hitting a hurdle, he actually felt the pain in his leg.

To further illustrate how powerful visualization can be, consider this amazing example. After the Vietnam War, a reporter interviewed an Air Force captain who had been a prisoner of war for over seven years. The former POW had just played a superb game in a golf tournament. When the reporter mentioned his surprise at the captain's skill after so long an absence, the captain said, "I've played this course perfectly for the last seven years." The reporter replied, "I thought you hadn't played golf in the last eight years." The captain said, "Well, actually I haven't physically played the game in the last eight years. However, for the last seven years in my cell as a POW I have been playing this course mentally."[7]

You can practice this same type of mental exercise. Positively affirm the feeling you want to create and visualize the outcomes you want to obtain. Think about what you will say and anticipate the prospect's responses. Create a mental image of the desired results, and then live it over and over in your mind. Practice out loud; your mind believes the sound of your own voice. *Remember that your mind cannot separate a real experience from an imagined one.*

"WELL, I'D SAY THAT SALE WENT PRETTY WELL!"

Used with permission from
The Boxcar Millionaire

Sources of Preapproach Information

When you know what information you need, you can identify a number of valuable sources for obtaining it. The information you gather will help you get in to make a presentation as well as guide you in preparing a strategy for the interview itself. For example, you can ask colleagues on your company's sales team for information they have on particular prospects. Current customers are also excellent sources of information, and they may be happy to share what they know. The quickest way to gain information these days is to consult online search engines, industry websites, and social media profiles. There is nothing wrong with calling on prospects without an appointment. At the very least, this cold call gives you the opportunity to observe their facilities and you learn something that validates them as, at least, partially qualified prospects. You cannot predict the most beneficial sources of information, so keep your eyes and ears open so you won't miss a great opportunity![8]

Here's a useful tip— read magazines and newsletters that are related to your customer's industry. You likely read publications that are pertinent in your field, so your clients probably also read publications relevant to their fields. You can also subscribe to email newsletters and updates from companies and organizations in your client's industry. This is a great way to uncover ideas to serve their needs better. However, just researching and reading are not enough. You must know what to look for.[9]

Here are six items to consider that may give you valuable information:

1. **Mergers**. Will new alliances give you better opportunities to see companies that have denied you access in the past?

2. **Personnel Changes**. Watch for new appointments by your customers, prospects, and competitors.

3. **Changing Product Lines**. Firms that drop or add products may be suggesting a new emphasis that gives you a reason to call.

4. **Advertising Plans**. Have your competitors or customers changed advertising agencies? Are they creating a new approach or pushing certain products? New advertising campaigns or revamped websites may signal a change in the company that elicits the use of your product.

5. **Online, TV, and Magazine Ads**. Online ads, television commercials, and print ads are a source of invaluable clues. Look at the features being stressed and the image being portrayed.

6. **Sales Training**. The news media highlights new sales training endeavors. Is your customer or prospect developing a sales training program of which you can make use?

On a more personal level, there are numerous online sites that have made pounding the pavement a thing of the past.[10] Even your fingers don't have to do much walking. Just a few mouse clicks and you can find thousands of employment opportunities on the Internet. If you are seeking employment in sales, or in any other career for that matter, Exhibit 8.3 lists four online sources to assist you in gathering a significant amount of preapproach information.

ΔExhibit 8.3

The Fast Track to Finding a Career

According to a survey of 100 executive recruiters conducted by executive job search and recruiting organization ExecuNet, 77 percent of recruiters use search engines to check the backgrounds of potential job candidates. Of those, 35 percent of recruiters have eliminated a candidate from consideration based on information they found online. For this reason, choose your words carefully so that you present yourself in the most accurate and best manner possible.[11]

Career Builder (www.careerbuilder.com)—Access is free to this website for job seekers. You can search opportunities by zip code anywhere in the United States. The site has the capability of notifying you via email of new listings that match your criteria.

LinkedIn (www.linkedin.com)—LinkedIn allows job searches in a way that highlights your existing professional network connections. You can conduct targeted searches among more than 50,000 job postings. Subscriptions to a Job Seeker Premium Account give access to Salary Filters and allow for direct contact with hiring managers through InMail.

Monster.com (www.monster.com)—Job seekers have access to interactive, personalized tools such as My Monster and Resume Builder. You can see real-time job postings and complete company profiles to guide you in your search for the "job."

TheLadders.com (www.theladders.com)—Online job search for positions earning over $100,000 a year. The site boasts more recruiters and hiring managers than anywhere else and more than 61,000 job postings across every industry and sector.

Excellence in selling requires an awareness that the hardest work takes place during the preapproach, but all that hard work leads to the desired end result—a yes. You must be prepared to answer the questions that are in the minds of prospects when you first contact them. Exhibit 8.4 lists ten questions that buyers have, although they don't often volunteer to ask you these questions.

ΔExhibit 8.4

Ten Buyer Questions ·

1. What are you selling?
2. Why do I need it?
3. Who is your company?
4. How much will it cost?
5. Who else is using it, and are they satisfied?
6. What kind of a person are you?
7. Is your price truly competitive?
8. How does your solution compare to other alternatives?
9. Why do I need it now?
10. What is your record for support and service?

Building Self-Confidence

A beneficial feature of preapproach planning is that it builds personal self-confidence. Knowing that you are prepared gives you an added measure of self-confidence that is transmitted to the prospect. The opposite of this confidence is fear, and fear comes primarily from the unknown.

A definite plan for each prospect means you are more likely to be accepted. A purchasing agent for a large, international food processing plant who sees many salespeople described his reactions like this:

> *I turn away salesman after salesman because they come in like lost sheep. . . . They hope that somehow they'll stumble into an order. I get the impression that they figure I'll do the selling for them. I haven't got time for people like that.*[12]

Salespeople call on professional buyers whose job is to make sound purchasing decisions for their companies. These professionals expect to interact with another professional, not an unprepared amateur. If you walk confidently into the buyer's office and get down to business immediately without wasting the prospect's time with unnecessary questions, you increase the likelihood of a successful close. And by emitting an air of self-confidence, you add to your perceived value.[13]

Setting Up the Sales Interview

Preapproach involves doing research, studying a company's website, and discovering other companies with whom they currently do business. It also encompasses the methods used to set up the face-to-face interview itself. There is more to consider than simply picking a day and time. Below are some factors that must be addressed and thoroughly planned to ensure you walk into the most ideal situation when you meet with a prospect.

Timing

With a little research, you can determine the best time to call a prospect you have not previously met. For example, Powell Kenney, vice-president of Clampitt Paper Company in Fort Worth, sees salespeople only between 5:30 and 8:30 a.m. each weekday morning. He does not want his regular work routine disrupted by listening to sales presentations.

Ordinarily, sales calls can be scheduled for almost any time during the business day. Like Mr. Kenney, however, most prospects have a time when they are more receptive to your presentation. Some like to see salespeople the first thing in the morning. Others prefer to handle routine matters first. Fortunately, prospects have different preferences to the extent that salespeople can fill the workday with appointments.

If every buyer insisted on appointments before 8:30 a.m., salespeople would be in serious trouble. If a particular prospect does not seem to have a preference for a time of day to see salespeople, try to discover when most salespeople call on this prospect. If most call in the morning, schedule your call for late in the afternoon. Many executives work past 5:00 p.m. and will see you. In fact, they may well appreciate your diligent work ethic.

The timing of your sales call also comes into play when calling or videoconferencing across time zones is involved. Whether you're scheduling a video chat with a buyer in India or calling the West Coast from your East Coast office, make sure that you keep the correct time difference in mind. World clocks can be found online or as apps for your smartphone, making it easy to check for the time in different selling areas.

Gaining Entry

Before you can arrange a face-to-face meeting, you must choose a way to contact the prospect and set up the interview. Appointments can be set up in several basic ways. You may send an email requesting an appointment, make contact through the appropriate social media, make a cold call, or telephone the prospect and schedule a specific time and date for the interview. Writing an email for an appointment may not produce an answer or may require several contacts to set a mutually convenient time. Cold calls have a low probability of finding the prospect available for an interview.[14] Often times, it requires a combination of several methods to get an agreement to meet.

With email, instant messaging, and social media replacing phones now more than ever, it's getting tougher to set up a meeting in the first place.[15] But the telephone still works with a little diligence. Often times, you will have to wade through a complex automated system, but eventually, you will get through to someone. After you make contact, in many cases, a few minutes are all that are required to make an appointment. Good telephone techniques and habits are important to anyone in professional selling. Using the telephone successfully requires the same basic selling skills as a face-to-face call, plus some additional skills to meet the special challenges of telephone use. Finding a prospect in a bad mood or under a time constraint, the surprise element of a call, and the lack of visual contact are some of the elements that may prevent you from feeling as comfortable with the telephone as you do in a personal contact.

Many executives have receptionists or administrative assistants who screen their incoming calls. These *gatekeepers* also do an excellent job of protecting and conserving the time of their superiors by determining who gets in and when. It is important to build a relationship with these gatekeepers, because statistics show that approximately 60 to 80 percent of them have significant influence over the purchase of certain products and services. It is a mistake to view them as barriers to overcome, and the best way to get to the main buyer is to sell yourself at the door. Exhibit 8.5 outlines eight ways to build rapport with gatekeepers.[16]

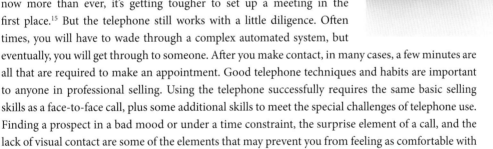

ΔExhibit 8.5

Building Rapport With Gatekeepers

1. **Adjust Your Attitude**. Be friendly, but not fake. Gatekeepers appreciate respect, and they can recognize insincerity.

2. **Honesty Is the Best Policy**. Don't lie to increase your chances of seeing the purchaser. Gatekeepers will inevitably discover your falsehoods, and once this happens the possible sale has ended before it has begun.

3. **Get Personal Information**. Find out the names of gatekeepers, their interests, and family names if you can do so without being too nosy. They appreciate being remembered by name.

4. **Sell to the Gatekeeper**. Gatekeepers have influence over buying decisions. So if you show them how their company can benefit by using your product or service, the chances of you making the final sale increase.

5. **Question Gatekeepers**. Ask them what are the needs and goals of their company, and they just might be willing to tell you.

6. **Be Thoughtful**. Remember to thank gatekeepers for their help, but also remember special occasions such as birthdays and holidays. Don't go overboard, and don't use these gifts as payoffs. Gatekeepers are intelligent and know what's going on.

7. **Keep a Sense of Humor**. This keeps things light, and maybe this will encourage the gatekeeper to accept you in a favorable way.

8. **Be Patient**. It may take longer than you expect to get through the door, but if you keep your patience and persistence, a positive outcome is the result.

Preapproach and Social Networking

The extent to which social media already plays a powerful role in business today is astounding. Surveys show that 62 percent of small and medium-sized businesses use social media for daily business. Of those using social media on an everyday basis, 92 percent say they use it to keep in touch with current customers, while 78 percent are using it to find new prospects.[17] With tens of millions of people logging on to social media sites each day, the potential for new customers is as great as the Web is wide.

One key to getting the most out of using social media for prospecting is by understanding the different uses for each type of networking site and catering your approach accordingly. LinkedIn is the largest professional network in the world, but its users tend to want to keep the site just that—professional. Exhibit 8.6 lists five ways that you can use the LinkedIn professional network to your advantage.[18]

Twitter, on the other hand, is known for being a more flexible site for those wanting to connect with new contacts for the first time. Work the characteristics of each of these sites to your advantage by approaching new contacts on LinkedIn via previously established professional connections in your industry and by interacting on a more informal basis with prospects through Twitter. Once rapport has been built, interaction can be carried over from one site to another.[19]

The door is wide open for social media to become a powerful tool for approaching new clients. As with approaching potential customers in person, on the telephone, or through email, advance research and self-confidence can go a long way toward showing people that you understand their needs and that you are offering a product or service they would benefit from.

Five Ways to Make the Most of Your LinkedIn Profile

1. **Connect with relevant people.** Bigger isn't always better as far as networks are concerned. A small network of people relevant to your business and goals is much better than a large network of people who you don't know or who are irrelevant.

2. **Seek out high-value connections.** Try to make connections with executives and decision makers so that you have access to their networks and so that your own network becomes more valuable to those seeking you out.

3. **Follow good invitation protocols.** Just as in-person sales should follow standard rules of etiquette, you should follow the rules of invitation on LinkedIn by not approaching high-level potential contacts too fast and too aggressively.

4. **Create a complete profile.** The more information you include in your profile, the greater potential you have to build your network. Include current and past companies, education, affiliations, and activities.

5. **Show your connections.** Why would you hide your greatest asset in networking? Your contacts are proof of your power to connect and help others. Make sure your security settings are working to your advantage.

Telephone Techniques

Direct marketing expert Bob Stone defines telemarketing in this manner:

> Telemarketing utilizes sophisticated telecommunications and information systems combined with personal selling and servicing skills to help companies keep in close contact with present and potential customers, increase sales, and enhance business productivity.

It is a marketing discipline that uses telecommunications technology as part of a well planned, organized, and managed marketing program that prominently features the use of personal selling, using non-face-to-face contacts. In the United States today, even with the array of communication technology available, 70 percent of all commerce (in terms of dollar volumes) involves phone calls.[20]

Because of the ever-increasing cost of a sales visit to a prospect, for many companies the telephone call has replaced the unsolicited or cold call approach to make the initial contact with a prospect. Proper telephone usage helps you qualify prospects, budget time, and save money. In addition, good telephone techniques enhance your image and precondition the prospect to receive you favorably. Phoning for an appointment implies that you are courteous and considerate of the prospect's time. The initial phone call helps to create a selling situation because, just by agreeing to see you, the prospect tacitly indicates interest in your product or service.

Getting the Appointment: A Mini Sale

You must regard the use of the telephone to set up appointments as a true sales activity and not just a necessary evil. You must also remember what you are selling. The mini sale is selling the prospect on the idea of giving you an appointment; your purpose is not to sell your product or service on the telephone.

You can make a large number of inquiries in a fraction of the time it takes to make personal visits. You will likely find that personal visits made with an appointment not only reduce waiting time, but prospects will be more receptive because those who are not really interested do not schedule appointments.

Making First Impressions

The quality of your voice, the hesitation in your voice, the volume, the strength of your speaking style all convey an image to another person. Do you come across as being sincere, honest, confident, strong, knowledgeable and likable? If you sound weak and tentative or use words like *well*, *sort-of*, *kind-of*, *maybe*, or *perhaps*, that says to the prospect, "I'm not one bit sure that this is going to a good investment of time for you." Some people even include phrases like, "Well, to be honest with you," which says to the prospect that you aren't always honest. Consider how you would react to this type of telephone call:

> *Hello, Mr. Fisher... uh, my name is... uh Adam Vinatieri... uh I'm with the Indianapolis Colts and... uh we've developed an...uh idea I...uh think you might find...uh interesting and...uh valuable. Uh...Jeff, are morning or....uh afternoon appointments more convenient for you?*

A salesperson with this type of delivery does not make a professional impression. Verbal hesitancy signals a weak personality.[21] An essential element in telemarketing that helps overcome this is a script, whether it is general or written out word-for-word. Scripts are helpful in guiding the salespeople by capturing the prospect's attention. The first ten to thirty seconds of a telephone sales call are crucial; they go far toward determining whether your request for an appointment will be successful or end with a dial tone.

People buy from the people they like. Remember you're projecting your personality over the phone.[22] *How* you say something can be as important as *what* you say. Put a smile in your voice and the prospect can literally hear it. The most successful salespeople project positive voice qualities such as sincerity, courtesy, and confidence. A survey conducted for Jacobi Voice Development revealed the type of voice characteristics by which prospects are most annoyed. Exhibit 8.7 illustrates the most negative or annoying qualities.[23]

ΔExhibit 8.7

Most Annoying Voice Characteristics to Prospects

Voice Characteristic	Percentage
Whining and complaining	44.0%
High-pitched or loud tone	28.0%
Mumblers	11.1%
Too fast or too weak	8.5%
Monotone	3.5%
Strong accent	2.4%

Evaluate Your Telephone Voice

Your voice is your personality over the telephone. It makes an immediate impression that can portray you as friendly or distant, confident or timid, spontaneous or mechanical, and relaxed or nervous. So, how do you come across over the phone? Make a recording of yourself while on the telephone and evaluate the following attributes:

Pitch. Do you speak in a monotone? In normal speech, pitch varies. These variations are known as inflection. The more inflection you use, the more interesting your tone of voice becomes. Keep in mind that when you are under emotional stress, the pitch of your voice will tend to rise and become shrill or strained. Watch it! The pitch of your voice is a gauge of confidence and poise.

Volume. Check the volume or loudness of your voice. You may even get a friend to help you determine this. Is it too soft or too loud? Often when people are tired or upset, their voices fade, and they will be asked to speak up. Be sure to speak loud enough to be heard, but not so loud that you sound overly forceful.

Rate. If you speak too slowly you'll likely lose the attention of the listener. Conversely, your listener won't be able to follow you if you speak too rapidly. In either case, your message won't get through.

Evaluate your volume so you give prospects the right impression.

Quality. The quality of your voice is its most distinctive and individual characteristic. This is where the essence of warmth, understanding and "likeability" come into play. Smiling as you speak enhances your vocal quality. Being angry, upset or in a hurry negatively affects your vocal quality.

Articulation. The price of poor articulation is high, particularly in business. You must enunciate or pronounce your words very clearly or your listeners will misunderstand you. Faulty articulation and incorrect word pronunciation give your listener the impression that you are sloppy, careless, and lack knowledge.

The telephone may be one of the most powerful, efficient, and cost-effective business tools you have at your disposal. Telephone manners and etiquette are critical components of a professional image. Through experience, you'll develop your own telephone style. You'll also find customers and prospects responding positively when you and your employees smile, listen and show personal interest!

Organizing the Call

Inadequate preparation reduces the effectiveness of your delivery. Ask yourself these four questions to help you stay on track:[24]

1. *Why am I calling?* Do you want to make an appointment, check on a customer's need to reorder, or follow up an inquiry?

2. *What is my proposal?* Your plan should have two parts: 1.What do you want from the person you call, and 2. What commitment you will make. Jot down some notes and be specific!

3. *What would make this person want to grant my request?* Before calling, determine why the person you are calling will do what you request.

4. *How does my telephone script sound?* Identify those key words or phrases in your telephone sales call that you can emphasize to make your message more convincing.[25]

Before you ever pick up the telephone, go through a mental checklist to ensure that you are fully prepared. Exhibit 8.8 presents ten strategic checkpoints to consider when you are preparing to use the telephone to set up appointments.

ΔExhibit 8.8

Key Points to Consider When Preparing to Use the Telephone

1. **Arrange a definite time each day to telephone.** Determine a specific number of calls to make during that time period.

2. **Arrange for privacy to avoid interruptions.** Make as many calls as you can in the allotted time. Your attitude is critical; without a positive attitude, using the telephone is mentally exhausting.

3. **Develop a well-written, structured script.** Know exactly what to say before you call. However, never make your call sound like a canned spiel. You can avoid sounding canned by doing one thing—practice, practice, practice!

4. **Verify that you are actually talking to the person that you intended to call.** Be sure you have the correct pronunciation of the name. Use the name several times during the call.

5. **Tell the prospect just enough to get the appointment.** You know a lot more than you need to tell at this time. Just peak his interest so that he agrees to a meeting.

6. **Show excitement and enthusiasm in your voice.** Give your voice the emotional feel of shaking hands over the telephone. Put a smile in your voice. You can even try placing a mirror by the phone to watch your expression.

7. **Never argue; be sure to ask for the appointment.** Always offer a choice of times so prospects can choose a time that is convenient for them.

8. **Sell your own name.** Ask the prospect to write it down so you are remembered when you arrive for the appointment.

9. **Be courteous.** Say thank you and begin sentences with phrases like, "May I ask …" and "If I may…."

10. **Watch your language.** Choose your words carefully for greater impact. Repetition of nonfunctional expressions like, "I see," "uh huh," "you know," and "fantastic" are irritating and unprofessional.

Plugging Contact Management Into the Phone

Of all the daily administrative tasks performed by a salesperson, using the telephone to set appointments is certainly one of the most critical. With sales force automation, telephone time becomes much more efficient and productive. All of the leading contact management programs have some integration with the telephone. This powerful tool can help you maximize the use of your precious phone time. A salesperson can quickly review preapproach information gathered or any past conversations with the prospect or client.

This chapter's *Developing Partnerships Using Technology* accentuates how contact management programs assist the salesperson in setting up appointments for a personal visit with a prospect or client. These programs give salespeople an integrated system for organizing prospecting information. The information might include the size and date of the previous purchases, when you contacted them last, and what happened in that interview—and even have the computer dial the phone for you.

Developing Partnerships Using Technology

A Day in the Life of a Salesperson: Making Cold Calls

With contact management programs, salespeople working out of their virtual office now have a virtual assistant traveling with them. Contact management software dials, answers, screens calls, and finds files in the blink of an eye. Software, such as the Maximizer™, a sales and contact manager software designed to manage and profile customers and prospects, allows you to easily access your email for phone numbers, track every sale, and maintain relationships for repeat business.[26] Take a look at how a salesperson can use the features available on various devices to help maximize selling time.

Unlimited Information. At the beginning of the day, the salesperson easily reviews preapproach information she gathered through Internet research. She also goes over notes from past conversations with her prospects. The contact manager app on her tablet computer makes it simple to open files to review price quotes and check inventory.

Auto Dialing. Most contact manager apps are equipped with automatic dialing features. From within the app on her smartphone, the salesperson has the option of dialing the contact's phone number with one touch. She doesn't have to exit the app to search her address book! Calling is faster and more accurate, especially for international contacts with complex dialing codes.

Note Taking and Synching. While the salesperson chats with prospects on her smartphone, she keeps her contact manager program open on her laptop. This way, she is able to type out notes as she talks, look up information as she needs it, and save time once the call is completed. With a couple of clicks on her laptop trackpad, she is able to synch her notes to her smartphone and keep her files current and accurate.

Check out these websites for additional information:
www.apple.com/webapps
www.blackberry.com
www.androidapps.com
www.maximizer.com
www.act.com

The Six-Step Telephone Track

The key to using the telephone effectively is to engineer conversations that sound like normal talk. They have to be two-sided, but simultaneously get people to sell themselves on seeing you. When you try to set an appointment by phone, you don't have the advantage of being able to show your prospect what a great product you offer. Instead, you need a careful strategy that allows the prospect to take an interest in what you're saying and agree to meet with you face-to-face. Use the six-step outline in Exhibit 8.9 to plan your appointment-setting calls so that the next time you talk to prospects, you're sitting face-to-face with them.[27]

ΔExhibit 8.9

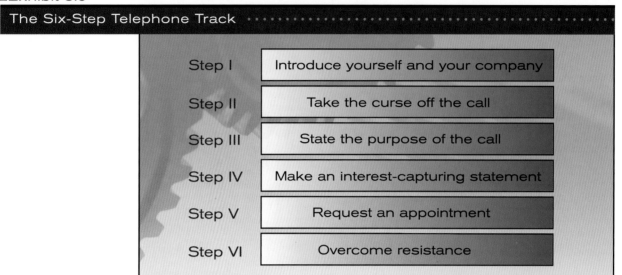

The Six-Step Telephone Track

Step I	Introduce yourself and your company
Step II	Take the curse off the call
Step III	State the purpose of the call
Step IV	Make an interest-capturing statement
Step V	Request an appointment
Step VI	Overcome resistance

Step 1: Introduce Yourself and Your Company

Most sales relationships depend heavily on initial impressions. When you place a call, the prospect will most likely make a judgment about you before your first twelve words are said.[28] How you introduce yourself, therefore, and what you say immediately thereafter are of vital importance. A weak or tentative opening puts you at a severe disadvantage throughout the rest of the call. Your opening words should tell who you are, indicate the company you represent, and confirm that you are speaking to the correct person:

> *Good morning . . . I am Will Brown, sales representative for iDesign. Am I speaking to Mrs. Teresa Ridings? . . . Good. Mrs. Ridings, . .*

Be sure the person you reach on the phone is someone who can make or influence a buying decision. Smile as you speak so that you transmit a warm, friendly personality. Watch the rate at which you speak. Prospects instinctively pay more attention to someone who speaks at a moderate and energetic rate. A too rapid rate of speech seems nervous or sounds as though you are reading a canned pitch. If you are too slow, you come across as lazy or unconcerned, or the prospect feels that talking to you will be a long, time-consuming process.

Step 2: Take the Curse Off the Call

A phone call is an interruption of your prospect's work. To sell people on the idea of granting you an appointment, you must detach their attention from what they were doing or thinking when the phone rang and attract it to what you propose. It helps if you think and talk about your call as a service you are offering rather than as an interruption for which you must apologize. You can take the curse off the call with a statement and a question to soften the impact of the interruption. For example:

> 1. *It will take just about a minute to explain why I'm calling. Is it convenient for you to talk now?*
> 2. *Mrs. Ridings, do you have a minute to speak with me now, or did I catch you at a bad time?.*
>   *(Then, if the prospect indicates the time is inconvenient) When would be a better time?*

A prospect who is totally preoccupied with other matters may refuse to speak with you. In this case, calling back at a time the prospect suggests is far better for both parties. When you do call back at the suggested time, the odds will be greatly improved that your message will receive a favorable hearing.

Step 3: State the Purpose of the Call

Assuming the prospect does have time to speak, follow with a brief, hard-hitting, lead-in statement about why you are calling—just enough to capture the prospect's attention, but short of describing the benefit(s) you will present in a later step. Use these ideas to spark your creative thinking about possible lead-in statements you can use:

- Refer to a direct-mail piece or email update you have already sent to the prospect.

- Mention the person who referred you to this prospect.

- Say that your company has designed a program or service to benefit clients like the prospect.

A letter, product literature, email newsletter, or any other direct mail piece sent to a select sampling of prospects gives you the opportunity to call and inquire if they received it. This tactic gives you a purpose for calling and provides an acceptable type of lead-in statement. Here is a sample, and whatever the answer, you can use this beginning to move on to the next step:

> *Mrs. Ridings, thank you for taking a minute of your valuable time to speak with me. My purpose in calling is to find out if you received the e-newsletter I sent you last week describing a specialized web design service that my company has recently developed for professionals like you.*

Perhaps the best reason you can give for calling is that a third party whom the prospect respects has referred you. The value of using a third party as an introduction is the immediate endorsement it provides. The prospect automatically assumes that you are reputable and reliable and that you deserve a hearing.[29]

In the majority of instances, a referral alone is enough to get the prospect to hear you out during this first telephone call. Then you must generate enough interest to motivate the prospect to agree to give you an appointment. Here is an example of how to use a referral as a purpose for calling:

> *Mrs. Ridings, we recently designed a new, interactive website for the DM Bass Company that was extremely well received by their customers and has doubled their online sales in the last month. The CEO, Murphy Bass, was so pleased with the results that she asked me to get in touch with you and see whether we might also be helpful to you.*

After you have established a legitimate purpose for the call, you are ready to move to the next step.

Step 4: Make an Interest-Capturing Statement

Once you have the prospect's attention, your task is to convert attention into interest so that you can expect a favorable hearing. Establish interest most effectively by promising a benefit or offering a service. Use product benefits, company services, or financial rewards to answer the prospect's unspoken question: "What's in it for me?"[30]

Offer the prospect a benefit from listening to you, offer a service, or offer to do something for—not to—the prospect. Be sure to say how long the actual personal visit will take, and assure the prospect that everything you have to say can be covered in that length of time unless the prospect wants to explore certain areas in greater detail. Here are three examples:

> 1. *Mr. Williams, we have designed a complete online package for companies similar to yours that could increase the effectiveness of your business from 10 to 25 percent with a decrease in the cost of your operations. It will take about 20 minutes for me to show you how.*

> 2. *The benchmarking results from our design department show that many managers have been pleased with the look and navigability of our custom designed web pages. Our clients report*

more online traffic and increased sales through their eCommerce stores. In fact one client, Parity Liquidators, saw their sales increase by $5000 in the week following the site launch.

3. Mr. Peterson, we've found that most people are just waiting for an invitation to come into a day spa, and we'd like to extend that invitation to you right now to come see how Blue Canyon Spa is changing the way our clients look and feel about themselves.

Rather than making a statement, you may ask a question to capture the prospect's interest:

My company has an idea that could give complete protection to your entire plant and decrease your present costs. You are interested in cutting costs, aren't you?

Most business people want to see their operations run more efficiently and would answer this question in the affirmative. You could then suggest that you have a specific plan and request a personal visit to discuss it with the prospect.

Step 5: Request an Appointment

Remember that your goal at this point is to secure an appointment with the prospect so that you can make a complete presentation. Avoid giving interview information over the phone; the more information you give, the more problems the prospect may see.

The prospect can easily say, "I'm not interested" over the phone. Then you have nowhere to go. The conclusion could be much different when you give an excellent presentation in person. Next time, try the "KISS" approach to setting the appointment: *Keep It Simple, Salesperson!* The telephone itself encourages brevity, so just ask for the appointment confidently and directly.

1. I'm sure you agree that we should get together to discuss how we can accomplish this for you. Would this Thursday at 9:00 be good for you? Or perhaps Friday morning would be better?

2. The best time for me would be tomorrow afternoon at 2:00 or Thursday morning at 11:00. Which would be more convenient for you, Mrs. Ridings?

Notice that in each example the prospect was given a choice of times rather than asked, "When would it be convenient to see you?" which makes saying no far too easy. You simply want to create enough initial interest to set up an appointment. Resist every temptation to get into specifics on the telephone. You are selling an appointment, not the product or service.

After you have set up the appointment, be sure to say "thank you" and then allow the prospect to end the call. It is important for you to hang up last, because the prospect may think of something at the end and should hear your voice instead of a click.[31]

Step 6: Overcome Resistance

Using the telephone to set up appointments gives rise to two types of objections: An objection to receiving the telephone call and an objection to granting an interview. A prospect who was engaged in an activity of interest or importance may feel irritated by an interruption and prefer to resume that activity. This prospect's goal is to get you off the phone by refusing to become interested in what you have to say.

Prospects who do not want to grant an interview often fear that they cannot successfully defend their own ideas or decisions when faced by an experienced salesperson. They are afraid that they will buy. This type of objection can be overcome in three steps:

1. Agree sympathetically with objections to build the prospect's ego.

2. Switch from the prospect's objection to your idea or purpose for the interview.

3. Ask for the appointment.

Case 8.2 – Gossip or Useful Information?

"Hey! Guess what I heard?" Running to catch up with Nancy, Hank was out of breath.

"What?" Nancy replied, wishing that Hank would dial it back a little.

"LongMeadow is merging with LD Mobile Homes! Do you know what that means?" Hank exclaimed.

"Well, it means that one of our clients is disappearing," Nancy answered. "What else?"

"No, no! You don't get it!" yelled Hank. He was becoming annoying. "We'll now have a shot at LD's business. We've never been able to even get an appointment before."

"What makes you think they'll see us now?" Nancy asked evenly. But her mind was turning. Her insurance company was, perhaps, about to lose a client; instead, she saw an opportunity to gain an even larger account. She wasn't sure how Hank knew about the merger, and she didn't want to know. Now, however, presuming that Hank's outburst was reliable, she needed a plan to turn his gossip into solid information that would elicit an appointment.

What information does Nancy need to gather? Presuming that the merger is still a secret, how should she go about obtaining the information needed to approach LD Mobile Homes? What strategies should she employ? And when should she make her initial approach?

The Face-to-Face
Relationship Model of Selling

9 10 11 12 13

Part 4

Consider this the "how to" portion of the textbook, the face-to-face segment of the sales cycle. The following chapters are the very heart of professional selling. It is the valuable time spent in the actual sales interview; and it is the time when a commitment is obtained and kept.

What happens in the opening minutes of a meeting is crucial to the overall success of the sales interview, and chapter 9 focuses on those opening moments—the approach. Chapter 10 is devoted to the art of asking questions and listening effectively. You will learn critical questioning and listening skills to help carry you through the entire sales interview. The SPIN® selling technique is explained and dramatized using a practical example. Chapter 11 then details techniques to use in the presentation itself. Units of conviction are the building blocks on which to build a meaningful sales presentation, and the five elements that comprise a unit of conviction are both explained and illustrated.

Chapters 12 and 13 present the psychology behind handling objections and closing the sale. You will be introduced to a plan to handle objections, and a portion of chapter 12 explains several ways to deal with the price objection. Chapter 13 stresses that closing the sale is the natural conclusion to a successful sales interview. The chapters in this section are:

9. Approaching the Prospect
10. Identifying Needs by Questioning and Listening
11. Making the Presentation
12. Handling Objections
13. Closing the Sale

First Impressions
You never get a second chance to make a good...

FOLLOW the river and you will find the sea. Determination is the key.

INDIVIDUALS cannot consistently perform in a manner which is inconsistent with the way they see themselves.

REMEMBER...If you fail to plan, you plan to fail.

SOME people dream of worthy accomplishments, while others stay awake and do them.

THE single most important ingredient in the formula for success is knowing how to deal with people.

IF you don't take care of the customer...somebody else will.

MANAGE your time and your choices—and you'll manage your life.

PREPARE yourself for leadership. Be a living example of the excellence you expect from others.

RUNNING a business is no trouble at all as long as it's not yours.

EVERYTHING you say and do is a reflection of the inner you.

SINGIN' in the rain of life is better than letting it dampen your spirits.

SELF-ESTEEM, commitment, and action determine your outcome.

IF we could kick the person responsible for most of our problems, we wouldn't be able to sit for a week.

ONE way to avoid criticism is to do nothing and be a nobody. The world will then not bother you.

NO one is useless in this world who lightens the burden of another.

Chapter 9
Approaching the Prospect

Learning Objectives

• Discover the purpose of the approach.

• Learn the importance of first impressions and ways to control them as a means of improving your performance.

• Understand how nonverbal language affects your ability to establish rapport with a prospect.

• Examine the elements of the greeting and how to control them.

• Discover ways to get the attention and capture the interest of the prospect.

• Explore different types of approaches and the best circumstances in which to use each one.

Use This Page for Taking Notes

Setting the Mood

You did your homework, and your prospecting and preapproach efforts uncovered potential clients. You successfully arranged a personal meeting with a prospect. So now what? What happens during the opening of the face-to-face encounter profoundly affects the success of the entire presentation and your ability to get a commitment to buy. The approach is the actual contact the salesperson has with the prospect. More importantly, it is your opportunity to set the mood of the presentation and perhaps even your future relationship with the customer.

This is the point of the selling process where the sales professional meets and greets the prospect, provides an introduction, establishes rapport that sets the foundation for the relationship, and asks open-ended questions to learn more about the prospect and his or her needs.[1] The approach is important because it determines the character of your future relationship with a prospect, including how receptive the prospect will be to your presentation and whether the close will be difficult or easy.

Although the overall success of the interview depends on more than the approach, an effective approach creates a favorable buyer-seller environment. The approach is often overlooked or taken for granted. Although the approach is usually considered in the context of the first call on a prospect, every meeting with a new prospect or an established customer begins with an approach.

Salespeople tend to use the same approach over and over, but prospects and situations are not the same; instead, salespeople ought to make a practice of using various types of approaches that fit the needs of a specific situation, whether calling on new prospects or on established customers. An effective approach achieves four key objectives:

1. To make a favorable or positive impression on the prospect.

2. To gain the prospect's undivided attention.

3. To develop positive interest in your proposition.

4. To lead smoothly into the need discovery phase of the interview.

First Impressions

In his book, *Contact: The First Four Minutes*, Leonard Zunin says that the first four minutes of initial contact with a prospect are crucial. He suggests that four minutes is the average time the prospect takes to decide whether to buy from you. Others say it takes even less time than that. However long this mental process actually takes, one thing is certain: Prospects start judging you from the moment you walk in the room.[2] Impress the prospect with a show of good manners, clear enunciation, good grooming, and appropriate dress; when you look and act like a professional, the prospect, consciously or subconsciously, begins to trust you. People make quick decisions based on feelings, emotions, or hunches. The more positive their feelings, the more they hear and accept what you say. The opening moments of the approach must be designed to create an atmosphere of trust. The first ten words you speak will reveal volumes about you.[3]

Your initial contact with prospects is crucial.

The initial impression you make on a new prospect is much like a homebuyer who looks at the potential home for the first time. Sellers and their realtors go to great lengths to present the home in the best light possible through a process called "staging." Staging things as seemingly insignificant as the optimal location of the furniture and other items in the seller's home can make a difference between a sale or no sale.[4] Remember that this is a business meeting, not a personal lunch with a close friend. You must put your best foot forward from the beginning in order to ensure that the prospect hasn't said "no" in his mind before he ever hears your presentation.

Successful salespeople know how to make other people feel important. It does not matter how knowledgeable they are about their product lines or how many closing techniques they have memorized. Unless they earn their prospect's trust and confidence, they are not going to make the sale—period.

A relationship salesperson must be able to work effectively with a prospect even in the presence of a personality clash. You also have to temper the first impressions you make about a prospect; spend some time and look further before making an unalterable judgment.

Prospects watch and evaluate virtually every personal characteristic you have, so your approach must be impeccable. Positive first impressions count. There's something about a good initial person-to-person contact that instinctively leads to more sales.[5] Exhibit 9.1 presents some guidelines for making the first impression a favorable one. After all, *you never get a second chance to make a good first impression.*[6]

ΔExhibit 9.1

There's Never a Second Chance to Make a Good First Impression

Visual Factors
- Correct any detail that could become a visible distraction such as a tattered briefcase, a messy car, or inappropriate grooming.
- Nonverbal communication is powerful. Pay attention to what the prospect sees in your body language as well as in what you wear.
- Don't wear jewelry such as lapel pins, tiepins, or rings that advertise your membership in a specific organization that may not be recognized or admired by some people.

Organization and Professional Habits
- Be prompt, or even early. Set your watch five minutes ahead if necessary.
- Present a clear agenda. State the purpose of your call right away. Make it clear that you are not going to waste the prospect's time.
- Be prepared with as much information as possible about the prospect (both the individual and company).

Building Rapport
- Pronounce the prospect's name correctly. A person's name is a personal identifier; mispronouncing it takes away some of the owner's status.
- If you pay the prospect a compliment, make it specific and of personal interest.
- Recall the importance of proxemics (use of space). Respect the prospect's personal space.
- Look for common ground like mutual friends, membership in the same religious or civic group, or similar hobbies.

Physical Actions
- Shake hands, maintain eye contact, and greet the prospect warmly, but never say, "How are you?" as it may sound contrived and insincere. Instead, open with a more specific greeting, including the use of the prospect's name.
- Refrain from personal habits like smoking or chewing gum, or from using careless language that might be offensive to some people.

Attitude
- Be enthusiastic. Enthusiasm is infectious if it is sincere.

Although first impressions may be dependable sign posts for the feelings you leave with a prospect, first impressions do have some weaknesses:

- They are likely to be based on feelings and emotions.

- All behavior traits do not show up simultaneously, and an initial short interview may not provide enough time for all traits (either favorable or unfavorable) to surface.

- The prospect may deliberately control behavior and allow you to see only certain chosen personality traits.

- Some event immediately preceding the interview may strongly influence the prospect's current behavior.

Be willing to wait before you conclude that you and a prospect are experiencing a personality conflict that cannot be overcome. Your job is to establish rapport, build confidence, and make the prospect feel comfortable. Do everything in your power to satisfy the needs of your prospects and refuse to allow first impressions to prevent a mutually beneficial sales experience.

Nonverbal Language

Nonverbal language—including grooming, clothing, accessories, posture, tone of voice, and time and space aspects—vitally affects first impressions, despite the fact that nonverbal factors actually provide limited or shallow insight into the true person. Salespeople must be sure the statements they make with their nonverbal language are favorable because the impressions formed during the first few minutes of an initial encounter between two people will last indefinitely. Successful salespeople increase the odds in their favor by taking advantage of the power of first impressions. Visual impressions almost always come first. Fortunately, you can do a lot to shape the visual impact you make when a prospect first sees you.

Projecting an Image

"You want your clothes to command respect, inspire credibility and create trust—you must come across as the authority on the product that is offered," points out Sherry Maysonave, head of Empowerment Enterprises in Austin, Texas.[7] Your clothes speak volumes about you, your company, your work, and how you relate to customers.

When you know that you are dressed appropriately, you feel good about yourself. When you are confident and at ease, you emanate an air of competence that the prospect unconsciously accepts and interprets as credibility.[8] Total appearance is important because the prospect's initial attention is focused on you and not on your proposition. If you want to be successful, you must look successful. A salesperson who wears an obviously cheap suit, for example, creates a negative impression and sets up this line of thinking in the mind of the prospect:

- This salesperson is dressed cheaply. He must not be making much money.

- Because he's not making much money, he must be having difficulty selling his product.

- If the product is not selling, something must be wrong with it.

- I don't want an inferior product.

Look the Part. We must look the part of a professional to be viewed as one. Lois Frankel, author of the bestselling *Nice Girls Don't Get the Corner Office*, says that research shows about 60 percent of our credibility comes from how we look.[9] Personal appearance and behavior are the easiest areas to address on the road to greater success, yet all too often sales professionals choose to ignore this aspect.

Unspoken rules for appropriate dress extend into every aspect of professional life. Optometrist Jerry Hayes says, "Your appearance greatly affects how patients feel about you."[10] When we go to the doctor, we want the doctor to be dressed in a manner that projects his authority and knowledge. Would you trust a surgeon to operate on you who is dressed in shorts and a t-shirt? Of course not! So how can you expect a prospect to buy an expensive product or service if you don't, well, look the part? Dress in such a way that commands respect and credibility; but remember, everything in moderation.

What do your clothes say about you?

Dress Conservatively. Your objective is to focus the prospect's attention on the benefits of buying your product or service. Anything that detracts from that focus works against you. Conservative dress gives the prospect the impression that talking with you is safe and that you are familiar and dependable. Although "conservative" varies from one region to another and from one industry to another, that variation is not extremely wide. Dressing conservatively suggests stability and dependability; following extreme fads of color, cut, and pattern may suggest just the opposite.

Corporate Casual dressing is the norm in today's business world, but the term itself can be confusing. Corporate casual does not mean yoga clothes! There are still guidelines every professional should follow, and many companies have written guidelines that take the guesswork out of getting dressed. Always make sure you research and follow your company's standards. Below is a set of guidelines for corporate casual dress from the ultimate etiquette source, Emily Post:[11]

For Men:
- Seasonal sport coat or blazer with slacks or khakis
- Dress shirt with optional tie, or casual button down shirt
- Open-collar or polo shirt
- Loafer or loafer-style shoes and socks

For Women:
- At or below knee length skirt, khakis or pants
- Open-solar shirt, knit shirt, or sweater (no spaghetti straps or décolleté)
- Casual-style dress
- No flip-flops

Remember, corporate casual style is not intended to convey a lack of professionalism, just a more comfortable, perhaps less boring way of projecting one's best. "Professional" is the key word to remember when dressing business casual. Always be aware that you do not dress too casually. Rather, make sure your clothes reflect your position and the message you wish to convey to your clients.

Choose Accessories Carefully. Accessories are intended to enhance your appearance. Make sure they do not call attention to themselves. Jewelry should be simple—one good piece is more impressive than three or four cheap pieces.

- Jewelry that announces your association with some organization or belief (unless shared by the prospect) may call attention to itself and away from the purpose of your call.

- Accessories should be of good quality. High-quality pen and pencil sets and top-quality leather attaché cases make a quiet statement of your personal pride in your profession and mark you as successful.

- Avoid sunglasses or lenses that noticeably change color with shifts in light. People may not believe what you are saying if they cannot see your eyes. Hiding your eyes seems to say you are hiding something else as well.

Dress Appropriately. You should plan to dress as well as your prospect. People feel comfortable dealing with those who seem to fit into their own lifestyle; but don't use your age as an excuse to dress more "youthfully" or casually. This is apparently a growing problem in the job market today, "It has gotten so crazy, a major pharmaceutical company called up and said, 'Help! People are wearing spandex to work!'" says Gail Madison, an etiquette and protocol consultant who regularly advises students at prestigious colleges on small but important details such as taking out their nose rings before a job interview or not dying their hair orange.[12] If your clothes are too formal or carry too much of an aura of power, you cause the prospect to feel overpowered; the result may be rebellion against what is perceived as your snobbish attitude. On the other hand, if you dress too casually or carelessly, wear distracting jewelry, or have an unusual hairstyle, prospects may unconsciously feel that you do not consider them or their business important.

Often men find it more difficult to talk and learn about dressing appropriately and with style than women do. If you fall in such a category, you may want to schedule an appointment with an image consultant or even pick up a copy of *GQ Magazine's* style manual. Don't be afraid to consult men's fashion websites or newspaper columns. Exhibit 9.2 is an adaptation of one such article, which gives the basics that every professional man needs in his wardrobe:[13]

ΔExhibit 9.2

The Well-Dressed Man: Shopping Checklist

Building a man's wardrobe starts with a few key items. Here's what to invest in first:

• Trim two-button wool suit with narrow lapels. Make sure the pants are flat front and are slimmer in silhouette. Start with navy or grey for most wear.

• A couple of slim white dress shirts with semi-spread collars. One or two check-patterned versions will add some variety.

• Two or three narrow ties. Make one black. (You can also try a silver tie bar.)

• Three or four pocket squares for your front jacket pocket. White will work for dressier occasions. A patterned print will add personality.

• A narrow black lace-up shoe. It will work for business and a formal dinner.

• Slim winter overcoat that extends just over your suit jacket.

• Pair of dark denim jeans cut slightly trimmer to the leg.

Whatever your gender, always remember that the clothes you wear speak volumes about who you are.[14] *What do your clothes say about you?*

The Proper Greeting

In order to increase the odds of making a good impression during the meet-and-greet, use the business etiquette *Rule of Ten*. The first ten words you speak should include a form of thanks: "Good morning, Mrs. Robertson. Thank you for agreeing to see me," or "Good afternoon, Ernie. It's a pleasure to meet you."

Casual questions like "How are you?" or "How ya' doing?" have lost all semblance of meaning. How does the prospect respond? "Great" or "Just fine, thank you," but what if the prospect is not feeling great and what if business is not going great? If a prospect covers up real feelings with a conventional answer, a vague feeling of uneasiness results from the untruth.

How would you answer the simple question "How are you?" You may want to try the response used by Pat Shemek. When prospects or clients ask Shemek, "How are you doing," Pat replies, "Super duper." The clients have come to expect this response, and even look forward to it. Shemek's attitude seems to be—*fake it until you make it!* Come up with your own unique response delivered with a smile on your face and enthusiasm in your voice. Your customers will appreciate your positive attitude.[15]

A proper greeting isn't just about a friendly face or the proper words, but an appealing surrounding also helps. Sometimes this is out of your control, especially if you are meeting the prospect on his turf. However, if you have the opportunity to select the meeting location, find a spot that is warm and inviting, and one in which you will not have to shout in order to be heard. Salespeople often meet clients at coffee shops. These are great neutral locations and often have free Wi-Fi for presentations done on your laptop or tablet. You may want to avoid coffee shops around the busiest times of the day (early morning and lunch) or outside distractions could diminish any good impression you attempt to make.[16]

The Handshake

Your voice inflection and pronunciation and how you shake hands are as important as what you say. Make sure not to inflect your voice up at the end of each sentence; you must project yourself as a leader, not as insecure or apologetic. Confidence signals to the prospect that you believe in what you sell. In order to have a leader's attitude, John Maxwell, the author of more than thirty books on leadership, says, "Leadership has less to do with position than it has with disposition."[17] What does your disposition say about you? Do you stand behind what you sell, or are you just trying to pay the rent? When combined with your tone of voice and facial expression, your handshake reveals to a prospect your mood. The business handshake is an essential selling technique to make a positive lasting impression. When the first handshake with a prospect is a firm one, you'll have the beginning of a strong business relationship.[18] Exhibit 9.3 presents helpful guidelines for an effective handshake.

ΔExhibit 9.3

Guidelines for an Effective Handshake

- Maintain eye contact for the duration of the handshake.
- You may wait for the prospect to initiate the handshake (to avoid offending those people who "do not like to be touched").
- If your palm tends to be moist from nervousness, carry a special handkerchief with powder and pat your hand several times just before entering the prospect's office. Be careful not to leave a residue of powder on your hand that might be transferred to the prospect's hand or to your clothes.
- Apply firm, consistent pressure on the hand and avoid limp-wristed, wet-fish, or bone-crusher handshakes.
- The hands should meet at an equal distance between you and the prospect in a vertical position. If you turn your wrist so your hand is over the prospect's, this nonverbal gesture implies the intention to be dominant. If you turn your wrist so that your hand is on the bottom, you are signaling a submissive nature.

The handshake is also an indispensable tool to consider when selling to customers around the globe. Several tips for international handshaking are presented in Exhibit 9.4.[19] The customs and mannerisms of our overseas partners are equally essential to understand and accommodate. Be sure to make use of this information as one aspect of surface language to assist you in establishing rapport with people regardless of nationality or personality style.

Shaking Hands Around the World

Here are three noteworthy tips when greeting international prospects and customers:

1. **Shake hands with everyone.** International etiquette demands that the salesperson shake hands with everyone that is in the room. Not shaking hands with someone will be noticed and considered a personal rejection.

2. **Initiate the handshake.** An American saleswoman should extend her hand to a European male. Not doing so may cause her to lose credibility. Women should initiate handshakes and shake hands with other women and men.

3. **Notice culture-to-culture differences.** Latin Americans tend to use a lighter, lingering handshake. In Arab countries, handshakes are limp and last longer than the average American handshake. Japanese salespeople shake hands with one firm gesture. The handshake is often combined with a slight bow.

Small Talk or Get Down to Business

In the initial face-to-face meeting, both parties may experience what might be called *relationship tension*. Prospects fear being sold something they do not want, and salespeople face the fear of being rejected. The opening few minutes of conversation are designed to find a comfort level for both parties so that rapport can be established. The purpose of small talk at the opening of the interview is to gain an advantageous, positive beginning that breaks the ice and eases the tension. Small talk may be a discussion of topics entirely unrelated to what you are selling. Al Angell, a successful sales professional in Boston, says this warm-up period usually takes him five minutes or more. Al calls this time "chit-chat with a purpose." He asks four basic questions that he feels are nonthreatening, easy to answer, and objective:

1. Are you a native of this area?

2. Were you educated there? (Based on answer to the first question.)

3. Are you a family person?

4. How did you happen to get into this business?

This type of socializing at the beginning of the interview eases tension and may give you some insight into your prospect's behavioral style. It warms up a cold environment and has the side benefit of providing additional information about the prospect. If the prospect seems withdrawn or even hostile, this warm-up conversation helps you determine whether that is the prospect's real personality or whether you have arrived on an especially bad day.

Speaker, trainer, and author James Malinchak teaches his clients this easy and simple rhyme when approaching a new prospect: *"When you meet someone new, they don't want to talk about you."* It's true! People love to tell you what they do in their spare time, talk about their accomplishments, or tell you about their families. So, remember this rhyme and it will remind you to let your prospects and customers talk about themselves or their interests. This non-selling conversation is important. An ideal topic for initial chit-chat is one that relaxes the prospect, is of interest, and relates, if possible, to your objective so that you can move easily into the attention getter and then into need discovery.[20]

> People have no confidence in salespeople whose only interest is self-interest, who seek to use their clients instead of being of use to their clients.

Use of the Prospect's Name

People do not like to have their names forgotten, mispelled (sorry, I meant misspelled), or mispronounced. Typically, when we meet someone, we hear our own name, but we may or may not hear the other person's name. In his book, *How to Win Friends and Influence People*, Dale Carnegie says, "A person's name is to them the sweetest and most important sound in any language."[21] If we forget a name or mispronounce it, we send out this message: "I care more about me and my name than I do about you and your name."

Imagine how a prospect feels when you say, "So you see, Ms. . . . ah . . . uh . . . excuse me (shuffle for prospect card or appointment calendar) uh . . . Mr. Hill, I mean, Lill." The prospect probably stiffens, the environment turns a bit frosty, and you may well walk out without an order.[22] Now recall how pleased you were when someone remembered your name after just a casual meeting several weeks previously. You would stand in line to do business with such a person.

Improving your memory for names is not as difficult as it may seem. Several books are available to help you devise a method to correct a careless memory for names. Exhibit 9.5 gives some suggestions for remembering names.

ΔExhibit 9.5

How to Remember Customers' Names

Associate
Relate a characteristic with some gimmick to help you recall the name.

Observe
Study people regularly to strengthen your ability to see characteristics and practice your imagination.

Pay attention
Ask to have the name repeated (even spelled). It will impress the person.

Repeat
Use the prospect's name several times during the interview.

Concentrate
Look for characteristics that distinguish this person from others.

Gaining Attention and Capturing Interest

As the cartoon states, first you have got to get their attention! Develop a carefully constructed, attention-getting statement that focuses the prospect's full attention completely on you and your proposition; remember that prospects are thinking, "What does this person want with me? Why should I allow my work to be interrupted?" Unless prospects want to listen, they won't—so give them a reason. Just as the newspaper uses a headline to make you take notice, you must also develop an attention getting opening that breaks through their preoccupation and focuses attention on the selling situation.

You can use two basic methods of getting attention: appealing to the senses and through the introduction of a benefit.

Appeal to the Senses. An appeal to the senses gets the prospect involved in the presentation. Be sure to use a little dramatization. Show something the prospect can see; hand the prospect something to hold.

Introduction of a Benefit. Introduce a benefit by a statement that relates to the prospect's need for your product or service. Highlight the value of the product or service especially in terms of how it may save prospects their most valuable resources—time and money. If you can modify the product to suit your prospect's particular needs, also be sure to outline this option.

An effective attention-getting statement requires preparation. If you have done your homework in gathering preapproach information, you already know enough to have some idea about both the needs and the behavioral style of the prospect. If you spend a few minutes in small talk you gain further clues to confirm or adjust your preapproach information. Use what you know to plan an effective attention-getting device to introduce the heart of your presentation. Exhibit 9.6 suggests ways to gain prospects' attention by appealing to their behavioral styles during your initial exchange.[23]

First you've got to get their attention!

ΔExhibit 9.6

Using Behavioral Styles to Choose an Attention-Getting Approach

Expressive—Open in terms of long-range goals or implications.
Mr. Arnold, I would like to show you how our innovative service will help your department reach its long-term potential.

Analytical—Open in very specific terms.
Mr. Arnold, I would like to give you the background on our service and then list the ways in which I think it will reduce your overhead, increase your productivity, and improve your profit margin by ten percent. (Be prepared to do so.)

Amiable—Open in supportive, people-oriented terms.
Mr. Arnold, I am aware of some of the pressing concerns you must be facing at this time, and I believe our service will help you and your people overcome some of these problems.

Driver—Open in results-oriented terms.
Mr. Arnold, our service will help you increase your sales by fifteen percent in just six months. Are you interested? (Be prepared to prove your statement.)

Suit the Approach to the Person

Most people today have more work than they can hope to complete during regular working hours. Individual consumers, purchasing agents, engineers—anyone a sales representative might contact—feel time pressure and quite naturally regard you as an intruder. Prospects may react with resentment toward anyone who appears intent upon "stealing" precious time to engage in "small talk." How much or how little time you give to small talk or chit-chat depends on the behavioral style of the prospect, the circumstances of the moment, and the nature of your visit. If you sense that the prospect wants to get on with the interview, move on.

Developing Partnerships Using Technology looks at the ways successful salespeople can integrate technology into their daily sales activities. Sales is a very mobile profession, and laptops, tablets, and smartphones can easily synchronize with company contact management programs (see Chapters 6 and 7 for a more in-depth look at these technologies).

Developing Partnerships Using Technology

A Day in the Life of a Salesperson

What does the use of technology look like in the everyday life of a salesperson?

You are a busy salesperson who utilizes the latest and best technology to help you gain accounts and exceed your client's needs. Over morning coffee, you open up your laptop to check in with your contact management program, which is synched to your email and your calendar. You double check prospect meeting times and open up the client detail files. You refresh your memory on important details and see if your prospect has posted anything on Facebook or Twitter. Your tickler alert beeps, so you open up the file of a new prospect you've been working with. Again, you check personal details, check Twitter and Facebook, and do a quick Google search to see if anything else comes up. You know this prospect is busy and on-the-go, so you send her a follow-up email asking to meet with her. However, make sure to set up another alert for a few days later in case she hasn't responded.

At 8:30, you reach for your tablet computer, and open up your presentation software to make sure it is ready to go and personalized for your first prospect meeting. You make a few tweaks, put it in your briefcase, and then grab your smartphone and keys. Programming in the first meeting place on your phone's GPS, you head out the door, pumped about another great day of meeting prospects' needs.

Consider Getting These Smart Technologies on *Your* Sales Team:

Slim laptops

Notebooks

Smartphones

Tablet Computers

Contact Management Software

Types of Approaches

Because every prospect and every selling situation is different, you must have several approach methods available in order to use the one that best fits the particular circumstance. Learn the principles of each of the different types of approaches so that you can use whichever one is appropriate for a particular situation. How many approach techniques are enough? The answer is simple—you cannot have too many. The personality style of prospects, the mood they're in as you greet them, and your own feelings and mood that particular day suggest the need to have an opening for every occasion and every situation. You may have to deviate 180 degrees from the opening and presentation you had planned.

Self-Introduction Approach

This approach is commonly used, but it is the weakest approach to use alone. A smile, a firm handshake, and a relaxed but professional manner should accompany the introduction. Address the prospect by name (pronouncing it correctly), state your name and company, and present your business card. Although the business card is optional, it is a useful reminder of your name, and the prospect will not have to ask you to repeat your name. Here is an example of a typical self-introduction:

Good morning, Blakele. My name is John Robbins. It's nice to meet you. I'm glad you could make time to see me today.." (Accompany this with a firm handshake and a smile to begin to establish trust).

To increase the effectiveness of the self-introduction approach, follow it immediately with one of the other approaches. The consumer-benefit approach, for instance, is generally a good fit.

Consumer-Benefit Approach

Give the prospect a reason for listening and suggest a risk for failure to listen. The benefit statement should be unique and appeal to the prospect's dominant buying motive. It should be sincere and must never sound like a gimmick. Something new and different about your product or service that paves the way for the rest of the interview is a good choice.

Good morning, Mr. Bricker. I am Kevin Dolan with Personal Best Gym and Fitness. I'm glad you stopped by to take fifteen minutes for me to introduce you to our facilities that will, first of all, give you 24-hour access—secondly, provide you with cardio, circuit, and free weights training, as well as give you access to professional certified personal training, and third—and probably the best part of all—is that it will help you reach and maintain your fitness goals.

This example combines both the self-introduction and the consumer-benefit approaches. Because most business people want to offer value to their customers, presenting this benefit statement may well cause the prospect to seek more information. Such a statement often sparks questions from the prospect that lead directly into the presentation.

Curiosity Approach

The curiosity approach works best when you know something about the prospect. Used sensibly, this approach is an effective opener. Suppose you are selling a telecommuting software package so a sales force can get up-to-date information on their laptops when they are out in the field selling. You might say something like this:

Mr. Sherrill, have you ever been in a meeting when a written report analyzing a new competitive product is brought to your attention for the first time, and you want to share parts of it with your salespeople immediately? Do you know how much time you are losing by having to edit the report manually?

People with certain behavioral styles, particularly analyticals and drivers, may find this approach offensive, especially if it sounds gimmicky.

Question Approach

The question approach quickly establishes two-way communication. It enables you to investigate the prospect's needs and apply the benefits of your product or service to those expressed needs. This type of approach suggests your interest in the prospect's problems and draws attention to the need to identify problems.

You may frame a leading question designed to obtain mental commitment from the prospect and at the same time show a major benefit. Here are two examples of how this might be done:

1. *Mr. Duerr, you want to have distinctive-looking, quality-driven reports and the most up-to-date pricing information to share with your customers, don't you?*

2. *Do you feel you could get more accomplished in meetings if you had complete and current information at your fingertips? Wouldn't you also like the capability to easily edit that information, thus enabling you to provide your customers the best support possible?*

Qualifying Question Approach

This variation of the question approach seeks a commitment from the prospect. This qualifying question approach asks the prospect to consider buying the product; it can help determine whether you have a prospect who is cold, lukewarm, or red hot toward your opportunity. Here are two illustrations of how this technique could be used:

1. *Mr. Armstrong, if I can satisfactorily demonstrate to you that the long-distance service provided by our company will save you at least $5,000 within the next three months, would you be willing to do business with us?*

2. *Mr. Mickelson, I am looking for individuals who have the discretionary funds to invest in an opportunity that will produce a return on their investment of at least 15 percent. If I can show you the evidence to support this claim, would you be willing to invest with us?*

These may seem like bold questions, but if the prospect says yes, you have a sale—provided you can back up your statement with valid proof.

Compliment Approach

Opening with a compliment is like walking on eggshells, but this opening is highly effective if used properly. Follow the same guidelines you would use in any situation: offer compliments with empathy, warmth, and sincerity. The purpose is to signal your sincere interest in the prospect. Sources of information for the compliment will vary. Information from a person who provided a referral or from an item you saw online, in a newspaper or trade journal about the prospect can tell you about significant accomplishments that you genuinely admire. You can also see hints in the company office as you arrive or see an item in the prospect's private office that suggests a potential basis for a compliment.

Camco Inc., with international headquarters in Houston, sells gas-lift equipment, well-completion systems, safety systems, and wire line tools and units to the oil industry. At a time when the oil industry is experiencing some instability, a Camco salesperson would be out of line to compliment a prospect on the company's "obvious prosperity." Instead, a compliment should center on some other commendable factor:

I have been impressed with your continuous emphasis on safety on your offshore drilling rigs.
I noticed the recent announcement that your company ranked first in safety ratings last year
You must be proud of that achievement.

This type of compliment not only builds rapport but also directs the prospect's train of thought toward safety and the related products that Camco has to sell. Whenever a compliment is used as an opening, it must be *specific*, of *genuine interest* to the prospect, and *sincere*.

Referral Approach

The referral approach is especially useful because it helps you establish leverage by borrowing the influence of someone the prospect trusts and respects. If you use a referral card signed by the person who provided the prospect's name, you can give it to the prospect to introduce yourself and your company. This approach enhances your credibility and increases the likelihood that the prospect will give you full attention. Here are two good examples:

1. *Miss Reid, your neighbor Rob Hibray has recently completed one of our courses in personal leadership. He told me that you are also interested in growing as a person and in becoming a better leader, and suggested that you would like to hear about what our company has to offer. (Give the referral card to the prospect.)*

2. *Mr. Flanders, I am Chris Elkins with Rivet Software Group. Rita Dadosky, who recently purchased an inventory software package from us, suggested that I contact you. She thought you would like to have an opportunity to consider whether our technology solutions and cost-saving features could also be of benefit to you.*

Educational Approach

The educational approach reflects the trend towards relationship selling. Here, salespeople research the field so thoroughly, they are able to present new information to the prospect by becoming an authority not just on the product, but on the industry or market the product serves. The presentation becomes less of a sales pitch and more of an educational lesson for the prospect. This shifts the power dynamic in favor of the one doing the teaching, which could be especially effective in a virtual meeting, where you can't develop your credibility, at least initially, face-to-face. Here is how this approach could be implemented:

Hello, I'm with Fit Mom magazine, and we've done some studies and found out that in your industry, there are five things that make companies fail and five things that make them succeed. I'm going to be sharing this information with [name their competitors here], and I wondered if you were interested in seeing this same data.[24]

Product Approach

This approach consists of actually handing the product or some physical representation of it to a prospect to produce a positive reaction. The product approach provides a visible image of the product or service. This approach should focus on the uniqueness of the product and, as far as possible, allow the product to tell its own story.

In the last five years, a unique phenomenon has literally "popped up" in the world of retail sales. Many prominent businesses —from Godiva chocolate, to Nike and Reebok, to Illy coffee, to Ebay—have created "pop up" stores, which are temporary, creative spaces placed in unexpected locations. Customers are invited to enter the space and try the products. Salespeople would be wise to incorporate this hands-on approach into their own meetings. If you have great software, make sure to give the prospect plenty of time to play with it. If you are selling a beauty product, bring the best samples to let the prospect try and keep. Whatever your product is, make sure it is beautifully presented and packaged and that you encourage discussion after the product is sampled.

Remember, bringing the product to the prospect stirs interest, permits a demonstration, makes a multiple sense appeal, and usually creates in the prospect a feeling of commitment to listen and to participate actively in the presentation. For example, a smartphone sales representative might say:

The Face-to-Face Relationship Model of Selling

"Mr. Stone, chances are, your busy field reps rarely have time to sit down. So why give them a computer that needs a lap? Our new smartphone helps them work better anywhere. Here, catch."

Sometimes you cannot bring the actual product with you because of size or other constraints. You can use other devices to simulate the actual product. A piece of literature, a sample of the output of the machine, a small working model, a flash animation or model, a picture—any visual tool that the prospect can hold or look at helps to focus his attention. If you are selling a service, such as a time-management program, hand the prospect a letter from a satisfied client that identifies specific benefits of the program. Statistical data that shows the return on investment earned by satisfied clients can accomplish the same purpose.

Transition from the Approach

Whatever approach you decide to use, it should be directly related to your plan for beginning the need discovery phase of the presentation. The exchange of conversation in the approach phase allows you to move smoothly into the questions you plan to ask to discover the needs of the prospect. If your opening has involved "chit-chat with a purpose," the transition is fairly simple.

Any compliment you offer should relate to the general area of your product or service so that the presentation grows naturally from the opening. A consumer-benefit opening obviously leads directly into need discovery. A product approach immediately gets the prospect involved in examining your offering. The referral approach focuses upon your product or service the approval of someone whom the prospect respects; it emphasizes the referring person's belief that the prospect will be interested.

Because the actual presentation of benefits cannot begin until the prospect agrees to having a need for what you have to offer, whatever you can do to make need discovery seem a natural process will be helpful. Chapter 10 deals with the critical task of discovering needs by asking questions and listening. The degree of rapport established between you and the prospect during the approach determines how willing the prospect will be to answer your questions and accept your buying recommendation.

SUMMARY

- What you do and say in the initial moments of the face-to-face or online interview has a profound effect on the success of the close. Plan those initial moments carefully. The first 10 words out of your mouth are crucial.

- Be aware of the power of first impressions. You never get a second chance to make a good one.

- Proper dress and grooming give the prospect the feeling that you are competent.

- Appropriate choices in dress and grooming let the prospect focus on your sales message instead of on your physical appearance.

- The greeting is important to create a favorable first impression. Use the prospect's name often and begin with some "chit-chat with a purpose" to feel out the mood and behavioral style of the prospect.

- Use a firm handshake, maintain eye contact, and make use of voice properties that reflect confidence.

- Confirm or modify your impressions of the prospect's behavioral style and adapt your plans for the presentation accordingly.

- A good approach forms a natural transition into the need discovery phase of the selling process. A number of different types of approaches are available:

    1. The self-introduction

2. Consumer-benefit

3. Curiosity

4. Question

5. Qualifying question

6. Compliment

7. Referral

8. Educational

9. Product

REVIEW QUESTIONS

1. What are the four objectives of an effective approach?

2. What are components of Nonverbal Language? Why are these items called Nonverbal Language?

3. What would you consider appropriate dress for calling on an insurance executive? A manager of a health and fitness facility?

4. What is the purpose of small talk? How can you use it to best advantage? For what kind of situation is small talk a negative?

5. Name and explain the nine types of approaches discussed in the chapter. Why does a salesperson need to master several approaches?

6. What are the advantages of bringing a product to the prospect? What are alternatives if bringing the product is not feasible?

7. Should the greeting you use be planned ahead of time, or should you depend largely on the inspiration of the moment? Justify your choice.

8. Under what conditions would you change the approach you had planned when you arrive for an interview?

9. List some guidelines for making a good first impression.

10. What are some weaknesses of evaluating a prospect totally on your first impression?

11. What can you learn about a prospect from a handshake?

ROLE-PLAY EXERCISES

The following role-play exercises help build teams, improve communication, and emphasize the real-world side of selling. They are meant to be challenging, to help you learn how to deal with problems that have no single right answer, and to use a variety of skills beyond those employed in a typical review question. Read and complete each activity. Then in the next class, discuss and compare answers with other classmates.

Role Play 9.1 – Dress for Success!

On a day selected by your instructor, come to class dressed for the role of salesperson to represent a company or organization in a field in which you would like to work. You should attend to the details of your attire and appearance as much as possible in order to make a good first impression. In addition, be prepared to role play greeting your prospective customer for the first time through the first words of your approach. Your instructor will invite other members of the class to critique your appearance and your initial greeting or exchange.

Alternatively, you can dress for a job interview with the company or organization for which you would like to work. You should prepare to role play your greeting and your approach through your response to a typical interview question, "So tell me about yourself." Again, your colleagues will be invited to critique your appearance and your initial greeting or exchange.

Role Play 9.2 – First Impressions

For this exercise, pair up with another student in the class.

In this role play, one of you will play the part of a B2B customer, while your partner will play the part of the salesperson. You may select the product or service to be sold.

According to Chapter 9, every salesperson has approximately 4 minutes to make a successful first impression and approach. Much depends on how quickly the salesperson can evaluate the personality or social style of the prospect so that the approach can be adjusted to fit the prospect's basic traits.

For this role play, you should work together outside of class to develop two brief scripts. For the prospect, you should select one of the basic social styles (review these if necessary). For that social style, create a script for both the prospect and salesperson that is *unlikely to work*. Create another script that you think is *likely to succeed*. Rehearse both scripts and be prepared to role play them in class.

CASE STUDIES

The following case studies present you with selling scenarios that require you to apply the critical skills discussed in the chapter and give you training through simulation, role-playing, and practical learning situations. They are meant to be both engaging and challenging, and like the role-play exercises, don't have one right answer.

Case 9.1 – A Referral Gone Awry

Rita Thurber represents a small publisher, Coastal Maine Publishing Co., that typically markets a small list of poets, travel magazines, children's books, and good, but relatively unknown, authors of fiction. Rita is opening up a new territory on Maryland's Eastern Shore, and is meeting the owner of an independent bookshop, Sam Wetherington, for the first time. Since the store is located in an upscale village to which the wealthy escape from Washington, D.C., and where tourists moor their sailboats, Rita surmises that the store's clientele would be a perfect match for her company's offerings.

Rita has prepared carefully for this interview. She is dressed stylishly in a navy blue blazer, grey slacks, a pink striped blouse, and low heels. She has researched Mr. Wetherington's online merchandise, and she comes armed with a referral from one of her own authors. The bell tinkles as she steps through the front door, and she immediately spots Mr. Wetherington sitting at a desk behind the counter.

"Hi. Mr. Wetherington? I'm Rita Thurber from Coastal Maine Publishing. It's nice to meet you," Rita says as she strides across the room, her hand extended in greeting. "Thanks for agreeing to meet with me."

"Welcome to my shop," replies Wetherington, shaking her hand. "Please call me Sam."

"You have a lovely store here. Just like Milton Stokes described it. In fact, Milton is the main reason I'm here. As you may recall, we feature his books of poetry."

"Oh, yes. Milton. We hosted a book signing for him once. Big mistake. He teaches at the local college part-time, and we thought it might get some new customers here from the college people and their families. But it never worked out. Milton's a terrible poet, and his stuff just doesn't sell. I took a large shipment of his latest volume, but had to return nearly all of it to your company. What a terrible experience."

"Oh, I'm sorry." Rita responded. Sam's negative criticism threw her for a loop. Using Milton's name clearly got things off on the wrong foot. What could she say to turn things around—and quickly?

Case 9.2 – Grasping the Relay Baton

Jamie couldn't believe her good luck. After accepting a sales position last month with OfficeDecor, Inc., a company that sells office furnishings to medium size companies and professional offices, she learned that she will be assigned to a different territory with sole responsibility for new and existing accounts. Sally, the salesperson previously responsible for that territory, left the company under something of a cloud (Jamie hasn't been told what the problem was); sales in the territory had declined during the past year as well. Still, Jamie was excited when Pete, her manager, called her in for a meeting. This was her big chance!

"Well, Jamie, I bet you're excited to be assigned to this territory," Pete said. "You know, however, that you're walking into a difficult situation. The territory has a lot of potential, but taking over from someone else under these circumstances can be challenging."

"I know, Pete," Jamie replied, sitting on the edge of her chair. "But I think I'm up to it. It's not like customers in this territory haven't heard of OfficeDecor. I know the product line, and most of the customers are already qualified."

"That's true," Pete agreed. "And I'm sure that you can break the ice with new prospects just fine. But Sally left some of her customers with a bad experience by overpromising delivery schedules. You're going to have some fence-mending to do, and I want you to think carefully about how you're going to approach these people."

"Well, I'm not going to make the same mistake that Sally did," promised Jamie. "But you're right: I've never had to deal with this sort of situation before. Introducing myself, getting their attention, reassuring them that I understand their needs and problems, and so forth will be a big challenge initially."

"Exactly," said Pete. "It's like running a close relay race when you're a couple of paces behind the leader. You can't afford to drop the baton. We're counting on you. Let me know what you come up with."

Recognizing that every situation is a little different, Jamie realized that she needed to develop a basic script that would launch her approach. She decided to consider basic sales approaches and to combine two or three that would help her to achieve her initial goals.

What should Jamie include in her script? Which approach(es) would offer the greatest promise in this situation? Why? Write out a one-paragraph script for Jamie and be prepared to explain your reasoning.

"The greatest motivational act one person can do for another is to listen."

Chapter 10

Identifying Needs
By Questioning and Listening

Learning Objectives

- Understand the purpose of asking questions.

- Learn how to select questioning tactics appropriate for the sales situation.

- Study specific questioning techniques.

- Examine SPIN® Selling and its applications.

- Understand the functions served by various types of questions.

- Appreciate the importance of listening in sales.

- Become acquainted with techniques for improving listening skills.

Use This Page for Taking Notes

Doctors of Selling

What is selling? Some may say selling is filling a need, while others say it's solving a problem. Some people say it's closing the deal as quickly as possible, and by any means necessary. None of those definitions really work!. Selling is ultimately asking people what they do, how they do it, when they do it, where they do it, who they do it with, why they do it that way; and then, and only then, helping them to do it better.[1] *Telling isn't selling—asking is!*

The problem created by the misconception that *talking equals selling* lies in its assumption that every prospect uses the product or service for identical purposes and in the same manner. But in actuality, each prospect has unique needs. Of the many benefits you have to offer, only a few will be the key motivators for a particular prospect.[2] The challenge is to determine their buying criteria before beginning your presentation and then use only the specific benefits that address their particular situation.[3] In addition, customers are less likely to become bored and disinterested if they are actively involved in the presentation.[4]

Salespeople should become *Doctors of Selling*. Physicians know they must clarify the patient's problem and conduct a pragmatic diagnostic process before they can prescribe any treatment. Doctors of selling follow an identical process: They diagnose potential buyers fully to uncover any needs for the salesperson's product or service.[5] If you went to your family doctor complaining of severe back pain, and the doctor—without asking any questions—wrote a prescription for a medicine to be taken three times a day for the next month, would you take it? Of course not! You would not believe the doctor could make an accurate diagnosis and prescribe the appropriate medicine without making a thorough examination and asking a number of probing questions about the problem. You would expect the doctor to understand your problem—not the problem of back pain in general—before prescribing for you. Your prospect has the right to expect the same professional attention.[6]

Need Discovery and the Sales Cycle

The evolution of relationship selling has reached the point where, in many cases, the need discovery step in the sales cycle is more important than making the presentation, handling objections, or closing.[7] Exhibit 10.1 shows the relationship between need discovery and the other basic steps in the face-to-face sales process. At this point of need discovery—not in the close—the sale is most often lost. The dotted line around need discovery in Exhibit 10.1 is a reminder that this step is often skipped or given inadequate attention by the traditional salesperson. In reality, more time should be spent in the approach and in discovering needs than in any other steps of the process.

ΔExhibit 10.1

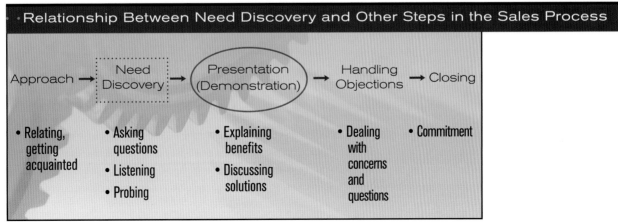

Relationship Between Need Discovery and Other Steps in the Sales Process

Need discovery is the foundation upon which a successful sale is built. Telling prospects what they need is a mistake.[8] Asking questions that allow prospects to discover their own needs and share them with you sets you up as a sounding board for the solutions they "discover" while considering your proposal. Prospects are more receptive when they feel that the solution is their own idea. Successful sales interviews contain more requests for opinions and suggestions by the salesperson and fewer statements of disagreement and tension. And in successful interviews, salespeople control the direction of the interview by the way they ask questions.[9]

People are often unaware of a problem until they are questioned about it. Here is a case in point: A professor at Grand Canyon College in Arizona conveyed an interesting story to the author of how an insurance agent sold him a policy by asking one simple question followed by an observation. The agent asked, "How much life insurance coverage do you have as protection for your family?"

When the professor replied that he had $75,000, the insurance agent shrugged his shoulders and remarked, "I guess you don't plan to be dead very long, then, do you!" This strong statement could easily offend some people. However, it caused him to realize for the first time the substantial disparity between what he had and the actual amount needed that would enable his family to maintain their current lifestyle, should something unexpected happen to him. The professor has continued to buy additional protection from this same agent as his family's needs changed.

Specific Planning of Questions

Asking the right questions is a skill all too often neglected. The majority of the time in sales situations it isn't about asking just *any* questions. It is about asking the *right* questions that help us to understand the perspective of the prospect, clear any misunderstanding, strengthen or break our assumptions, lead to new discoveries, and even close the sale.[10] You must retain control of the questioning phase of the interview so that you obtain the required information and do not detour into irrelevant areas. The old standbys—who, what, when, where, why, and how—are a vital part of the sales interview. Decide in advance what you need to know, and then plan what types of questions will elicit that information in the quickest and most efficient manner consistent with the prospect's social style and situation.

Don't ask just *any* questions. Ask the *right* questions.

Because the sale is made in the mind of the buyer and not in the mind of the salesperson, using the questioning process to gain agreement on key issues is paramount. Once you have gained agreement on key issues, you must assist the prospect in prioritizing those issues and agree that those are the problems or concerns that must be addressed before they make a decision to buy. Prospects are more likely to buy if you establish points of agreement early in the interview. To accomplish this:

- Plan your questions in sequence to gain information in a logical order.
- Predict beforehand all the possible answers to each question so that you are never left wondering what to do next.
- Prepare a smooth transition from every possible answer into the next question.

Some salespeople hesitate to ask questions because they are afraid the prospect will refuse to answer. However, prospects that refuse to cooperate during the need discovery phase are unlikely to cooperate at the end of the sale either. Communication is a two-way street that demands participation by both you and the prospect. If you are to involve prospects in the sales process, you must be prepared to ask the questions that maximize participation. The right questions never materialize out of thin air. Your questions should attempt to achieve four objectives:

1. To discover the prospect's "hot button" or dominant buying motive.

2. To establish the purchase criteria or specifications.

3. To agree on a time frame for completion of negotiations.

4. To gain prospect agreement on the problem(s) before making the presentation.

Andrew Rudin understands the value of asking the right questions

Andrew Rudin is the CEO for Outside Technologies, Inc. and has over 20 years of direct sales experience selling software, services, and hardware. His company caters to large clients, commercial small business owners, and public-sector organizations. He is responsible for developing successful plans to identify and mitigate sales risks. He does this through providing tactical sales execution services as well as sales training and development programs for his clients. Through innovative technology, his team and partners help companies solve strategic and tactical sales challenges, define the value of their product or service, establish strategic business goals, and develop a vision for strategic priorities in the future.

A key aspect of his job involves instructing his clients on how to figure out the right sales questions to ask. Rudin says that the right answers are the result of asking the right questions. Being visible and connected with each client allows him to ask "how" and "why" questions in order to dig deeper into situations and business problems where Outside Technologies, Inc. can assist their customers to compete and win.

Rudin operates and instructs his clients using the following principles: 1. Need discovery begins with an objective, 2. Your company's culture reinforces discovery, 3. Discovery requires establishing a mutual trust between vendor and customer from the beginning, and 4. Before you meet with a prospect you must develop a question and answer roadmap. The roadmap represents the top questions that you want answered. When creating the question and answer roadmap, the questions can be separated into four related groups that Rudin outlines for each of his clients. These groups involve qualification, network and contact, attitude and sentiment, and validation.[11]

Strategic Recommendations

As you select specific questioning methods, keep these four tactics in mind:[12]

1. **Avoid Technical Language That Might Confuse the Prospect.** An account executive selling ad space to a small business owner should avoid terms such as kerning, bodoni extra bold, mistral fonts, or bleed page unless certain that the prospect is technically sophisticated and would expect to use such terms. In the same way, using company stock numbers, codes, or abbreviations may confuse the client. Your goal is to promote understanding and not to demonstrate your own personal erudition.

2. **Establish a Clear Agenda.** Chapter nine presented four specific objectives of the approach: To make a favorable first impression, to gain attention, to create interest, and to serve as a logical transition into need discovery. This transition into need discovery requires that you tell the prospect exactly what you intend to accomplish during the interview session. You are to provide a clear agenda for the sales interview. Always let the prospect know what you want to accomplish. You can set up the

desired atmosphere by requesting permission to ask questions. Here are two practical permissive questions:

1. *I believe I can offer you a service that will be of considerable value to you, but in order for me to be sure, and to know a little more about your particular situation, would it be okay if I ask you a few questions?*

2. *The only way for us to know how my company can best serve your needs is for you to give me permission to ask a few personal questions. Will that be all right with you? Oh, and may I make some notes while we talk?*

3. **Phrase Each Question So That It Has One Clear Purpose.** An ambiguous question or one with multiple meanings creates misunderstanding between you and the prospect. Proceed logically, one topic at a time. Murphy's Law operates here: Anything that can be misunderstood will be misunderstood. A corollary to this principle is equally important: Phrase each question to produce the maximum amount of information so that the number of questions needed to elicit the required information is as small as possible. Exhibit 10.2 gives a good example of how not to do it.[13]

ΔExhibit 10.2

Focusing the Questioning Process

A real estate agent wants to find out how many children the prospect has, their ages and gender. Poor planning produces a scenario like this:

AGENT: Do you have any children?

PROSPECT: Yes.

AGENT: How many?

PROSPECT: Three.

AGENT: How old are they?

PROSPECT: 11, 9, and 7.

AGENT: Are they all boys or all girls?

PROSPECT: Two boys and one girl.

AGENT: What age is the girl?

PROSPECT: She's the 7 year-old.

At this rate, the agent will be asking questions all day. Why not simplify the process with one straightforward question:

AGENT: What are the ages and genders of your children?

4. **Use the "Repeat a Fact" Technique.** Sometimes a prospect will share a piece of information that may be buried in the context of other information or in an answer to another question. For example, let's say a prospect is discussing returns from last year and mentions a number like 15 percent. Repeat the number back to him, pause, and let the prospect elaborate on what that number means to the company. There was a reason the prospect told you this, so allow him the opportunity to reveal what that motive was and it may lead to a way you can help improve that number.[14]

The Spin® Technique

Neil Rackham is president and founder of Huthwaite Inc. and the author of the book *Spin Selling*. His corporation's 12-year, $1 million research into effective sales performance resulted in the unique sales strategy, the SPIN® method: **Situation**, **Problem**, **Implication**, and **Need-Payoff** questions. Successful salespeople don't ask random questions. This model represents how relationship salespeople probe. These are guidelines, not a rigid formula. There is a distinct pattern in the successful call. The answers you get will be used during the presentation to help underscore how the benefits you give support, reinforce, and provide answers to the questions you have asked during need discovery. Its questioning sequence taps directly into the psychology behind the buying process. The questions provide a road map for you, guiding the sales call through the steps of need development until explicit needs have been agreed upon. You want to allow customers to discover for themselves the problems they have. People don't like to think, and certainly don't want to admit, their problems are that obvious.[15]

SPIN® Selling in Action

Let's take a specific example of a company and demonstrate the SPIN® method just as they might use it. A business with overdue accounts receivables has three options: It can hire a conventional percentage-based agency, a flat-fee agency, or do the collecting internally. Transworld Systems Inc. (TSI) is one of the largest collection agencies in the country. TSI works with over 60,000 clients helping them to recover their slow-paying and delinquent accounts without having to pay up to 50 percent of the collection as charged by a conventional agency. Many clients with a wide range of account balances have found the TSI system to be the only economical method of obtaining professional third-party collection results. TSI pays the money they collect directly to the client, the client maintains control of their accounts, and they do not have to pay a percentage. TSI has a low flat fee that enables clients to assign their accounts in the early stages of delinquency, thus providing the best opportunity for successful recovery.[16] Here is the SPIN® technique in action:

Situation Questions. These questions are designed to find out about the customer's situation. These are data-gathering questions. They ask about the prospect's general state of affairs or circumstances as it relates to the services TSI has to offer. They help the TSI sales rep get to know the prospects and obtain initial information about their background and situation. You are looking for a general understanding of the prospect's needs. The following questions have an important fact-finding role, are non-threatening, and help to build an atmosphere of trust and cooperation:

- Do you make the purchasing decision?
- How many active accounts do you bill each month?
- Do you do all the collection of overdue accounts internally?
- About what percentage of your customers do not pay their bills on time?
- Do you have out-of-state accounts?
- Is the billing and follow-up done in this office?
- Do you currently use a collection agency?

Problem Questions. Once the TSI sales reps feel comfortable about the buyer's situation, they move on to a second type of questioning technique. These questions explore needs, any difficulties they may be having, and dissatisfactions in areas where TSI's service could be the solution. The goal in this step is to have the prospect say, "I really do have a problem with the collection of my accounts receivables."

TSI wants to determine explicit needs or uncover the prospect's "hot button." Remember: The sale is made in the mind of the buyer, not in the mind of the TSI salesperson. Customers don't want to be told they have a problem; allow them to discover it for themselves. Whatever they say is true; when you say it, they doubt it! You're searching for areas where the services TSI offers can solve their specific problem. If you can uncover problems your service can solve, then you're providing the buyer with something useful. Ask these kinds of problem questions:

- Do you know how much it costs to do your collecting internally?
- Do you ever get mail back? Wrong address? No longer at the address?
- When do you consider an account to be a concern or problem?
- Do you ever get checks back NSF or ACCOUNT CLOSED?
- Do you have a service to help recover these checks? If yes, is it a guaranteed service?

Implication Questions. Implication questions build up the magnitude of the problem so that it's seen as serious in the mind of the prospect, and then the sales rep uses need-payoff questions to build up the value of the solution. Implication questions are the language of decision-makers, and if you can talk their language, you'll influence them. In larger sales you need to ask this third type of question. The phrasing of implication questions is critical because you want the prospect to discuss the problem and how it might be improved.

Attach a bottom-line figure to the implication questions. The TSI sales rep wants the prospect to agree that the implications of the problem are causing such things as loss of revenue, ill-will with some of its customer base, prohibitive cost of time and money in trying to do the collection themselves, and expensive percentage-based collection agencies. The prospects must see that the problem is serious enough that it outweighs the cost of the solution, namely, using the services of TSI. The TSI sales rep might ask these questions:

- Would it help if the money was paid directly to you? In the last five years, we collected over $2.4 billion for our clients and the money was paid directly to them.
- Do you know most collection agencies deposit the money they collect into their own bank account and hold it up to 60 days?
- Would it be important to you to recover a larger share of delinquent accounts and bad checks faster than a conventional collection agency and put the money directly into your hands and let it work for you?
- Is it safe to say that you would like to collect delinquent accounts quickly, without disturbing ongoing relationships with those customers?

Need-Payoff Questions. How would that help? What benefits do you see? Why is it important to solve this problem? Is it useful to solve this problem? These questions get the customer to tell you the benefits that your solution offers. These types of questions actually get prospects to name benefits and tell you why they should buy. These questions help you build up the value of your proposed solution in the customer's mind. You want to focus the customer's attention on the solution rather than on the problem. This creates a positive problem-solving atmosphere.

In the words of an eight-year-old named Quincy, "Implication questions are always sad; while need-payoff questions are always happy." That's because implication questions are problem-centered, while the following need-payoff questions are solution-centered:[17]

- Would it be useful to speed up the rate of collection, and at the same time be guaranteed that you will recover at least twice as much as you pay for our service?
- If you could create the perfect agency, what would you want them to do for you?
- If I can show you how TSI has been able to help others in your industry, and we can determine what kind of results you might expect, can we get started today? Let's take a look at your aging report.
- We automatically send out a report detailing the status of each account assigned for collection. Does this sound like something that would interest you?
- Do you want the account handled diplomatically or intensively? We have another division that handles the hard-core collection problems. Would you like to have that option?
- Would you like us to send a "thank you" card to the debtor after the account has been paid?

Common Questioning Techniques

The major types of questioning techniques are summarized in Exhibit 10.3. Questions are generally classified by the type of answers required and by the purpose they are intended to serve. Begin the questioning process with closed-end questions or fact-finding questions that are easy to answer and therefore not threatening to the prospect. If the first few questions are reasonable, the prospect begins to gain confidence and feel comfortable with the questioning process. The next questions then, although progressively more challenging, seem easier to handle.

ΔExhibit 10.3

Types of Questions and Probing Techniques

General types of questions

1. *Closed-end questions.* Provide a series of responses from which the prospect selects one, are easy to answer, used to get feedback, and can be used to get prospect commitment.

2. *Open-end questions.* Identify a topic but do not provide structured alternatives for responses, usually begin with "how" or "what", cannot be answered "yes" or "no", and are designed to stimulate the prospect's thinking.

Classification of questioning techniques

1. *Amplification questions.* Ask prospect to expand on an answer; do not direct thoughts but encourage prospect to continue talking. (Double-check, nonverbal gestures, silence, and continuation questions)

2. *Internal summary questions.* Assimilate information presented, put it in perspective, and ask if the interpretation is correct; may repeat all of prospect's last response in the form of a question. (Reflective or internal summary question)

3. *Getting agreement on the problem.* Make a formal statement of the problem, get prospect to agree, and attempt to get commitment. (Formal statement of the problem)

Closed-End Questions. These questions are direct, fact-finding questions that are designed to reveal background information about the prospect's business and/or family. They ask an either-or question or request a choice from a series of suggested responses. Closed-end questions are usually answered with a very brief response, often a single word. They often ask for a yes or no response or a choice between two alternatives. They are directive questions for which you want specific answers:

- How many employees do you have working the day shift?

- With what interconnect companies are you familiar?

- Is a rear-window defogger important to you?

- Does your company pay the full cost of employee health insurance, or do the employees pay part of the cost?

You may also phrase closed-end questions to get feedback or to gain commitment:

- Would you like delivery Friday, or is Monday of next week all right?

- Are you responsible for making the decision to purchase from us or will there be others involved?

- Do you know what your customers do with your product after buying it?

- Do you prefer to pay cash, or would you like to arrange a monthly payment plan?

Closed-end questions may be used as a substitute for telling the prospect something. A question can sometimes make a point in a more telling manner than a statement because the prospect must think to answer it, and thinking makes a stronger impression than hearing. Consider these two ways to impart the same message:

1. Our procedure will completely eliminate waste in your welding operations.

2. How much savings would you have if you used a procedure that completely eliminates waste from your welding operations?

The first method tells the prospect something. The salesperson hopes the prospect is impressed, but that may not happen. Unless the prospect reacts strongly enough to the statement to break in with a comment, any skepticism is buried until some later point, where it emerges as a vague objection or stall like, "Well, we're not thinking of making any changes just now."

The question method, however, gains attention because the prospect has to think about an answer. Disbelief surfaces immediately where it can be dealt with instead of being postponed until later when the salesperson is trying to close. Exhibit 10.4 lists the various purposes served by asking closed-end questions.

ΔExhibit 10.4

Purposes of Closed-End Questions

- Uncover specific facts.

- Reduce prospect tension because they are easy to answer.

- Check for understanding and receive feedback.

- Maintain control by directing the flow of conversation.

- Reinforce prospect commitment to a specific position.

Open-End Questions. These broadly phrased questions allow prospects plenty of room to answer as they wish. They call for explanations. Open-end questions encourage prospects to discuss their needs by explaining their preferences, expectations, or judgments. Open-end questions tend to be general rather than specific. Use them when you want the prospect to talk freely. You can encourage the prospect to verbalize feelings by asking questions that begin with "What do you think?" or "How do you feel?" Talking out loud often helps people clarify and organize their thoughts. Real feelings are often not in the conscious awareness until they are verbalized.[18]

Open-end questions help you and the prospect sort out ideas and begin to make decisions. Here are some examples of questions that give prospects the freedom and responsibility to express their own thoughts and use their own information in the decision-making process:

- What options would you want on your new Mercedes?
- How do you think I might be able to help you?
- In a perfect world, what would you like to see us deliver?
- What are five unique characteristics of your business?
- What benefits would you expect from our ten-week, self-paced time-management program?

Open-end questions reveal attitudes that a salesperson must be aware of if the sale is to be closed. You cannot easily ask a prospect, "Are you motivated by pride?" but you can ask open-end questions designed to detect this emotion, and you then have the answer to the direct question you cannot ask. Exhibit 10.5 lists the properties of open-end questions.

ΔExhibit 10.5

The Properties of Open-End Questions

- Allow the prospect to move in any direction.
- Cannot be answered with "yes" or "no".
- Ordinarily begin with "how" or "what".
- Designed to stimulate the prospect's thinking and increase dialogue.
- Help determine dominant buying motives (rational or emotional).
- Uncover the social or behavioral style of the prospect.

Classification of Questioning Techniques

The questions salespeople ask can be classified by the purpose they are intended to perform. Three basic classes of questions can be used: Amplification, internal summary or reflective, and questions to gain agreement on the problem. Either open-end or closed-end questions may be asked for any of these purposes, depending upon the situation. If one type of question does not provide all the information needed, another type can be used to get a more specific response or to elicit a better sense of the prospect's point of view.

Relationship selling is more than a process in which two people sit together in a room and take turns talking. As the salesperson, you must be certain that the prospect knows what you are talking about and understands it. You must also be sure that you understand the prospect, know that person's needs and desires, and be certain you can satisfy them. You need feedback, and asking questions is the method for receiving feedback.

Be careful how you phrase the questions you ask. Place the responsibility for not understanding on yourself rather than on the prospect. "Do you understand what I said?" or "Did you get that?" or "Are you with me?" seems to imply that the prospect may not be too bright. You must take responsibility for any possible misunderstanding by asking, "Have I explained this clearly enough? Is there some part I need to clarify or go over again?"

Amplification Questions

Ask probing questions and listen to your customer.[19] These questioning techniques encourage prospects to continue to provide enlightening information and encourage them to explain the meaning of a statement made. Amplification questions help both salespeople and prospects. At times prospects may not make themselves clear; they may wander off the subject or may stop talking before you can fully understand their position. In a subtle manner, these techniques ask the prospect to expand on or clarify the meaning of a statement and help identify the frame of reference used. There are four types of amplification questions:

Double-Check Question. A double-check question is a means of giving feedback to the prospect. It involves taking the information the prospect has provided, rephrasing it, and handing it right back. A prospect might tell a motor freight salesperson, "Every Tuesday and Thursday the whole yard is backed up with trucks for the entire afternoon." The salesperson might offer feedback by saying, "Now as I understand it, you find that your loading platforms get badly jammed at peak hours." This statement is actually a question because it evokes an answer. It serves the dual purpose of clarifying the salesperson's impression of the situation and solidifying the prospect's opinion.

Nonverbal Gestures. Visual cues such as nodding the head or leaning forward show that you are listening, believe the prospect is on the right track, and understand what the prospect is saying. You may also inject appropriate words or phrases to encourage the prospect to continue: "You don't say?" "Is that right?" "That's interesting!" You may imply a question by the nonverbal choice of silence accompanied by a slightly raised eyebrow or furrowed brow.

Silence. Silence is a powerful sales tool. When prospects avoid telling you the whole truth, the knowledge that they are being less than honest makes them uncomfortable. Your silence convinces them to go ahead and tell you the whole story. Silence allows you to slow down and relax the pace of asking questions. Some prospects want to think and contemplate longer than others before responding to your questions. Give people time to reply at their own pace. Silence also gives you valuable time to formulate your own next question or comment.

Continuation Questions. Continuation questions encourage prospects to keep on talking by making a positive request for more information. Such questions do not push for a particular response or for agreement; they just encourage more communication from the prospect. Here are two examples:

1. What additional thoughts or questions do you have regarding our shipping policies?
2. Could you tell me in a bit more detail why you feel that way?

Exhibit 10.6 lists the advantages of using amplification questions.

Δ**Exhibit 10.6**

Advantages of Using Amplification Questions

- Encourage the prospect to continue to provide revealing information.
- Allows the salesperson to rephrase what the prospect appears to have intended.
- Invites the prospect to expand or clarify any point of disagreement.
- Narrows down generalizations and clears ambiguities.

Internal Summary Questions

Probes designed to get prospects to think, see, and consider your interpretation of the situation may be called internal summary or reflective questions. Summarize what you understood the prospect to mean. You want to assimilate the information provided, place it in the perspective that suits your purpose, and ask if the interpretation is correct.

You achieve this by repeating all or part of the prospect's last response in the form of a question or by rephrasing the entire idea expressed by the prospect, feeding it back in a slightly different form, and asking for confirmation. Consider the following example in which a company president explains why the firm may not be able to sponsor an in-house blood drive. Note how the salesperson empathizes and rewords or echoes the president's remarks but suggests the process can be accomplished without disruption:

> **Prospect (company president)**: My company has always felt the need to support the charitable activities of organizations like yours. But where do we draw the line? I am constantly besieged with requests for my company's time. We have only so many hours a day.
>
> **Salesperson (donor consultant)**: I certainly understand how you feel. If I were in your position, I'd probably feel the same way. I sense that the blood donor program is something you wholeheartedly endorse. But with only so many hours in the working day, humanitarian concerns take a back seat to the realities of the business world. However, if you thought this could be accomplished with a minimum of time lost, and you felt your employees really wanted to do it, it could be done. May I tell you how we manage it?

These types of questions are useful throughout the interview. Every salesperson knows about summarizing the key benefits just before asking for the order: "Now, as I see it, we've agreed that a complete line, with these particular items featured, will move for you with the proper promotion. Am I right about that?" Such summary techniques are especially useful during the close.

The summary question may be used to underscore points on which you already agree. An occasional summary of the points to which the prospect has already agreed will fix them firmly in the mind of the prospect and demonstrate just how wide an area of agreement there is between the two of you.

Getting Agreement

In *Open the Mind, Close the Sale*, John Wilson says that the salesperson's failure to confirm the problem is one of the biggest mistakes in selling. The underlying purpose of asking questions is to determine whether the prospect has a problem or need that you are capable of solving. State the problem in your own words and get the prospect to agree, "Yes, that's it." Never begin the actual presentation phase of the sales interview until the problem has been clearly established in the minds of both you and the prospect. Begin the formal statement of the problem by using such phrases as these:

- Let me attempt to summarize what we have been saying.

- As I understand it, here is (are) the problem(s) we must solve.

- Based on your answers to my questions, I see the problem as . . .

After you pinpoint the problem, you must seek confirmation. Get the prospect to agree by following your summary of the problem with questions like these:

- If I show you some comparisons demonstrating that my company can save you money without sacrificing quality, would you commit to our program?[20]

- Is that a fair statement of the way things stand?

- If I can satisfactorily demonstrate a solution to these concerns of yours, would it be enough to earn your business?

If the prospect agrees with the problem statement, you are ready to present the specific benefits of your product or service that can solve the problem. Even if the prospect disagrees with your summary of the problem, you have both learned by sharing information.

Listening

Everybody wants the secret to closing more sales, but it's no secret. If you're not closing sales, you're not listening to the customer. Salespeople are so busy telling their prospects or customers all the wonderful things that their products or services will do for them instead of being quiet and

You were given two ears and one tongue. So listen twice as much as you talk!

letting the prospects tell them what they need.[21] Prospects are not patiently sitting at their desks waiting for you to call so they can buy your product. People are not easily sold, which is why you must do more than mechanically go through your script. Prospects can sense insincerity, and they will know if you are not really listening to them and giving only scripted generic responses. Listen—your prospect will reveal his needs and show you how you can help him.[22]

Eighty percent of waking hours is spent communicating, and about half of that listening. Effective listening is not just hearing what the prospect is saying. Faulty listening results in misunderstanding and lost opportunities.[23] Research indicates that 60 percent of misunderstandings in business are due to poor listening.[24] Fortunately, improved listening skills can be learned. When a salesperson listens intently to prospects, they are likely to have a very positive reaction when it is the salesperson's turn to speak. Actively listening to prospects not only increases the effectiveness of the interaction, it also greatly increases the chance of making a sale.[25]

To succeed in professional selling, you must be able to offer a product or service that satisfies the buyer's needs. Presenting features and benefits is not always enough. How they are presented may be as important as what is presented. Listening is the key to finding ways to present benefits that enhance the possibility of a close. Effective listening helps sales professionals catch verbal and nonverbal signals indicating a prospect who is interested in buying their product or service. "Unfortunately, good listening skills usually require a change in our behavior," says Barry Elms, CEO of Strategic Negotiations International.[26]

Psychologists claim that listening uses only about 25 percent of our brain. The other 75 percent either thinks about what to say next or stops listening if the conversation is boring or of no interest. Exhibit 10.7 is an example of the kind of listening that destroys any credibility you have or ever hope to establish.[27]

Are You Listening?

Ed Milligan called on the drugstore every week to fill inventories and check new items. He always greeted the owner with a big smile and the question, "Good to see you. How's the family?"

The storeowner answered, "Fine," and Ed always replied, "Terrific. Let me show you what we have for you this week."

Wondering if Ed really cared about his family, the owner decided to give a new answer to Ed's standard question. When Ed showed up on schedule the following week and said, "Good to see you. How's the family?" the owner said, "Well, my mother-in-law jumped off the cliff, the children are lost in a forest, and my wife had to go to a leper colony."

Without missing a beat, good old Ed answered, "Terrific. Let me show you what we have for you this week."

Improving Listening Skills

To improve your listening skills, practice these five mental activities as you listen:

Avoid Prejudgment. Not only should you allow the speaker to complete a message before you comment or respond, but you should also wait until you have heard the entire message before judging it. Making value judgments colors your thinking and creates emotional blind spots that can block your ability to make a solid buying recommendation. Jumping to conclusions is a common fault of poor listeners. As the cartoon indicates, assuming you know what is coming next can seriously damage your understanding of the actual meaning intended.

Be Patient. Listen more and give "verbal nods" of encouragement. This allows speakers plenty of time to answer questions and encourages them to express their ideas. Speak at the same speed as the other person: Matching speed is a rapport builder. In addition, find the person's mental rate of speed and then adjust or modify your thinking to that rate. Even though the speaker is saying something exciting, wait until the message is complete and you are sure that you understand it all before you contribute your own thoughts.

Take Notes. Remembering everything a person says is difficult. Use the pen-and-paper approach to selling. Divide your notepad into two columns. On one side note what the prospect says. Then, in the other column, sketch out your proposal to meet those expressions of needs, requirements, or desires. The mere physical action of writing down a few key words reinforces your memory and understanding. You can go back to the prospect's own words to help you show your product's applicability to the problem.[28]

Reinforce. Anchor, in your mind and in the prospect's, the points made by the prospect. Use your own reinforcing responses to achieve this purpose. If the prospect says the mileage per gallon a car gets is important, respond, "Yes, that is very important." Later, tell what mileage the prospect could get with your car. If the prospect says, "Our secretaries spend too much time making copies," respond, "That has to be a problem." Then later emphasize how your copier cuts secretaries' time by copying on both sides of the paper in one operation and by running more copies per minute.

Capitalize on Speed of Thought. We can process about 600 words a minute, but even a fast talker gets out only 100 to 150 words in that time.[29] Thus you can think about four times as fast as the average prospect talks. All that spare time is valuable. The poor listener uses it to fidget impatiently, to think about what happened earlier in the day or what will happen later, or to plan what to say as soon as the prospect takes a breath. Successful salespeople have a plan to follow for using this time profitably:

- *Anticipate where the prospect is going.* If you guess right, your thinking is reinforced. If you are wrong, compare your thoughts with those of the prospect; look for the point the prospect is making.

- *Mentally summarize the message.* Pinpoint problems, misconceptions, attitudes, objections, or misunderstandings. What you learn can be an excellent guide to the items that should be stressed in the presentation and at the close.

- *Formulate a response.* Be careful not to formulate one before you hear everything the prospect wants to say. Listen, understand, and then turn the prospect's words to your advantage.

- *Listen between the lines.* Nonverbal messages are as important as verbal ones. Watch facial expressions, body movement, and position; listen to the tone of voice and volume changes.

SUMMARY

- Asking questions is the primary tool for identifying problems. Need discovery lays the groundwork for the presentation and close. When you ask the right questions, prospects clarify problems in their own minds as well as in yours.

- No standard set of questions is universally applicable. The product or service, your preapproach information, and the prospect's behavioral style help determine the questions you ask.

- Questions may be either closed-end or open-end. A closed-end question asks for a yes-no response or a choice between alternatives. Open-end questions ask for opinions, explanations, or judgments.

- Ask questions according to their structure: Amplification, internal summary, and questions designed to gain agreement.

- Listening is one of the most neglected skills in any type of training program. Taking notes focuses your attention on what the prospect is saying and avoids prejudgment of ideas. Reinforce what you hear by comparing the prospect's ideas with your own.

- People can think at a rate much faster than they talk. Use this spare thinking time to anticipate where the prospect is going, mentally summarize what you hear, form a response, and refine the message as your listening continues.

REVIEW QUESTIONS

1. What factors determine a salesperson's ability to formulate the right questions?

2. What is the difference between manipulation and consultation? Which is most useful to the successful salesperson? Why?

3. What kinds of questions allow the salesperson to discover the prospect's behavioral style? How does this information aid the salesperson?

4. What tactic is useful as a transition from the approach into need discovery?

5. Who should control the needs-assessment phase of the interview? How is control maintained?

6. What is the purpose of the open-end question? Formulate an open-end question that might be used to sell investment property.

7. Describe in detail all the instruction you have had in school, at home, or elsewhere in listening skills.

8. In what situations do you find it hardest to listen? Easiest? What makes the difference?

9. Is listening easier if a visual factor is added? For example, do you prefer to talk to someone in person or on the phone when you have something serious to discuss?

10. Educators say learning that involves more than one of the senses is more effective. Explain how this applies to listening and taking notes, to simultaneously listening and looking at visual aids, and to listening to radio versus watching television.

ROLE-PLAY EXERCISES

The following role-play exercises help build teams, improve communication, and emphasize the real-world side of selling. They are meant to be challenging, to help you learn how to deal with problems that have no single right answer, and to use a variety of skills beyond those employed in a typical review question. Read and complete each activity. Then in the next class, discuss and compare answers with other classmates.

Role Play 10.1 – 10 Questions

Pair up in class with another student as directed by your instructor. Imagine that the two of you are seated next to one another on a flight from Hawaii to San Francisco. You represent a company that supplies electronics components for jet engine controls, while your seat mate is a procurement officer for a company that manufactures jet engines. Since your companies are well known to one another, you are aware that your flight companion's company is not a client of your company. This is a once-in-a-career chance: you are determined to gain an appointment with the other company to make a full-scale presentation.

On the spur of the moment, compile a list of no more than 10 questions along with anticipated responses that you can ask your seat mate that will secure the appointment.

Role play your questions. Did they succeed? What type of questions did you ask (your partner can help categorize the questions)? Would other questions have been more successful? If you role play your questions in front of other class members, what do they think of your effort?

Role Play 10.2 – A Need for Questions?

For this exercise, the class should be divided into teams of 4 persons each.

On each team, 2 persons will undertake the following role play:

Select a technical device such as a smartphone. One person, acting as salesperson, will sell the phone to the other, but without asking the customer any questions. This process should take no more than 5 minutes. Whether the sale is closed successfully does not matter. The other 2 members of the team will simply observe.

Thereafter, the remaining 2 members of the team will undertake the same role play, but this time the salesperson will conduct the sale by asking questions in order to determine the customer's need. The 2 nonparticipants will simply observe.

After both role plays have been concluded, the team will discuss and critique both. Which role play—without questions or with questions—seemed to go more smoothly? Which felt better or more natural to the participants? To the observers? Why? If you were employed to sell this product, which approach would you use, and why?

CASE STUDIES

The following case studies present you with selling scenarios that require you to apply the critical skills discussed in the chapter and give you training through simulation, role-playing, and practical learning situations. They are meant to be both engaging and challenging, and like the role-play exercises, don't have one right answer.

Case 10.1 – Clanging Pots and Pans

Jack Lund couldn't figure out what had happened. As a representative for WearStrong Restaurant Supplies, he had been supplying equipment to Midwest Diners for the past 15 years. Midwest ran a string of 88 Greek diners in 10 major metro areas from Detroit through Indianapolis and Des Moines. They had been one of Jack's first major clients, and he counted the owner, Mark Antonopoulos, a friend. He and Mark had attended trade shows together and on many occasions had golfed together whenever Jack was in the Chicago area. From the time that Mark had opened his first diner, Jack had come through with a good deal as Mark expanded his business one location at a time. That's why the phone conversation just a few minutes ago was so disturbing.

Jack had just called Mark to let him know that it was time once again to begin his regular replacement rotation. Every 5 years, Mark's diners had to replace their aluminum cookware. Although sturdy and capable of being scrubbed to a mirror finish, WearStrong's top-of-the-line, heavy aluminum pots and pans could withstand only so much abuse. The replacement schedule called for replacing every pot and pan in each kitchen every 5 years, but stretching the process out over 3 years for all 88 stores. When Jack mentioned to Mark that another replacement round was due to commence, he was met with a long silence.

"Jack, I just don't think we're going to do that this time," Mark finally sighed. "You see, we've decided to go with a 3-ply line offered by one of your competitors. They have a durable, non-stick finish with a copper lining underneath. It can save us cleanup time and still provide an even heat."

"I don't get it, Mark. You know that WearStrong manufactures the same sort of item, but you never expressed any interest in it. You said that our aluminum pan had been a workhorse for you, and you saw no reason to change."

"I know. I know. But do you remember, Jack, when you met last with our operations people here in Chicago? They mentioned that they were interested in saving time in cleanup costs, among other things."

"I think I recall something along those lines, Mark, but since you didn't say anything, I figured everything was all right the way it was," replied Jack.

"Well, it wasn't. You really need to pay closer attention, Jack." Mark paused. "Tell you what. The deal isn't done yet. In light of our long-term association, I'll give you one more shot. You can meet with our people next Tuesday, but bring your 'A' game." With that, Mark clicked off.

What do you think had gone wrong? What can Jack do to save the situation? If you were advising Jack, how would you suggest that he prepare for next Tuesday's meeting? Precisely how should he approach Midwest Diner's operations executives? What sort of questions should Jack be prepared to ask next Tuesday?

Case 10.2 – Smothering the Sale

Kurt Edwards had just landed on his feet. After working for 15 years as regional manager for a major moving and storage company, he was laid off when the housing bubble burst. People couldn't afford to sell their homes for a loss in order to move, and Kurt's company had to downsize. Kurt's supervisory responsibilities had included maintaining the company's fleet of moving vans in good working order. Now, however, he had been hired in sales by a major truck parts distributor in the Northwest. Kurt was poised to make more money than he ever had in his previous management position. After all, he knew firsthand what his new clients would need.

As part of his training, Kurt accompanied his district manager in the field. Today, they were calling on the WashMont Hauling Co., a major carrier in Washington and Montana. As they got out of their car, Kurt's manager told him, "After I introduce you, you're on your own. You know the product line. I'm just going to sit back and watch. Go ahead as if I'm not there."

"Ok," Kurt replied, eager to show his manager that he knew his stuff.

Once inside, they proceeded to the office of Bruce Olds, fleet operations manager. After the usual pleasantries had been exchanged, Kurt turned the conversation to the purpose of their visit.

"As we get started, Bruce, I want to assure you that, with me, you will be dealing with someone who understands your situation. I managed a fleet of moving vans for 15 years; so you can be confident that I know what you're facing these days."

"Well, I'm glad to hear that," Bruce replied. "You see, . . ."

"I'll bet your chief problem is delivery of spare parts on time, especially those that wear out more quickly," Kurt interrupted. "That's always the way it was for me. But our company has solved that problem so that you'll never have to worry about having portions of your fleet stranded for lack of parts."

"That's wonderful," Bruce said, "but, you know, . . ."

"And for a large account like yours," Kurt continued, "we can warehouse the parts for you for daily delivery. The large volume allows us to absorb that cost for you. Would you like to solve your major problem today for the next six months?"

"Well, Kurt, I'm not sure that I'm ready to go there just yet. Perhaps you could call back once I've got a better handle on just what our needs are," Bruce said, standing and extending his hand.

Back in the car, Kurt's manager exploded, "What was that about? You don't know the first thing about sales! You smothered the guy!"

"What do you mean?" asked Kurt. "I solved his problem for him. He just wasn't ready."

Based on what you've learned from Chapter 10, what happened here? Why was Kurt's manager so angry? Why didn't Kurt's knowledge and connection with Bruce produce better results? What do you think Kurt's manager should recommend in terms of additional training for Kurt?

Chapter 11
Making the Presentation

Learning Objectives

- Understand how to make a presentation.

- Learn how units of conviction help prospects reach a buying decision.

- Discover effective tactics for making a sales presentation.

- Study different methods for involving the prospect.

- Understand the significance of using a demonstration and effective virtual tools.

- Examine the different types of sales aids available.

- Recognize the value of using technology in making presentations.

Developing a Persuasive Presentation

With the ever-increasing popularity of online buying, some experts say that salespeople are soon to be corporate relics on the road to extinction. This is simply not true! Relationship salespeople will continue to prosper in the future if they understand one simple concept: There is a big difference between presenting data versus information. In the past, traditional sales reps simply presented data—facts and figures that can often confuse or complicate a presentation if their significance is not explained. How "data dense" are most sales presentations? Here are some interesting and surprising facts about most sales presentations:

- The typical salesperson presents six to eight features or benefits during the sales presentation. Twenty-four hours later the average prospect remembers only one benefit.

- In 39 percent of those cases they remember the one benefit incorrectly.

- In 49 percent of the cases they remember something that wasn't mentioned at all.

Prospects demand a product that does what they want it to do, explained in a language they understand.[1] The future of professional relationship selling is going to be based on real-time value and how well sales professionals become trusted advisors in guiding clients to solutions to their problems. The future belongs to those sales pros that can present and share their knowledge, offer wisdom, and create value in a way that benefits the prospect.[2]

Strive for Passion, not Perfection. More often than not, customers buy because of the rapport building established over time. "Selling is all about relationship building. There are hundreds of competitors chomping at the bit," says Diane DiResta. It all comes down to the way you present yourself and your product or service and the value you create for the customer. Sales presentations must be listener-centered. People want to have their problems solved.

In his book *What They Don't Teach You at the Harvard Business School*, Mark McCormack said there are three fundamental selling truths: (1) If you don't know your product, people will resent your efforts to sell it; (2) If you don't believe in your product, no amount of personality or technique will cover that fact; (3) If you can't sell your product with enthusiasm, the absence of it will be infectious.

Nobody buys from a dispassionate seller; if you don't believe in the product, no one else will. The more options a sales rep creates for the prospect, the greater the chance for a sale.[3] Don't worry about making the perfect presentation. It probably will not happen! Prospects are looking to you for knowledge of what you're selling and how it can help them solve a problem or become more successful. You must truly believe in what you're selling and show some passion when doing it—that is far more important than perfection.

Calling on Regular Customers. If you are calling on the same person or dealer on a regular basis, you may tend to give the same old presentation over and over or even skip the presentation entirely and merely ask, "What do you need today?" If you are unwilling to put some real work into your selling and are content just to "take orders" all your life, your best opportunity to become rich is to win the lottery! Vary your presentation. Provide new ideas to help your customer make money, save time, or increase efficiency. Plan to use ideas like these:

When you believe in your product, your prospects will too.

- Give the customer a new advertising or merchandising idea.

- Help the customer develop an overall marketing plan for improving the business.

- Tell some new product fact that the customer needs to know.

- Share a piece of industry or trade news of personal interest to the customer.

Begin with Planning

Everything important begins with planning. Over the last few decades, sales professionals strived to find ways to quantify best planning practices and ways to target key prospects. The best salespeople learn to dutifully target, segment, and measure inputs, outputs, and performance. AC Nielsen has built a multibillion-dollar business of gathering and distributing sales data to analyze and report with perceived expertise; consumers and management eat it up. Some even refer to this research and planning as a science.[4] This may seem like an overstatement to some, but effective planning, in fact, has become highly methodological and even scientific in its approach.

Exhibit 11.1 is one man's account of the results he suffered from his failure to plan his immediate future. Random, haphazard action never leads to success in any worthwhile endeavor, and in this respect, selling is no different from any other undertaking. How well you plan what takes place during the sales interview plays a major role in the success you achieve when closing time arrives.

ΔExhibit 11.1

Failing to Plan My Immediate Future

I am writing in response to your request for additional information. In block #3 of the accident form I listed "not planning my immediate future" as the cause of my accident. I trust the following details will be sufficient.

I am a bricklayer. On the date of the accident I was working alone on the roof of a new six-story building. At the end of the day, I discovered about 500 pounds of bricks left over. Rather than carry them down by hand, I decided to lower them in a barrel by using a pulley that was fortunately attached to the building at the sixth floor.

Securing the rope at ground level, I went to the roof, swung the barrel out, and loaded the bricks. Then I went back to the ground and untied the rope, holding it tightly to ensure a slow descent of the 500 pounds of bricks. Block #11 of the accident report shows that I weigh 135 pounds. Due to my surprise of being jerked off the ground so suddenly, I forgot to let go of the rope. Needless to say, I proceeded at a rapid rate up the side of the building. In the vicinity of the third floor, I met the barrel coming down. This explains the fractured skull and broken collarbone.

Slowed only slightly, I continued my rapid ascent, not stopping until the fingers of my right hand were two knuckles deep into the pulley. Fortunately, I had regained my presence of mind enough to hold tightly to the rope in spite of my pain.

At approximately the same time, however, the barrel of bricks hit the ground and the bottom fell out of the barrel. Devoid of the weight of the bricks, the barrel now weighed approximately 50 pounds. I refer you again to block #11. As you can imagine, I began a rather rapid descent down the side of the building.

In the vicinity of the third floor I met the barrel coming up. This accounts for the two fractured ankles and the lacerations of my legs and lower body. The encounter with the barrel slowed my descent enough to lessen my injuries when I fell onto the pile of bricks. Fortunately only three vertebrae were cracked.

I am sorry to report, however, that as I lay there on the bricks, in pain, unable to stand and watching the empty barrel six stories above me, I again lost my presence of mind and let go of the rope. Now the empty barrel weighed more than the rope, so it came back down on me and broke both of my legs.

I hope these details explain sufficiently that my accident was caused by failure to plan my immediate future.

In reality, planning and preparing for the sales presentation begin when a name is first recorded in your contact management system. As information is gathered about the prospect, you are subconsciously planning how to approach this person, what features and benefits are most appropriate, and what kind of close is likely to be most effective. The final step of preparing for the sales interview is to crystallize all your plans and decide exactly how to proceed with making the presentation. You really need a clear, focused objective for your message, and that's determined by the type of individual or company on which you are calling.

When planning your presentation, here is a good rule of thumb to follow: When you are developing a brand new sales talk, plan on spending one hour of preparation time for each minute of presentation time. For example, if you are speaking for twenty minutes, you should invest twenty hours in research, development, organizing, outlining, fleshing out, and rehearsing your presentation. It sounds like a lot of time—and it is—but it's necessary if you want to deliver a dynamite presentation. If you invest the time to construct a superb, researched presentation, you'll be able to deliver the same or a similar version to other prospects. As Dr. Norman Vincent Peale said, "I give the same mashed potatoes for each speech, I just change the gravy."[5]

Call Objective

The most successful salespeople have specific objectives for each sales interview. In many instances, the call objective is to present your product or service and secure an order. In others, your objective is to discover the prospect's needs so that you may prepare a proposal for later consideration or to persuade the prospect to set up a presentation to a group of people who are jointly charged with the responsibility for a buying decision. In these latter instances, you will probably plan several interviews that, taken together, contain all the elements that may be considered parts of "the presentation." The difference is that you accomplish the various steps in successive interviews rather than in a single meeting with the prospect.

Whether you intend to complete the presentation and the close in a single call or in a series of calls depends upon the type of product or service you sell and the size of the expected order. The single-call close is appropriate for selling items that can be ordered upon the decision of one person; if a buying center is involved, multiple calls are usually necessary.

Tanis Cornell is a Global Enterprise Manager for Network Appliance, a leader in the data storage industry. She manages one of their Top Enterprise Accounts, AT&T. Tanis has a team of 25 people either partially or totally dedicated to selling and supporting this one account. Her approach to selling a major account involves a complex interview process. The sale may be closed on any one of the calls, but often it requires many more than four calls. Here is her system:

1. **Initial call**. Develop rapport and establish a need. Judge how far to go by how quickly a relationship is established. Take notes all along to help build a trust level.

2. **Survey call**. Interview all key decision makers to get information. The decision is ultimately based on three factors: cost, quality, and service. Discover which one is most important to this client.

3. **Proposal call**. Present a buying recommendation. Recognize the fact that this is a joint or buying center decision, and give each person what that individual needs to reach a decision. Use trial closes.

4. **Closing call**. Get verbal and/or written commitment.

5. **Follow-up calls**. Continue meeting with executives, managers, and department heads until a solution is reached. Consider each meeting as a mini contract negotiation.

Sales Call Planning

Many companies, especially those whose product or service entails extensive research into customer needs, require salespeople to prepare a presentation plan in written form. The plan reveals the need for any additional information, makes it possible to check needs and goals against suggested solutions, and makes sure you have a clear picture of the entire situation before arriving for the personal interview. Planning for sales calls can be low tech—written on a sheet of paper—or high tech, using a call planning app compatible with iPads or iPhones or a plug-in that is compatible with your CRM system.

Using a high tech call planning will produce added benefits. The Professional Selling Skills® Call Planner, for instance, plugs into Salesforce CRM and can track accelerated sales cycles, collaboration with sales teams, minimizing productivity losses, storing and sharing best practices in call planning, and gaining insights into sales strengths and weaknesses. As the cost of a sales call has grown from an average of $126 per call in 1980 to $379 today, sales managers will be particularly interested in researching and choosing these products. In fact, using a sophisticated call planning tool in combination with excellent online business resources can increase profit margin by 33 percent.[6] Whichever sales call tool you choose to use, however, you should keep in mind the key questions your planning process should answer. Exhibit 11.2 is an example of a sales call planning sheet that may be used for this purpose.[7]

ΔExhibit 11.2

Sales Call Planner

1. Company Name _____
2. Type of Company _____
3. Address _____
4. Individual(s) to contact
   _____ (position) _____
   _____ (position) _____
5. Background and profile of buyers _____
6. Major competitors to be aware of
   _____ (sales rep) _____
   _____ (sales rep) _____
7. Objective for this particular call _____
8. Best time to see buyer _____
9. Expressed needs or problems _____
10. Strategies and tactics useful for this situation _____
    a. Best approach to use _____
    b. Specific fact-finding questions _____
    c. Features and benefits to stress _____
    d. Anticipated objections _____
       (and techniques to answer them) _____
    e. Closing techniques to be used _____
11. Sales tools to take (audiovisual, flip-chart presentation, etc.) _____
    _____
12. Results of this sales call _____
    _____

Presentation Styles

As long as people have been attempting to analyze the selling process, a running controversy has raged over the use of "canned" presentations. Opponents point to presentations that are obviously memorized and delivered in a hypnotic manner likely to produce a mesmerized listener in the shortest possible time. Supporters of memorized presentations point to the many advantages of knowing exactly what to say and when.

The question is not likely to be settled once and for all because the difference lies more with the salesperson than with the method of delivery itself. In deciding how you will deliver the message you want the prospect to receive, consider the advantages and disadvantages of three basic choices: The memorized presentation, the outline presentation, and the extemporaneous presentation.

Memorized Presentation

Some companies supply their salespeople with a printed presentation and require them to memorize it. A few words of caution are in order when considering the use of a memorized presentation. Even though it is memorized, the presentation should never sound memorized. A memorized presentation should be practiced and its delivery polished until it becomes natural. It should be internalized to the point that it is a normal, personal message that can be conveyed in a conversational tone. The memorized presentation must be used as a framework or guide to lead you and your prospect through the sales process. Most companies that make use of a standardized presentation provide a list of suggested questions to help discover buying motives, suggest options to use in different types of circumstances, and caution the salesperson to remain flexible. A well-prepared, memorized presentation offers a number of important advantages, especially to new salespeople.

A memorized presentation gives you confidence.

Quick Productivity. If salespeople are new to the company or to the selling profession, they can memorize a good presentation in much less time than one can be developed. Using a standardized presentation gets the salesperson into production quickly. Enough sales can be made during the initial learning period to supply basic income needs while they gain knowledge and experience.

Reliable and Proven Effectiveness. The memorized presentation makes sure you give the right information to the prospect. Nothing vital is omitted, and nothing erroneous is inserted. The presentation a company supplies to salespeople has usually been tested and refined over a period of years in actual selling situations.

Confidence Building. Using it is a confidence builder for the inexperienced salesperson. When you know the presentation has worked for others with no more experience than you have, you feel capable of using it successfully. When you succeed in closing a sale with the presentation, you gain even more confidence. Each success builds on the previous one, and you are earning and learning at the same time.

Memorizing your presentation as well as your answers to the most commonly asked questions or objections prevents you from committing pitfalls from which you may never recover. Neil Rock, a district sales manager for pharmaceuticals giant GlaxoSmithKline, said, "I had a representative talking to a group of ten neurologists, and she began to answer a question she didn't know. Her response was a hesitant, 'I think the answer is...' "[8] Salespeople are not expected to know every last detail about a product, but starting a response with, "Um, I think..." is not an option. You have to be confident in your answer. By memorizing your presentation and learning the answers to common concerns, you can attain that much needed confidence and set yourself apart.

Outline Presentation

The outline presentation takes a great deal of thought and preparation. With this presentation technique, exact words are not planned in full detail. You know what content will be presented at each stage of the presentation but are confident enough of both knowledge and skill to believe that the right words will be available as needed. This is the same process that most experienced public speakers use.

Using an outline presentation successfully depends upon the development of numerous units of conviction that are thoroughly internalized. The outline is built by considering all the information available about the prospect. Most salespeople who use an outline method follow the same general outline for most presentations. They may, however, have several approaches or openings from which to choose, numerous features and benefits to present, and all sorts of evidence to present—all of which can be combined and recombined to meet the needs of the specific situation. Ideally, you make the choice in advance and know which pieces of material will be used. The use of the outline presentation generally calls for more judgment about people and broader product knowledge than the memorized presentation.

Many companies, especially those whose product or service entails extensive research into customer needs, require salespeople to prepare an outline presentation in written form. Any type of written plan you use reveals any existing need for additional information, enables you to check needs and goals against suggested solutions, and makes sure you have a clear picture of the entire situation before arriving for the interview. Procter & Gamble is one company that recommends its sales reps follow an outline plan for presentations. Exhibit 11.3 is an outline for a presentation written by one of its sales managers in Cleveland, Ohio.

ΔExhibit 11.3

Procter & Gamble Sales Plan ·····························

Purpose of the Sales Call—Sell 40 cases of Folger's one-pound for display.

Background of Account—Chain store with $100,000 weekly volume. Store is allowed to select displays in addition to headquarters' displays. Store's current need is to increase dollar volume per customer transaction. Manager has also expressed concern with labor cost. This particular store has a back stock of eight cases of canister creamers.

Summarize the Situation—The store manager said several weeks ago that they want to increase dollar volume 7 percent in the next three months by increasing the average amount of each customer transaction. I want to suggest a way to sell more Folger's coffee to help achieve this goal.

State the Idea—My idea is for the store to display 40 cases of one-pound Folger's coffee with eight cases of canister creamers from the store's back stock.

Explain How It Works—Last year's records show that the store displayed 30 cases of Folger's one-pound coffee during this time, and it sold out quickly at regular shelf price. Now in the cold months, coffee consumption is the number one dry grocery item. Capitalize on customer appeal of Folger's, which has proved popular in the past, and enhance it with an appealing display with the canister creamers. Store now moves 10 cases weekly, and a special display will move 40 cases easily. I'll help build the display and save time and labor for the store.

Reinforce Key Benefits—Show calculations of contribution this display can make to help reach the 7 percent increase desired: $2,678.40 in sales on coffee. Add the quality image created by Folger's TV advertising. The related item display will increase movement on creamers that are now sitting in back stock. The result is an increase in the average per-customer sale, which is the goal.

Suggest an Easy Next Step—Ask for a decision on which truck to send the 40 cases of Folger's and suggest Tuesday.

Extemporaneous Presentation

Some highly successful salespeople, particularly those who have many years of experience, may be heard to say that they "don't prepare" for a sales presentation. Actually, their preparation time is distributed in a different way than that of the less experienced salesperson, but they do prepare.

The extemporaneous presentation follows the same principles that any other presentation would incorporate, but experienced salespeople who use the extemporaneous approach are master people watchers. They understand people; they ask questions and listen. They are experts in discovering problems and identifying dominant buying motives. They know their product so thoroughly that they can seize almost magically upon the one feature or benefit that will best appeal to the prospect. They possess such charisma that the air of trust and credibility they create makes objections nonexistent and painlessly places the client's name on the order form. People love to buy from them. As a result, these master salespeople spend most of their "preparation time" in gathering additional information about the prospect rather than spending time in consciously matching features and benefits to prospect qualification information. This step is almost automatic and subconscious as a result of their long experience.

You can use the extemporaneous presentation when you have paid your dues over a period of time. It takes up-to-the-minute product knowledge, intensive prospecting, thorough preapproach qualifying of prospects, and a full background of selling experience upon which to draw. Although salespeople who use the extemporaneous method sometimes claim not to prepare, listening closely to presentations made by these masters shows that they have, over time, developed some uniquely personal tactics for conducting a sales interview. Many of the same phrases and sentences appear over and over—because they work! Conscious preparation, for these people, consists of learning about the particular prospect. Then automatically the tactics, the procedures, and words themselves surface from the well of experience and provide the "extemporaneous" inspiration that accomplishes the goal.

Product-Analysis Worksheet

Prospects have neither the product knowledge you have nor an understanding of the type of service you are prepared to render. You must not only know all the facts about your product but also be able to relate your knowledge directly to the specific needs of the prospect. If you can quote prices, catalog numbers, shipping dates, delivery schedules, and credit terms but have no solid, convincing evidence of the product's value to offer upon which the prospect can base a buying decision, you are afflicted with what has been called the *salesman's curse*: "You know your product better than you know how your client's business can use it."[9] A salesperson who suffers from the "salesman's curse" is in the same league as a math student who can recite all the formulas in the algebra book but never knows which one to use to solve the problem. Before you can expect a signed order form, you must figure out how to improve your customer's business and then find a way to persuade the prospect that the solution you offer is the best possible. You can do this by preparing *units of conviction*.

Units of Conviction

Units of conviction are concise, carefully prepared "mini-presentations" used as building blocks to construct the information you present. When the individual units of conviction are combined, they form what is referred to as a *product-analysis worksheet*.

Preparing a written product-analysis worksheet helps you evaluate the various characteristics of your product so that you are better able to present it to your prospects. When you prepare units of conviction and add them to your store of available options, they become a permanent part of your selling arsenal. A single unit of conviction consists of five elements:

1. A feature of your product or service

2. A transitional phrase

3. The benefits the feature provides

4. Evidence to support your claims

5. A tie-down question to gain the prospect's agreement

Features and Benefits. *Features* are the tangible and intangible qualities of the product or service you sell. Features are facts that are the same no matter who uses the product or service. The tangible features of a product include observable factors such as color, size, capacity, speed of performance, material from which it is made—anything that can be detected through one of the five senses.[10] Intangible features are also important: the service given by the company, price, delivery, availability of service, and even the service and support that you promise.

Benefits, however, are the value or worth that the user derives from the product or service. Of the numerous benefits a product or service has to offer, only four or five will be key motivators to a prospect, and these will be different for each prospect.[11] Your task is to find out which ones are the key motivators.

Every feature of your product has numerous benefits. Remember, *one feature does not equal one benefit*. Examine the insert that follows and challenge your mind to perform some mental gymnastics to prove this point.

> **Every feature of your product has numerous benefits.** Here's an exercise to give your mind a healthy benefit workout: What are the benefits of a 270-horsepower engine in a luxury car? They could include a smoother ride, power to spare when passing a slower car, quick acceleration away from a hazard, the feeling of being in charge, less wear and tear, higher resale value, etc. The point is, one feature does not equal one benefit. List your product's top ten features, and then come up with at least five different benefits for each feature. Remember, features only justify the price; benefits justify the purchase. This gives you 50 new ways to close more sales.

Transitional Phrase. The ability to translate features into benefits is one of the strengths of a relationship salesperson. Even if you know which feature can fulfill the buying motive, you cannot expect the prospect to make the connection automatically. You must make the verbal transition. The prospect does not know your product as well as you know it and has to have features and benefits connected by transitional phrases. Some salespeople call these bridges.[12] While the actual words may vary, they are all designed to accomplish the same purpose: To connect, in the prospect's thinking, features and benefits. These phrases all serve the purpose of answering the prospect's question, "What's in it for me?" Some common transitional phrases are:

- "This is beneficial to you because . . ."

- "This lets you . . ."

- "This heads off all the problems of . . ."

- "What this means to you . . ."

Begin preparation of units of conviction by listing in writing all the features of your product or service. If you sell more than one major product, make separate lists for each one. Then go back and list all the ways the first feature can benefit your prospect. If you neglect this preparatory step, you will find yourself confronting prospects who listen to the features you describe and ask, "So what?" and you will have no appealing answers. When you have prepared units of conviction in advance, finding the right one is just like reaching into your briefcase and pulling out a sample; you know what is there and all of it is at your fingertips for instant use when you need it.

Exhibit 11.4 shows a features and benefits card prepared by Hartmann Luggage Company of Lebanon, Tennessee, for their carry-on luggage and carry-on totes. These cards are distributed by the company's marketing managers to retail salespeople to help them sell the product.

ΔExhibit 11.4

Unique Features and Benefits of Hartmann Carry-On Totes

Features	Benefits
1. Seven pockets or compartments	1. Lots of places for all those extra items when you need the space (organizing your packing).
2. Two-way carry	2. Comfortable strap that adjusts to hand-carry or shoulder strap. Lets you decide how to carry the bag most comfortably for YOU.
3. Full-opening front pocket	3. Easy access and even has room for a small laptop or tablet.
4. Carry it on a plane	4. Your clothing/contents will arrive when you do, and you won't have to wait for baggage.
5. Easy-access large center compartment	5. Makes packing and unpacking easy and fast.
6. Waterproof pocket on inside of center compartment	6. Great storage for an iPod or cell phone. Can also be used as a cosmetic/toilet bag. Keeps inside dry and separates "spillables" from the rest of the contents.
7. Large outside back pocket PLUS a zipper pocket	7. Large pocket allows you to put in those last-minute items for easy access, and the zipper pocket gives you a secure place for your keys, wallet, passport, etc.
8. Lightweight, yet strong	8. Light weight permits you to carry on more clothing and strength of bag protects its contents.
9. Teflon-coated fabrics	9. Stays attractive. Easy to clean.

Evidence to Support Claims. Just as you present benefits to head off the prospect's question "So what?" about the features of your product or service, you must present evidence to support the claims you make to head off the questions "Can you prove it?" and "Who says so?" Even if you have been unusually successful in establishing a high degree of credibility and trust with the prospect, you are unlikely to be looked upon as an all-knowing sage with all the answers whose statements are to be accepted without question. You must be prepared to back up what you say with: (1) demonstrations, (2) testimonials, (3) facts and statistics, (4) samples, and (5) examples or case histories.

1. Demonstrations. Show the product being used. The demonstration is especially effective for some types of prospects if they have hands-on use in the demonstration. Just as audio and stereo salespeople encourage prospects to listen to their speakers to hear the high definition sound, more and more technology companies are offering their products through free trials. You, as a salesperson, for example, are the target prospect for CRM programs. It may be well worth your time to watch their online demos and sign up for free trials of each product to find out which is the best match for your company. As a prospect, you know how much you appreciate this opportunity; so you can be certain your own prospects will, too.

Use testimonials from satisfied customers to build credibility with new prospects.

2. Testimonials. The best possible testimonial is for one of your satisfied customers to call the prospect ahead of time and suggest that you be given an appointment. At this time, your customer expresses satisfaction with the product or service; this predisposes the prospect to accept what you say. Other types of testimonials are also effective with the right type of prospect. Use customers' letters expressing their pleasure with your product and the service you have provided. Such letters are easy to get. Just ask for them! You may even write the testimonial yourself and ask the prospect to read and sign it to save the client's time and make sure the letter is worded to fit your needs. When a client thanks you for some help, just say you would appreciate a letter saying the same thing. This kind of testimonial is especially helpful when it comes from a person who has influence in the community or with the particular prospect or when it is written on the letterhead of a respected company. You may have pictures of your clients using your product, with their signatures on the back.

3. Facts and Statistics. Call attention to manufacturer's ratings, such as the energy ratings of air-conditioning and heating units and the estimated mpg ratings of automobiles. Show earnings of stocks or other investment vehicles over the past five years. The U.S. Census Bureau projects that the 65-and-older group will grow 75 percent by the year 2050. Hispanics over 65 will increase by 150 percent, faster than any other ethnic group in that age bracket. This type of market segmentation data is useful to a wide variety of companies in various industries.[13]

4. Samples. A sample of the product itself or of the material from which it is made gives the prospect something concrete to use as the basis of decision-making. Supermarkets offer customers a taste of a featured food: Cheese, sausage, pizza—anything that can be served from a small table, cooked in an electric frying pan, or stuck on the end of a toothpick. The demonstrator then displays the food item and asks the customer to try it. A salesperson for operating room scrubs for hospitals might give the purchasing agent a swatch of the material from which they are made to feel as the quality is described. Samples are intended to provide an appeal to one or more of the five senses.

5. Examples or Case Histories. The use of examples or case histories is another way to present the satisfaction of other clients and customers. You may tell the prospect about other people whose circumstances are similar and how you were able to solve their problems or how they are enjoying some benefit from using the product. Use these guidelines when planning this type of evidence:

- The case history must be authentic. It should be about someone the prospect knows or can contact for verification.

- Use many details to let the prospect know you are intimately familiar with the situation.

- Back up the example with pictures, personal letters, newspaper articles, and other evidence.

- Relate it directly to the prospect's circumstances.

The evidence used to back up the features and benefits you present must be as carefully tailored to the needs, problems, and personality of the prospect as the features and benefits themselves. For example, use cost-saving evidence for a prospect who is especially interested in economy; but use testimonials from prominent people for a prospect who is largely motivated by the desire for status. Use everything you know about the prospect's social style as input for every step in the sales process.

The Tie-Down. The "tie-down" is an essential step in building units of conviction, although it usually consists of no more than a single question that asks for the prospect's agreement. Your goal is to translate features into benefits for the prospect, to provide the necessary evidence to prove your points, and to gain a commitment to act. Here are some examples of tie-down questions:

- *Considering these facts, you agree with me that this is a safe tire, don't you, Ms. Craft?*
- *I believe you will agree with me, Mr. Osinski, that this is a better way for handling this process than your present method, won't you?*
- *I think you can get an idea of the enormous advantage you will have with one tenth of a minute billing, can't you, Ms. Grimmett?*

The tie-down is important throughout the presentation to check on understanding and agreement and to make sure the prospect is ready to proceed to the next point. One of the functions of the tie-down is to ask a series of questions, all of which the prospect can be expected to answer yes. Then when you attempt a close, the prospect more easily says yes again. Suppose, however, that you ask, "You agree with me about this, don't you?" and the prospect says, "No, I don't." Where are you now? You are in a better position than you were before you asked the question because you now know you have a problem. Had you not asked this question and found out about the lack of agreement, you would have pushed on to the close and to failure. Now you are warned about the existence of a problem and can go back to find its source and correct it, ask another tie-down question, and move forward again when agreement is reached.

Exhibit 11.5 is a complete unit of conviction for a wireless phone company. Notice the tie-down at the end—the question that leads the prospect into agreement.

ΔExhibit 11.5

Unit of Conviction: Cell Phone Service

Feature	While most cell phone companies count your minutes in full, our cell phone plans round down on the minutes used.
Transitional Phrase	What this means is...
Benefit	If a call goes to 1:46, we will only bill you for 1 minute, instead of rounding up to 2 minutes. With minutes that round down after the first minute, not up, consumers get more minutes for their money.
Evidence (Facts and Statistics)	Here's an illustration of the extra savings you could receive: If you place 10 calls in a day that are just over 1 minute, other companies would count that as 10 extra minutes a day—and that amounts to 300 extra minutes a month! With our round down billing method, you can use a plan with fewer minutes, saving you as much as $75 a month, not to mention all the overage fees you'll save by no longer going over your minutes. And for someone whose business relies as heavily on your cell phone as yours, the savings could be enormous. Even a few minutes saved per day could add up to a sizable amount of minutes saved.
Tie-down	I think you can get an idea of the enormous advantage you will have with rounding down the minute billing, can't you, Mr. Mauck?

Effective Presentation Tactics

You have the option of approaching the task of telling your story to the prospect using a variety of sales tactics. Which tactics you choose depend upon what you have learned about the prospect during preapproach qualification, what you observe in the opening minutes of the interview, what you personally want to do, and what kind of environment you find in the interview location. The only limit to the number of different presentation tactics is your own creative imagination. The most common tactics are presented here; you will use all of them at one point or another as they fit into your sales activity. You will probably find yourself developing your own personal mixture of tactics—a blend that fits your personality, your product, and the needs of your prospects.

Participation

Every presentation—no matter how it is organized or what other method is used—must get the prospect involved. When prospects are shut out of the presentation process or choose to remain aloof, say nothing, and contribute nothing, they also buy nothing. The prime tactic for gaining the participation of the prospect is asking questions and then listening to the answers. Plan the questions to be asked during the presentation to gain maximum participation by the prospect.

Beyond asking questions yourself, you should encourage prospects to ask questions about any benefit of the product you present or any factor involved in its application or use. Their questions prevent misunderstanding and give you the opportunity to direct your presentation to the problem or need that is most important to them.

Demonstration

Showmanship sells if it is more than mere carnival hoopla. There is a big difference between showmanship and *show-off-manship*. A well-timed dramatic touch seizes and holds the prospect's attention. A demonstration is an effective method of adding showmanship to the presentation while achieving the purpose of the presentation. A good demonstration provides you with these benefits:[14]

1. Catches the buyer's interest

2. Strengthens your selling points

3. Helps the prospect understand the proposition

4. Stimulates your own interest

5. Cuts down on the number of objections

6. Helps you close the sale

The value of a demonstration is that it involves more than one of the physical senses in the selling process. Remember these three points when determining how you will deliver your message to the prospect:

1. If you rely solely on "telling" the prospect about your product, only the auditory sense is involved. If you add a demonstration, you include the visual sense.

2. If you involve the prospect in the demonstration, you add the sense of touch. The more of the senses you can involve, the more quickly the prospect absorbs the information that leads to a sale.

3. People remember 20 percent of what they hear and 20 percent of what they see, but they remember 50 percent of what they see and hear. By mapping your information out visually, you unquestionably increase how much your clients retain.[15]

Here are four principles to follow in using a demonstration as a part of your sales presentation:

Concentrate the Prospect's Attention on You. The CEO of a large corporation once called a meeting of his associates in his office. When they came in, he was juggling several tennis balls. Finally, he tossed aside all but one and said, "We all have many things on our minds—like these tennis balls. But we must put them aside and concentrate on one problem at a time or we'll waste time trying to juggle them all." This demonstration illustrates the situation when you go to call on a prospect. You must focus the prospect's attention on one thing—what you are saying. A planned demonstration is an excellent tool for accomplishing this purpose.

Use a hands-on demonstration to capture the prospect's interest.

Follow the "Tell 'Em Three Times" Rule. At the beginning of a presentation: 1) tell prospects what you're going to be sharing with them 2) then tell it to them during the demonstration and finally 3) at the end, tell them what you just told them. This is probably the oldest rule in speechmaking—and with good reason. It works. Using this structure makes it easier for your listeners to follow the details and easier for you to stick to the point.[16]

When you fill your prospects in on the agenda and key points in your introduction, you send a signal as to what "files" your audience should open in their minds. When you cover the points in the body of your presentation, you place the data you wish them to comprehend and retain in those "files" they have opened. When you repeat the salient points at the end, you are essentially hitting the "save" button and reinforcing the data already presented. Remember that your prospect, unlike the reader of a written document, cannot "re-read" a passage they did not comprehend or look up a word not understood.[17]

Get Your Prospect Into the Act. Invite the prospect to operate your device, taste your food, smell the fragrance, feel the depth of the tread on the tires, or listen to the quiet sound of your machine in operation. If you are selling an intangible, hand the prospect photos, charts, or a prospectus. Get as many senses as possible involved. The Gulf Coast Regional Blood Center in Houston asks a prospect to put a thirty-letter word puzzle together. The sales representative hands the prospect a small box full of letters that, when properly arranged, spell: WILL YOU HAVE BLOOD WHEN YOU NEED IT? This demonstration dramatically illustrates how crucial a company-sponsored blood drive is to the community and to individuals.

Keep Your Prospect Glued to The Screen. As technology becomes more advanced, more salespeople are engaging in virtual meetings—often called webinars—through Cisco, Skype or any other web-based application. A webinar can be mutually beneficial for both parties because it dispenses with the inconvenience of travel time and costs. Virtual conferencing also enables prospects and salespeople to form sales relationships over great distances.

Virtual meetings do have some pitfalls. As virtual presentation expert Tom Drews, CEO of WhatWorks Communications, says, the average person has a 5 to 8 second attention span, which itself is decreasing as we integrate the Internet into our daily lives. Think of all the ways—Facebook, Twitter, news sites, or email—your prospect could be distracted by what's on their screen! It's your job to ensure that your presentations are riveting. While much of the preparation you will do for a virtual presentation remains the same as for a person-to-person presentation, there are key points you should keep in mind. These are discussed in Exhibit 11.6.[18]

ΔExhibit 11.6

Guidelines for Making A Virtual Meeting Presentation ·······················

Keep your slides simple. If a slide takes more than 3 or 4 seconds to read it is too long.
- Break your points into smaller components, so you have a point per slide.
- Use annotation tools like highlighters and laser pointers.

Think of your slides as mini-movies. Make sure to add photos, graphics and other visuals to help emphasize your point.

Make the most of your voice. The old adage *practice makes perfect* is key. Make sure to practice enunciation, articulation, inflection, volume, tone and pace and, most important, enthusiasm! Practice eliminating fillers like *um, uh, like*.

Interact Often. Give prospects control of the keyboard and mouse so they can control applications on their own desktop. Use annotation tools and the chat room whenever possible.

Ask Questions. Make sure they are relevant—and make sure to use the prospect's name during the presentation. We love to hear the sound of our own name.

Do a dry run. Get a colleague to participate, or record yourself and play it back so you know what parts needs to be changed or practiced more.

Start your meeting early. Set everything up and running smoothly so you are calm and collected when the meeting begins.

Use two or more computers. Have a backup running in case the primary one crashes.

Paint a Mental Picture Using Metaphors. Metaphors imply comparisons between otherwise dissimilar things without using the words "like" or "as", often creating a dramatic visual image. Remember, "facts tell, stories sell." Painting a mental picture is a hook that grabs prospects and reels them in. Steve Becker, west regional manager for Amersham Life Science, has used this creative metaphor with prospects:

> *Picture yourself in a desert without a canteen. In the distance you see a water well. There's a bucket with a rope nearby. Now, would you jump into the well headfirst or would you use the bucket and rope? What my firm can do for you is supply you with the bucket and rope—the tools you need to succeed.*

Metaphors, analogies and similes can bring special life to sales presentations. These are effective ways to reinforce concepts, while building rapport and winning people over to your way of thinking.[19]

Presentation Sales Tools

Sales aids fall mainly into the categories of audio, visual, or audiovisual. Many people are visually oriented. That's why exciting, illustrative slides, and computer-driven programs are effective presentation tools. Sales aids are used primarily to help the prospect visualize or otherwise experience the benefits of the product or service or to help you organize the presentation so that your prospect receives an ordered, logical message that is easily remembered. There are two things to remember when using sales tools to enhance your presentation: 1) low tech items like flip charts are simple, but effective and reliable; 2) with today's technology, the sky is the limit when using audio-visual tools.

The Organizer or Flip Chart

Companies may provide their salespeople with standard visual sales kits in the form of a small flip chart suitable for standing on a desk or in the form of a ring binder. This is especially helpful if the meeting environment is not conducive to a computer or audio-visual based presentation. When such an organizer is provided, a planned sales presentation usually accompanies the visual and is coordinated with it. The presentation and visual help you cover all the features and benefits and overcome objections. The organizer not only provides additional input for the prospect but also prompts your memory about what to cover next and keeps the interview on track.

A well-designed organizer has these characteristics:

1. It is built around user benefits.

2. It fosters two-way communication because you can concentrate on listening attentively to the prospect rather than worry about what to say next.

3. It increases the closing rate by leading naturally to that point.

4. It helps you tell the complete story in less time.

5. It helps the interview get back on track after an interruption by reminding both you and prospect what was being discussed.

Although the company-prepared organizer is a good beginning tool, most successful salespeople develop additional visuals that are useful for their personal style and type of selling. Here are some of the visuals you can prepare for yourself:

1. Letters from existing customers expressing satisfaction with the product, the company's responsiveness, and your personal service.

2. Business cards of existing clients, preferably with a note thanking the salesperson for service.

3. Pictures of clients actually using the product.

4. Pictures of product installations in customers' plants or offices.

For presenting more complicated equipment or processes and for presenting to a group instead of a single prospect, visual aids are especially helpful. Exhibit 11.7 presents some useful guidelines to follow when preparing visuals.[20]

Creativity is thinking up new things.

Innovation is doing new things.

-Theodore Levitt

ΔExhibit 11.7

Guidelines for Preparing Visuals

- Keep your visuals simple.
- Don't use complete sentences. Text should be in short phrases.
- Leave plenty of white space and place text in a similar location on each slide or overhead.
- Use colors that are functional, not decorative. Colors should be easy on the eyes (use red sparingly).
- Never put the whole presentation on a visual and simply read it to the prospect.
- Tables or charts with complex data must only be used for groups that need to study the information closely.
- Each chart or graph should present only one idea at a time to ensure clear understanding.
- Use *line charts* to show how several variables change over time.
- *Bar charts* show relationships between two or more variables.
- *Pie charts* are used to show relationships among parts of a whole at a given point in time.

Audiovisual Presentations

With the portability and capability of today's phones, laptops and tablet computers, there is no reason why any salesperson should not have an up-to-the-minute, creative and engaging presentation a click away. PowerPoint, while being accessible with any Office suite, may not be the answer anymore in terms of quality and professionalism. Instead, you and your company may want to invest in a professional, designer-quality presentation program. These are often compatible with your CRM system, so dates of presentations, presenters, and other variables can be tracked. In addition, web-based presentations are currently gaining momentum because they take the fear of system crashes out of the picture. If you've got a reliable Internet connection, you've got the capacity for a great presentation. Better yet, some companies offer a free trial or tiered subscriber services, so you'll only have to pay for what you need (how is that for customizable sales?). Check out the website links in the *Developing Partnerships Using Technology* section on the next page for examples of these programs.

> "The world is but a canvas to the imagination."
> -Henry David Thoreau

Developing Partnerships Using Technology

A Day in the Life of a Salesperson

What would your day look like with presentation technology?

Brian Thomas has a big day ahead of him. As a new rep for pharmaceutical company, he has two key meetings today—one online and one face-to-face.

He starts his day by checking his email through CRM on his smartphone. Fabulous! A client has emailed him back confirming an interview for the next day, so he makes sure it is scheduled into his calendar. Brian follows through on his tickler alerts then grabs his tablet to review his Sliderocket presentation for his face-to-face meeting. He's amazed again at how professional it looks and how much user interaction it has. Then he's off to the coffee shop to meet his prospect. Brian knows the value of preparation and runs through the presentation in his mind one last time in the car. He gives the prospect a top notch presentation and closes on the sale.

That afternoon, it's back to the office, where Brian will host a virtual meeting. He makes a few adjustments to personalize the presentation for his next prospect. Then he logs into his conferencing service site, greets the operator who will assist him, and double checks that all technical aspects are geared to go and running smoothly. When the meeting begins, he greets the prospect enthusiastically and makes sure to give her keyboard and mouse control so she can interact as much as possible with the presentation. All the while, he asks her key questions and takes the time to listen to her responses. He's made sure to embed whitepaper files into the presentation, which present her key benefits she can't refuse. Another sale closed, another key account opened.

It's been a great day helping people meet their needs. Brian opens CRM again: Who else can he help today?

Check out these websites for additional information:

www.ontrapresentations.com

www.presentiafx.com

www.sliderocket.com

www.cisco.com

Situational Selling

Master salespeople have a specific plan for every sales interview, but they never feel slavishly bound by that plan. Relationship selling requires flexibility. No matter how much you learn about a prospect before you appear for the interview, you can never be absolutely sure what kind of situation to expect when you arrive. Instead of finding a calm, receptive prospect ready to listen and evaluate your product, you may find one who is angry, resentful, or emotional. If planning has been adequate, you can shift gears and make a different kind of presentation, switch to another purpose for the interview, or even delay the presentation until a better time.

John Zavitz finds his smartphone ideal when making sales calls. This way he doesn't walk into a buyer's office "lugging equipment" during the initial call. Instead, he can reach into his pocket and be prepared to take an order, calculate it, offer "what ifs," and make any changes right on the spot.[21] The ability to exercise this type of flexibility is called *situational selling*—fitting yourself to the situation and making each contact with the prospect beneficial to your ultimate purpose of closing a sale.

The Setting

Where the sales interview takes place is often a vital factor in determining its success. The prospect's own office is usually the best place if interruptions can be controlled. If the prospect has a private office, the door can be closed and calls can be held. The prospect feels at ease and in control in familiar surroundings and is not required to put forth effort or travel time to accommodate you. You are a guest and automatically a person to be treated politely and with respect.

If your information tells you that this prospect customarily tries to control every interview and every person, however, you might decide that meeting at a place where you are the host or even on neutral turf would give you more potency. Some salespeople make effective use of what is called a *power lunch*. Inviting the prospect to lunch at a carefully selected restaurant gives you an opportunity to present your product or service with several distinct advantages:

- You are away from an office where interruptions may occur.

- You are the host, and the prospect, as your guest, feels obligated to listen politely.

- The atmosphere is nonthreatening.

- Relaxing over the meal relieves some of the stress of making a decision.

Let's review in detail what we discussed last time.

Interruptions

No matter how carefully you schedule an interview, your best-laid plans often go astray. Asking the prospect at the beginning of the interview if the secretary could hold all routine calls until later can prevent many interruptions. This tells the prospect that you believe the interview is more important than routine matters, but that you know some important duties could take precedence over the interview.

When preapproach information indicates that a particular prospect's duties involve continuous supervision of a work group's activities or that the prospect does not have a private office, consider arranging the interview away from that environment. When an interruption does occur, your sense of timing will tell you whether the discussion can be resumed or whether scheduling a later interview would be better.

If you decide to continue, summarize what has been said up to the point of the interruption. If a problem or need has been identified, state it again and ask a question designed to gain the prospect's agreement. Review in more detail the last major point made in your presentation, and again check for agreement or commitment by asking a question. Be sure the prospect is back on track and is following your planned path of reasoning. If you decide to come back later, attempt to set up a time for the interview. If the interruption is caused by some real crisis that demands the prospect's immediate attention, say you will come again later and leave so that the prospect may give full attention to the urgent problem.

When you do come back, begin the presentation all over. You can safely assume that the interruption has probably completely erased the effect you had built. Preface points with phrases like these: "You will remember that we discussed," "As I told you the other day," or "I believe you told me that." Intersperse your remarks with questions that check on what the prospect remembers, and you can quickly discover what needs to be repeated in depth and what can be quickly reviewed.

SUMMARY

- You can memorize a presentation or use an outline that allows you to present each of your selling points in an orderly and systematic way.

- Personalize each presentation to the needs of the prospect. One of the most important tactics available is prospect participation – even in virtual presentations.

- One way to choose what you will present is to develop units of conviction. Each unit of conviction includes:

  1. A feature of your product or service

  2. A transitional phrase

  3. The benefits the feature provides

  4. Evidence to support your claims

  5. A tie-down to gain agreement

- Sales aids include all sorts of visuals and audiovisuals. The web and cutting edge presentation software make anything possible. Many people are visually oriented, which is why exciting, illustrative graphics are effective presentation tools.

- Interruptions represent anything that distracts the prospect's attention from your message. The setting of the sales interview requires that you be prepared to take advantage of any situation. You must learn to control these distractions and transform them into buying opportunities.

REVIEW QUESTIONS

1. Describe the types of evidence that may be used to back up a claim.

2. Define "salesman's curse." Why is it a problem?

3. How does a salesperson learn to personalize units of conviction? Why is this important?

4. Distinguish between a feature and a benefit. Why is it important to know both?

5. What is a tie-down and why is it an important part of the sales presentation?

6. How can a novice salesperson prevent a memorized sales presentation from sounding memorized?

7. Why must the prospect become involved in the selling process?

8. What are the pros and cons of using a well-designed organizer as an integral part of your sales presentation?

9. What self-prepared visuals could be used by a salesperson selling a landscaping service?

10. How can a salesperson get back on track after an interruption?

ROLE-PLAY EXERCISES

The following role-play exercises help build teams, improve communication, and emphasize the real-world side of selling. They are meant to be challenging, to help you learn how to deal with problems that have no single right answer, and to use a variety of skills beyond those employed in a typical review question. Read and complete each activity. Then in the next class, discuss and compare answers with other classmates.

Role Play 11.1 – Presentation Planning

The class should be divided into teams of 4 persons each. This role play requires your team to plan (not deliver) a presentation of MimioPad™, a product in the MimioClassroom™ family of products from DYMO™/Mimio® ITT (http://www.mimio.dymo.com/en-US.aspx). This major sales presentation is to be delivered to the buying center of a community college so that the product will be placed in the hands of every full-time faculty member. Each member of the sales team should produce a portion of the presentation plan in one of the following areas:

- Presentation style, including persuasive reasons for the recommended style.
- Product analysis, including features and benefits, proof of claims, and tie-down question for each unit of conviction.
- Presentation tactics.
- Presentation sales tools.

The team should discuss and modify each section as necessary and present everything in a unified document.

Each team's presentation plan should be shared with other teams online or in hard copy. In a subsequent class session, discussion will focus on differences among the plans, the reasons for such differences, and which planning features are optimal.

Role Play 11.2 – Features and Benefits

For this exercise, you will work independently.

Select a product of your own choosing. After conducting appropriate research (online or otherwise), prepare a "features and benefits chart" for the product (see discussion in Chapter 11, including Exhibit 11.4). Make the chart as complete as possible, and for every feature, list at least one customer benefit (bear in mind that each feature can have more than one benefit).

Once the chart is complete, write out a one-page summary of a sales presentation approach in which you structure at least two units of conviction (see discussion in Chapter 11).

Be prepared to share and discuss your chart and sales presentation approach in class or online.

CASE STUDIES

The following case studies present you with selling scenarios that require you to apply the critical skills discussed in the chapter and give you training through simulation, role-playing, and practical learning situations. They are meant to be both engaging and challenging, and like the role-play exercises, don't have one right answer.

Case 11.1 – Teaching is Selling!

Dave Casper's dean was not happy. From the moment that Dave walked into the dean's office, he knew that this would not be a convivial meeting.

Peering over the top of his reading glasses as Dave sat on the edge of the sofa, the dean asked, "Have you had a chance to review your student evaluations from last semester? They're substandard once again."

"I know, Dean Farber. You'll notice, however, that I get high marks for knowing the material and for being prepared for class. I just don't know what to do about the rest," Dave replied.

"Well, you're going to have to figure it out," the dean retorted. "Too many students are withdrawing from this course. Since macroeconomics is required for business majors, we can't have that because it delays completion of their program. If you can't solve the problem, I'll have to find someone else who can get the job done."

Dave realized that defending his teaching approach and arguing with the dean was not the right strategy. "Do you have any suggestion? I'm not above trying something different."

"I'm not an economics professor. But your colleague, Martha Oakshott, has stellar reviews. Moreover, her average assigned grade is 'C+'; so she's not bribing the students with high grades. Go talk with her and see if you can learn something useful." With that, the meeting was over.

When Dave knocked on Martha's office door, she greeted him warmly. "Hi, Dave! What brings you here today?"

"Dean Farber suggested that I talk with you. My student evaluations are low again, and he thought you might have some suggestions for me."

"OK. Tell me what you're doing now," said Martha.

"As you know, I have a reputation for thoroughness and organization. I always get through the required material, and I'm extremely organized in class. For years, I have copied a detailed outline of my lecture on the chalkboard, and then I go over each point in order, embellishing whenever I can. I've refined my system so that I always finish on time. You know how students hate to be late getting out of class."

"Wow! You sure are organized," she said, struggling somewhat unsuccessfully not to wince. "I can never stick to the material that well. But tell me, what exactly are you selling?"

"Selling? I don't know. I never thought of teaching as selling anything."

"Oh, but we're all selling something," said Martha with a twinkle. "Just for starters, aren't you trying to convince your students that macroeconomics is important for them as individuals, that what happens on a macroeconomic level will affect their careers directly, and that they should therefore pay attention to national and international economic developments?"

"I guess so. But how do you sell an idea like that? It's so abstract."

Martha then proceeded to explain in some detail what she meant by selling an idea. What do you think she told Dave? What sort of strategies did she advise him to try? How could Dave improve his classroom presentation in order to engage his students more effectively? Do or should selling techniques as outlined in Chapter 11 play any role at all in Dave's approach to teaching?

Case 11.2 – Dorothy's Debut

The president of Dorothy Strong's company, SurgiMax, decided that it was time to make a splash. The company had just developed a new, high-intensity fiber-optic light and lens system, called a laparoscope, for surgical use. The new laparoscope was much smaller, but could generate a higher resolution image for viewing on a monitor. This would allow surgeons to perform noninvasive microsurgery in places that were impossible before. Since there were already hundreds of thousands of older laparoscopes already in use, surgeons would need to be convinced of the advantages of the new model before significant sales could be generated.

A convention of West Coast surgeons was coming up in San Francisco, and SurgiMax was on the program. The president himself usually made these presentations, but this time he thought he would call on Dorothy, his new vice president for sales and marketing, to do the honors. It would be an impressive way to introduce the new product: Dorothy was energetic, passionate about improving health care, and extremely successful as a salesperson in her own right. There was only one catch: there would be over 1,200 surgeons in the audience, and Dorothy had never addressed such a large group. While Dorothy was an expert at relationship selling, she had never had to anticipate the needs of so many people in a situation where no interaction was possible.

As Dorothy planned her presentation, she realized that she needed to accomplish three major objectives: (1) seize and hold the attention of 1,200 surgeons (who were typically skeptical and jaded) for at least 30 minutes, (2) present the features and benefits of the new laparoscope without appearing to be a medical authority, and (3) convince as many in the audience as possible to contact her or SurgiMax for more information.

How would you advise Dorothy regarding the following questions or issues pertaining to her big day?

- Should she memorize her presentation, or should she use an outline approach?

- What sort of visual or audio/visual aids should she use, and how much?

- Are there any kinesthetic aids that she might be able to supply or use?

- Should she use technical jargon and medical terms in describing the laparoscope's features?

- What sort of evidence should she introduce to back up her claims that surgeons would find convincing?

- As she moves through the presentation, what sort of tie-down questions should she introduce (even if no immediate responses are possible)? Or should she just forget about tie-down questions in this situation?

- How should she end her presentation so that her audience desires more information?

Chapter 12
Handling Objections

Use This Page for Taking Notes

Defining Objections

The problem with the word objection is that it conjures up an adversarial relationship between the salesperson and the prospect—someone must win and someone must lose. Just mentioning the word may send some sales veterans into a state of panic or anxiety. But what many fail to understand is a "no" and an objection are two vastly different things. The most successful salespeople look positively at the objections prospects offer. Objections move prospects nearer to the close and reveal what they are concerned about. An objection often reveals the key to closing the sale.

> **Always bear in mind that your own resolution to succeed is more important than any one thing.**
> —Abraham Lincoln

If the prospect has been properly qualified, objections are really buying signals. Offering an objection is another way for the prospect to say, "Here are my conditions for buying," or "I want to buy as soon as you answer a few more questions or reassure me that buying is the smart thing to do." Welcome objections! They are the verbal and nonverbal signs of sales resistance that give you the chance to discover what the prospect is thinking. These objections later become leverage for closing the sale.[1]

Objections actually indicate that the prospect is interested in what you are saying. Successful sales presentations – those that end in a sale – have twice as many objections as those presentations that are unsuccessful.[2] Qualified prospects will not raise objections to a proposal in which they have no interest. They simply wait and say no.

An *objection* is anything the prospect says or does that presents an obstacle to the smooth completion of the sale. Sounds simple enough, right? It's not quite that easily defined due to the fact that sales resistance, or an objection, contains elements of both logic and emotion. When people really want something, logic goes out the window and emotion takes control, and the heart tends to rule the head when it comes to making decisions. Objections are a normal and natural part of almost every conversation—not just in sale situations, but whenever people discuss any current topic. Without this resistance to buying, there would be no need for salespeople.[3] A purchasing decision usually involves risk. To ease the fear of risk, people object, raise concerns, or ask questions in hopes of getting answers that will convince them that the buying decision is in their best interests. Objections are so common that research indicates a prospect will say "no" at least five times before they actually buy.[4]

> **When you don't have an objection, you don't have a client.**

The first task in answering an objection is to calm the prospect's emotions by proving that you are open to reason. Pause before responding; then acknowledge that you respect the prospect's opinion and find the views expressed worthy of consideration.[5] People are open to changing their opinions and attitudes when they are convinced that others value their opinions, understand how they can feel that way, and grant them the right to those opinions.[6] Show a measure of empathy; thus, the key to maintaining a positive sales environment is to *disagree without being disagreeable.*[7]

Your purpose is to remove the objection without being objectionable. Arguing with a prospect, particularly in response to objections, is one of the easiest and most disastrous mistakes you can make. Remember that relationship selling is a win–win proposition. The negotiation process is not a battle that you win and the prospect loses; rather, it is a situation of mutual cooperation and mutual benefit. You may well win the argument and prove that

There is a vast difference between a "no" and an objection.

you are right but lose the sale in the process. People who are forced to agree seldom actually change their minds. Never force a prospect into making a decision; prospects are more likely to stay sold and come back to you for repeat business if the decision to buy was their idea.

Types of Objections

The difficulty with objections is that they have the tendency to sound like obstacles that will stop the sale. When the prospect objects, you must understand what type of sales resistance is being offered before you can handle it effectively. Sales resistance may be separated into four general categories: the *stall* or *put-off*, the *searcher*, the *hidden objection*, and the *stopper*.

The Stall or Put-Off

When prospects offer a *stall* or *put-off* objection, look for the true meaning behind their words. Oftentimes, the prospect is simply trying to avoid making a decision; the stall is a way of saying, "I really don't want to think about your proposition right now because I would then be forced to make a decision."[8] Other times, the prospect is "*not* convinced that your offering will help his bottom line."[9] *However*, you should rarely experience this kind of stall if you have properly qualified a prospect at the beginning. The stall could mean that you have not presented a compelling enough reason to buy, or, in other words, that "you don't yet have a clear understanding about the problem your product or service will solve."[10] A stall is a classic sales killer unless you can build on the sense of rapport you've established with the prospect. If you hear a stall, ask a relevant question, and truly care about the response. You are much more likely to gain a sale if you ask questions, uncover the prospect's genuine concerns, and focus on the relationship, not the sale.[11] In fact, studies have shown that customers have increased purchasing confidence when rapport is developed.[12] Here are some examples of how stalls are phrased by prospects:

1. "I have to leave in fifteen minutes; I have an important meeting."

2. "Just leave your literature with my secretary. I will look it over in the next day or so and then call you."

3. "I must talk this over with my partner."

How you handle a stall is really a test of your *attitude*. If you believe you have a qualified prospect whose needs will be satisfied by your product, then you do not allow a put-off to put *you* off. You should try to uncover the real reason behind the stall. Here are some suggestions for responding to the stalls given above:

1. "I understand—we are both busy people. Allow me a few minutes to ask you about the specific product features your company needs? I may have a solution that could save you hundreds, perhaps thousands of dollars."

2. "Mr. Crowder, I thought that I had adequately covered the points summarized in the literature. Obviously, I have not made myself clear at some point. Would you tell me which points require further clarification?

3. "I certainly understand wanting to involve your partner in a decision like this. Can we ask him to join us now, or may I drop by his office this afternoon?"[13]

The Searcher

The second type of objection is called a *searcher*, which is a hidden request for additional information.[14] Some prospects object simply to get more information even though they have already mentally decided they want to buy. The customer just wants to be convinced that buying your product or service is the right thing to do.

Handle Searcher Concerns With Finesse
Responses to Four Common Searcher Objections:

1. I'm not interested.

There is no reason why you should be interested until I show you how my service can help you make money and solve your problems. May I show you how the product can do that for you?

Do you mean you are not interested at this time, or at all? I'll call back in four weeks; hopefully, things will be less hectic for you.

2. I don't have the money for this.

I can certainly respect that. If I could show you two ways the product will pay for itself, would you be interested?

If you did have the money, would you want it? Good! Allow me to present some facts and statistics illustrating just how affordable our product really is.

3. We are satisfied with what we have now.

What do you like most about the product you are using now? Then demonstrate how your product is better.

You don't like to change without a good reason, right? I can certainly understand that. Here are five reasons why more and more managers are switching to our online sales training material.

4. I really like the competitor's product.

I am not surprised to hear you say that. Their product does have some interesting features. I know some of my happiest customers are people who used to own that other company's product.

The Hidden Objection

The third type of sales resistance is called the *hidden objection*. This kind of resistance is often more difficult to overcome. They can be defined as hidden problems or unspoken hesitations, which, if they are not addressed, can delay or prevent a sale.[15] The prospect refuses to let you know the real concern. Many times the reason is actually quite personal, so the prospect prefers not to reveal it or has a vague feeling that cannot be articulated easily. Exhibit 12.1 pictures the hidden objection as an iceberg lurking below the surface. Just the tip of the iceberg is revealed. You know the prospect has a hidden objection when the answers fail to make sense.

ΔExhibit 12.1

The Hidden Objection

Based on the presentation up to that point, the reasons for not buying are not logical. That means the prospect likely has other reasons for objecting that are not directly related to something specific in your presentation or your product. For example, a prospect may simply not feel comfortable revealing these four real concerns:

1. "Circumstances have changed since you first spoke with me. Recent family problems have caused severe financial hardships, and I do not have the ability to pay for your product."

2. "I find this whole situation distasteful, and I don't want to deal with you. I don't like you, but social convention prevents my being blunt enough to tell you so."

3. "I really don't know what my objection is. It just doesn't feel right. Quite frankly, the product looks like a cheap imitation to me."

4. "I really wasn't in the market for your product. I just wanted to hear what you had to say for future reference."

The Stopper

Prospects often have legitimate reasons why they feel unable to buy. This fourth type of objection is what can be called a *stopper*.[16] Even Houdini couldn't solve this one. The stopper is an objection to which no satisfactory solution can be found. For instance, if you can promise delivery no sooner than six months from now and the prospect absolutely must have the product in three months, you cannot—or at least, you should not—make that sale. Not every prospect is a fit for your product or service. This is inevitable, and if you encounter such a situation, simply recognize this and move on to a more qualified prospect with a real need for what you sell and the ability to buy.

The Heart of Sales Resistance

The relationship salesperson must get to the heart of the prospect's objection before it can be negotiated successfully. Before you can assemble the appropriate facts, logic, and evidence to resolve a vaguely stated objection, you must know the basis for the prospect's point of view.[17] To make intelligent responses to customer resistance, you must know the underlying circumstances.

Most objections that an experienced salesperson hears are not original. If you have been selling for any length of time, your chance of encountering an objection you have not heard before is remote. Eighty percent of buyers will give you the same five or six objections. You should therefore be ready to handle each one in advance and have practiced handling them in a training course or sales meeting first.[18] You should also consider what salesperson and author Jeffrey Gitomer considers the one word key to success: *Attitude.* Here is Gitomer's list of the ten attitudes top salespeople should have before they enter a meeting with a prospect:

1. **Sales Attitude:** The belief you will make the sale.

2. **Value First Attitude:** The customer wants value, not a sales pitch. Are you thinking of what value you can bring others?

3. **Relationship Attitude:** It's more than a sale; it's a long-term, value driven association.

4. **Winning Attitude:** Do you think and believe that you are a winner?

5. **Profit Attitude:** There are two sides to profit. Do you believe you will get your price and that others will profit from dealing with you?

6. **Service Attitude:** Are you thinking about how you can serve others?

7. **Loyalty Attitude:** You know loyal customers breed more sales and profits. Do you believe the actions you're taking will lead to more business and referrals?

8. **Money Attitude:** You know it's not just about making money, it's about earning money. Do you think about getting it before you've earned it?

9. **Success Attitude:** Everyone strives for success in his or her own way. A huge part of success is believing that you will achieve it.

10. **Five Year Attitude:** You must have a vision for your future. Where you will be five years from today will be determined by the actions you take today.[19]

Adopt these 10 attitudes, and you will know you have the proper mindset to answer every legitimate objection. Prior preparation and a servant's heart allow relationship-oriented sales pros like Jeffrey Gitomer to adapt such positive attitudes toward objections.

To deal effectively with the objections you hear, develop a worksheet to categorize them and the responses you use to answer them effectively. Write out your responses word for word, commit them to memory, and practice delivering each one so that it becomes a responsive, intrinsic action. Polish and refine your responses; keep a record of how they are received. You will soon be able to choose the best possible response from your prepared list for each situation you encounter. Exhibit 12.2 lists six basic categories of buyer resistance with examples of what the prospect might say or, in the case of hidden objections, might think.

ΔExhibit 12.2

Categories of Buyer Objections ·······················

Product Objection
- The materials are not up to industry standards.
- The product is poor quality.
- The product won't hold up over time.
- The product has the same features as your competitor but is priced higher.

Objection to Salesperson (Hidden)
- You are poorly prepared.
- You are not listening to my concerns.
- You are trying to sell me too aggressively.
- I don't like you.
- You have tried to dominate me from the very moment you arrived.

Company Objections
- Your company is not very well known; I prefer to deal with a large, established company.
- You represent a brand new company—I don't know anyone who has dealt with you.
- Wasn't your company charged with some unethical sales practices?

Aversion to Decision Making
- See me on your next trip.
- I want to think it over.
- We don't have room for your line.

Service Objection
- I can't live with your delivery schedule.
- We need same-day response on all service calls.
- Your maintenance contract doesn't meet our needs.

Price Objection (Possibly Hiding Real Objection)
- I can't afford it.
- Your pricing structure is out of line.
- I'm going to wait until prices come back down.

When To Answer Objections

A lot more has been said about how to overcome objections than about *when* to answer them, but choosing the proper time to answer them is just as crucial as the answer itself.[20] In determining when to answer an objection, you must consider the type, why it has been raised, the mood of the prospect, and in what phase of the interview it is raised. Timing is important in any negotiation. Prospects introduce an objection at a time that favors their position. Why shouldn't you choose to handle it when the timing favors your position? Normally, there are four logical times for responding to the buyer's concerns:

1. Anticipate and forestall objections
2. Postpone the answer until later in the presentation.
3. Answer it immediately when it is raised.
4. Do not answer an excuse.

Anticipate and Forestall Objections

Every product or service has both strengths and weaknesses. Because no product is perfect, a prospect may well identify a negative feature or shortcoming in what you sell. Hoping that the prospect will fail to notice a negative feature is futile. Instead of waiting for the prospect to raise a specific objection, anticipate the objection and forestall or answer it in the presentation before the prospect can ask. Just as companies want to stay ahead of the curve in technology and product advancements, you must strive to stay ahead of the "objection curve."[21]

Weave into your presentation factual answers to anticipated objections, so they are answered before the prospect verbalizes them. Anticipating objections requires a well-thought-out, planned presentation delivered from the prospect's point of view and focusing on value. Don't just identify potential roadblocks; spell out how to overcome them as well. The more obstacles you remove in advance, the easier it is for others to welcome your suggestions.[22]

As an example of how you might forestall objections that come up over and over again, consider this approach as described by Wendy Weiss, a sales trainer and coach:

> A frequent objection that salespeople hear is: "It's too expensive." You can eliminate this objection's power by addressing it first. If your product or service is more expensive than the competition, there is probably a good reason for it. What is the reason? Does your company use superior quality in the manufacturing process? Does your company offer special services? Identify the reason that your product or service is more expensive—and bring it up yourself.

A good strategy for anticipating and overcoming objections is to do your homework first: Before you meet, **make sure that your prospect is indeed a viable prospect**—that the prospect matches your ideal customer profile. "When you call on a prospect who is not a good match for your offering, you make things harder for yourself. Such prospects don't even need or want what you have to offer—so naturally they have objections![23]

Of course, dealing with an objection early in the presentation does not guarantee that it will not be raised again. However, you are at an advantage in such a situation for two reasons:

- The objection has much less impact the second time.
- You may recall the original answer, expand upon it, and then move on into a close or back into the presentation if necessary.

Postpone the Answer

Some answers to objections are better postponed. This tactic is logical when you are planning to cover that very point further along and the prospect has simply jumped ahead. To answer early might disrupt the flow of the presentation and make the answer less effective. For example, the prospect may ask about price. "How much is this going to cost me?" This often occurs before you have had the chance to establish the value of your product. If you answer immediately, the price may seem too high because the prospect has not yet learned enough about the product to make a value judgment. The price may depend upon options selected; in that case, you cannot quote an accurate price. You may need to build a better foundation before risking a confrontation with the prospect.[24] You can postpone answering an objection by saying something like this:

> *That's an excellent question, and I can certainly understand why you want to ask it. Let me write your question down so I don't forget to answer it. I'm positive, though, that your question will be best answered during the presentation. You can make a more informed decision after you've been presented with all of the facts and benefits. Is it all right with you if we continue?*

> "Nothing will ever be attempted if all possible objections must be first overcome."
> - Samuel Johnson

Salespeople often get price questions early in the interview. Here are two ways to postpone the premature price question:

1. I can appreciate that you would be interested in the price, and I assure you we will discuss it completely, but before we even consider the price, I want to be sure that my service can satisfy your needs. Will that be all right?

2. Mr. McCreary, your concern for price is quite understandable. The actual amount paid for the product, however, will depend upon the options you ultimately select. Let's consider the price for the system after we establish the specific features you will require. Is that fair enough?

The price question should be answered near the end of the presentation, after need, value, and benefits have been discussed. Should the prospect absolutely insist that you answer immediately then by all means do so. You do not want to risk the question remaining in his mind to block out everything else that follows.

Answer Immediately

Most valid objections should be answered when they are raised unless you have a logical reason to postpone them. If you feel the objection is valid and postponing an answer could cause problems, then obviously it should be handled immediately. Answering an objection right away prevents it from festering in your prospect's mind and blocking out the more important information you are presenting. Never answer until you are sure of the real concern, and once it is discovered, answer in 30 seconds or less. Answer questions briefly and honestly; be congenial and intelligent.[25] A sincere and immediate response conveys professionalism, respect for the prospect's point of view, empathy, and listening skills. The right answer removes the resistance and promotes the sale.

Do Not Answer an Excuse

A final alternative is to simply not answer an excuse. After all, some issues don't have a worthwhile answer. On some sales calls, prospects raise concerns that have nothing to do with your discussion. They say things that have no relevance to the point you are trying to make. In reality, they are offering excuses for not buying rather than valid resistance. Never try to answer an excuse. By acknowledging excuses, you may actually turn them into real objections in the prospect's mind. If you must reply to excuses, suggest to the prospect that you will answer them at the end of the presentation. If the question is a serious objection, the prospect will repeat it later. Exhibit 12.3 summarizes the factors to consider in choosing the best time to deal with objections.

ΔExhibit 12.3

Timing Considerations for Objections

Anticipate the Objection and Answer It Before It Arises
- This option should be considered only when you are fairly certain that the prospect will bring up the objection.
- Anticipating the objection prevents a future confrontation and shows your objectivity.

Postpone an Answer Until Later
- Postponing an answer allows you to present many more benefits that have the effect of reducing the significance of the objection.
- Postponing an answer allows you to maintain control of the interview by keeping to your agenda rather than to that of the prospect.
- Postponing an answer gives you time to think about how you will answer it.

Answer the Objection Immediately
- Answer immediately so the prospect can concentrate on the rest of the sales story.
- Answering the prospect immediately shows them your sincerity.
- An immediate answer prevents prospects from inferring that you are unable to answer.

Do Not Answer an Excuse
- Not acknowledging an objection is one way to separate it from an excuse. The serious prospect will repeat it.
- By not answering, you suggest that the excuse is not relevant and imply that bringing it up again is not necessary.

A Six-Step Plan For Identifying Objections

Why do salespeople need specific plans to handle objections? The answer rests in maintaining control. If you allow a prospect to derail you from your presentation with every question or comment, you lose the power; when this happens, your perceived value decreases—and so do your chances for making the sale.[26]

You can best handle prospects' objections successfully by first identifying them, and then placing them in the proper perspective—then the well-handled objections become powerful aids. To handle them skillfully, you need a definite negotiation strategy so that you react naturally to buyers' concerns. Knowing that you have a strategy gives you confidence; then you can welcome objections instead of shuddering at the very thought that the prospect may not go along with your proposition. The six-step plan presented in Exhibit 12.4 should be internalized so that you use it instinctively and automatically.

ΔExhibit 12.4

A Strategic Plan for Overcoming Buyer Concerns

1. **Listen carefully and hear the prospect out**. Learning to listen is not difficult, just unusual. We were born with two ears and one tongue. Listen twice as much as you talk. The buyer will tell you what you need to know. Just listen!

2. **Confirm your understanding of the objection**. The key is to clarify and classify the objection. What type of objection is it and into what category does it fall?

3. **Acknowledge the prospect's point of view**. Prepare the prospect for your answer. Don't just tear into your answer. After all, the buyer must have a reason for stating the objection. Show concern for his or her feelings. Practice empathy.

4. **Select a specific technique**. No one technique works best for all prospects. It must fit your behavioral style as well as that of the prospect.

5. **Answer the objection**. The answer must satisfy the buyer if a sale is to result, and it must be complete. Get a commitment from the prospect.

6. **Attempt to close**. If the close is not completed, continue the presentation. After answering a major objection, ask for the order. The worst that can happen is that the buyer will say no. If that happens, continue with the presentation.

Hear the Prospect Out

Be happy when the prospect raises an objection, because it provides the information needed to complete the negotiation. Never interrupt a prospect who is expressing an opinion; rather, listen carefully to what the prospect says. Observe the prospect's verbal and nonverbal behavior, and listen to what is not being said. Recognize the prospect's right to express opinions and concerns. The prospect is really telling you what to do and their objection is actually saying to you:

- "Give me more information."
- "Go over that service agreement again—it wasn't clear."
- "Reassure me one more time that this is a good decision."

Let me see if I can explain that in a different way.

Simply paying attention is the first step in becoming more responsive to your prospect's objections. Active listening will help you to better respond to what your prospect is really saying. If you really listen, then you can pinpoint what the source of the objection is. This process will help you to better explain the ways your product or service can serve your prospect's needs and be of value to them in the long term.

Confirm Your Understanding of the Objection

Restate the prospect's objection to make sure you understand just what it is; this is a critical negotiation tactic. Use your own words and repeat what the prospect was saying to clarify and classify the real objection and to indicate to the prospect that you understood what was said. In addition, you give yourself time to formulate an answer. Restating the objection in a sympathetic manner dissolves the prospect's defensiveness and helps you avoid the temptation to argue. Say, "Now as I understand it, your position is... ," and then explain the prospect's position in your own words. When you prove you understand, the prospect is ready to listen to you.

Your purpose in this phase is to evaluate and isolate the stated concern. Determine whether the reason given for not buying is the real reason, simply an excuse, or a statement hiding the actual objection. You may decide to answer immediately, not answer an excuse, or seek more information. If you need more information before you can answer, ask questions until you have the information you need. There are a number of questions you might ask the prospect that can help you isolate the real issue and confirm your understanding.[27] These questions include:

1. Other than that, is there any other reason that would prevent you from purchasing?

2. I am glad you brought that out into the open. Is this your only concern?

3. If we can work together to find a solution to this important concern, would that help you make a purchase decision?

It may help to ask the prospect to explain the objection. At times, the prospect may not know fully what they are objecting to, and explaining it will help clarify the issue for both you and the prospect.

Acknowledge the Prospect's Point of View

All successful negotiations find points of agreement with the prospect before you begin to answer an objection. Agree as far as possible before answering, and take responsibility for any misunderstanding. If the prospect indicates a bad experience with your company or your predecessor, believe it. Find a way to cushion your response so that it has a chance of convincing the prospect. After all, prospects believe they have good reasons for not buying and give you those reasons. Instead of arguing directly, soften your answer and say something like this:

1. I can certainly understand how you feel, Mr. Keenan. Others have had much the same feeling when I first presented the concept to them. (Then provide a plausible explanation.)

2. I appreciate your concern, Mr. Keenan, and you do have a relevant point. Thank you for bringing it to my attention. (And you really should appreciate it.)

Select a Specific Technique

In the next section of this chapter, seven techniques are detailed for use in formulating answers to the types of sales resistance you may encounter. Not all of them work all the time. In deciding which of the techniques to use, take these factors into consideration:

- The prospect's behavioral style

- The stage of the negotiation process in which the objection is raised

- The mood (argumentative or receptive) of the prospect

- How many times the objection has come up

- The type of objection (searcher, excuse, stall, product or service)

You must decide quickly on the technique you will use and avoid showing that an objection has upset you. Keep in mind that far too many variables operate in a given selling situation to guarantee that every objection can be answered satisfactorily.

Answer the Objection

Negotiation is persuasion, not manipulation. Avoid explanations that merely cloud the issue and cause prospects to feel that you are trying to pressure them. The answer, however, must be conclusive; don't close off your answer with the question still up in the air. Present only as much information as required to gain the prospect's cooperation and commitment. Minimize the objection by not dwelling on it. Say just enough to dispose of it to the prospect's satisfaction. Be honest and factual, and do not promise anything that you, your company, or your product or service cannot deliver.

Prospects have their own needs, viewpoints, and ways of looking at things. Be sure to consider the prospect's ego and help the prospect to win. Your answer should include a benefit and should be shaped to fit the behavioral style of that prospect. Finally, confirm that your answer satisfied the prospect. Gain agreement by suggesting, "Am I correct in assuming that I have completely satisfied you regarding...?"

Attempt to Close

Closing opportunities exist at various times throughout the entire negotiation process. Recognizing those times and capitalizing upon them is up to you. When you have successfully answered a major objection, you have created an opportunity to close, especially if you are near the end of the presentation. Attempt a trial close before continuing with the presentation. The *trial close* gets a prospect's reaction without exerting any pressure for making a definite decision. It may be used at any point in the sales presentation to test the water to see whether you have presented enough information for the prospect to make a decision. Typical trial closes start with "If you were to buy," "In your opinion," or "How do you feel about..."

If you receive positive buying signals from the prospect at this point, you can attempt to close. If the close proves unsuccessful, get back on track and continue the presentation until another opportunity presents itself.

Seven Techniques For Negotiating Objections

Keep in mind that with any technique you must produce evidence to prove the validity of what you say. Techniques do not establish belief and credibility; that is your job. Techniques are merely vehicles for organizing your answer and your support for it.

After an objection has been clarified and classified, you are in an excellent position to respond by using one or more of the following techniques.

1. Feel, Felt, Found

This practical technique overcomes a stall or a very personal concern. It can offset prospect hostility, pacify an unhappy customer, or inform someone who does not yet clearly understand the value of the product or service. Answer the prospect with this language:

I can understand how you feel.... I have had other customers who felt the same way until they found out....

This approach serves several purposes. It shows prospects that you understand their concerns, and it reassures the prospect that having this kind of objection is normal. Now the stage is set to introduce information that can change the prospect's way of thinking. This technique says that other people who are now customers had similar misgivings but changed their minds after they found out some new information. These new facts allow the prospect to reevaluate your proposition. The following example illustrates how a bank executive in a sales role might use this negotiation technique with an unhappy client:

Banker: Good afternoon, Mr. Reznor. I am Porter Brown with Fifth Third Bank. I have been assigned to your account and would like to ... (suddenly interrupted!)

Client: So your bank is playing musical chairs with its loan officers again. It took Lily Allen six months just to learn about my business needs and now I have to train someone new. Why can't you people give me a banker who will stay with me?

Banker: I certainly understand how you might feel that way. Some of Lily's other clients have indicated that they felt the same way. However, the bank has found that someone with Lily's experience is an invaluable asset to our Problem Loan Division. I have previously worked with firms in your line of business (mention them and provide testimonial letters) and from my review of your account, I feel I have a pretty good understanding of your operation. (By the way, here are my credentials.)

A word of caution when using this method: The feel, felt, found technique is commonly used in a vast number of industries, and if you are dealing with a seasoned professional, he or she may likely recognize that you are using this "technique" and get annoyed if they are aware of what you are doing. Then again, such a prospect might be impressed and even have a good laugh with you, not at you, because they will know what you are trying to accomplish.[28] Here is an example of how to rearrange your words slightly in these situations:

"Mr. Blunt, I do understand how you must feel. Frankly, lots of my customers have felt the same way when they first heard about our program, but what they discovered after further discussion was the benefits heavily outweighed the limitations."

2. Compensation or Counterbalance Method

At times, a prospect may buy in spite of certain valid objections. The prospect may be partly right or may have misunderstood a portion of what you said. Accept and admit any truth in the objection. Admit that your product does have the disadvantage that the prospect has noticed and then immediately point out how the objection is overshadowed by other specific benefits of the product. Your job is to convince the prospect that the compensating benefits provide enough value that the disadvantage should not prevent the prospect from buying. By admitting the objection, you impress the prospect with your sincerity and sense of fair dealing. Then you can select the real strengths of your offering to offset the prospect's negative feelings.

A good way to deal with this situation is to provide documentation such as statistical evidence, a third-party endorsement, or the case history of someone who faced a similar situation. This method works because the prospect is approached positively with an acknowledgment of expressed concerns, and then given a series of logical, compensating benefits to counterbalance the stated objection.

3. Ask "Why?" or a Specific Question

This method is helpful not only for separating excuses from real objections but also for overcoming objections. You can use questions to narrow a major, generalized objection to specific points that are easier to handle. If the prospect says, "I don't like to do business with your company," ask, "What is it that you don't like about our firm?" The answer may show a past misunderstanding that can be cleared up. If the prospect complains, "I don't like the looks of your product," ask, "Why do you object to its appearance?" The objection may be based on a relatively minor aspect that can be changed or is not true of all models.

4. Deny the Objection

One way to answer buyer resistance is simply to assert that the prospect is wrong. This technique must be used with caution or it will antagonize prospects. You can sometimes tell prospects they are wrong but you have to be careful how you do it. You could win the argument but lose the sale.

The denial technique is useful when the prospect clearly has the wrong information. Either a portion of the presentation was misunderstood or someone else has supplied incorrect information.

Point out that the prospect's information is wrong, but not by means of a direct, frontal assault. Present the denial thoughtfully and with dignity. Listen attentively to the buyer's concern, and then begin by saying:

I don't believe I fully understand what you are saying.

This response allows the buyer time to cool down emotionally and perhaps to soften the statement. It also gives you the opportunity to regain your composure. After the prospect repeats the incorrect information, respond in this manner:

I don't know how you could have gotten that impression. I really must have stated my position poorly; please let me correct it for you.

A bit more forceful statement would be: Fortunately for me, that is not the real situation. I have some other information that does not support what you just told me.

Your attitude is critical when using this technique. Your goal is to earn the prospect's respect and avoid an angry reaction. However, you do want the prospect to know that you will not be intimidated. Sometimes a direct denial is your only recourse. There are times when you must fight fire with fire. A direct denial is a high-risk method of dealing with any objection, but it is necessary at times even if you lose the sale.

A successful salesperson can agree with prospects while still showing them that their concerns need not prevent a purchase.

5. Boomerang Method

The *boomerang method* allows you to agree with prospects yet show them that their objections need not prevent a purchase. This method is often used in a situation where the point to which the prospect is objecting is actually a sales point in favor of buying the particular product or service. The boomerang method involves agreeing with the objection and then making another statement that translates the objection into a reason for buying. For example, a sales representative for Blue Bell Inc., located in Brenham, Texas, might hear this type of objection:

"Blue Bell Ice Cream is too new to this area. My customers will not buy something they have never heard of before."

Then turn the objection into a sales point:

"There is no question that our ice cream is new to your area; that's why we are eager to build consumer awareness for the product. We intend to spend over $100,000 to tell your potential customers about our ice cream. Blue Bell uses its advertising messages to presell the product for you. If you agree to carry the product, we will generate a great deal of customer demand (and increase store traffic) for you."

The boomerang method works well when the prospect lacks complete information or perceives a drawback that actually may not exist. Be careful of the image you project when using this technique. If prospects feel that you are directly challenging them or perhaps patronizing them, then you could be in for a real battle. In that case, you might as well pull out your boxing gloves because you will have more use for them than you will for your order book.

The *tongue-in-cheek method* is an adaptation of the boomerang method. It uses a bit of humor that may soften up the prospects and turn away their anger. A salesperson for Strickfaden's Nursery in Sandusky, Ohio, used the technique this way:

Prospect: "I'm not going to buy any more shade trees from you; every time I plant one I have too much dirt left over!"

Salesperson: "Yes, that is a concern. But the way to solve your problem is to dig your holes a little deeper."

6. Curiosity Method

By now, you already know that prospects and salespeople work best together when prospects believe their specific needs are being addressed. The curiosity method works inside this relationship-driven approach. In other words, you should already be asking your prospects questions, so if they raise an objection, it will be natural for you to answer that objection with a question of your own. Take a look at the following scenario in which a web-based invoicing software system salesperson is trying to close on a sale:

Prospect: "I don't think my clients will easily accept such a complex electronic billing system.

Salesperson: I wonder why that is?

Notice the salesperson did not simply ask "why," which could seem aggressive and does not reflect an active listen attitude. Instead, the salesperson demonstrated a genuine curiosity about the prospect's objection. This curiosity allows for an exploration and identification of specific needs. The salesperson can then more meaningfully explain the value of the product features.

7. Deflection Method

It is always important to address prospects' valid objections in the best way you can. You may find, however, that sometimes prospects bring up objections that don't relate specifically to your product or service, or they bring up objections in an effort to take control of the situation. In cases like these, you may want to use the deflection method. Here, you listen to the concern, acknowledge it, and then simply carry on:

Yes, I see what you mean—how interesting. So as I was saying.

This method may initially make you feel like you are ignoring your prospect's concern, but if it was truly an objection that didn't relate to your product or was raised in order to take control of the meeting, using the deflection method can help you move on from it and not get you off track with the rest of your presentation.

Handling Price Objections

One type of objection surfaces so frequently that it requires additional examination: *The Price Objection.* Your prospects and customers want as much for their money as they can get. While that's not unexpected, you can't provide value-added service at reasonable prices if you give up too much at the negotiating table. How many times each week do you suppose a salesperson hears, "I just think your price is too high." To succeed in selling, you must see this type of sales resistance for what it is and overcome it.

The price objection is more difficult to pin down because it can mean many different things. The final price paid for a product or service depends upon the type of discounts available, advertising and promotional allowances paid by the seller, service after the sale, free trial periods, warranties or money-back guarantees, sales support service and training, delivery charges, and myriad other price-related variables. Then, too, the prospect may not really be objecting to the price but may just be hiding the real reason for not buying. When prospects says, "I can't afford it" or "Your prices are just too high," they may just be saying, "You have not convinced me that the value I will receive is worth the price I have to pay to get it." Often the buyer's concerns or questions about price represent an incomplete sales job!

Your company priced the product or service so it would sell. Never be afraid to ask the full value for your offering, but be prepared with solid evidence to support the price you are asking. Do not be defensive or apologetic. You must believe that the price you are quoting is actually much less than the value your product will give the prospect. If your product has exclusive features that are not readily apparent, convert them to benefits and sell those benefits as this classic example of Ma McGuire in Exhibit 12.5 illustrates.[29]

ΔExhibit 12.5

Sell Benefits to Overcome the Price Question

Two farm wagons stood in a public market. Both were loaded with potatoes in bags. A customer stopped before the first wagon.

"How much are potatoes today?" she asked the farmer's wife, who was selling them.

"A dollar and a quarter a bag," replied the farmer's wife.

"Oh, my," protested the woman, "that is pretty high, isn't it? I gave one dollar for the last bag I bought."

"Taters has gone up," was the only information the farmer's wife gave. The woman went to the next wagon and asked the same question. But Ma McGuire "knew her potatoes," as the saying goes. Instead of treating her customer with indifference, she replied:

"These are specially fine white potatoes, madam. They are the best potatoes grown. In the first place, you see, we only raise the kind with small eyes so that there will be no waste in peeling. Then we sort them to grade out culls so you get only full-sized, good potatoes. Then we wash all our potatoes clean before sacking them, as you see. You can put one of these bags in your parlor without soiling your carpet—you don't pay for a lot of dirt. I'm getting $1.75 a bag for them—shall I have them put in your car or will you take them now?"

Ma McGuire sold two bags, at a higher price than her competitor asked, in spite of the fact that the customer had refused to buy because she thought the price was too high!

Ma McGuire certainly understood how to sell value. People have a perceived price-quality relationship. They do not mind spending money when the quality and value of the purchase have been successfully established.

Four Methods for Overcoming the Price Question

A product often has hidden qualities, and the prospect cannot see these qualities and does not fully appreciate them until they are pointed out. You usually get what you pay for. A low price is probably low for a good reason. Competitors can undersell you only temporarily because they have the same basic costs, they are cutting corners somewhere with lower standards of product quality, service, or delivery. A bargain price can turn out to be quite expensive.

You must face the fact that you will not always have the lowest-priced product or service to sell. Be prepared to justify your asking price and show that it is fair. Understand and be able to apply the differential competitive advantages you have in product, source, people, or service superiority.[30] There are a number of negotiation tactics that can help you overcome the price obstacle. You may respond to the question of price by using one or a combination of the following methods.

1. Price Breakdown

The price that sounds intimidating in its entirety often sounds much smaller when you break it down into weekly or monthly payments and compare it to how the customer normally spends extra money. If the prospect is really objecting to the absolute magnitude of the price, then a logical response is to break the total cost down over a period of time. Here is an example of how you might use this technique to convince a physician:

I am glad you mentioned price, and I can certainly appreciate your concern. The upfront cost of the Adobe software system does seem like quite a bit of money. And you know how essential a professional graphics suite is for your practice. Adobe recognizes this and has just implemented a

You can be confident when your firm does quality work.

monthly payment plan. Just imagine, for the price of a yearly subscription to a magazine for your waiting room, your office staff will have access to the best software on the market.

Compare the one-time price of your product to the amount of money the prospect will save after years of using it. The clearer you make the distinction between what your prospects pay and what they get, the easier it will be for them to recognize your product's great value. That's your job—to establish value, not price.[31] Talk about the initial and ultimate costs. Look at the price-cost-value comparison from two perspectives: Price represents the initial amount paid for the product; cost is the amount the buyer pays as the product is used over time.

2. Presumption of Exclusivity

What can you do when the price for your company's product is higher than that being asked by a competitor? Stress those features that are exclusively yours. What does your product have that the competition cannot offer? No two products are exactly alike. You will find strengths and weaknesses in any offering. Analyze your competitor's offering to see why the same product has a lower price. If your analysis indicates that you are offering more, then drive home those exclusive features. You may have to show more interest in the prospect than the competition that concentrates only on price. Go out of your way to isolate other needs of the prospect for which you can provide assistance.

If your company has a higher price, then it must be because you offer more to your customers. Identify your advantages and convince the prospect that the extras can be obtained only from you. In other words, justify the price with facts. Determine what the prospect wants more than anything else from your product, and then identify the features that satisfy those wants. This is called the *presumption of exclusivity*. Concentrate on those features until the prospects feel that only you can satisfy their needs.

Consider this example of how one cell phone salesperson's lack of product knowledge prevented a sale. A prospect was not convinced that the newest arrival in the wireless company's product line was offering him a better deal, and was reluctant to change providers. With every question that the prospect posed to Ron, the sales rep, it became evident that the prospect knew more about the various options and offers in the cellular services than Ron did. "Really?" Ron would say, "That's their new scheme?"

For every answer, he went into a huddle with his boss, who appeared equally clueless. The prospect thanked him for his time and left without purchasing. The prospect had the upper hand because Ron did not understand the concept of the presumption of exclusivity. A visionary salesperson will be able to not just anticipate knowledgeable prospects, but be so educated about his own industry and product line that he can show his product's unique features in such a way that prevents this objection from even surfacing.[32]

If a prospect gives you a hard time about price, stop selling price. Show what the money buys. Make the price seem unimportant in comparison to the value received. You may proceed something like this:

Mr. Dykes, allow me to share some information with you. The lower price of our competitor may not be the best buy for you. Let's look at the quality of our product and why we are more expensive. We pay our employees a fair wage, purchase superior-grade raw materials, and have a multimillion-dollar advertising program that has made our product nationally known.

Our price includes training for your people; our staff is skilled at maintaining and upgrading the product over time. You will have easy availability of parts and a one hundred percent guarantee. We stand behind our product. We don't fight your complaints; we settle them promptly and equitably. The price paid for a solution to your problem should be based on what gives you the best solution. Don't you agree?

Draw the picture clearly and convincingly. Sell quality and exclusivity when the prospect argues price. If you sell the exclusive features properly, the prospect is not even thinking about price by the end of the presentation. Most buyers are fair-minded if you show why your company must get the price it does.

3. Comparison

Be prepared to present logical reasons for the price you are asking. One way you can do this is to compare the quality of your product to that of the prospect's company. For example, you could stress that both are selling superior products:

> *Mr. Givens, your own company makes a high-grade product that commands an exceptionally high price and deservedly so. Your tool-and-die products warrant their outstanding reputation because of the top-quality materials used to make them. Our high-viscosity, high-grade motor oil is naturally suited for your machines. While it's true you can buy less expensive brands than ours, you would not be satisfied with their performance.*

Acknowledging the superior nature of your prospect's product and suggesting that the prospect's company and your company are two of a kind makes considerable sense. This approach elevates your product to the same level of pride the prospect's company has in its products.

If you choose to make comparisons, be sure you have facts to substantiate your claims. Case histories and testimonials are useful for this purpose. For example, Dick Randolph sells X-ray equipment to hospitals and clinics by focusing on company performance and referrals to build trust. "My customers are more concerned about what happens after they sign a purchase order than the actual price," says Randolph, account manager at NXC Imaging. He provides prospects with current customers and a referral list encouraging them to contact any or all of them. Randolph uses his company's reputation to build trust and justify the higher price.[33]

Your price may be more, so focus on your superior quality.

A demonstration could also work effectively to show a comparison. Let the prospect see personally how your product compares to other alternatives. Visual evidence and verifiable case histories produce powerful comparisons regardless of what you are selling.

4. Sell Down

All prospects have a buying range, and because you've done the research on the prospect, you should have a good idea of what that range is before you make a presentation. It's a good idea to have a variety of options or benefits available for your product or service. Present the best, most comprehensive product or service first. This will accomplish two things. First, your prospect will know the quality of features available to them should they choose that option. Second, it gives you the opportunity to reduce the price by removing features or lowering quality. As an added benefit, it gives prospects a sense of control over the buying process without placing you in a position of devaluing the product or service offered. Here is how you can present the sell-down should a prospect present a price objection:

> *Although I believe our premium package is still the best for your company, we can certainly address your need to have a lower-priced option.*

Always remember when dealing with price objections that your prospects know it is unwise to pay too much, but it is actually worse to pay too little. Your customer may pay too much and lose a little money, but when they pay too little, they could lose everything, because the thing that was bought was incapable of doing what it was bought to do. The common law of business balance prohibits paying a little and getting a lot—it can't be done. So be patient with your prospects and focus on the benefits if they still seem fixated on price.

SUMMARY

- Success in handling objections depends on your attitude. If you assume that the sale is over when you hear an objection, it will be. If you regard an objection as an invitation to continue negotiating, you are likely to enjoy a successful close.

- Buyers offer objections for a number of reasons, most of which are psychological. Objecting to something enables them to avoid the risk of making a decision that has potentially unpleasant consequences.

- Some objections are valid and indicate either a logical reason for not buying or a need for you to present additional information before the prospect makes a buying decision.

- Classify and clarify the objections according to their type and apply the appropriate plan to overcome them.

- The six-step strategic negotiating plan for identifying objections gives you the opportunity to handle whatever objection you encounter.

- Experts in overcoming objections record the ones they hear, study them to determine which ones they hear most often, and develop logical answers to use whenever these objections come up.

- You will not always have the lowest-priced product to sell. Apply the competitive advantages you have in product, source, people, or service superiority and respond to the question of price by breaking the price down, employing the presumption of exclusivity, use comparison, or stress the sell down method.

REVIEW QUESTIONS

1. How does a salesperson sometimes cause a specific objection to be raised? What can be done to prevent this?

2. Who is responsible if prospects misunderstand part of the presentation or are not convinced that the product is applicable to their needs? Give examples of how objections reflecting these conditions are likely to be stated.

3. If you were selling homes in the price range of $200,000 to $250,000, how would you anticipate and forestall price objections?

4. In deciding when to answer objections, what factors would lead you to choose to answer them before they arise, postpone the answer until later in the presentation, answer them immediately, or ignore answering at all?

5. List the seven steps in the strategic plan for handling objections.

6. List and discuss several strategies for coping with price objections.

7. How can an objection be considered a buying signal?

8. What are some underlying causes for psychological sales resistance?

9. Why might a prospect raise objections even when that prospect has already mentally decided to buy?

10. In what phases of the relationship sales cycle does negotiation play a part? Describe its purpose in each.

The following role-play exercises help build teams, improve communication, and emphasize the real-world side of selling. They are meant to be challenging, to help you learn how to deal with problems that have no single right answer, and to use a variety of skills beyond those employed in a typical review question. Read and complete each activity. Then in the next class, discuss and compare answers with other classmates.

Role Play 12.1 – Anticipating Objections

Working with the same team of which you were a member for Role Play 11.1, review your presentation plan, but this time try to anticipate objections that your buying center counterparts might raise to various points in your presentation. For each objection that you identify, be sure to classify it according to category of objection (see Exhibit 12.2). Next, decide on when you intend to answer each objection and why. And finally, describe the technique or approach you would take toward answering each objection. In the case of price objections, be especially careful to describe how you would handle them. Be prepared to discuss the results in class.

Role Play 12.2 – Which Objections Are Truly "Stoppers?"

For this exercise, the class should be divided into as many teams as possible of 2 persons each.

In categorizing objections, Chapter 12 mentions that there is one type, the "stopper," that actually calls a halt to the selling process because it cannot be answered successfully. One example of a "stopper" objection is provided.

In class, Team A (a 2-person team) identifies a product or service and begins to present its features and benefits to Team B. During the presentation, Team B interrupts with an objection. Team A then consults briefly and responds appropriately to the objection. The presentation continues, and Team B poses another objection to which Team A has an opportunity to respond. Whenever a "stopper" objection is posed—that is, an objection to which no appropriate response is possible—the presentation is stopped. Then the teams reverse roles so that Team B presents a product to Team A, and Team A poses objections. The team that responds appropriately or successfully to the largest number of objections wins.

The following case studies present you with selling scenarios that require you to apply the critical skills discussed in the chapter and give you training through simulation, role-playing, and practical learning situations. They are meant to be both engaging and challenging, and like the role-play exercises, don't have one right answer.

Case 12.1 – Don't Let the Bedbugs Bite!

Research shows that people hate purchasing mattresses more than any other item for the home. There are good reasons for that. A mattress showroom is intimidating: all of the mattresses are laid out in rows, and they all seem to look alike. Moreover, there are thousands of brands, types, models, and price points, making it almost impossible to compare one store's mattress directly with another store's product. And, finally, there is no way for an ordinary customer to "look under the hood" in order to check independently the features built into each mattress. All the customer can do is lie down on the mattresses to test their comfort; and even that doesn't work well, because all mattresses begin to feel the same after about 5 tries. No wonder people hate the process, and no wonder bedding salespersons encounter so many objections!

Bob Driscoll's store, Mattress Mavens, carries only mattresses on the medium to high end of the pricing scale—$2,300 to $6,000—on the theory that customer satisfaction will be better. This not only cuts down on complaints and returns, but it also improves word-of-mouth marketing. Still, Mattress Mavens faces stiff competition from Doug's Discounts. Doug's produces a lot of TV ads that blare, "Why pay more for just a name? Come on down to Doug's for a quality night's sleep at a fraction of the cost!"

The ads drive Bob nuts because prospects who come into his store don't know what they are looking at or for. They don't have a clue about the shoddy materials that go into Doug's no-name bedding or, worse, about what a $500 mattress will do to their spine over time. Professional ethics prevent Bob from trashing the competition, but he has become frustrated at dealing with pricing objections day in and day out.

When Bob approaches his manager about the problem, he receives some really good support (pun intended!). The manager says that he has just requested some cut-away displays from StarCrest, the store's high-end vendor, so that customers can see and feel just how these fine mattresses are constructed. These will be displayed on the showroom floor along with a few cut-aways of disgustingly cheap mattresses for comparison. In addition, the company is sending videos that show the entire construction process, including the harvesting of wood for the frames, the production of the memory steel coils, the production of foam and cotton layers, and the stitching and packaging. Mattress Maven will play the videos in an endless loop on 6 monitors at various locations in the store. "But," says the manager, "when it comes to handling pricing objections directly, Bob, you're on your own!"

With all of the above support, what should Bob be prepared to do? How can he handle the pricing objections creatively and effectively? What strategies should he employ?

Case 12.2 – "I Must Check with My Spouse"

Charlie Brandon had been selling home furnishings for 8 years. He had worked for high-end companies and discount outlets. And throughout his career, he had encountered more objections than even he had thought possible. Some people wouldn't buy leather furniture because they thought it felt hot; others thought it felt cold. (The truth was that leather always conforms to room temperature.) Charlie had worked out responses to most objections. It didn't mean that all customers actually bought, but Charlie never blamed himself for being unable to help most customers make a buying decision in their own interest. But there was one objection that stumped Charlie nearly every time, and that was some variant on, "I must check with my husband/wife."

There were, in Charlie's experience, two problems with this objection. In the first place, it could often be used to mask a more important, yet hidden, objection. And second, by invoking the privacy of the marital bond, a customer could thwart probing questions that might be considered offensive. Moreover, whenever this objection surfaced, Charlie knew that a customer rarely returned with spouse in tow. Even if they did return together, the second spouse was often grumpy and usually found some pretext to veto a purchase: the merchandise was always "the wrong color," "the wrong size," or "too expensive." It just never worked.

Now that Charlie had accepted a new position with a mid-level retailer, he thought he would attempt to address the problem again. Perhaps Tanya, his new manager, could shed some light on how to handle the spousal objection.

Having explained his previous difficulty with this objection, Charlie complained, "I just don't know what to do, Tanya. Now, every time a customer raises this objection, I just freeze."

"Well, Charlie, I have two suggestions for you," Tanya replied. "First, you need to qualify your customer more carefully and earlier in the process. When a man or woman comes in alone, find some way to ask who the merchandise is for, who is involved in the selection process. If another person must be consulted for whatever reason, then make just enough of a presentation to keep the customer in front of you interested and press for a definite appointment so they can be assured of your full attention."

"What's the second suggestion?" asked Charlie.

"The second suggestion applies later in the process, when your attempting to close after having made a presentation. Perhaps you couldn't qualify the customer for some reason. But now, you need to probe whether this is a real objection on its face or whether it masks some other concern," answered Tanya. "You need to come up with a list of gently probing, inoffensive questions."

"Ok, I'll try," Charlie responded, somewhat apprehensively.

Knowing what you've learned from Chapter 12, what sort of questions should Charlie ask? When should he stop, and why?

Chapter 13

Closing the Sale

Learning Objectives

- Develop productive attitudes and a professional perspective toward the close.

- Know the function of the close.

- Discover the importance of reassuring the prospect.

- Appreciate the value of persistence.

- Gain knowledge of how to deal with rejection.

- Develop a sense of timing in knowing when to close.

- Recognize buying signals.

- Study the different types of closes.

Use This Page for Taking Notes

Success in the End is What Counts, Not Failure in the Beginning
Abraham Lincoln's Failures Far Exceeded His Successes

1831 - Lost his job

1832 - Defeated in run for Illinois State Legislature

1833 - Failed in business

1834 - Elected to Illinois State Legislature

1835 - Sweetheart died

1836 - Had nervous breakdown

1838 - Defeated in run for Illinois House Speaker

1843 - Defeated in run for nomination for U.S. Congress

1846 - Elected to Congress

1848 - Lost re-nomination

1849 - Rejected for land officer position

1854 - Defeated in run for U.S. Senate

1856 - Defeated in run for nomination for Vice President

1858 - Again defeated in run for U.S. Senate

1860 - Elected President

A Closing Frame of Mind

Finding new prospects, successfully making appointments through referrals and other prospecting techniques, establishing trust, and effectively explaining features and benefits can be difficult enough. But when it comes time to close, the results can be crushing, especially to inexperienced salespeople. After all, even the pros often have trouble wrapping up the sale.

A *close* can be defined as a question asked or an action taken by a salesperson designed to elicit a favorable buying decision from the prospect.[1] It is always related to the specific objective you identified for the interview. Closing the sale is not really difficult for the salesperson who is conducting a professional sales interview held under favorable conditions, including the presence of a qualified prospect.

Although closing a sale is actually quite natural, far too many salespeople have adopted such a distorted view of the close that they dread trying, even though the close is their only reason for being there. In fact, in 63 percent of all sales interviews, salespeople fail to ask for the prospect's business.[2] The usual scenario goes like this:

Well, Dr. Bickley, that's about all I have to tell you. Is there anything else you would like to ask me? No? Okay, I guess I'll call you again in a few weeks. Have a good day. I enjoyed talking with you.

Then the salesperson is standing outside the prospect's office wondering, "What happened? I thought sure I had that order. What did I do wrong?" The usual answer is that the salesperson did not do anything wrong. The salesperson just did not do anything.

> Many of life's failures are people who did not realize how close they were to success when they gave up.
> -Thomas Edison

Closing is not a separate event tacked onto the end of a sales interview—it is something that happens all along during the course of the presentation. Closing might be easier to understand if someone had devised a better name for it. The word close suggests something that occurs at the end of a process, so salespeople seem to feel that it is an isolated segment of the selling process that must be approached in some exact manner to produce success; but the opportunity to close may occur at any

By meeting the prospect's expectations and desires from the start, **the close will occur naturally.**

time during the sales interview. The wise professional watches for and takes advantage of every closing opportunity. Take the order as soon as you can get it!

Always Be Closing

Closing begins the moment you speak the first word to the prospect and continues throughout the whole process until the order is signed, sealed, and delivered. You close on many points: the prospect's agreement to grant an interview, confirming the existence of a need, permission to make a survey or an on-site visit, permission for a trial installation, and acceptance of your explanation of product benefits.

The sale has actually been made or lost long before the time arrives to sign the agreement. The final step should be just a formality—a necessary step, but not one that requires making weighty decisions. Unless you complete the selling process by asking for the order, the only title you deserve is *conversationalist*. Ultimately, it's a simple concept; you must close from the beginning. Don't confuse this idea with the hard sell. A cutthroat approach alienates many potential customers. Instead, explain your agenda. Tell the prospective customer exactly what you're selling and how it can benefit their business. Being up front about your intentions promotes an honest, mutually respectful and rewarding discussion, paving the way for a smooth close.[3]

Failure at the close is the result of inadequate completion of the prior steps in the sales process: Inadequate prospecting, incomplete qualifying of the prospect, or too little probing to determine the prospect's needs. As a result, the presentation has focused on the wrong features and benefits, or the wrong evidence has been supplied to support claims for the product. A prospect's failure to buy, then, does not automatically brand you as a poor closer. Studying your entire performance to find the weak link in the chain is necessary. Focusing only on closing as an indicator of sales skill is like expecting to hear Phil Mickelson say that putting is all that matters in golf. Of course, that final putt that wins the championship is the most obvious success moment, but obtain agreement throughout the sales process and the final step is the easiest one.

Learn the art of diagnosing prospects to find their real needs–and then fill them.

Functions of the Close

Even when all the steps leading to the close have gone well, the prospect may still hesitate. Logically, the prospect would gladly sign the agreement when a professional salesperson has a good product or service to offer, has presented meaningful benefits, has a carefully planned strategy for servicing the prospect's account, makes an impressive sales presentation, and successfully answers all of the buyer's concerns. However, the moment of decision is difficult for most people. Buyers take many risks: They must live with the purchase and pay for it; they may be forced to justify the buying decision to someone else; they may be responsible for an important impact on the company's productivity or profitability as a result of the purchase. Risks are threatening to most people. Of course, you may also feel some strain at the moment of decision. You may be asking yourself, "Have I told the prospect enough? Did I find the real need? Did I read the verbal and nonverbal clues correctly? Is this the best moment to close? What if the answer is no?"

The *salesperson-prospect* relationship is much like the *doctor-patient* relationship. The patient knows something is wrong and looks to the doctor for advice about diagnosis and treatment. The doctor guides the patient to a course of action to which the patient gladly agrees. Closing a sale requires a similar guidance of the prospect by the salesperson. Just as a doctor urges the patient to follow the treatment closely, a salesperson must make wise decisions about the prospect's needs.[4] If you believe that the decisions you recommend are in your prospects' best interests, then you must support buyers and help them make the decisions that will solve their problems.

Reassure and Close. Consider how the prospective buyer is probably feeling and thinking. Do you remember the first time you jumped off a diving board? You thought, "The board is too high; I can't swim that far; I'll choke on some water; I think I see sharks." You thought about all the possible bad consequences. Perhaps a friend in the water encouraged you to try. When you finally jumped, you discovered that the water was fine, just as your friend had said. In the sales situation, you are the friend in the water, you know how the prospect feels and you offer the needed reassurance: "Come on in; you'll be glad you took that first dive; I'm here to help if you need me." Your attitude must be that you respect prospects and their decisions, whether or not they decide to jump in. You continue to reassure them until they finally make a decision. The next time you advise them to make a buying decision, they will trust your recommendation more readily.

> **Wife:** Honey, do you have difficulty making decisions?
>
> **Husband:** Well, yes and no.

Once prospects agree that they can benefit from using your product or service, your responsibility is to guide them to a close. You must never be discouraged by a no. If you honestly believe that a sale is an exchange of mutual benefits, then a no should set up this train of reasoning: The prospect is asking me to explain once more that this decision will work, so I will continue to reassure and close. Do not be discouraged when the buyer hesitates. People do not like to make decisions; without assistance and reassurance, some simply cannot make decisions at all.

A Closing Consciousness

The most important factor in successfully closing a sale is not having the lowest price or the best product. Your attitude is the crucial factor. You must have an absolute belief in what you are selling, and you must expect to be successful. If you assume that you will successfully close the sale, the prospect interprets your confidence as reassurance that the product will provide the needed benefits. Your positive attitude makes the difficult decision, "Yes, I'll buy" much easier. All they have to do is say, "Yes, you're right" when you recommend that they buy. Confidence is contagious; it infects prospects and draws them to your side. Confidence at the close allows you to ask for the order in a straightforward manner.

Indecision is the graveyard of good intentions.

> *Mr. Eastwood, we have agreed on the capacity of the printer, its speed capabilities, and the cost of supplying paper, and we have clarified your questions regarding the service contract. We could significantly speed up the process if we could settle now on a delivery date. Is Friday okay with you?*

Closing is only frustrating if you have not identified customer needs, shown the right mental attitude, made a memorable presentation, and were perceived as a genuine help.[5] If you and the prospect have together defined the problem and worked out a solution, then the final question, the close, is nothing more than the last step in a sequence. After all, you have provided a quantity of solid information and helped the prospect study the existing situation and work out solutions to personal and/or business problems. You have been working for the prospect as an unpaid business consultant. The close is payday.

The art of closing is not the process of persuading, but the art of making decisions with which people agree.

When you maintain a positive mental attitude, a high level of self-confidence, and belief in your product, you create an atmosphere within which you can handle the day-to-day rejections that are inevitable in the world of selling. Steve Simms, noted author and speaker, reveals how to *shake off the shackles of rejection*. Simms says that when prospects fail to follow your buying advice, you know that the rejection is seldom directed toward you personally but is instead a reflection of their own differing opinion about what will best fill their needs or a result of their personal hesitancy to make a decision that they perceive as a risk. In other words, you have lost nothing except a little of your time, but the prospects who say no have lost the opportunity to benefit from using your product or service and of being your personal customer. The bigger loss is theirs. Take the following attitude tips from Donald Trump on the NBC series, *The Celebrity Apprentice*:[6]

- **Be Positive**. People like being around those who give off good energy. John Rich and Marlee Matlin did so well because they gave off such positive energy and wanted to win badly, but win fairly, for their respective charities. Gary Busey got fired in large part because no one could stand to be around his eccentric personality. (Although his behavior in the boardroom didn't help his cause).

- **Have the Courage to Speak Your Mind**. Don't mistake being positive for going with the flow. For example, during a negotiating session Meat Loaf was stubborn and quite emotional that his was the best idea. He simply could not see anyone else's point of view. Expertise is worth nothing if you don't know how to use it.

- **Stand Up For Yourself**. As "The Donald" says, "If you don't stand up for yourself, no one else will." He fired one of his favorite celebrities, Hope, because she didn't defend herself when her team told Trump she'd been a poor project leader, even though her team won that project. Trump told his TV audience afterwards, "If you don't fight for yourself, the accusations must be true."

Persistence

Jim Duerr, a sales rep for Chris-More, Inc., says, "You should push, but never be pushy." Duerr calls on Nashville commercial builders to convince them to use his company's line of plumbing supplies in their construction projects. Jim suggests that, "making repeat, meaningful calls demonstrates to prospects that you are not going to give up. *The idea is to be graciously tenacious—without being obnoxious.*"[7] Focused persistence involves asking whether doing this today will get you that tomorrow.[8] Successful salespeople like Jim Duerr never take no for an answer unless it is in everyone's interest to do so. If the business is worth having, it is worth going after repeatedly—with repeated calls or repeated attempts to close during a single call. The extra effort often makes the difference between success and failure. Jim was able to win a substantial amount of the plumbing needs of the Opryland Hotel after the terrible floods that hit Nashville in 2010.

By permission of Syndication International Ltd., London.

Gerhard Gschwandtner, founder and publisher of *Selling Power* magazine says that, "When you are at the point where you think it's not worth it, that's when you need to redouble your efforts. Customers are looking for someone who is dependable, who is persistent and who will do what it takes to get the best solution implemented within the customer's organization." When sales are slow and you feel like every step is an uphill battle, that's when you shouldn't quit. Salespeople who redouble their efforts will be rewarded handsomely by the payoff. "The pain goes away the minute you are victorious," says Gschwandtner, "but if you give up, the pain will persist for the rest of your life."[9]

How often do you ask prospects for their business? The answer often given is "one more time." Realistically, you should be prepared to ask at least four or five times. A study of several thousand salespeople demonstrates how important persistence really is:

1. 48 percent of those interviewed quit after the first contact with a prospect.

2. 73 percent give up after the second contact.

3. 85 percent quit after the third contact.

4. 90 percent give up after the fourth contact.

The most dramatic statistic from the study shows that the 10 percent of salespeople who continue past the fourth contact, end up with eighty percent of the business.[10] Selling should be a side-by-side, step-by-step process, involving both prospect and salesperson, in which the salesperson earns the right to close. When you understand the problems faced by prospects, stay with them through the problem-solving process, watch for buying signals, and time the close to fit the prospect's behavioral style, your chances of a successful close skyrocket. Opportunities to close occur a number of times during the sales process; recognize them, persist, and ask for the order. Exhibit 13.1 describes the kind of persistence needed for success in sales.

ΔExhibit 13.1
Persistence

One of the best examples of persistence is a story you probably loved as a child—*Green Eggs and Ham*. This Dr. Seuss classic describes the attempt of the "salesman," Sam I Am, to induce a wary "prospect" to try a meal of green eggs and ham. When his first straightforward offer is rejected, Sam I Am tries one assumptive close after another: "Do you want them here or there? Would you like them in a box or with a fox? Do you want them in a house or with a mouse?" Finally, the prospect tries green eggs and ham and is surprised to find them quite delicious. His no's seemingly never registered with the persistent Sam I Am. If you have not read *Green Eggs and Ham* lately, visit the children's section of the library and learn the story's important lesson about persistence.[11]

Dealing With Rejection

Many would-be salespeople leave the profession because of their inability to cope with the day-to-day sense of rejection they experience. They interpret a prospect's refusal to buy as a message that says, "You are personally worthless." Mary Crowley, founder of Dallas-based Home Interiors, Inc., would often tell her salespeople what Eleanor Roosevelt was quoted as saying: "No one can make you feel inferior without your permission." She feels that this concept is especially important for not only her people, but all sales reps, to internalize.

My great concern is not whether you have failed, but whether you are content with your failure.
-Abraham Lincoln

Sales professionals must learn to deal with rejection by keeping a positive attitude about themselves and how they make their living. True, they feel disappointment if they fail to close, but successful salespeople focus in on the sense of accomplishment they feel when they do close a sale.[12] To keep from being overwhelmed, accept the fact that rejection exists, see it for what it really is, and never make the mistake of allowing it to serve as a measure of your own self-worth.

What is a good *batting average* in selling? Professional baseball players who average .300 (three hits for every ten times at bat) or more for a full season are a small minority of players in the major leagues. Imagine failing to get a base hit 70 percent of the time. Consider some of the great names in baseball history:

- Babe Ruth hit 714 career home runs, but struck out 1,330 times.
- Cy Young won 515 games, but lost 313.
- Ty Cobb stole 96 bases one year but was caught stealing 38 times.

Baseball fans ignore the failures and instead concentrate on the successes of their favorite players. The attitude of all true professionals is, "I may have failed, but that does not mean I am a failure."

A salesperson who never hears a 'no' is not a salesperson, but merely an order taker. Rejection is as much a part of sales as getting dressed in the morning, and salespeople who can't or won't deal with it had better find another career. The first thing to remember when handling rejection is that you just can't take it personally.[13] Refuse to permit anyone else to make you feel bad about yourself. Exhibit 13.2 describes nine specific tactics for coping with rejection.[14]

ΔExhibit 13.2

Nine Tactics for Dealing with Rejection ························

1. **Remind yourself that you are not alone.** Remind yourself of exceptional salespeople and how many hundreds or thousands of rejections they had to face on their journey to success. You see, you are not alone!

2. **Forgive yourself.** When you make mistakes, forgive yourself. Mistakes are great learning experiences, but to benefit from them you have to keep moving forward. Continue to generate, gather and harvest prospects. The more prospects you have, the better you feel.

3. **Give yourself a pep talk.** Replace negative thoughts with positive ones such as, "I'm a great salesperson, and after they hear what I have to say, they'll want to buy from me."

4. **Refuse to give up**. Remind yourself constantly that persistence is key to success, and that rejection may not be pleasant but you won't let it stop you. Stubbornly refuse to let it get to you!

5. **Remember you are important because of who you are, not what you do.** Remind yourself of the difference between self-worth and performance. Never equate your worth as a human being with your success or failure as a salesperson.

6. **Engage in positive self-talk**. Separate your ego from the sale. The prospect is not attacking you personally. Say to yourself, "This prospect doesn't even know me; the refusal to buy cannot have anything to do with me as a person."

7. **Positively anticipate rejection and it will not overwhelm you.** Expect it, but don't create it. Think in advance what your response to rejection will be.

8. **Broaden your definition of success**. Instead of looking at outcomes, or being attached to how things turn out, look at success as getting out there in the first place.

9. **Commit to routinely attracting more customers than you need**. "No, thanks" is much easier to handle when you have a steady flow of qualified prospects streaming in. If you aren't in this position, be sure to revisit your marketing plan and recommit to daily marketing actions.

When To Close

Most of the sales you make will not close themselves. The true superstars of selling do not find it necessary to ask overtly for orders. Many factors go into the successful closing of a sale, from timing to presentation style.[15] The closing curve shown in Exhibit 13.3 illustrates how the closing process works. The will-buy line (WBL) shows that some sales will be closed almost at once, others are easy sales, and that most can be closed with an interest-building presentation. A few can never be closed. The key is recognizing the spots at which a close can be made—when the buyer gives a buying signal. The appearance of a buying signal is the critical moment during the presentation when a successful close is more likely.

ΔExhibit 13.3

The Closing Curve

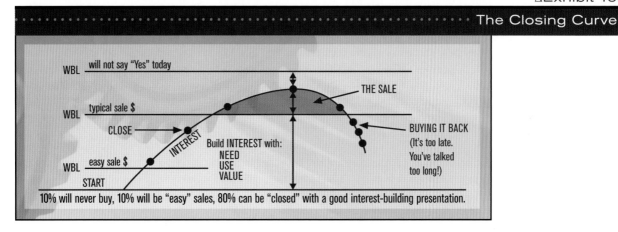

WBL — will not say "Yes" today

THE SALE

WBL — typical sale $

CLOSE → INTEREST

BUYING IT BACK
(It's too late.
You've talked
too long!)

Build INTEREST with:
NEED
USE
VALUE

WBL — easy sale $

START

10% will never buy, 10% will be "easy" sales, 80% can be "closed" with a good interest-building presentation.

When you sense the psychological moment to close do so immediately. A delay of even a few seconds may give prospects a chance to change their mind.[16] If you fail to recognize these critical moments at which the prospect is most nearly ready to make a buying decision and continue to talk past them, the close becomes steadily more difficult. After a critical point is passed, you must buy back the prospect's readiness to decide. In other words, you must once again convince the prospect that buying is the proper decision. Talking too much and overselling is a much greater danger than underselling. Your attempts to close early and often eliminate the possibility of going past the point at which the prospect is ready to buy.

The professional salesperson guides and directs the prospect's behavior. As you reach the point where the final decision is to be made, it's just as important for you to know when to ask for the order as it is for you to know how to ask.[17] Instead of just watching passively for signs of interest, you must create situations in which interest can be generated and revealed.

The best psychological moment for closing may occur at any time during the presentation. When it does come, prospects signal in some way that you have convinced them and they are ready to buy.[18] You never have only one possible moment to close. You may be in the early stages of the presentation, you may have completely exhausted all the selling points you planned to present, or you may be somewhere in between.

Recognizing Buying Signals

A *buying signal* is anything the prospect does or says that indicates readiness to buy. Buying signals are all around us if we learn to recognize them.[19] Unfortunately, it's all too easy to become focused on your presentation that you overlook these signals even if they are obvious. Buying signals occur quickly and may be verbal, nonverbal, or both. Genuine buying signals show that the prospect has moved from evaluating your proposal to an appraisal of it.

A buying signal may come in the form of a question. A prospect may ask you to repeat some point or benefit previously discussed or stop you right in the middle of the presentation to ask how long delivery will take. However a buying signal comes, take advantage of it and close immediately. Always remember that when the prospect is ready to buy, you will receive a signal.

The CHEF Technique

Just as the experienced chef in a fine restaurant knows precisely the right ingredients to blend to produce exquisite cuisine, similarly professional salespeople can exhibit chef like characteristics as they try to translate the combination of gestures fed to them by their prospects. With the traditional method of selling, salespeople were taught to close, close, close. They were told to spend most of their time closing the deal. Trainers taught salespeople fancy closes to handle and overcome objections. Over the years, a new school of thought has evolved: the school of possibility. Imagine what would be possible if all the objections you typically hear at the 'closing table' were prevented and defused throughout the course of your presentation.[20]

In addition to this new mindset, it is essential to decipher prospects' physical buying signals to determine your level of effectiveness through the presentation in bringing them to a point of decision. Use the **CHEF** method (Cheek or Chin, Hands, Eye Contact, Friendly Prospects) to identify these verbal and nonverbal buying signals.[21]

Cheek Or Chin. When prospects touch or stroke their chin or cheek they are signaling satisfaction and gratification. Leaning forward and nodding the head in agreement says, I'm almost persuaded. In this instance, ask if you've answered all their questions, move quickly and ask for their business. Prospects that tighten their jaw muscles or cover their mouths suggest that they are not receptive to what you have to say. This is a critical time to ask questions to open them up.

Hands. Open and relaxed hands, especially with palms facing upward, are a sign that prospects may be ready to buy. Rubbing their palms together signals that they are already assuming ownership. Those individuals who steeple (like a church steeple) their hands together are indicating confidence or superiority. When the prospect's hands are fidgeting or forming a fist, they're more than likely skeptical, or worse yet, irritated. You must stop talking and find out what is wrong!

Eye contact, or the lack of it, can signal to the salesperson a prospect's level of interest.

Eye Contact. Maintaining consistent eye contact with you indicates that the prospect is probably paying attention to what is being said, and the handling and examination of any visuals shows the intensity of that commitment. This is a good time to request a buying decision. When the pupils of the prospect's eyes are dilated this signals relaxation, and you are on the right track. However, rolling or squinting of the eyes often means irritation or confusion. In addition, the rate at which a prospect blinks can indicate anger or excitement. A raised eyebrow can mean the prospect doesn't believe what you are saying.[22] Something is wrong and you had better find out what that something is. If you sense this you might say, "You seem a bit uneasy with this. Please tell me what concerns or questions you have."

Friendly Prospects. Prospects who are smiling, relaxed, or engaging you in conversation are telling you that you've earned their trust. A prospect indicates readiness to purchase by saying, "It sounds good, but I ought not to buy." Give this prospect another reason to buy. Reassure and ask for a decision. When prospects turn unfriendly, try to be sensitive and empathetic. After all, the basic reason for becoming experts at relationship selling is to *create an atmosphere within which an act of trust can take place*! People like to buy from people who are like them.

The Trial Close

A *trial close* asks for an opinion; a *closing question* asks for a decision. A trial close, by asking for an opinion, serves as a thermometer that tells you whether the prospect is warm, hot, or cold to your proposition. It is designed to help you read the prospect's feelings and predict probable reactions. In Chapter 11, the tie-down question was discussed as one element in a unit of conviction. The tie-down and the trial close are used for basically the same purpose. When you get the prospects agreeing with you throughout the presentation they are much more likely to agree with you when you ask the closing question, that is, when you make the formal request for their business. You want to be careful not to talk past the sale. Close when the prospect wants to buy.

Many salespeople think of closing as the last phase of a sales call. If they do, they may not get all the sales that they should. During every sales call there will be a number of opportunities to close the sale. How do you know the proper time? When in doubt, test the prospect with trial closes such as:

1. "Is this what you're looking for?"
2. "Can you imagine how this will boost your productivity?"
3. "Do you have the necessary budget for this?"
4. "What else do you need to make a decision?"
5. "Does this sound like something you would like to do?"[23]

Although it resembles a definite attempt to close, the trial close is used to probe and to reveal how far along the prospect has gone in the decision-making process. You do not need to ask a closing question if you know the prospect is not ready to buy. The time to ask for the order is when the prospect is fully ready to buy. You can, however, ask for an opinion at any time.

A Closing Question

A closing question, in contrast to the trial close, is designed to produce an answer that confirms the fact that the prospect has bought. Look at these two examples:

1. Would it be better for you to receive shipment of a full month's supply right away, or would you prefer to receive half at the end of this week and the other half in about ten days?

2. We can have the product delivered to your warehouse next week. Is Monday a convenient delivery day for you?

When you ask a closing question, say nothing else until the prospect gives an answer. The pressure of silence is enormous. Silence is golden because of what it brings you in terms of the information you need. Never miss the opportunity not to say something.[24] If you can remain silent after asking the closing question, only two outcomes are possible: 1) The prospect says yes or 2) the prospect gives a reason for not wanting to buy. In either instance, you are better off than you were before you asked the question. If the answer is yes, you have a sale. If the prospect gives you a reason for not buying, a concern has surfaced that you can convert into another opportunity to close.

Technology and Closing. Technology can make closing the sale quicker for salespeople. Smartphones often eliminate the need to return to the office for price approvals or price calculations. When several individuals must approve a price or bid before the salesperson can close, smartphones and Wi-Fi connections can give a time-saving edge to your deal. For instance, the Falconite company sells cranes and lift equipment to industrial and commercial users. In the past, days or weeks might pass before all the individuals involved study, make corrections, and approve a bid on a large purchase. Today, the bid is sent to each person's smartphone. Each one makes changes and returns the bid to the salesperson with applicable comments or notes. The changes are incorporated, and the bid is sent back for final approval. Less than a day may be required for complex bids even though everyone involved is at widely separated locations in the field.

Developing Partnerships Using Technology examines how computer networks shorten the selling cycle and facilitate the purchasing function. Computer-to-computer systems link customers and suppliers, providing a one-stop communication tool for the salesperson. These systems are referred to as Electronic Data Interchanges.

Developing Partnerships Using Technology

Make an Electronic Data Interchange a Member of Your Closing Team

Electronic Data Interchanges (EDI). Today's salesperson can leave his order book at home. With EDI, it's like having your own personal sales team member along on your calls. When a salesperson uses EDI technology, he has a one-stop communication tool for the ordering, production, delivery, and billing of a product, right at his fingertips. EDI allows the computer system of the salesperson's company to communicate with the prospect's system. Companies can electronically exchange business documents like purchase orders and invoices.

With this digital exchange of data, the salesperson is freed up to provide quality customer service and keep track of any order and its status. Instead of dealing with cumbersome paperwork, the salesperson can focus his time on listening to the customer's needs and developing a more personal level of interaction.

Here is just a sampling of what this EDI tool can do to help a salesperson:

1. Shorten the overall selling cycle and simplify the purchasing function between the salesperson and his clients.

2. Allow automatic replenishment of inventory on a just in-time (JIT) basis.

3. Recording of all production, ordering, and delivery communication.

4. Automatic processing of information through computers without human interference.

Check out these websites for additional information:

www.edi-network.com

www.cticomm.com

www.truecommerce.com

Types Of Closes

There are a multitude of closing strategies, and as a professional, you should become familiar with as many types of closing techniques as possible. One or two standard closes are not enough in the competitive selling arena that is filled with many different kinds of buyers, all with varying needs and personalities. You need a specific close for every occasion and for every type of prospect. If you attempt to use the same close for every prospect, you will walk away from much of the business that should be yours. The sales plan for each interview calls for a specific type of presentation strategy; your plan should also extend to the type of close you use. Just as circumstances often dictate some changes in your presentation, however, they also point up the need for shifts in your closing plans. Your sales call plan should provide the preferred closing routine to fit with the presentation you expect to deliver. Be sure to plan some alternative closing routines you can use in the event you find it is necessary to modify your presentation.

For example, an insurance agent had prepared a comprehensive insurance program to present to a client. Upon arrival the agent finds an excited prospect who shares information that he and his wife are actually expecting triplets. This prospect's needs have changed dramatically in just 24 hours. The presentation now becomes a work session to devise a new program, and the close the agent anticipated may not be appropriate. A master salesperson with a full repertoire of closing techniques merely chooses one that fits the revised situation and moves on as though nothing unusual is occurring. The various closing methods shown in Exhibit 13.4 and described here are not the only methods available. Most of them are subject to combination with other methods to fit your unique personality, your product, and your market. Learn the principles upon which these techniques rest and adapt them to your needs.

ΔExhibit 13.4

Successful Closing Techniques

1. **Assumptive close**—Throughout the presentation, assuming that the prospect will buy allows the prospect to make the decision more easily by presenting opportunities to make smaller or easier choices.
2. **Impending-event close**—Stress the urgency to make a decision because something is about to happen that means the opportunity to buy with the present advantages may be lost.
3. **Direct close**—Make a straightforward request for the order. Many buyers appreciate a no-nonsense approach, but be mindful of each prospect's behavioral style and use this approach only with those who welcome such tactics.
4. **Summary close**—Review the features and benefits of the offering with particular emphasis on selling points that generated the most prospect interest earlier in the presentation.
5. **Call-back close**—Most sales are not closed on the first attempt. Offer to call back on a prospect with a specific purpose in mind and with new information.
6. **Trial-order close**—Either guarantee the prospect's money back or offer to absorb all expenses if the prospect tries the product or service and decides not to keep it.
7. **Balance-sheet close**—The salesperson takes an active part in the decision-making process to help the prospect understand that the reasons for buying heavily outweigh the reasons opposed to buying.
8. **Never-the-Best-Time Close**—This is ideal for prospects who are sitting on the fence and unable to make a decision by showing them that delaying will either get them no advantage or may even be to their disadvantage.
9. **1-2-3 Close**—For those prospects who are "straight shooters" and don't want you to have to woo them into buying, this can be an effective close. You simply summarize the best benefits in sets of three and ask a closing question.
10. **Cost of Ownership Close**—If you have a product of superior quality and can offer low service costs, you can emphasize the total cost saved over time, rather than the high up-front cost that may scare away customers.
11. **No-Hassle Close**—Do everything you can to make the buying process as simple as possible for the customer. Fill in all forms for them, and provide delivery and installation.

Assumptive Closes

In a sense, every close is assumptive. You do not attempt to close until you have received one or more buying signals from the prospect and have reason to believe you have a better than even chance of success. When you enter every sales interview with a positive expectation of success, you are assuming that the prospect will buy at the close. Your attitude throughout the interview is assumptive. Say, "When you use this product" and "As your program progresses." Avoid words like *if* and *should* because they are conditional and block closing action.

The assumptive approach to closing establishes a positive environment in which the prospect can more easily say yes. These closes work well with indecisive buyers who tend to be nervous about making a final decision. Present them with minor decisions that give them the opportunity to appear decisive in a small matter while they are actually painlessly making the big decision at the same time. The closes described below are common assumptive closes.

Continuous-Yes Close. By asking a series of questions throughout the sales presentation, all of which are designed to be answered in the affirmative, it becomes more difficult for buyers to say no when they've already said yes a number of times. That is why you must get agreement on minor points before you ask for the order.

These questions begin in the need discovery phase. For example: "I'd like to ask you a few questions that help me understand your particular needs. Would that be okay with you?" Yes. Then continue them during the presentation: "Do you like the idea of our billing in six-second increments on all your long distance calls?" Yes. During the closing phase you may ask: "Are you satisfied with the comprehensive service contract that we offer?" Yes. "Does the financing of this telecommunications system seem fair to you?" Yes. "Then it seems we can go ahead with our plans to begin the installation process." Yes. These are all closed-end type questions, so you must be confident that you will receive an affirmative response before you ask them. When the final closing question is asked, the prospect is inclined to keep on agreeing with you. You have a sale.

Physical-Action Close. The physical-action close is quite simple, but can be most effective. Without directly asking for the prospect's order, begin taking some action that assumes the sale is completed. For example, you can begin filling out paperwork and ask the prospect for a signature when you finish. A retail salesperson may simply begin wrapping the merchandise or move to the cash register to ring up the order. If the prospect does not object or stop your action, the sale is made.

Order-Blank Close. Begin to ask the prospect a series of questions and write the answers on the contract or agreement form. You might ask, "Do you use your complete middle name or just an initial?" Continue to fill out the information and then ask for a signature. "Now that we have reached agreement, I know you will want to expedite delivery. Just indicate your approval by placing your name right here."

Ownership Close. With this assumptive close, you act as if they already own what is being sold. Talk about your product and what they are going to do with it. Discuss how it already fits into their lives. Do not talk about whether they are ready to buy or have already bought it. Just act as if it has always been theirs.[25] Here are some examples:

- Now where will you put your new wardrobe?

- What will people say about your car?

- What do you like most about your camera?

The ownership close uses an assumptive principle, acting as if they already owned the product. This seeks to create mental closure on the principle of already owning it.

Alternate of Choice Close. In general, people like to exercise their freedom of choice and salespeople like to lead their buyers toward an easy agreement. This well-known close consists of giving the prospect a choice between two positive alternatives. Here are some suggestions:

1. Would delivery be convenient on Thursday, or would you prefer Friday?

2. Do you prefer to pay cash or is our monthly payment plan more convenient for you?

3. Where would you like the order sent—directly to your warehouse or to the main office?

The idea behind the alternate of choice close is to offer the prospect a choice between buying A and buying B instead of a choice between buying and not buying. The question is not "Will you buy?" but "When?" or "Which one?"

Impending Event Close

This close uses the sense of urgency that is suggested by some impending event that will affect the terms or the effectiveness of the buying decision. Use this close with discretion. It must be based on truth and must not seem manipulative. The most common inducements are concerns that prices are going up or that resources will be in short supply.

My company has announced that prices on this product will go up about five percent next month because of an increase in supplier costs. If I can call your order in now, you can stock up before the price increase becomes effective.

Never use this close deceptively! Whatever the impending event is, it must be real and in the prospect's best interests to take advantage of an order placed now. Because this close is often abused by manipulative and scheming salespeople, prospects are likely to be skeptical of it. When you have good information to work with, you can prevent a customer from running short of inventory or from facing an unexpected price increase, and this gains the appreciation and the loyalty of the customer. Properly applied, this close can work wonders for your long-term credibility.

The Direct Close

The direct close is a straightforward request for an order. Once you have covered all the necessary features and benefits of your product and matched them with the buyer's dominant buying motives, you can ask with confidence, "May I have your business?" This type of close is quite common when selling to industrial buyers. Many buyers appreciate a no-nonsense approach. Of course, be mindful of the buyer's behavioral style. Amiables, for example, could find this approach threatening.

Be sure to keep the direct close positive. Avoid the word *don't*. "Why don't we begin next week?" and "Why don't you try the product for a while and see what happens?" are open invitations to additional objections. Insertion of a negative into the close may implant doubt where none existed, and the prospect may try to tell you why not. Use positive statements like these:

1. I will schedule delivery for next Tuesday?

2. It comes in five-pound, ten-pound, and twenty-pound bags. I suggest you take five of each to begin.

3. Let's run your first ad beginning Friday of this week.

When you use this type of closing statement, then you and your customer can make positive plans together.

The Summary Close

One of the best closing tactics is to summarize the major selling points made during the presentation. This method is especially good when the prospect must defend a purchase to someone else. The repetition of benefits at this point overcomes the prospect's tendency to forget or overlook points previously identified as important to satisfying existing needs. Review the benefits and ask the prospect to confirm again that they are important. Avoid mentioning any new benefits during this close. Bring up additional points only if the summary fails and you need additional ammunition to answer new objections.

Concentrate in the summary close on those items that were of most interest to the prospect and that related directly to the dominant buying motives.[26] For example, a sales rep selling advertising space in an industrial magazine might use the summary close like this:

Mr. Russell, let's review the major points on which we have agreed:

1. An ad in our magazine will give you maximum effective circulation coverage.

2. Your ads will enjoy high readership.

3. We saw that businesses similar to yours have had a great deal of success advertising with us (indicate testimonials or case histories used during presentation).

4. Our marketing staff will help you develop ads for all the media you use, not just our magazine.

5. You'll receive free artwork and layout help. These services are included in our basic price.

This summary puts into capsule form the highlights of your sales story. It gives both you and the prospect an opportunity to reconsider what was covered throughout the sales interview.

Give the prospect an opportunity to agree that the summary is correct. Once agreement has been expressed, the prospect is in a positive frame of mind, and the time is ripe to get some sort of formal commitment. The summary close must be combined with some other closing technique to complete the sale. For example, you might use the alternate of choice close like this:

Mr. Russell, with all of these major benefits available, you can see that advertising with us is a sound investment. Do you want to run your first ad on October fifteenth, or would November first be better for you?

Call-Back Close

Many sales opportunities are lost every day because salespeople take the prospect's decision not to buy as permanent. Studies show that many accounts are won by salespeople who call five or more times on the same prospect. Each time you return, you must present new information or ideas that will stimulate the prospect to buy. If you have the same old story told in the same old way, you probably will not make a new impression. If you walk into the prospect's office and say, "Well, have you thought it over?" the prospect's natural tendency is to restate the original objection: "Yes, and I still feel it is not a good time to spend that much money." In other words, "No deal." Here is an effective plan for a call-back situation:

1. **Approach**. Begin by giving a reason for calling back: "Coach Blevins, after I left the other day, I realized that there is some information I did not give you that has a real bearing on your situation." Be sure you do have something different to present—new data, additional evidence in the form of testimonials, or whatever. Be sure it is pertinent and logical.

2. **Review**. Next, review the whole presentation. Begin with, "Let me review briefly the items we talked about last time." The last meeting may be fresh in your mind, but the prospect will not remember ten percent of what you presented. Throughout the review, use phrases like as you remember, you will recall, and we said that to suggest points of agreement from the previous meeting.

This approach may not always work, but you know that you cannot sell to someone without face-to-face contact. Being there gives you the only opportunity you will ever have to sell this prospect.

The Trial Order Close

This technique involves asking the prospect for a trial order with no obligation. You either guarantee the money back if not completely satisfied or absorb all expenses and make the offer free. Prospects like it because they can simply refuse to pay for any unsatisfactory merchandise. Their risk is low and yours is minimal because only a small quantity is shipped with the possible result of establishing a satisfied customer who will give you repeat orders. Sometimes salespeople call this the *puppy dog close*. How could you ever return a puppy to the pet store and get your money back after the children have played with it for a week? By then, everyone is in love with it.

Suppose you are selling Dave Ramsey's 13-week Financial Peace University™ program to financial planners, and one prospect says something like this: "I have never used material like this in my teaching or consulting activities. Let me think about it before I decide." Respond with this trial order close:

> *I can certainly appreciate that. One thing we do that might be helpful to you is to make the program available on a fifteen-day, satisfaction-guaranteed basis. This enables you to work with the material firsthand and see if it is something that would be useful in your career consulting and training classes. We encourage you to listen to some of the audio, view the introductory DVD, go through the manual, and try it out in some actual financial counseling sessions. After you have done that, if you find that you can benefit from using it, then just hang on to it and we will bill you next month. In fact, you can even spread the payments out over six months; that would mean just $99.00 per payment. But if you find that you can't use the material or that it's not suitable for your situation, we'll understand. All we ask is that you return it to us. Is that fair enough?*

Follow this statement with one of the assumptive closes to get the prospect to take action that will allow you to actually enter the order.

The Balance-Sheet Close

This practical, decision-making format is familiar to most prospects, and they will feel comfortable as you use it. The procedure involves using a blank sheet of paper with a line drawn down the center to form two columns. In the first column, list all the reasons for making an affirmative decision in favor of your buying recommendation. These are the assets. In the second column, list all the questions or concerns about a buying decision— the liabilities involved in saying yes. The closing process is an analysis of the two columns to show the prospect that the reasons for buying heavily outweigh the reasons for not buying. Give the prospect the opportunity to express agreement with your conclusions.

As you build the balance sheet, resist the temptation to hurry. As you list each advantage for buying, pause and allow time for the prospect to absorb the idea. Be sure that you have many more ideas in favor of buying than opposed to it so that the number of reasons will be so impressive that you won't have to deal with the relative weights of individual reasons.[27] To use the balance-sheet method, you can begin like this:

Mr. Leno, the decision you are about to make is important. I know you want to be sure you are making a sensible choice. So that we will be sure to make the decision that is best for you, let's look at all the reasons in favor of buying this product and any questions or concerns about it. We can then determine which side weighs more and make your decision accordingly. Let's begin with the ideas that favor a positive decision today. Is that fair enough?

Take out a sheet of paper and begin to list the reasons for buying. Be sure to avoid the word objection. Instead of talking about the prospect's objections to buying, state them as concerns or questions to be answered: "You expressed concern about delivery schedules." When you use the word objection out loud, you are setting up the prospect and yourself as adversaries; if you are adversaries, one of you must win and the other must lose. Exhibit 13.5 shows a partial balance sheet for selling a mutual fund.

Δ**Exhibit 13.5**

The Mutual Fund Decision

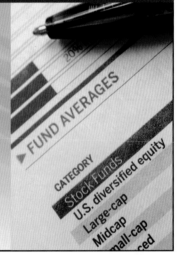

Reasons for Buying

1. This fund will grow faster than a money market account.

2. Diversification lowers risk.

3. Professional management lowers risk.

4. Blue chip portfolio lowers risk.

5. Stocks are a hedge against inflation.

6. You can quickly redeem or borrow on shares.

Questions or Concerns

1. Higher risk than a money market account.

2. Less liquidity than a money market account.

Never-the-Best-Time Close

When people are procrastinating or indecisive over whether they should buy now or buy later, show them that delaying will either get them no advantage or may even be to their disadvantage. You can discuss what they will miss by not having it over the coming period. If you have some, give examples of people who waited for the best moment, which never came.[28] Here is what this close may sound like:

- If you leave it until next year, you'll have one year less to enjoy it.

- The best time to buy is when you need it—which I'd say is now, wouldn't you?

The never-the-best-time close works by reframing delaying tactics as value-destroying procrastination.

1-2-3 Close

In this close, you summarize in sets of three items and word it as, We will give you this, that, and the other. The three items may be features of the product, benefits, or add-on "sweetener" items such as bonuses or rebates. There are two ways to do this: the items may either be closely related (to reinforce a single point) or may be relatively separate (to gain greater coverage, especially if your presentation is long or your product is complicated). Most customers ideally want the impossible:

products that are free, perfect, and available immediately—the classic business measurement trilogy of cost, quality, and time.[29] That is why this close can be effective; you are naming a bundle of benefits, the flawless "trifecta" of reasons to buy your product. Here is how to phrase this close:

- This product is cheaper, faster, and more reliable than the competition.

- Our homes are better-looking, better-built, and better-equipped than those in other subdivisions.

- If you buy today, we will give you free tickets to the Symphony, pay the sales tax, and provide a full tank of gas.

The 1-2-3 close works through the principle of triples, a curious pattern where three things given together act as a coherent triple threat that, when grouped together, give a compelling message.

Cost of Ownership Close

Rather than talking about price, the technique for this close focuses on the total cost of ownership, including service, replacement of the product, and so on. These costs are totaled and compared to the prices of competing products. It is a good idea to compare your price to the annual, monthly, or weekly cost of your competitors. Some examples of using the cost of ownership close are the following:

1. *Competing systems may seem cheaper, but when you take into account installation, maintenance, and the lifetime of the product, this system is about half the price!*

2. *Because we are so confident about the reliability of our systems, we only charge about 80 percent of what our competitors must charge. That means your monthly cost is quite a bit less.*

3. *If you buy a competing product you'll more than likely be replacing it in two years. Our product will last you twice as long.*

Because people often focus on the immediate price, they miss the longer term cost that may be incurred. The cost of ownership close works by comparing costs over time rather than up-front payments. If possible, this can be put into effect along with staged payments. Lower service costs mean that you should be offering a more reliable product, and it helps to have evidence of your product's superior quality.

No-Hassle Close

"No hassle" means you make completing the sale so easy for the customer that they give no thought to potential steps in the buying process that might put them off. Fill in all forms for the customer. Do all the paperwork. Include delivery, installation, and setup. How much easier could it be for the customer? Examples for this close are very straightforward:

1. *I've filled in all the paperwork, and all you need to do is to sign here.*

2. *It will be delivered Tuesday, at a time of your choosing, and fully installed by qualified technicians.*

The no-hassle close works because of its simplicity. Any anticipated difficulty or hassle that may be holding the customer back is blown away. The customer is also encouraged to return the favor as an exchange for your help with the completion.

Getting Creative with Closing

It is always a good idea to have as many of the closes memorized as possible. But salespeople should also be coached and trained to use an adaptive approach to selling.[30] Highly adaptive salespeople use a little creativity to close the really tough prospects. The following list is a few out-of-the-ordinary strategies you can use to influence customers to put pen to paper:[31]

1. Looking for one phrase to reassure customers that you will always do right by them? Try this: "I will spend your money as if it were my own."
2. As you close, hold up a $50 bill, tear it in half and give one half to the customer. Then hold up the remaining half and say, "If you can find a better value for your money, I'll give you the other half."
3. Put it in writing. Print up a list of services (think of 4 or 5) that you can personally guarantee to the customer: "I will return all phone calls the same business day," "I will always treat your time as a precious commodity," are two examples. Offer this sheet to customers in exchange for their business.

After the Close

Once you have closed the sale and have completed any necessary paperwork, you have no further business with the prospect at this time. Learn to leave gracefully. Don't become afflicted with *"lingeritis."* You may be tempted to stay and enjoy the company of a new customer you especially like. You feel like celebrating a successful sale. However, the customer has other work to do, and so do you! If you linger, you invite second thoughts and perhaps even regret. Leave while the client still has good thoughts about you and your efficient, professional manner. Thank the client for the order, say you are looking forward to meeting again, and leave.

SUMMARY

- Closing the sale is a natural conclusion to a carefully prepared and well-conducted presentation to a qualified prospect. Successful closing is often a matter of attitude.

- Learn to recognize buying signals. These enable you to close at the earliest possible point in the presentation. Learn the CHEF technique.

- The most threatening element in the sale for many salespeople is the fear of rejection. Develop a plan for dealing with rejection.

- Both verbal and nonverbal clues point to the prospect's readiness to buy. The buying signals often suggest the type of close that would be appropriate.

- Close when the prospect is ready to buy.

- One effective tactic is a trial close that asks for an opinion rather than a commitment; this allows the salesperson to determine just how ready the prospect is to say yes!

- Use words like when or as during the close. Avoid words such as *if* and *should* because they are conditional and block closing action.

- The summary close consists of restating the major selling points made during the presentation. This repetition of benefits overcomes the prospect's tendency to forget or neglect main points.

- The balance sheet close works well because it also allows you to present a summary of the main selling points, but in a pro and con format. Many of us tend to think this way and this close is well received by the analytical and amiable social styles.

REVIEW QUESTIONS

1. Discuss some strategies for handling the feeling of rejection that salespeople tend to experience from missing a sale.

2. Why do many prospects naturally say no when a close is attempted?

3. Why do many salesperson dread the close? Why is this fear unfounded?

4. When should the salesperson decide what kind of close to use? Why?

5. Should the planned close ever be changed in the course of the interview? Why or why not?

6. Timing is crucial in closing. Is attempting a close before the prospect is ready more harmful than trying to close past the critical point? Why or why not?

7. Distinguish between a trial close and a closing question. When is each appropriate?

8. What is the purpose of reassurance in connection with the close?

9. How many times in one interview should a salesperson ask for the order? How many times should you call on the same prospect to ask for an order?

10. What is the difference between persistence and pushiness?

11. Describe some typical verbal and nonverbal buying signals.

ROLE-PLAY EXERCISES

The following role-play exercises help build teams, improve communication, and emphasize the real-world side of selling. They are meant to be challenging, to help you learn how to deal with problems that have no single right answer, and to use a variety of skills beyond those employed in a typical review question. Read and complete each activity. Then in the next class, discuss and compare answers with other classmates.

Role Play 13.1 – Planning Closes

This is the final planning exercise for your team; therefore, you should use the same team that worked on role plays 11.1 and 12.1.

Review your presentation plan as amended by your approach to handling objections. Now you need to insert appropriate closing attempts. Although you are dealing with more than one person in the buying center, your experience of the chief decision maker should allow you to identify his/her personality type (driver, expressive, amiable, analytical). With all of the other information about the buying center's needs and concerns that you have developed, insert closing opportunities into your plan. Specifically, note the following points:

- When will you introduce trial closes (calls for opinion) and why? Which type of trial closes will you use?

- What sort of buying signals will you look for throughout your presentation?

- What type of final close (call for decision) will you attempt? Why? When?

- What will be the objective of your final close, your call to action (sale, trial order, call back, etc.), and why?

Role Play 13.2 – *A Sign of True Love?*

For this exercise, the class should be divided into teams of 4 persons each.

Beginning salespersons often have difficulty remembering and noticing verbal and nonverbal buying signals. But put them in a social situation in which they are trying to attract the romantic attention of someone they admire, and they notice every little twitch and nuance!

As a team, you should brainstorm about various verbal and nonverbal cues (*excluding overt verbal expressions of love or affection, or nonverbal expressions such as touching, hugging, or kissing*) that indicate personal attraction of one individual for another. As you create your list, think also in each case of a corresponding or analogous buying signal, verbal or nonverbal, based on what you have learned from Chapter 13. (Use the CHEF technique to get you started.)

The team with the greatest number of legitimate pairings (as determined by your instructor) wins.

CASE STUDIES

The following case studies present you with selling scenarios that require you to apply the critical skills discussed in the chapter and give you training through simulation, role-playing, and practical learning situations. They are meant to be both engaging and challenging, and like the role-play exercises, don't have one right answer.

Case 13.1 – *"Don't Tell Me No Lies!"*

Harold was not feeling good about his last sales presentation. A customer who was somewhat interested in purchasing an entire season's worth of lawn care and landscape maintenance service had proved in the end to be indecisive. Harold had gone through all of the benefits of his company's service for the customer—how it would save him time and effort, how his lawn and shrubs would recover faster after the harsh winter, how his plantings would withstand the summer drought better—but the customer wouldn't pull the trigger.

Because getting new customers was so difficult for McPhee's Landscaping Service due to increased competition, especially from two large home improvement centers that had just opened, the company sent Harold to Atlanta for sales training. In light of the nature of the business, the trainers emphasized hard, aggressive selling that was designed to close the deal in one visit. Giving a customer an opportunity to think things over, they said, was the same as handing your business to your competitors. Needless to say, this meant that the trainers emphasized closing techniques as the heart of the entire sales process. When Harold returned to home to Cleveland, he told his boss that he was ready to try the new techniques.

The Atlanta trainers had emphasized the "physical action" and "order blank" closes as particularly effective when dealing with amiable or expressive types who were otherwise indecisive. Harold's latest customer fit that mold perfectly, but didn't respond to the order blank close that Harold tried. So Harold turned to his last trick and told the customer that if he didn't purchase the contract today, the price would go up by 25%. He explained that the lower price was only available for those who signed on the dotted line in advance of needing the service. The customer signed and wrote out a check for the full, discounted amount. Harold thought to himself that this is like shooting fish in a barrel. It would be a good year.

Two weeks later, Harold's boss angrily reported that the customer had called to cancel the contract and demand a full refund. Apparently, the customer had learned from friends who had purchased later, after the lawn-mowing season had begun, that no price increase had occurred. At least one person had waited 10 days before signing a contract for the same price that Harold's customer was offered! The customer canceled because Harold had lied to him.

Should Harold have been surprised by this turn of events? What was the matter with Harold's attitude toward selling? Which closing techniques should he have used that would have been more effective and that would not have involved deception?

Case 13.2 – Always Be Closing Means . . . What?

James Arnold sells airplanes, big ones. He heads a large team of salespersons, financial experts, contract attorneys, and aviation engineers that sells fleets of planes to major airlines around the world. In the current global economy and in light of increasing caution on the part of financially pressed airlines, his team has had to become more aggressive and focused on closing business. When James broke into sales at his father's auto dealership, the mantra, "Always Be Closing," was drummed into his head. Now, 30 years later, he realizes that something like this must be imparted to his team. But what can "always" mean for a sales cycle that can take as long as 7 to 12 months? In order to get a handle on what this might mean for the entire team, James calls a meeting of the primary team leaders.

"How can we keep ourselves and our clients directed toward completing the final transaction?" he asked. "What might 'Always Be Closing' mean for our respective roles?"

"Well, I know one thing," said Sherm Atkins, the chief engineer on the team. "If we are in a position of having to persuade anyone to buy our planes, we've already lost the sale. As we work out answers to problems and questions, some of which come from our clients, it must be one seamless process, in fact, a process of ceaseless assent."

"Very well put, Sherm," James answered. "But how do we make sure that happens?"

"I think the answer to that is really rather simple," interjected Marian, lead attorney. "We all work in very disparate areas and on long-term, complicated negotiations. But toward the end of every meeting with our counterparts from the airlines, we need to confirm agreement on what the next step is— whether that is merely to keep working on the same problem or to move on to something new—and get a commitment to keep moving forward. Every time. Without fail. If we do that, signing the final contracts will be a mere formality."

"I think your onto something, Marian," said Jim. "Let's try to unpack that a little."

What do you think? Given what you've learned from Chapter 13 about different types of and strategies for closing successfully, have Sherm and Marian captured what their team should be doing? Do you have any additional suggestions to refine or correct their approach?

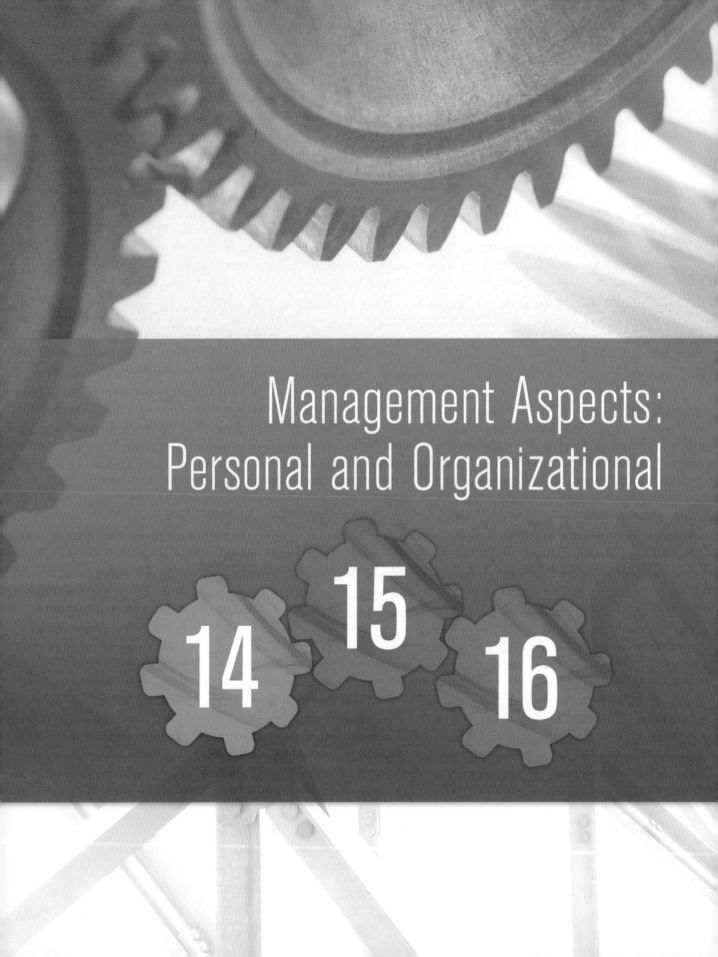

Management Aspects:
Personal and Organizational

14 15 16

Part 5

The service you give the customer after the sale has been completed can be as important, or even more important, than the sale itself. Keeping current customers happy and regaining lost clients is the focus of chapter 14. The customer absolutely defines quality in every transaction. Great salespeople don't talk customer service—they live perfect service.

Chapter 15 shows you how to get better control of your time and your activities. The chapter really is all about personal organization and self-management. You cannot manage time, but you can manage yourself and your personal activities. Administrative ability on the part of the salesperson is fundamental to success. Statistics indicate that only about 20 percent of a salesperson's time during a typical day is spent in face-to-face interviews with prospects.

Finally, chapter 16 details job responsibilities of the sales manager, and provides a useful introduction for classes in sales management. The chapters in this section are:

14. Service After the Sale

15. Personal, Time, and Territory Management

16. Sales Force Management

WHAT IS EXCELLENCE?

Excellence is never an accident. It is achieved in an organization only as a result of an unrelenting and vigorous insistence on the highest standards of performance. It requires an unswerving dedication to continuous quality improvement.

Excellence is contagious. It infects and affects everyone in an organization. It charts the direction of programs. It establishes the criteria for planning. It provides zest and vitality to the organization. Once achieved, excellence has a way of penetrating every phase of the life of an organization.

Excellence demands commitment and a tenacious dedication from the leadership of the organization. Once it is accepted and expected, it must be nourished and continually reviewed and renewed. It is a never-ending process of learning and growing. It requires a spirit of motivation and boundless energy.

Excellence inspires; it electrifies. It potentializes every phase of the organization's life. It unleashes an impact that influences every program, every activity, every committee, every individual. To instill it in an organization is difficult; to sustain it, even more so. It demands adaptability, imagination and vigor. But, most of all, it requires from the leadership a constant state of self-discovery and discipline.

Excellence is an organization's lifeline. It is the most compelling answer to apathy and inertia. It energizes a stimulating and pulsating force. Once it becomes the standard of performance, it develops a fiercely driving and motivating philosophy of operation.

Excellence is a state of mind put into action. It is a road map to success. Success is getting what you want. Happiness is about liking what you get. Successful people form the habit of doing what unsuccessful people don't like to do.

Excellence in life is important—because it is everything. The quality of a person's life is in direct proportion to their commitment to excellence regardless of their chosen field of endeavor.

Chapter 14

Service After the Sale

- Examine the purpose of total customer service.

- Determine what constitutes service quality.

- Know when and how to service.

- Understand your role in servicing.

- Appreciate how to upgrade and cross-sell current customers.

- Develop a systematic plan for follow-up activities.

Use This Page for Taking Notes

Building Partnerships with Customer Service

How do you sell your products or services and keep them sold when there are so many others fighting to do the same thing? Customer service is the answer. According to Dun and Bradstreet, the single most important reason for the failure of businesses in America is lack of sales. And this refers to re-sales and up-sales as well as initial sales. So your company's job is to create and keep a customer, and your job is exactly the same.[1] Remember, no matter what your official title may be, you are a salesperson for yourself and your company. And the best way to increase your value as a salesperson is to build a loyal customer base through first-rate service. The customer absolutely defines quality in every transaction. Don't talk customer service—live perfect service.[2]

> A lot of people have fancy things to say about customer service, but it's just a day-in, day-out, ongoing, never-ending, unremitting, persevering, compassionate type of activity.
>
> –Leon Gorman, L.L. Bean

Because meeting and exceeding customer expectations is so vital to success, companies must develop customer service strategies. This usually involves segmenting customers because they generally have different service needs. So you must inform specific customers what kind of service they can expect, and the key to success is exceeding what you promise.

Keeping customers happy, and coming back, takes more than smiles and a thank you. It takes outrageous service. Allen Endres of the Juran Institute explains, "Customers have an increasing rate of expectation for services and a decreasing tolerance for poor service, and as a result are more likely to migrate to the vendors who provide the highest-quality service."[3]

Second-Mile Action

Be willing to give your customers more than they demand, more than they expect, and even more than you feel they deserve. Exhibit 14.1 depicts one salesperson with such an attitude. Act from the desire to serve—not the desire to gain. When you make this your policy, you will do whatever you must to be of service to your client. This means that you sometimes deliver an order in your own car so that you get it to the customer sooner than your company could deliver it.

ΔExhibit 14.1

Second-Mile Service

Going the second mile may involve a service for the customer that is unrelated to the business. Atlanta-based fast-food chain Chick-fil-A has adopted a policy of "second-mile service" for all of its 1,240 nationwide locations. Jon Lech, manager of Chick-fil-A in Phenix City, Alabama, took the policy to heart when he changed a customer's flat tire in the restaurant's parking lot while she ate, saving her the headache and expense of calling a towing company. Though Lech's act is only one example, Chick-fil-A prides itself on being a company known for its "second-mile service." When Lech's branch recently saw a 13 percent sales growth over one year without any menu or aesthetic changes, he couldn't help but believe the growth was due to Chick-fil-A's exceptional service philosophy.[4]

Paul J. Meyer, founder of SMI International, once had a client who made a hobby of collecting rocks containing fossils. When Meyer was on a vacation trip one year, he found a rock with a particularly interesting fossil on it. He packed the rock carefully and mailed it to his client. That kind of extra service, when given from sincere interest, pays rich dividends. Exhibit 14.2 highlights a company who truly understands the value of second-mile service.

Δ**Exhibit 14.2**

Doing The Right Thing

One company that understands the importance of second mile service is John Laing Homes. CEO Larry Webb sets the bar high with a simple credo: Do the right thing. The company places top priority on near-constant communication with buyers. "It's a lot more important today than a few years ago," says Vic Goochey, operations vice president in the Inland Empire division of the company.

George Hammond, vice president of Laing in Colorado Springs, pioneered a new standard for response time to warranty service requests: 15 minutes—that's 15 minutes for a phone call or visit from a customer-care representative after the request is received. Now the whole company aims for it.

Inland Empire division president Terry Neale came up with an innovative idea to raise customer satisfaction scores. He budgets $100,000 a year and one of his best customer service reps to keep Laing's homeowners even happier than they already are. The rep calls home owners, makes appointments to stop by, and then gives them gifts and asks if he can do touch-up painting or preventive maintenance. He also drops off a gift certificate and walks the house looking for something to do. "We think we're doing pretty well with customer service and trade relations, but we're only scratching the surface of what we could do."[5]

Determining your client base's level of satisfaction and keeping a constant flow of feedback is the best way to know if you and your company are consistently going the extra mile. *Benchmarking*, in which organizations evaluate various aspects of their processes in relation to best practices, is an excellent method of performing "preventative maintenance" in your processes and interactions with customers and prospects.

The Hylant Group, one of the nation's largest privately held insurance brokers, decided it needed a formal process for determining the level of client satisfaction with its products and services. It retained the services of Active Retention, a company that specializes in retention, renewal, and cross-selling. Active Retention's hallmark product is the Client Service Review™, which includes a complimentary national benchmarking module. The Hylant Group conducted a client survey first and then began the benchmarking process. "When we were out with clients, we'd ask, 'How's it going?' Our approach had been basically opportunistic, as opposed to inviting feedback in an organized fashion," says Toledo office President Richard Hylant of their traditional feedback methods. With the new benchmarking strategies in place, "We were able to see exactly how we stacked up with other participants in the program," vice president of sales John McDermott said. "In some cases the results were surprising, and in other cases they weren't. Overall, our loyalty factor was very strong, at 95 percent, and the majority of that was favorable or exceptional. That was very gratifying."[6]

It pays to go the extra mile. Here are a few additional ideas that could be seen as going the extra mile to follow up with the customer if there is a problem after the sale:[7]

1. *Offer* to pick up or deliver goods to be replaced or repaired.

2. *Give* a gift of merchandise to repay for the inconvenience. The gift may be small but the thought will be appreciated.

3. *Reimburse* for costs of returning merchandise such as parking fees or gas.

4. *Provide* discounts on office supplies, car rentals, or express shipping.[8]

5. *Acknowledge* the customer's inconvenience and thank him for giving you the opportunity to make it right. Make the wording of the apology sincere and personal.

6. *Follow up* to see that the problem was taken care of. Don't assume the problem has been fixed unless you handled it yourself.

Moments of Truth

Awareness of quality service by your customers and prospects can be a great advantage. Salespeople are far more likely to make a sale when they can truthfully say, "If you buy from me, I will never let you down. Servicing your account is my top priority." In his book *Moments of Truth*, Jan Carlzon writes of his time as president of Scandinavian Airlines (SAS), "Each of our 10 million customers come in contact with five SAS employees. Each contact lasts about 15 seconds. Thus, SAS is created in the minds of our customers 50 million times per year, 15 seconds at a time."[9]

> Customer service is like a daily election
> and customers vote with their feet.

Those 50 million moments of truth, when customers are made aware of service quality, are the moments that ultimately determine the success of SAS. All employees must realize and care that their work affects customers' perception of service quality and even product quality, no matter how far they are removed from the "front line" or from direct communication with customers. Customer satisfaction is measured as moments in time. Plenty of customers do not come back unless the service you provide is consistently better than service provided by competitors. You must create a trust-bond relationship. Sixty-five percent of a typical firm's sales volume is done by loyal customers who return to buy again and again because of the service quality provided.

There are many ways a service organization can determine when service recovery efforts are likely to be needed. For instance, one simple method is to provide customers with an opportunity to voice their dissatisfaction by providing customer response cards, or supplying a toll-free telephone line, email address, or website. Such means make it easy for an unhappy customer to express a complaint. For example, El Pollo Loco, a fast-food casual dining chain, rewards customers with discounts on purchases or chances at a cash jackpot in exchange for feedback through online focus groups or toll-free phone surveys.[10] Exhibit 14.3 spotlights one company who has truly created trust as well as a place for themselves in their customers' hearts.[11]

ΔExhibit 14.3

Environmentalism Begins at Checkout ···

Recreational Equipment, Inc. (REI) is a leading outdoor equipment retailer and not just because of their wide selection of quality gear. Their commitment to customer service begins with their commitment to their employees' satisfaction, earning REI a spot on FORTUNE Magazine's list of "100 Best Companies to Work for in America" for nine years in a row. Education and environmentalism are top priorities for REI in attracting customers who desire to do good while shopping for the equipment they need for their outdoor activities. To that end, REI pledges to use a portion of their annual profits to support outdoor causes and environmental conservation programs. In any given year, REI's donations and grants amount to $3.7 million—talk about an incentive for customers to spend money in order to give back!

Service Techniques That Support Relationships

Value Added

Many companies can attribute their sales success to the ability of their salespeople to engage in value-added thinking. This type of thinking occurs when companies become less focused on promoting their own agenda and instead become more "shopper-centric." One such company is leading grocery retailer Kroger, whose "Customer 1st" rewards program recognizes the value that lies within their loyal customers and rewards customers with offers relevant to their own shopping preferences. Kroger CEO Dave Dillon says, "We target our existing customer base because of the opportunity we see, that even in our very best customers, there are still a lot of purchases they [may] make outside of Kroger."[12] Recognizing value added is much easier than defining it. When you are in the position of the customer, you recognize value added when you receive it—and you remember it! Here are two additional examples of value-added service:

- Salespeople from Caterpillar Tractor promise that their customers will receive ordered parts within forty-eight hours anywhere in the world. This after-sale service is both appealing and highly successful. The promise is not an idle one; if the delivery is not made within the forty-eight hours, the part is free.

- The air conditioner in your car goes out, and you take it in to the service department of a car dealership to be repaired. They find they must order a part that will not arrive for two days. You mention to the service manager that you really need to get the car fixed before the weekend because you are planning a trip. Two days later when you take the car in to have the new part installed, the mechanic finds that the wrong part was shipped and they will have to reorder. The service manager asks you to wait for a minute and returns with a set of keys and says, "Here, we want you to use one of our demonstrators for the weekend. The new part will be here early Monday morning, and you can pick up your car by noon."

When an automobile service department repairs your car's air conditioner, that isn't service. It's what you paid them to do. When you are provided with a car while they wait for a replacement part, that is service—and you remember it. The delay in getting the part was not their fault, but they knew the delay was not your fault either. Their concern was helping you have a comfortable trip. One weekend's use of a demonstrator was a small price for the dealership to pay for the kind of goodwill that will bring you back to purchase a new car next year.

Some companies are recognizing that customers appreciate having their time and effort respected as valuable. Staples gave their customers that extra bit of respect by moving their paper and printer ink—the perennial best-sellers for any office supply store— to the front of the store, saving customers the time it takes to walk from the entrance to the back of the store where printing supplies are traditionally located. Staples realized this would mean a short-term loss in sales from impulse purchases, but in the long run it means customers may choose to shop at Staples because of their commitment to saving time and making life easier. If time is money, then that's value added![13]

The automobile industry estimates that a brand-loyal customer represents a lifetime average revenue of $300,000 to the dealer. If they refer two other customers and the revenue for service is added to these amounts, over $1 million of sales is gained by one satisfied customer.[14] The professional salesperson has numerous opportunities for follow-up activities that determine whether particular customers will reorder as well as whether they will tell others of their satisfaction or provide referrals to other prospects. The relationship sales rep is sincerely and unselfishly helpful to clients and prospects alike. Sometimes value-added service costs nothing except thoughtfulness and a few minutes of time.

Herb Kelleher founded Southwest Airlines to set itself apart from other airlines. Since inception the company has been known for its low fares and attention to customer service. Southwest has maintained a high level of customer satisfaction not just because of its flights, but also because of its value-added service. Exhibit 14.4 shows how Southwest Airlines adds value to its service and develops a loyal customer base.[15]

ΔExhibit 14.4

Going Above and Beyond

At 9:00 p.m. one Christmas Eve, customer service agent Rachel Dyer was working the ticket counter at Southwest Airlines when a man with a cane approached her. In a faint voice he told her that he had to go to New Orleans. It seems that his sister-in-law had dropped him off with some cash and a plastic bag full of clothes, and told him to go to New Orleans where he had some relatives. Confused and worried, the man explained that he'd also recently undergone bypass surgery.

Dyer responded by reassuring him that they would work everything out. She booked him on the earliest flight to New Orleans the next morning, got him a hotel and a meal ticket for dinner and breakfast, and tipped a World Services employee to take the man to the airport shuttle. Dyer bent down to explain his itinerary to him and told him everything would be okay. He told her, "Thank you," then bowed his head and started to cry.

In Southwest's monthly employee newsletter, Dyer wrote, "I am so proud to work for a company that not only allows but encourages me to help people who really are in need. I truly believe the success of this company has to do with the fact that it was founded and is run by kind, honest and loving people."

Get More From Current Customers

Managers are telling their sales forces to get out of the office and start building personal relationships with their customers. Chick-Fil-A founder Truett Cathy knows how important the customer base can be for business. "We can outperform [the competition] because we teach our employees the importance of being kind to customers. Your customers become cheerleaders for you, and you have to do little advertising. They're worth more than TV and radio," Mr. Cathy says of his customer base.[16] Thus, not only can current customers be sources of additional income themselves, they can in essence become part of your marketing team!

Sell current customers more of what you're already selling to them. Other departments may have a need. Sell them upgrades, enhancements, or additional products. Needs change over time. Sell your current clients something new. Keep them up-to-date on new products. Sell customers on you. Strive to become a trusted member of their team and opportunities will present themselves.[17]

Upgrading or Up-selling. Upgrading, also known as *up-selling*, is the process of persuading the customer to purchase a better-quality product or, perhaps, a newer product. Upgrading is largely a matter of selling your company and pushing the quality factors of your product and customer image. You ask for the upgrade because the newer or higher-quality product will serve the needs of the client better than the less expensive version of the same product. Most firms have products that vary in quality and price. And most buyers like to have choices when making a purchase. The only way you can succeed in upgrading is to believe one hundred percent in what you're doing, think ahead, service your clients, and create win-win relationships.

The cornerstone of selling—especially when trying to upgrade a client—relies on continuously qualifying the prospect throughout the buying process. It's ultimately the customer's choice and you don't want to oversell, but giving them options is just logical, especially given the statistics that up-selling leads to more purchases by the customer 58 to 72 percent of the time.[18] You want to sell to the real needs of the prospect. Salespeople need to remember they don't sell products—they sell results. Sadler Evans, account executive for Comcast Cable Advertising of Huntsville, Alabama, says he is "more of a consultant instead of just a salesperson scrambling to make his monthly numbers."[19] Evans attempts to upgrade his clients to the point where he thinks the advertising schedule will work. One of his clients wanted to start out at $600 per month, but Evans was convinced that at least $750 was needed for the advertising to be effective. The client took his recommendation. It worked, and now the company is a really solid account, spending about $2,500 per month. When a salesperson takes the time to act as a consultant who understands the customer's needs, the result will be more than just a slightly larger one-time sale. Instead, the salesperson will be rewarded with the on-going benefits of a sales relationship with a truly satisfied lifelong customer.

Cross-selling. Cross-selling is the process of selling products that are not directly connected to the primary products being sold to new and/or established clients. For example, *cross-selling* occurs when in a conversation with your bank's loan officer about a loan for expanding your business, you casually mention how expensive it is to keep your two elementary school children in a private school. Several days later, you receive a note in the mail from that same loan officer with materials describing how a limited trust fund could be used to help pay college expenses and offering the bank's services to help set it up.

Cross-selling and upgrading have become increasingly important to many companies in this information age. Customers have to be convinced that what you have available is going to solve a problem or save them money before they're even willing to talk. "To be truly customer-focused you have to make as many channels available as your customers are demanding," says Ann Vezina, vice-president of customer relationship management at systems integrator EDS. To do the best job of fostering lifetime loyalty, you need to know exactly what your customers are thinking. The ideal scenario goes like this: When a customer contacts our customer service hotline via email or telephone, the agents in our call center can call up a comprehensive record of every interaction, no matter how, why, or when. And the most profitable callers are identified and directed to the most knowledgeable agents right away. Our agents get a view of our customers that is so granular they can cross-sell and up-sell products to our customer base.[20]

It really does pay to go the extra mile for the customer; not just for their benefit, but for yours as well. In fact, the payoff of exceptional, consistent customer service can be summed up in four primary categories, called the "Four R's." They are:[21]

1. **Referrals**. Loyal customers encourage others to choose your company or product over the competition, saving you the substantial cost of acquiring new customers. Where yesterday's "word of mouth" could influence a dozen individuals, today's "word-of-mouse," via email or blogs, can influence thousands.

2. **Retention**. Customers who continue to do business with you provide a solid base for success. Your most loyal customers should cost you the least to service because they are not as sensitive to competitive pressures.

3. **Reputation**. Loyal customers speak well of you to others. They increase public support and positive interest from investors, suppliers, future employees, the media, and even regulatory bodies.

4. **Revenue**. Loyal customers give you a larger share of their business, which increases overall revenue and the recognition that comes with success. As mentioned previously, cross-selling and up-selling to existing customers can be the primary growth strategy for an organization and is particularly lucrative with loyal customers.

Retain Or Win Back Unhappy Customers

A customer calls and launches into a tirade, complaining and whining about everything. Who needs an account like this? But then you stop, catch your breath, and think, "When clients are rude it's usually because they are having a problem with some aspect of our product or service." No matter how badly clients behave, avoid responding angrily. You must learn not to take their rudeness personally. Maintain a positive attitude and an even tone of voice. This serves to disarm them and they will generally follow your lead. For all the steps you may take, some may inevitably be unhappy with whoever services them. Sometimes a resolution isn't always to the consumer's satisfaction—this isn't a perfect world.[22]

Restate the client's concerns to demonstrate that you were listening. Employ empathy by putting yourself in their shoes and seeing it from their perspective. Remember that this customer is reacting to a real or perceived problem with your product or service that they feel has let them down. Thank the customer for bringing the issue to your attention and then recommend a plan to solve it while the client is still on the phone. Make sure your proposed solution meets with the customer's approval. Lastly, follow up with a personal visit to ensure the issue has been resolved and the client is completely satisfied.

When customers are angry, try to see things from their perspective.

This tends to build a stronger relationship and greater loyalty with clients.[23] The following is a list of additional ideas to keep your customers smiling no matter what the circumstance was surrounding the sale:

1. **Be genuine in your efforts**. First and foremost, customer service can't be lip service.

2. **Be proactive**. Anticipate any further problems and their needs every step of the way and take care of those needs.

3. **Communicate thoroughly and frequently**. Don't give your customers the chance to call you to inquire about a late order or faulty merchandise. Be the first to communicate with them.

4. **Go the extra mile to do what's not expected**. Consumers can be a pretty jaded bunch. If you go above and beyond to offer what they need but least expect, you're sure to gain many, many fans.

5. **Create a memorable experience**. In today's business climate, "good" is as good as dead. You have to be the best to succeed, so you have to do whatever you can to leave an impression in your customers' minds.

6. **Be professional**. This is the best medicine for an upset customer.[24]

Service in Response to Needs

Your customers might explode if you don't let them blow off some steam.

When you are practicing ongoing service, you can anticipate complaints and handle them promptly before they become serious sources of customer dissatisfaction. A customer who is dissatisfied with a product or service tells an estimated nine or ten other people. Always respond immediately to the possibility of a complaint or to one that is actually expressed. The salesperson who assumes that a customer must be satisfied because he has voiced no gripes over an extended period, is living in an unreal world. Instead of leaving the customer with no option but to complain to the people around them (who are other potential customers), the salesperson must make "customer-saving opportunities" by giving them the chance to voice complaints directly to someone who can do something about it.[25]

Washington D.C.-based Technical Assistance Research Programs Inc., one of the nation's top customer service research firms, conducted research among manufacturing concerns that produced overwhelming evidence of the value not only of "handling" complaints but also of going out of the way to encourage and then remedy complaints. Their key findings include these:

- Of unhappy customers, only four percent of them complain to company headquarters. For every complaint received, the average company has 26 customers with problems, six of which are "serious," who do not complain.

- Among customers with problems, complainers are more likely than non-complainers to do business with the company again, even if the problem isn't satisfactorily resolved.

- Between 54 and 70 percent of complainers will give repeat business if their complaint is resolved, but a staggering 95 percent are repeat customers if they feel the complaint was resolved quickly.

- Dissatisfied complainants tell 9 or 10 people about their experience. 13 percent recount the incident to more than 20 people. Customers who have their complaints satisfactorily resolved tell an average of five people about the treatment they received.[26]

Retaining Existing Customers

Service after the sale is critical to retaining existing customers, particularly in technical selling. In many technical sales, up to fifty percent of the sale involves the follow-through stage of the selling cycle. More technical sales are lost through inadequate follow-up than from any other cause. When so much time is invested in making a sale, attempting to save time by neglecting follow-up is a costly mistake. A bad buying experience can be a bitter and enduring memory. There is no substitute for salespeople asking their customer base how they feel about the service the company is providing.

All the efforts to retain customers is certainly not without benefits. Customer retention results from customer satisfaction. The average business loses about 15 to 20 percent of its customer base a year, forcing them to put money and effort into attracting new customers. It has been estimated that reducing customer defections by as little as five percent can double a firm's profits.[27] The apparel industry is one area that recognizes the importance of keeping and communicating with current customers. Retailers such as Nordstrom and Kohl's have worked hard to develop successful customer advocacy systems and rewards programs to increase customer retention and achieve higher profits.[28]

> **Those who enter to buy support me.** Those who come to flatter please me. Those who complain teach me how I may please others so that more will come. Those only hurt me who are displeased but do not complain. They refuse me permission to correct my errors and thus improve my service.
>
> -Marshall Field

Win Back Angry Customers

No one enjoys losing a customer. Winning back a customer who has turned to a competitor helps your feelings as well as your bank account. The first step in regaining a customer is to discover why you lost the account. If customers leave because they feel they've been badly treated, it is your responsibility—not the customer's—to mend this relationship. Exhibit 14.5 gives some of the most common "excuses" given by salespeople for losing accounts. If you put aside such excuse making, then some real soul searching can show you why the account was lost.

ΔExhibit 14.5

Excuses Salespeople Give for Losing Accounts

- If it isn't price, then it's because the competition uses unfair or unethical tactics.
- My company fails to back me up; delivery is late, or quality deteriorates.
- That customer is just too difficult for anyone to get along with.
- The customer never cared about anything but price, so I was helpless.
- I just don't have time to make all the service calls I'd like to make.
- There can't be anything wrong with my sales techniques. I'm doing exactly what I've been doing for years.

You will find helpful questions to ask that relate directly to the product or service you sell. Listen carefully to what the customer tells you in answer to each question. Do not contradict what the customer has told you, argue, or become angry yourself, no matter how angry or unreasonable the customer may seem to you.

When faced with an angry customer, you have two choices. One, you can walk away and consider the account lost; or two, you can resolve the conflict and further reinforce the relationship.[29] If you listen politely, ask additional questions, and probe for hidden feelings, the mere act of telling you what is wrong often defuses the negative feelings of the customer. The former satisfaction that was experienced in doing business with you surfaces and the customer may be quite happy to consider reestablishing your relationship.

Do your best to glean every bit of current information you can regarding this angry customer, along with what you know of your relationship with the customer in the past, in order to decide what went wrong. Here are some possible reasons that you might lose an account:[30]

Something You Have Done. No one is at top effectiveness all the time. Without intending to do so, you may have said or done something that offended the customer or damaged your credibility in some way. Exhibit 14.6 illustrates a sure-fire way to offend a customer and destroy a relationship. Customers appreciate promises kept as much as you do—*so don't promise what you can't deliver.*

ΔExhibit 14.6

Destroying Credibility with the Customer ∙∙

Something You Fail To Do. Failing to tell the full story about what the product can or cannot do, failure to keep the customer informed about product or delivery changes, failure to meet promises, failing to follow up or waiting too long to follow up—all these omissions destroy the customer's faith in you, your product, and your company.

Something The Company Does. If the company delivers only a portion of an order, substitutes some items in the order without telling the customer or makes errors in billing, the customer may become dissatisfied enough to change suppliers.

Something The Company Fails To Do. The company may fail to meet the promised delivery schedule without warning, fail to provide necessary training and technical backup as promised, or fail to meet maintenance agreements.

Take some time for problem solving. Until you discover and acknowledge the real problem, you cannot solve it. Sometimes the answer is unpleasant. If the problem lies in your actions or attitudes, you must accept responsibility so that you are free to solve the problem and regain the account. If you deny your obvious responsibility, you escape into excuse making and are blinded to the options available for regaining the customer's goodwill. When you know what the problem is, you can plan strategies for rebuilding the account.

A Systematic Plan For Follow-up

Your tracking system for servicing should be as well-organized as your prospecting system. Use a calendar software program to set up files listing the customer's name (company and individual with whom you deal), the date of each service contact, and the form it took (telephone call, email, visit). Whatever organizing system you choose, be sure to have a specific, written plan for servicing. Your plan should include these four elements:

1. Stay Informed

The process of buying and selling does not end with the purchase—unless you intend for the current purchase to be the only possible transaction you will ever have with this customer or with anyone this customer can influence. Service is the marketing concept in action. Service is the activities you do to keep customers sold permanently. The sale is not complete until the customer is satisfied. You have a responsibility that goes far beyond closing the sale. You may carry the responsibility for customer satisfaction a long time after the sale has been made. It is not enough to "pass the buck" to a service representative; tell your customers how to get in touch with them and be prepared to help them make initial contact. Giving the customer the name of a person to contact when things go wrong is an excellent idea. If something goes wrong, your client has the right to expect you to help him put things right.[31]

Frequent service calls on existing customers help you keep up with personnel changes in their company. If you meet new personnel early, a relationship can be developed and your credibility established before you ask for a new order. Make sure you do not continue to send mail addressed to a buyer's predecessor. Keeping up with personnel changes not only helps you solidify your presence with the existing company client but also gives you an ally in the company where the former employee now works.

You also learn about anticipated changes in the company structure when you make frequent service calls. Perhaps a merger or an acquisition is about to take place. Your customers may be planning to introduce a new product line that will increase their need for your product or service, or they may be expanding their whole general operation as a result of increased sales. All of these conditions affect you as a salesperson, but you will not hear of them while the information can help you unless you are there. It takes days, weeks, even months to get a customer. Regaining a lost customer after poor service will be much more expensive than keeping a current customer satisfied.[32]

> GAINING A NEW CUSTOMER COSTS **FIVE TIMES** MORE THAN KEEPING A CURRENT ONE.

2. Make Phone Calls

The telephone is still one of your best service tools. Although everyone seems to communicate solely by email and networking sites these days, nothing can replace an actual phone call to ask how a customer is doing. The phone allows you to give the customer personalized attention with less investment of time for both you and the customer than would be required by a personal visit. Customers respond positively to the fact that you are interested in them and how the product is meeting their needs, and they are also pleased that they did not need to spend half an hour in a personal visit with you. Here are some of the items of service you can handle through phone calls:

- Verify delivery
- Check for problems
- Inform the customer of price changes or possible shortages
- Check customer's inventory level

A Variety of Communication Devices. "Make it possible for your customers to reach a live person—even when you aren't available," advises Eric Harris, sales manager at Benefit Partners in Roseville, California. His job is to offer independent insurance agents or brokers and their customers access to a wide selection of health insurance plans. The brokers need fast, accurate information when they call, and for that reason Harris' phone does not have voicemail so that callers can always talk to a live person. If their specific rep is not available, brokers talk to another member of the sales team who can answer their questions.

The telephone isn't always enough. Use a variety of communication media to make sure you reach your customer and that your customer can reach you. Exibit 14.7 illustrates the value of using a variety of media to interact with your customers.[33] When you secure a new client, learn the person's schedule, best times to call, email address, fax number, cell phone number, other office telephone numbers, home telephone number, and social media usernames.

ΔExhibit 14.7

Personalized Contact and Customer's Preferences ·····················

Personalized contact in the social media age means knowing which platforms your customers prefer. For Zappos.com, the online shoe retailer, this means a wide presence on Twitter. Zappos main Twitter account has 1.8 million followers, but their contact with customers goes beyond the corporate presence in social media. Zappos has encouraged its employees to "tweet" from their own accounts, from CEO Tony Hsieh down, giving customers more opportunity to interact with the company on a personal level. It can be argued that this individualized attention through social media is part of what turned Zappos from a small Internet upstart in 1999 into a giant with $1 billion in annual sales ten years later. What a huge return on the investment of a few minutes a day of contact through Twitter, Facebook, or other social networking sites!

3. Determine Contact Frequency

Decide how often you will contact each customer. Base this on your experience with each customer and with customers in general in your business. Consider account penetration (current and potential volume) and customer need. Rate your accounts as A, B, and C, much as you rate prospects, according to how much business you can expect to develop with each one and how many referrals that customer can generate for you that will produce business in addition to what that account provides. Also consider the personality and needs of the customer and determine what care is needed to maintain goodwill and a solid relationship. Decide also whether contact will be by email, social media, telephone, in person, or a combination.

4. Send Mail (Email, Letter or Card)

When your customer has no specific problems or need to reorder, keep your name before the customer with direct-mail items like these:

- New promotional material your company produces that will help the customer use the product more successfully.

- Information about new products from your company that might interest your customer.

- Your company in-house newsletter that could include trade information, promotional articles, and stories that might interest your customer (Be sure to write a few words of greeting).

- A letter with a self-addressed business reply card on which the customer can check the level of satisfaction (excellent, good, fair, poor) with your product.[34]

Give close attention to the effectiveness of each type of service contact you offer to your customers or clients. Discard methods that do not work, and repeat methods that do. Keep your service records as meticulously as you do your data on prospecting. Know what you have done for each customer, what you plan to do next, and when.

Hallmark keeps in touch with their customers by regularly sending personalized cards. They developed a division called Hallmark Business Expressions that caters specifically to businesses and consulting services. The salespeople send welcome cards to new customers, as reminders of their purchase and to begin the relationship. Scott Robinette, the director of business development for Hallmark Business Expressions, says, "We don't attempt to get a sale. When we send a card to a customer we do so with the intent of developing a relationship." The company also sends cards to clients marking their "anniversary" as customers. Exhibit 14.8 illustrates how a thank-you card and a follow-up phone call paid off for a creative salesperson.[35]

ΔExhibit 14.8

It Pays to be Prompt

Thank each client you visit promptly! This is what Julie Puckett, a sales rep with Home Buyer Publications in Fairfax, Virginia, does. And it is something worth emulating. Before Julie travels, she addresses an envelope to each customer she plans to visit. After each appointment, and while the details are still fresh in her mind, she immediately creates a handwritten card thanking them for their time and expressing how much she enjoyed the meeting. The note is mailed that day in their city! In a world of virtual communication, a handwritten note is still the best way to differentiate yourself and stand out in the customer's mind.

By the time she returns home to make follow-up phone calls, the clients have received the "thank you" cards. Puckett says, "It's surprising how often my customers refer to my note and express appreciation for its timeliness." It doesn't surprise the authors! It may seem like a no-brainer, but it certainly is effective for her.

SUMMARY

- The right kind of customer service brings you repeat business over time. A buying decision is a one-time action unless you turn it into a habit with effective follow-up and follow through procedures.

- Service after the sale adds value to what you sell by showing the customer that you are willing to take care of any problems. Service after the sale can be more important to your client than the actual sale itself.

- Sell current customers more of what you are already selling to them. You do this by cross- selling or up-selling to your customer base.

- After sale service gives you an opportunity to keep up with personnel and other company changes so you will know who to contact for reorders and what additional opportunities you have for supplying this customer.

- Service is an ongoing activity. It is never too soon or too long after the sale to provide service.

- Plan, execute, and track any personal visits, telephone calls and mailings to your customers and measure how effective they were.

- Service is the key to winning back lost accounts. No matter what causes the loss of an account, that loss is a signal for renewed service activity. Contact the former client with sincere concern and interest.

REVIEW QUESTIONS

1. List ten elements of service after the sale and give a concrete example of each.

2. What is meant by value added in connection with selling? Can you give an example of a time when you experienced value added as a customer?

3. Think of a situation in which failing to keep up with personnel changes could cause loss of sales for a salesperson.

4. List some types of problems a customer might have that you, as a salesperson, could solve before they become serious by following a regular servicing program.

5. What is the salesperson's responsibility if a piece of machinery or equipment is installed and then is found to be defective or has some part missing?

6. Discuss the importance of service as an ongoing activity.

7. Explain how you would go about setting up a systematic plan for follow-up activities.

8. Describe some of the particular services that are beneficial to buyers for a retail business.

9. Is prospecting for new customers or servicing existing ones more important? Justify your answer.

10. Describe some specific servicing activities that could be used to win back a lost client.

ROLE-PLAY EXERCISES

The following role-play exercises help build teams, improve communication, and emphasize the real-world side of selling. They are meant to be challenging, to help you learn how to deal with problems that have no single right answer, and to use a variety of skills beyond those employed in a typical review question. Read and complete each activity. Then in the next class, discuss and compare answers with other classmates.

Role Play 14.1 – Maintaining the Loop

You will work independently on this exercise in class.

Imagine that you own a website development, marketing, and hosting company that employs 8 people. Five of your staff work in sales and marketing, while three manage the technical backend. There is no separate customer service department. All 5 of your sales staff, yourself included, do it all: prospect for new customers, sell your services, respond to requests for assistance, and follow up with customer requests and needs. You don't sleep.

As you acquire more customers, you realize that you need to systematize serving their ongoing needs and problems. In other words, you need to develop a customer follow-up and service plan. For the next 15 minutes, jot down as many items as you can think of that you will include in your service plan for this business. Be prepared to explain or justify the items on your list.

Role Play 14.2 – How Far Should One Go?

For this exercise, you should work independently.

Case 14.2 raises questions about corporate customer service practices. Similar questions can be raised about attitudes and practices regarding customer service for individual salespersons. Chapter 14 offers several examples of salespersons who "go the extra mile" for their customers. As you think about the responsibilities of yourself as a salesperson, jot down brief answers to the following questions:

- Should there be limits on what a salesperson is expected to do by way of customer service?

- If so, what are those limits, theoretically speaking?

- What limits, if any, would you personally adhere to?

- Provide some concrete examples of actions that you would refuse to take in the interest of customer service.

- Provide some concrete examples of actions that you would consider taking that would be considered extraordinary ("going the extra mile") by most persons.

- Should salespersons be rewarded or compensated for customer service actions that exceed company requirements?

CASE STUDIES

The following case studies present you with selling scenarios that require you to apply the critical skills discussed in the chapter and give you training through simulation, role-playing, and practical learning situations. They are meant to be both engaging and challenging, and like the role-play exercises, don't have one right answer.

Case 14.1 – To Tweet or Not to Tweet

Nutmeg Appliances operates 35 stores throughout the State of Connecticut and southwestern Massachusetts. They offer complete lines of kitchen appliances, TVs, and home entertainment centers. Competition in this business is fierce. Customers are always shopping for bargains for such products and are often complaining about missed deliveries and malfunctioning equipment. The pace on the sales floor, in operations (delivery and installation), and customer service is, to say the least, brisk. In this environment, however, Nutmeg executives take the enlightened and financially prudent view that increasing customer loyalty must be a top priority. Living off new customers who walk in the door is not a viable option, especially in a stressed economy. Customer retention is vital.

Therefore, Nutmeg routinely holds meetings involving representatives from sales, operations, and customer service to see how they can improve service to their existing customers. This morning's meeting addresses a controversial matter: how to position the company vis-à-vis the burgeoning social media, especially Facebook™ and Twitter™. Questions for discussion and decision include the following:

1. Should Nutmeg establish corporate accounts on Facebook? On Twitter?

2. How can these accounts be utilized to the best advantage of the company?

3. Should Nutmeg assign someone to monitor these accounts to filter out negative or critical comments? Why should negative comments be filtered out? Why should they be permitted?

4. Should these accounts be monitored in such a way that individual employees from sales, operations, or customer service are alerted whenever there appears to be a comment posted by a customer with whom an employee has had contact?

5. Should all employees be encouraged to participate through these accounts, or should Nutmeg restrict participation to designated company spokespersons?

As a representative of sales, you immediately recognize that the decisions taken in response to these questions will affect the company's bottom line and your livelihood. What do you recommend for each of these questions, and why?

Case 14.2 – The Nordstrom™ Way

Sandra was so frustrated that she was ready to quit on the spot. She loved selling, and she loved selling computers and related equipment. It was her company's lack of commitment to customer service that she hated. She was convinced that the company's refusal to take customer complaints seriously was hurting sales and depriving her of a chance to develop long-term relationships with her customers. And that, in turn, deprived her of commissions. She took her complaints directly to her regional vice president, Ernest.

"Ok, Ernie," Sandra declared upon taking a seat in front of Ernest's desk. "I'm here to renew my demand that this company begin to change its policies and devote some resources to customer service."

Clasping his hands behind his head, Ernest (Ernie) replied, "Well Sandy(!), you and I have had this conversation before, and the company hasn't changed its mind. Why do you keep pressing?"

"I'm on your case because I know that customer service works," said Sandra. "When I started out in sales, I worked for Nordstrom™, a company that has won awards for the highest quality customer service since they were founded in 1901. Not only am I convinced that I made money because of their policies, but it's a fair bet that customer service helped them expand to 115 department stores in 28 states today. This company is missing out. I'm missing out."

"Well, how do you expect a computer company to adopt Nordstrom's policies and survive?" asked Ernest. "From what you tell me, we'd go bankrupt in a matter of months."

"I know that Nordstrom's policies are counterintuitive," responded Sandra. "As you may know, Nordstrom instructs all of their sales associates to use their own judgment in accepting returns of merchandise for any reason or no reason; and in case of any doubt, to err on the side of the customer. In practice, that means virtually unlimited returns are allowed."

"We can't begin to do that. Our merchandise costs hundreds, sometimes thousands, of dollars per unit," Ernest replied, leaning forward in his chair.

"Well, you should know that at Nordstrom, I regularly accepted $3,000-coats and $800-shoes as returns, even when they showed signs of wear and couldn't be resold," Sandra answered. "But over the long term, these same customers bought more than they returned. The company made money and I made money."

"Sandy, this isn't Nordstrom, and we don't sell shoes." Ernest stood, indicating that this meeting was over. "It appears that you have an important decision to make. Call me to let me know what it is."

So, based on your understanding of Chapter 14, who is correct? Should Sandra's computer company adopt Nordstrom's customer service policies? Does the difference in product matter in deciding this issue, as Ernest claims? Would a Nordstrom-like policy of customer service mean more sales for the computer company in the long run? What sort of changes in customer service might the computer company make short of adopting Nordstrom's unlimited return practice? What should Sandra do? Should she quit, or not?

Chapter 15

Personal, Time, and Territory Management

Learning Objectives

- Discover how to develop an effective time management attitude.

- Recognize the need for organizing your activities and surroundings as a means of controlling your time.

- Develop a procedure for getting organized.

- Establish an effective organizing system for all activities.

- Learn how contact management and mapping programs increase productivity.

- Examine the need and the process for managing travel time in your sales territory.

Time Control and Self-Management

The term time management is a contradiction. Because every minute has sixty seconds and every hour has sixty minutes, time itself cannot be managed—it can only be used. What can be managed, however, are you and your activities. So in actuality, time management is really personal organization as well as self-management; and it involves three areas:

- Self-management (also known as self-discipline)

- Planning and organizing

- Systems and techniques to form routines

Manage your time as you would manage your money.

Time itself is a precious commodity. Although a continuous supply of time is available, it cannot be stored for future use, and it cannot be reclaimed if it is wasted. When you realize that life itself consists of time, the value of time becomes clear. We loudly denounce attitudes or practices that show a lack of respect for human life, but we don't seem to notice when we throw away priceless hours in useless activity or idleness.

Use your time instead of simply spending it. Time is made up of a series of events. The key to managing time is controlling these events to your advantage.[1] Time control and self-management can be learned; you have the ability to control your present thoughts and actions and to decide how to use your time. Here are some symptoms of time mismanagement. See if any of these sound familiar to you:[2]

- Letting papers pile up on your desk and emails pile up in your in-box.

- Delaying decisions, thus frustrating both your superiors and your co-workers.

- Getting farther behind every day.

- Working late and having to work weekends.

Most of us can relate to some or all of those symptoms; so, here is an easy visualization exercise that may help you get a better grip on time's worth. Pretend that the president of your bank informs you that you have been chosen to receive a special prize: Every day for the rest of your life $86,400 will be deposited into your account. The only stipulation is that it must all be spent every day. Anything left at the end of the business day goes back to the bank. You can't hold anything over from one day to the next. Those first weeks are exhilarating. By the end of the first month, you have received over $2 million. After a while, however, you begin to have trouble spending that much every day. Think how you would feel the first time $20,000 slipped away from you and went back to the bank because you failed to spend it all. You would quickly realize that using this much money every day calls for some serious planning.

This imaginary scenario is not entirely fantasy. The old adage is true: Time is money. Every day, 86,400 seconds are deposited in your account and into the accounts of everyone else. You cannot save any unused time for another day. How many of your 86,400 seconds go back to the "bank" unused depends on your skill in planning and managing your time. The important questions are these:

1. How will you spend your time?
2. How will you invest your time?
3. How much time will go to business, to service for others, to family, to leisure?
4. How much time will be reserved just for you, for the things you want to do?

> Dost thou love life? Then do not squander time, for that's the stuff life is made of.
>
> -Ben Franklin

A Time Management Attitude

Your most important asset is time, and how you use it is crucial to your success. Renowned speaker Ira Hayes once said:

"The inability or lack of desire to become organized is responsible for the vast majority of failures. It is why otherwise bright people turn out to be only mediocre performers and achieve only a small degree of the success that they rightfully could achieve. A disorganized desk, car, or way of life leads to rushing around and confusion and generally results in a poor attitude which makes people around you question the advisability of doing business with you."

Everybody has the ability to manage his or her time. The *desire* is the variable that makes the difference, and taking charge of your life depends on your personal choices. Like most success factors in selling, time management depends on attitude. The first line of defense to protect your time is to identify precisely how it can be eroded, and then learn effective means for managing it.[3]

Nearly everything that we think, say, or do is governed by patterns of behavior that we develop over the years. We develop most of them early in life and rarely change them. The only way to lose a habit is to stop practicing it. Stop practicing negative habits and start practicing positive ones, and your life will improve automatically.[4] If you want to achieve high-quality results in professional sales, establish healthy habits and patterns. The people who most efficiently control their time have the best idea of what they want to accomplish.[5]

In sales—more than in many other professions—the management of time is a matter of personal choice and responsibility. Here's an idea to try: Get to work by five o'clock in the morning three times a week, and you'll gain an extra day. You will realize a great feeling of satisfaction at eight o'clock when you have already finished what would have taken you at least six hours to do during normal working hours because of the interruptions.[6]

> "The average American worker has fifty interruptions a day, of which seventy percent have nothing to do with work."
>
> -W. Edwards Deming

Mental preparation is necessary to win the race against time. Developing a time management attitude helps to overcome life's obstacles. Just as Olympic champions practice diligently and relentlessly to perfect their athletic techniques, you can practice time management techniques and maximize the benefits to be enjoyed from both professional and personal pursuits.

You can let the whole subject of time management assume such proportions that the mere thought of attempting to master it becomes frustrating. It is estimated that the typical salesperson spends an average of only two hours a day in productive selling. However, just increasing the time spent with a customer doesn't do very much for you, it's what you do with the time that's important. Focus your time so that it matches opportunity. Perhaps it is a better strategy to target five large accounts, rather than target 50 accounts and divide your time trying to get each one of them. You don't have enough time or enough protection, and competitors swoop in and take them away.[7]

Keep a positive perspective toward time and your use of it. Here are some suggestions for establishing the kind of time attitudes that will bring you success:

1. Make a list of the activities you want to complete during the next week to achieve the results you desire.

2. For an entire week, keep an hour-by-hour record of exactly what you do with your time. Summarize your record and compare what you actually do to the list you made of what you want to do to achieve your goals. (Exhibit 15.1 illustrates a form you can copy to use for this purpose.)

3. At the end of each day and at the end of each week, take a personal accounting of what you have accomplished compared to what you set out to do.

4. List the five habits or attitudes that were the biggest obstacles to the achievement of the results you wanted. Write out a plan for changing these habits or attitudes. Conduct another time analysis study three months from now and compare the two. Determine whether you are making progress in replacing these habits or attitudes with new ones.

ΔExhibit 15.1

Daily Time Survey

	Prospecting	Telephone for Appointments	Sales Interviews	Travel	Reports and Paperwork	Meetings	Sales Training	Servicing Accounts	Preparing for Interviews	Studying Product Info.
6 am										
7 am										
8 am										
9 am										
10 am										
11 am										
12 pm										
1 pm										
2 pm										
3 pm										
4 pm										
5 pm										
6 pm										
7 pm										
8 pm										
9 pm										
10 pm										

Conducting a detailed personal time-analysis study at least twice a year is a good habit to establish. Just as you schedule a regular medical checkup (or at least you should), plan for a time management checkup to keep you aware of how well you are using your time resources.

Getting Organized

Many professionals have the skills to be successful, but they are often held back by their bad habits. If you are disorganized or inefficient, the first step towards organization is to determine what type of "time abuser" you are. There are three types:[8]

1. **Procrastinators**—Do you leave assignments until the eleventh hour and then throw yourself into a panic, working round-the-clock in a vain attempt to meet a deadline?

2. **People Pleasers**—Do you chronically take on more and more responsibility out of a fear of confronting authority and eventually commit too much time to unproductive projects?

3. **Perfectionists**—Do you take more time than is allotted to satisfy extremely unrealistic but deeply internalized standards of excellence?[9]

Once you identify what type or types you may be, and before you can gain any measure of control over your time, you must lay the groundwork for effectively handling the onslaught of information you encounter every day. The following techniques can help you:

Remove the Clutter

You can think more clearly and more creatively if you remove as much clutter as possible from your life and your living space. Remove unnecessary papers from your work area—your desk, your attaché case, and your car. Even if the stacks of paper are neat and appear to be well organized, they promote a subconscious psychological tendency to review and think through the items in sight. According to a national Harris Interactive survey by Cambridge Home & Office Accessories in Stamford, Connecticut, more than 84 percent of salespeople polled are *pilers*—they regularly stack up their paperwork instead of filing it.[10]

"Simplicity is the ultimate sophistication."
~ Leonardo DaVinci

In a few seconds you can think through all of the tasks that are represented by a sizable stack of paper. For all practical purposes, however, your mind does not differentiate between doing a task physically and doing it mentally. If you mentally review a big stack of paper a dozen times a day in the process of deciding which one to tackle next, or which one to avoid, you are exhausted long before the day is over. Once you decide to dispense with clutter, tackle the job at once. Follow this plan to eliminate the disorder from your surroundings and your life:

1. **Collect the Clutter**. Gather up all the clutter that affects you and take it to one convenient work area. Empty your car, bedside table, pockets, and any other cubbyhole where you stick things that are waiting to be done. Dump all the clutter into one container.

2. **Sort the Clutter**. Divide the clutter into two categories: Time-critical material (that is, items with a specific due date) and "someday" material (that is, items that need to be addressed but have no specific due date). Removing clutter allows you to think more clearly and creatively.

3. **Deal With Priorities**. Deal first with the time-critical items. Provide a series of thirty-one folders to represent the days of the month. (This is commonly called a 1-31 file.) A computer master calendar is just as handy and can quickly retrieve each day's notes or retrieve items by subject. You may still need the 1-31 file to collect reports, memos, and other written items. Examine each of the items you have identified as time critical. If it involves a meeting or a specific hour of the day, write it on your calendar. Then put each item in the folder for the day that the first action must be taken to meet the due date. Each

day check the appropriate folder as you make your daily to do list. Then each item will be accomplished on time.

4. **Set Up Categories for the Rest**. Now begin to organize the someday material. Set up two convenient files—the stacked in-out file boxes are helpful. Label these files reading and projects. Go through your someday items and sort them in the two files according to their nature. Pull out a reading item to take along when you are going somewhere that might involve a wait, and then use waiting time to catch up on reading. The material in the projects box may then be sorted into folders for each separate project.

Handling Interruptions

To handle interruptions properly, you must first determine whether an occurrence is truly an interruption or part of your job. Only when you understand this difference are you able to control your attitude toward the people and the circumstances that threaten to get in your way as you are doing your job. Once you determine that an interruption is part of your job, decide whether it is more important than what you are currently doing or whether it should be postponed. This will help you keep your priorities straight and reduces procrastination.[11]

Interruptions typically fall into three categories, each of which you can handle with the right attitude. Exhibit 15.2 lists the three types of interruptions and examples of the most common ways that people experience them.

ΔExhibit 15.2

Types of Interruptions

People	Paper	Environmental
• Superior	• Notes	• Telephone calls
• Associate	• Memos	• Visual distractions
• Subordinate	• Correspondence	• Comfort factors
• Client or customer	• Periodicals	-temperature
	• Messages	-light
	• Projects	-clothing

People Interruptions. People interruptions are the most frustrating because they are the most difficult to solve, and who the person is makes a difference in the way you respond. If your superior interrupts you, remember that that person probably has the right to interrupt you. If you are working on an item of extreme importance with a tight deadline or are due to leave for an appointment with a prospect, however, you can properly ask respectfully whether your superior might wait until your project or call is completed. It's okay to say "no" to your superiors.[12] Because your work is important to the success of the organization, and therefore to your superior as well, most bosses consider such a request to be a mark of both effectiveness and self-confidence on your part.

When a client interrupts you either by phone or in person, adopt the attitude that this contact is not an interruption. You do not automatically put your full day at the disposal of a client's whim, but you do give full attention while the client is talking and then do whatever is necessary to take care of the situation.

Paper Interruptions. People who work in a disorganized environment experience both confusion and frustration when confronted with necessary paperwork. They feel confused because they have no automatic method for handling the item; they spend too long thinking about how to handle it. Then, because they dislike feeling confused, they become frustrated with the repeated inroads made on their time by additional paperwork. Before very long, disorganized people decide they just hate

Learn how to say NO to interruptions.

all paperwork. Salespeople are often among those who say they hate paperwork because they feel that it is less important in producing their income than their direct selling activities.

Businesses are increasing their use of technology and moving more toward a 'paperless' environment where they can enter orders, product information, and account information from their iPads, tablet PC's, smartphones, and laptops. These businesses are looking to the Internet for file storage, communication, and lead generation. In a recent study by Godfrey Phillips, the vice president of research at American City Business Journals, small business owners are using fewer traditional computers than they did three years ago. Instead, they are opting for the mobility offered by laptops and tablet PCs. According to Phillips, nine percent of business owners are now using iPads.[13]

Environmental Interruptions. Distractions in your work space can wreak havoc on productivity if not properly addressed and controlled. Instead of feeling overwhelmed by environmental distractions such as frequent phone calls, schedule a specific telephone time each day to set up appointments for sales presentations and to take care of other sales related business.

Email and social networking are notorious time zappers. Some organizations have tried to impose 'no email' days to cut down on interruptions and have banned the use of social networking sites such as Facebook and Twitter for non-business related communications. The starting point is to ban any casual use of email. Next, take the time to audit incoming mail and don't be afraid to be selective. Try to set aside specific periods to deal with it. Turn the sound off on the computer, so you are not alerted every time a message arrives.[14] Then the remainder of the day is free for those vital selling contacts. When you have a particularly important piece of work to complete, take everything you need to do the job and go to a place where you can work without any kind of interruption.

> Ordinary people think merely of spending time.
> Great people think of using it.

An Organizing System

The challenge for salespeople is to discover the methods that work for them, and typically this will be different for everyone. What's important is that you take the guesswork out of the sales process and replace it with a defined business process. Recognize that success is a percentage game; sales is a profession in which there can never be 100 percent success. Just because you have a clean desk and an organized filing system won't guarantee you will make more sales; but it certainly won't hurt. If you find a certain system that works for you, just keep doing it—in other words, repeat successful behaviors.[15] This is a secret of success at any level of competition. Selling is not a game that requires perfection. You only need to figure out ways to stay ahead of the competition. Identify the behaviors that will consistently improve your performance and you will be well on your way to creating a powerful sales discipline.

In order to be on your way to staying ahead of the competition, you must first remove the unnecessary disorder from your environment. Once you remove the clutter and the incompletions from your work area and get a firm grip on controlling interruptions, two simple tools will help you organize your activities.

1. The Master Calendar

Your master calendar should list only specific time commitments such as appointments with clients and meetings to attend. When using a computerized calendar, you can link your master calendar with your cell phone or smartphone so that you can access the information no matter where you are. There are numerous calendar software applications that can be downloaded onto your cell phone, smartphone, tablet PC, or laptop. All of your information can be stored in these calendars and can be accessed easily for your review. Most of these programs also have a notes feature where you can enter additional information about the appointment.

2. Daily To-Do List

The second time-organizational tool you will need is a daily to-do list. Be sure to prioritize each item on your list. Highlight those activities completed, and carry forward the uncompleted items.[16] These lists can either be generated on paper or you can generate electronic versions using your cell phone, your smartphone, or your iPad. A story about Charles Schwab, former president of Bethlehem Steel, shows the impact of this simple tool. Schwab called in consultant Ivy Lee and proposed a challenge, "Show me a way to get more done with my time, and I'll pay you any fee within reason."

"Fine," said Lee, "I'll give you something in twenty minutes that will increase your output at least fifty percent."

Lee then handed Schwab a blank sheet of paper and said, "Write down the six most important tasks that you have to do tomorrow and number them in order of their importance. Now put this paper in your pocket, and the first thing tomorrow morning look at item one. Work on it until you finish it. Then do item two, and so on. Do this until quitting time. Don't be concerned if you have finished only one or two. You'll be working on the most important items. If you can't finish them all by this method, you couldn't have finished them by any other method either; and without some system, you'd probably not even decide which was the most important."

Lee continued, "Use this system every working day. After you've convinced yourself of the value of the system, have your men try it. Try it as long as you wish and then send me a check for what you think it's worth." Several weeks later, Lee received Schwab's check for $10,000—an impressive sum of money some 80 years ago.

As much as we may want to, no one can alter time. The trick to managing your time is to manage not your time, but your activities. Keep a daily to-do list of what needs to be accomplished and use the list to make sure you are moving the sale forward.[17] The value of a to-do list is apparent, but it becomes even more valuable when you use it not only to identify needed tasks but to establish priorities for them. Putting top priorities first is the only way to be sure that your activities are making a direct impact on your goals. Sales success depends on establishing and steadfastly pursuing a series of goals. When you develop specific and measurable growth goals, you gain the determination and drive it takes to succeed.[18]

Use the To-Do list app on your smartphone to keep you organized.

Charles A. Coonradt, president of Western Leadership Group, says, *"In the absence of clearly defined goals, we are forced to concentrate on activity and ultimately become enslaved by it."* Using a to-do list helps you develop the automatic habit of attaching a when to every thought, idea, commitment, or promise. Exhibit 15.3 is an example of a format you can use for your to-do list. If you are using a computerized master calendar, you can print out your daily to-do list. The form is not nearly as important as the practice!

ΔExhibit 15.3

To-Do List with a Daily Plan to List Appointments ·

Priority	Done	Date ——— Important	Priority	Done	Date ——— Imperative

The Integrated System

Your notes, master calendar, and to-do list can be merged into one file that is capable of being synchronized with all of your technological devices so that you can access the information whenever you need reminders. You can safely forget about incomplete tasks until they surface in your system. Together these organizing tools form a system that makes organization of your daily activities an automatic process. At the close of each day's work, transfer any leftover items from today's to-do list to the new list for tomorrow. Then consult your notes and your master calendar to find all the items you have scheduled for tomorrow. Check any specific times associated with those items, such as the time for an appointment or meeting. Now you are ready to begin work tomorrow without even thinking about what to do first. You are ready to begin your day with the task of highest importance.[19]

Identifying Priorities

An important concept for good time managers to understand is the Pareto Principle. It states that 80 percent of the value (or the frustration) of any group of related items is generally concentrated in only 20 percent of them. In other words, "a minority of the input produces a majority of the results." The principle, named for the Italian economist who proposed it, holds true for many areas of today's experience. For example:

In Measuring Value, You Receive...

80% of:	From 20% of:
• Sales	• Customers
• Productivity	• Activity
• Profit	• Products
• Referrals	• Clients
• Commission Income	• Orders

In Measuring Frustration, You Experience...

80% of:	From 20% of:
• Absenteeism	• Employees
• Errors	• Workers
• Servicing Problems	• Customers

Likewise, 80 percent of your success comes through the achievement of the top 20 percent of your goals. In managing your time effectively, you must recognize that which items you complete, not how many items you complete, determine your success.

To identify the special 20 percent of your activities that have the potential for producing the greatest success, practice establishing different categories of priorities.

"A" priority items are the most pressing. They include the items that must be done by a specific date if you are to reach one of your major goals and items that would damage the reputation of your company or your personal credibility if you failed to accomplish them.

"B" priority items are any items that can be done at any time within the next week or month without causing any repercussions.

"C" priority items would be nice to do at some time when you have nothing else pressing to do, but you would suffer no real loss if you never got around to them.

Obviously, you want to give first attention to your "A" priorities and carefully number them in the order of their importance. Your goal is to complete as many "A" priorities as you possibly can each day and then supplement them with any "B" items you can.[20]

Time Goals

Once you have established the habit of using a to-do list, begin to record next to each item your estimate of the amount of time you will need to complete it. Estimating the required time lets you judge whether you can complete everything. If you can't, you have the possibility of getting someone else to help before you fail to complete some vital item. Time studies have shown that even people who know which items are most important and set priorities still waste an average of fifteen minutes between items of work in simple procrastination or in trying to decide what to do next.

A second benefit of estimating completion times is to help in avoiding procrastination. A deadline—even an informal estimate of the time required—pushes you to complete the work in the allotted time. Northcote Parkinson, a British naval historian and author of *Parkinson's Law*, is noted for his observation that *work expands to fill the time allowed for its completion*. Something about a stated time allotment seems to establish a mental set that causes you to use just that amount of time. If the time is short, you work efficiently and push for completion. If the time allowance is too generous, you procrastinate, spend extra time getting ready to work, and find a dozen small interruptions to make sure you don't finish too early. By estimating times for completion, you eliminate the tendency to procrastinate.

Positive Attitudes Toward Time

Anyone who expects sales success should also expect hard work and long hours. If you always seem to have more work than working hours, though, you may be due for a refresher course in time management. These techniques can't give you more time, but they can help you make the most of what you've got. Follow them to help you get—and keep—time on your side.

Place a Time Limit on Meetings. If you or your salespeople tend to dread meetings, maybe it's because they drag on too much and accomplish too little. Knowing your meeting lasts only an hour should help keep things moving. Before each meeting, decide on a limited number of topics to discuss and a limited time period for discussing them. Exhibit 15.4 looks at how two top executives learned to reign in abuse of meeting time.[21]

ΔExhibit 15.4

Meetings: The Best Way to Avoid Real Work · · · · · · · · · · · · · · · · · · ·

As the new executive vice president at Barnhart/CMI, a marketing and advertising firm based in Denver, Cheryl Akright's first order of business was to cancel all of the company's regular meetings. "It was ridiculous," Ms. Akright said. "Every person in the company was in some type of meeting three to four times per day."

Samuel J. Palmisano, chief executive of IBM, was concerned about how many meetings his company's sales representatives attended each week, Specifically, he was concerned that more than 30,000 members of the company's sales force were spending six hours a week, on average, preparing for and attending meetings. The company is so serious about its new rule on meetings that top executives must now approve any unscheduled sessions. Executives at IBM estimate that the sales force has doubled the time spent with customers as a result.

Set Deadlines and Beat Them. When you've got a lot to do and not a lot of time to do it in, deadlines can help you to stay on schedule. Prioritize your tasks, and then draw up a schedule for completing them. Don't make the mistake of waiting to start on a task just because the deadline seems far away. Chances are, something will come up to fill the extra time you think you have.

Take Advantage of Your Peak Time. To be most efficient at the jobs you like least, tackle them at the time of day when you feel most productive. Pay attention to your moods and work output throughout the day to find out when you're most productive, and save your worst jobs for when you're at your best.

Don't Overload on Overtime. If your workweek consistently exceeds a reasonable number of hours, ask yourself why. Identify the tasks that take up the most time and look for ways to complete them more efficiently. Also, compare the number of hours you're working to what you're actually getting done. A too-small return on your time investment indicates a problem.

Do Some Delegating. Don't feel guilty about delegating responsibility—if you take on a job that someone else could handle more effectively, you're not making the best use of your company's resources.

It's Okay to Say No. When it comes to time management, many of us are our own worst enemy. You'll never have enough time to finish your work if you're always biting off more than you can chew. When people ask you to take on extra projects, they are putting a monkey on your back. *If you agree to take on too many jobs for others, you are soon carrying an impossible load of monkeys and accomplish nothing.*

Put It in Writing. To remember phone numbers, important dates or anything else, write them down. Freeing your mind of clutter helps you think more clearly, and concentration is key to productivity.

Cultivate Helpful Relationships. Create and keep lasting relationships that result in people gladly working to assist you, and this can be one of your most powerful time-management strategies.

Ultimately, it's all about balance. If you are going to be an effective time manager, you need to balance the driving forces with the limiting forces in your life. Live within the zone between these two pressures so that you can be your most effective all the time.[22] Time is like talent—you can't create more of it, you just have to make the most of what you've got. You need self-discipline from the time you wake up in the morning until you go to bed that night.[23] Spending your time more wisely starts with paying attention to how you spend it. Once you decide to take control of your time, you'll have the power to stop squandering it.[24]

Managing Travel Time

One of the most important considerations for field salespeople is protecting their time for making those vital sales presentations. Travel through a territory is, in a sense, nonproductive although necessary time. Linda Meyer, sales director for Oakstone Publishing Company in Ohio, says, "Organize your time before you hit the road, not while on the road."[25] She plans for time blocks—how long it will take her to write letters, do reports or recap a meeting. Look at your time as a 24-hour cycle of fragments. Travel time must be kept to a minimum.

As you learned earlier, the Pareto Principle says that 80 percent of your business will come from 20 percent of your customers. Thus, you must determine how much time and energy each account receives. Scott Gander, a sales rep for Geneal, a company selling restaurant supplies, divides all accounts into A, B, C and D accounts. He tries to spend 40 percent of his time helping A's, 30 percent with B's, 20 percent with C's, and 10 percent with the D's—the D accounts are only interested in price.[26] Be sure to categorize your accounts in a priority ranking such as:

"A"—High-volume, repeat customers.

"B"—Moderate sales volume, but reliable customers.

"C"—Lower volume accounts.

"D"—Accounts that cost you more time and energy to service than you receive in profits.

Outside salespeople travel through time and space, so it will help if they set themselves in motion on the most efficient route between customers and prospects. Sales professionals pay close attention to the routing and scheduling of their calls. They take into consideration the proper mix of accounts on each trip. Prioritizing is useful for determining a profitable mix of account visitation and servicing. A common mistake is to call on "D" accounts simply because they are located near "A" accounts, and require little travel. These customers do not need to be called on with the same regularity as the "A" accounts. Instead use your time to prospect for new high volume, repeat customers.[27]

Organize your time before you hit the road, not while on the road.

Computer Mapping Systems

GPS (global positioning systems) provide geographical information to users through their computers, smartphones, handheld devices, auto units, and even watches. The use of GPS mapping systems is a rapidly growing market of sophisticated products that put numeric data into visual form, making the data much easier to understand. These products create computer-generated maps of geographic areas of interest to both sales managers and their salespeople. This software is used to balance sales territories, optimize driving time, and then target new markets and new accounts. This GPS mapping software lets managers do in minutes what used to take hours, or even days to complete.

Unless you have intimate knowledge of all the Zip codes in every sales territory, it's impossible to know which areas border one another, and which don't. Territory mapping software such as Terralign can help map out the Zip codes in a way that is easy to read and visualize. This type of software has updating features that allow you to match business records to updated geographic Zip codes.[28] Spreadsheets and databases tell you how much and what kind, while mapping software tells you where.

Samantha Miller, sales manager for Precision Wiring, downloads a trip planning application for her iPad. She records her point of origin, her final destination, and multiple stops along the way. Within seconds, she has access to personalized maps indicating alternate routes for her to choose from. The program she has chosen can help track expenses and budget costs for hotel, gas, meals, and also includes information on current traffic conditions.[29]

The Smartphone—Your Travel Companion

The smartphone can do many things including reading and sending email, reading and sending text messages, finding a nearby Starbucks, checking a stock portfolio, taking a picture, recording voice memos, playing games, accessing Internet sites, maintaining contact lists, keeping a calendar, listening to music and audio books, looking at and sharing a picture, and making telephone calls.[30] They can also be used to plan your entire sales trip from determining the route to securing your reservations. There are also GPS mapping programs available for download to your smartphone that will help you budget your costs, find restaurants and hotels, and provide real-time traffic updates.

Strategize Your Sales Calls

Like a leaf blowing in the wind, many salespeople leave the office with no idea where they're going. They go where the wind blows and when the wind changes direction, so do they. The solution to this is a quality contact management system coupled with a good mapping system.[31] The goal of all the various mapping programs is to minimize your travel time and maximize your selling time.

For example, Gabriel Smith, outside salesman for Apple™, uses a mapping system called BusinessMap™ to plan his road trips more efficiently. Smith covers a Southeastern territory that spans seven states, requiring him to spend 70 percent of his time on the road. He says, "If I know that I will be visiting a customer in Alabama, I can map out my route so that I can call on customers on the drive out there as well as on the way back."

The uses of computer mapping systems are limited only by your creative imagination. For example, when prospects ask you for referrals, really impress them by trying this: Use your mapping system to place the prospect on a map, and then use the system to draw a circle that identifies every one of your customers in a 25-mile radius. By doing this, you provide your prospect with a comprehensive and organized list of referrals who are nearby. Proximity is important when providing referrals to potential customers.

In-dash navigation systems take the guesswork out of planning your sales call route.

This mapping technology also enables a sales rep to get a list of every potential customer in a geographic area and map it against a display of the company's existing accounts. The result is an up-to-date analysis of how well you have penetrated your territory and the opportunity that remains. Maximizing travel time is an obvious and critical competitive advantage for today's traveling sales professsionals.[32]

Developing Partnerships Using Technology examines mapping programs and GPS (Global Positioning Systems). Getting lost is no longer an excuse, and there is no need to be flipping through an atlas on the side of the road. Just plug in your computer, and type in the address you wish to find, and let your GPS do the rest.

Developing Partnerships Using Technology

Here are some of the features found on most quality mapping programs:

Destination Routing. To plan an entire sales route and help budget your time and gas expenditures, you can enter the physical locations of each prospect or customer into your GPS system, and the system will calculate the mileage and timing between them. The system will also give you alternate routes such as the shortest, longest, or most scenic.

Points of Interest Database. Imagine trying to close a sale and finding out that your prospect loves to play golf. You can conduct a search of local golf courses and schedule a tee time for you and your prospect using your GPS software, thus helping you to win the favor of your prospect and increasing your chances of closing successfully.

Real-time Traffic Information. When you need to get to the airport in a hurry during 'construction season' you can download up-to-date traffic information and suggested alternative routes directly to any of your devices.

Synchronizing Capabilities. You can download territory mapping software and have your sales routes synch directly to your in-car GPS, hand-held GPS, smartphone, tablet PC, or laptop. Sales managers can even synch the sales routes of all their salespeople to have a better visual of the information all on one screen.

Check out these websites for additional information:

www.google.com/maps

www.infousa.com

www.randmcnally.com

www.delorme.com

www.bing.com/maps

www.mapblast.com

maps.yahoo.com

www.terralign.com

Territory Routing Patterns

You may not realize it, but traveling in your territory involves more strategic planning than merely getting from point A to point B. Several popular scheduling or routing patterns have been developed and are used by field salespeople to cut travel time in their territories and maximize face-to-face selling opportunities, and they are:

The Cloverleaf Pattern

Exhibit 15.5 illustrates how this travel pattern might look. The starting point may be your home or the district or regional sales office location. One "leaf" is covered at a time. Each leaf or quadrant could take a day, a week, or longer to complete. A new leaf is started on each subsequent trip, until the entire territory is covered.

ΔExhibit 15.5

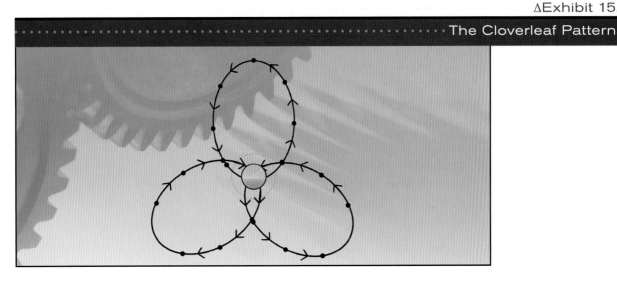

The Cloverleaf Pattern

The Hopscotch Pattern

Exhibit 15.6 is a graphic illustration of this travel pattern. You begin at the most distant point from your home base and make prospect and client calls on the return trip. Depending on the size of the territory (some sales reps have territories that encompass several states), you may fly out to the starting point and drive back. Outside salespeople can vary this pattern and cover different directions on subsequent trips.

ΔExhibit 15.6

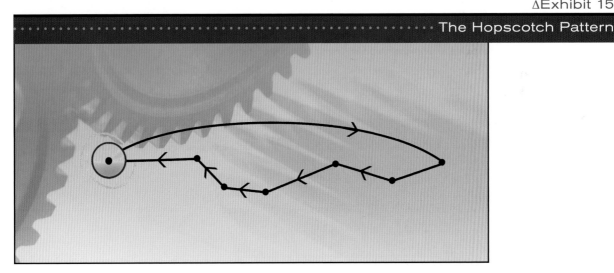

The Hopscotch Pattern

The Circular and Straight Line Patterns

Two other routing patterns are the Circular Pattern, where the salesperson starts from base or home office and moves in a specific pattern to make sales calls, and the Straight-line Pattern, where the salesperson starts from base or home office and makes sales calls in one direction.[33] See Exhibit 15.7 for an example of these two patterns. Dividing the territory into several segments and scheduling appointments for a single day in one segment of the territory makes considerable sense. Controlling your schedule in this manner does not preclude flexibility to meet an important prospect or client regardless of location; occasionally, you will choose to readjust your plan for an important reason. Without a plan, however, you are so flexible that you are soon all bent out of shape.

∆Exhibit 15.7

The Straight Line and Circular Routing Patterns ·

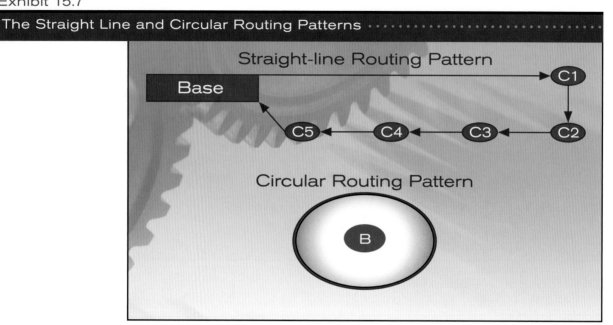

Heuristics Patterns

Other routing patterns are based on mathematics and heuristics, or the trial-and-error method. Two prevalent heuristics that may be used to create sales routes are the *Largest Angle Heuristic* and the *Closest Next Heuristic*. The Largest Angle Heuristic involves traveling from Point A to Point B and then to the point that generates the largest angle. In the figure for this heuristic, the next point traveled to would be Point D. The Closest Next Heuristic is similar, however, after you have traveled to Point B, you will then travel to the point closest to where you are now, which would be Point D in Exhibit 15.8 below.[34]

∆Exhibit 15.8

Heuristics Routing Patterns ·

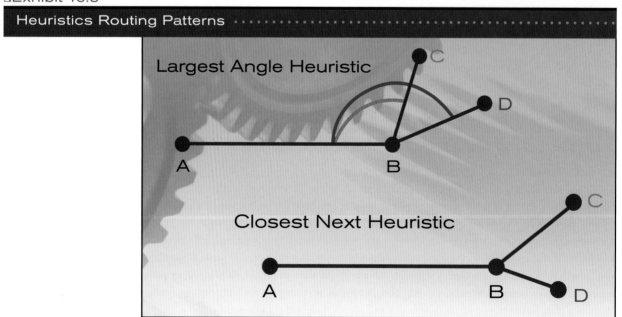

SUMMARY

- The ability to manage time efficiently and effectively is fundamentally a matter of attitude. Time is money. If you seek advancement and a comfortable income, managing time properly is one of the best skills you can develop.

- Interruptions are ultimately just time wasters, so handle them with planning and control. Interruptions come from everywhere—including people, paper, and environmental factors.

- A workable system for time management includes at least three elements:

    1. A master calendar for scheduling commitments.

    2. A daily to-do list to record activities to be done each day to reach your goals.

    3. A reminder file to hold items that will become important at a specific later date.

- Smartphones allow you to download mapping software onto your tablet PC, laptop or vehicle navigation system to make getting around and tracking appointments more convenient.

- Use GPS mapping systems and territory routing patterns to balance sales territories, optimize driving time, and target new markets and accounts.

- Routing patterns and heuristics can be used to create territory maps for contacting prospects and customers.

REVIEW QUESTIONS

1. Write a hundred-word statement giving your opinion about the importance of effective time management and its possible impact on your future in professional selling.

2. What three activities must your mind perform that affect how you use time? How does a system for time management make each of these tasks easier?

3. Describe an effective method for handling incomplete tasks.

4. How does a cluttered desk or briefcase affect time use? What kind of impression do you think a cluttered office or briefcase gives your prospects?

5. How does the appearance of a salesperson's car and briefcase affect professional credibility?

6. Describe the necessary elements of an effective organizing system.

7. Explain how a computer can be used to help with time management.

8. What three main sources of interruptions cause time problems? Give some strategies for handling each type.

9. What can be done to limit the time needed for telephone calls?

10. How can the time needed for travel in the sales territory be kept to a minimum?

ROLE-PLAY EXERCISES

The following role-play exercises help build teams, improve communication, and emphasize the real-world side of selling. They are meant to be challenging, to help you learn how to deal with problems that have no single right answer, and to use a variety of skills beyond those employed in a typical review question. Read and complete each activity. Then in the next class, discuss and compare answers with other classmates.

Role Play 15.1 – Doing A, B, C.

You will work individually on this exercise in class.

Whether you are a full-time or part-time student, whether you are working or have family responsibilities (or both!), you are busy. Chapter 15 offers several suggestions for managing your activities more efficiently. During the next 20 minutes, you will construct and think about one of them: the To-Do List.

On a blank sheet of paper draw a grid with three columns: "A – Imperative," "B – High Priority," "C – Priority." Add three rows, one row for each of the next 3 days.

- "Imperative" means that an activity must be completed by a certain date/time within the 3-day period and that if it is not, dire consequences ensue.

- "High Priority" means that an activity must be completed anytime during the next week.

- "Priority" means that an activity can be completed at your discretion as you have time.

Next, enter activities in each cell of the grid and note an estimate of how long it will take to complete each activity. (You can allow time for daily activities such as eating and sleeping, but don't enter them into the grid.) During the next 3 days, keep an accurate record of which activities in each column were completed.

Examine which activities were not completed and the reasons why. What challenges regarding management of your activities did your analysis of this brief to-do list reveal?

Role Play 15.2 – Where Are You?

For this exercise, pair up with another student in the class.

Many persons are geographically challenged. That is, they have little or no notion of where they or anything else is physically located on the planet. Such a condition is disastrous for salespersons who must manage a physical territory, and in today's global economy a sales territory can be very large indeed!

Imagine that you and your partner are a small sales team for a multi-state region. In order to arrange your sales calls most efficiently, you decide that you must know exactly where you are at all times. To accomplish this, you agree to put a "location kit" together to help you plan and execute your travels.

- After some research, which GPS device will you purchase? What sort of features must your system have, and why?

- What happens if your device fails or the satellite signal is unavailable? Do you have a map? Do you know how to read it?

- Assuming that your territory is too large for you to return home each evening, how will you go about making sure that your travel time is minimized? What sort of considerations must you keep in mind to answer such a question?

Jot down your responses and be prepared to discuss them in class or online.

 CASE STUDIES

The following case studies present you with selling scenarios that require you to apply the critical skills discussed in the chapter and give you training through simulation, role-playing, and practical learning situations. They are meant to be both engaging and challenging, and like the role-play exercises, don't have one right answer.

Case 15.1 – The Pesky Client

While she was busy working on her computer at 3:30 p.m., trying to complete two spreadsheets that she had to forward to her sales manager in a couple of hours, Janice's phone rang. With a groan, she reached for it, "Yes, Alice? What is it?"

"I'm sorry, Janice," replied Alice, "but it's Mr. Caruthers again. He called earlier around noon, but you were out."

"Do you know what he wants?" asked Janice.

"Something about those bearings that he talked about with you last week. I tried to refer him to Ed, but he said that he would only deal with you."

"Ok, Alice. I'll take care of it." Janice was perturbed. She had to submit her bi-weekly sales report and expense report by 5:30; otherwise, she wouldn't get paid and the numbers wouldn't make it into the company's monthly totals. Caruthers was one of her largest accounts, but he could be a blowhard and take up too much time.

Janice looked at her reflection in the small mirror that she kept next to the phone, put on a big smile, and pushed the lighted button. "Hello, Mr. Caruthers. It's nice to hear from you again. I'm sorry that I was out when you phoned earlier. What can I do for you?"

"Hi, Miss Stokes. I'm calling about those bearings that you promised me last week. I told you that if I don't get them by next Tuesday I'll have to shut down the line. Here it is, Friday, and I haven't heard anything from you." Caruthers was upset and worried.

"I'm sorry, Mr. Caruthers. I do know how important delivery of the bearings is to your operation. Let me check with our people, and I'll get right back to you," Janice replied in her most reassuring tone.

"All right. But I can't wait much longer." With that, the line went dead.

What should I do? Janice thought. If I discover that there's a problem with meeting Caruthers's deadline, there's really nothing I can do about it today. But if I call him back with that news, he'll never get off the phone. I might as well trash my reports. On the other hand, if there is no problem, I'm certain that Caruthers will be so relieved that he'll talk forever. He knows he's a good customer, and he expects me to give him a lot of attention. Either way, I'll miss my deadline.

What would you advise Janice to do? Should she take care of her reports before dealing with her best customer's problem? Or should she handle the Caruthers matter and explain the circumstances to her manager, hoping that he'll understand? What would you do, and why?

Case 15.2 – "I'm Late, I'm Late . . . for a Very Important Date"

The White Rabbit's song in *Alice in Wonderland* had become the mantra for Roberta's current existence. No matter how hard she tried, she just couldn't get her act together. It seems she was always late getting to the office, late for appointments with clients, and late meeting her boyfriend for dinner. And this morning was no exception: at 9:20 a.m., she was just pulling into the parking lot. Greg, her manager, was sure to be on her case.

And he was. "Nice of you to work us into your busy schedule, Roberta," Greg growled.

"I know. I know. No matter how early I leave, I always get stuck in traffic." Even as she said it, Roberta realized how lame that sounded.

"Well, I can't let it slide. My boss has been reviewing time sheets, and you know what that means." Greg softened his demeanor a bit. "Come on in, and let's chat about it."

After they both settled in with their lattes, Greg asked, "So tell me, why do you think you have such a problem being on time?"

"I don't sleep well, Greg. I go to bed at a reasonable hour, but then I wake up around 1:00 or 2:00 in the morning, worrying about what I didn't get done and what needs to be done for the next day. I sometimes watch the clock tick over to 4:30 before falling back to sleep."

"Not good. Not good at all. You must be exhausted," Greg responded with some sympathy. "And I know that telling an insomniac to get more sleep doesn't help."

"I know," said Roberta. "I've tried prescription and over-the-counter sleep aids, but nothing gets me through the night. I really don't know what to do. When the alarm goes off, I can barely drag myself out of bed, let alone to work."

"Maybe your problem is stress. And it sounds to me like your stress might be occurring from lack of organization," remarked Greg. "What do you think? Shall we try to work on that a little?"

"Ok. I've tried everything else," Roberta admitted plaintively.

In light of the discussion of activity management in Chapter 15, what do you think Greg suggested to Roberta in order to relieve her stress? What suggestions would you make to someone in similar circumstances? How do you manage stress so that you can get sufficient rest in order to function at a high level? If lack of organization is a problem, what can you change to better manage your affairs?

Chapter 16

Sales Force Management

Learning Objectives

- Examine the function of sales management in a company.

- Understand what is required of a sales manager.

- Learn the differences in qualifications between sales managers and salespeople.

- Determine the specific responsibilities of the sales manager.

- Examine the distinctions of various compensation plans.

- Discuss the recruitment and selection process of salespeople.

- Study orientation, training, and motivation practices used by managers.

The Role of Sales Management

Sales force management plays a vital part in the overall success of any company. If salespeople do not sell the company's products or services, no amount of effort in sales or marketing planning will produce success. Although the failure of an individual salesperson to sell may occasionally be attributed to lack of ability or unwillingness to work, the failure of an overall sales force is more likely to result from a basic sales management problem: *The salespeople were improperly recruited, selected, trained, compensated, or motivated.* The costs associated with managing a sales force are often the largest single operating expense item for a company.

Most companies would agree that a good salesperson—someone who represents his company well, sells above expectations, and treats his position like a career and not just a stopping point between jobs—is invaluable. But most sales managers also know that those types of salespeople are often hard to find. So, the real question then becomes, how much does it cost to hire the *wrong* salesperson? Exhibit 16.1 shows the actual dollar investment spent in hiring the wrong salesperson for your open position.[1] The numbers are astonishing!

The cost of hiring the wrong salesperson can really add up, but when it comes to team leaders, the costs can escalate even more rapidly. One Senior VP estimated the cost of losing a single product development team leader at $29 million, due to the necessity of getting a product rapidly to market.[2] In addition, the time invested in training a new salesperson ranges from eight weeks to two years. You begin to get a clear picture of just how truly critical are the recruitment, selection, and training processes. And when you add in the *turnover factor*, you begin to fully understand that companies must have a process in place that provides them with salespeople who are committed and loyal for the long run.

ΔExhibit 16.1

The Real Cost of Hiring and Turnover

Let's say you have an open sales position, and it has to be filled immediately to meet your market demands. After spending time sifting through the myriad resumes you received from your monster.com and theladders.com job postings, you think you've found the perfect fit. But after making what appears to be a terrific selection, you begin to have some doubts about your choice. You want to give him some time to adapt and adjust, and so you commit even more of your time to coach him. By the time you're sure it's a bad fit, six months have passed, and it's time to start over again. So, what did that process really cost? Let's look at some numbers:

Direct Cost:		Indirect Cost:	
Base Salary and Benefits for 6 months	$45,000	New business opportunities lost	$$$$
Recruiting Cost	$6,000	Future lost revenue (unhappy customers)	$$$$
Training and Development	$4,000	Time, effort & cost to get customers back	$$$$
Coaching Time and Effort	$15,000	Lost market share (stronger competitors)	$$$$
Doing It All Over Again	$25,000	Impact to forecast	$$$$
Lost Revenue	$300,000	Impact to sales measurement indices	$$$$
		Impact to sales team	$$$$
		Finding the time to do it over again	$$$$

The rule of thumb is that hiring the wrong salesperson will cost your business 10-12 times annual salary and benefits. So, the cost of making this one wrong choice will likely be close to $600,000!

The sales function is the responsibility of the sales manager, who is involved with all aspects of selling, including planning, organizing, controlling, and evaluating the sales force. The sales manager is the link between individual salespeople and their customers and the organization's upper management. In a smaller firm, the sales management function may be assigned to the marketing manager. A larger, more diversified company may have several sales managers classified by geographic area, customer type, or product line, and each may report to a district or regional manager who, in turn, reports to the chief sales executive of the company. Increasingly, sales managers in companies of any size interact with marketing personnel to develop and carry out marketing campaigns using email and social media, both with existing customers and with prospects.

Both sales ability and management ability are required regardless of how broad or how limited the sales manager's job may be. The management ability required of a field salesperson is primarily applied in the area of personal time and activity management. The sales manager needs excellent management ability in addition to the basic sales abilities that everyone in sales needs. The amount of time spent in actual *sales activity* versus *administrative activity* changes at each level of management. The manager who directly supervises field salespeople spends more time in selling activities than in administrative duties, but a chief sales executive who is separated from field salespeople by several levels of sales management may be almost completely involved in administrative activity. In any case, today's sales managers and executives need a firm grasp of the available technologies to maximize their effectiveness on the job.

Managing In Today's Business Climate

Marketing and sales companies historically used the 4P's—*Product, Price, Place, and Promotion* to formulate strategy. Now a fifth P is needed: *People*. A sales manager's job is no longer to rule over the sales force using the traditional authoritative management style. Individuals entering the sales world today have a different set of values. They have more education and sophistication, desiring managers who listen, encourage, teach, coach, and give them a voice in how they are managed. If the sales environment does not meet these requirements, they will search for one that does.

According to Dr. Ken Blanchard, co-author of the *One-Minute Manager*, young sales professionals are foregoing other aspects of the job, including financial considerations, to work in a caring, supportive environment. In a study by the Families and Work Institute, 3400 randomly selected men and women ranked their three most important job considerations, which were:

1. **Open Communication**. Information is power; do not withhold information as a way to abuse your management position. Tell your sales force everything you know that is pertinent to their job. Involve them in the decisions that affect them.

2. **Effect on Personal and Family Life**. The explosion of two-wage-earner families and the growing number of families with single parents makes it more stressful to juggle all the demands of work and home life. Problems that did not impact the work place a generation ago, such as sick children or scheduling a day-care provider, means managers must find new ways to allow for greater flexibility and autonomy in individual jobs.

3. **Nature of the Work**. Workers want to feel their job is important to the success of the company. A wise sales manager takes every opportunity to let the sales force know how critical their efforts are in meeting company goals. Saying "thank you" frequently is easy, and best of all, it's free.[3]

The sales manager's challenge is to walk the fine line between pleasing top management and keeping the sales force motivated. Sales managers must be coaches, facilitators, and cheerleaders for their people. Their main concerns must be how to shape a more supportive work environment and to find ways to help each salesperson be more productive.

Sales Managers and Technology

Sales managers have an increasing array of options to choose from as they communicate with their remote sales forces: smartphones, teleconferences, email, videoconferencing, voicemail, instant messaging, text messaging, and of course the standby, face-to-face.

The salesperson's use of technology was covered extensively in chapter 6, but technology's uses for sales managers have enough extra benefits to warrant mentioning here. Exhibit 16.2 shows a few ways the benefits of technology apply to sales managers.[4]

ΔExhibit 16.2

Sales Management Made Easier

Ease of communication. For complex organizations, smartphones and laptops are a must-have for sales managers to communicate between divisions and with their sales personnel. Technology allows sales managers to authorize changes in the terms of an offer with only a few taps on the touch screen of a phone or tablet. There's no need to fill out new forms; the paperwork will catch up after the sale.[5]

Increased productivity. Sales managers can benefit from many of the same contact management tools used by sales personnel. Whether managers are accessing sales and contact information on the company server or through a cloud-hosted CRM system such as Salesforce.com, the wide availability of information saves time and frustration for managers dealing with multiple personnel and clients on a daily basis.

Enhanced training and demos. The latest training and file-sharing software allows managers to share screens between salespeople during meetings, as well as conduct polls and surveys to keep a finger on the pulse of the training group.

Videoconferencing. In today's global marketing economy, the salesperson must sell to a more diversified and geographically spread-out customer and prospect base then ever before. Finding the time and resources to have a face-to-face meeting can be difficult and expensive. With the advent of videoconferencing, the salesperson, sales manager, or customer can have the "face-to-face" meetings that are so critical to success in professional selling. A skilled sales manager can conduct an interactive meeting with sales reps in offices from New York City to Perth, Australia. No expensive plane tickets are necessary, and the sales reps never have to leave their territories.

Previously, expensive video equipment was required for videoconferencing, but today all you need is an Internet connection, computer, webcam, and microphone. This enables the sales manager to conduct a meeting with his salespeople who might be anywhere in the world. Salespeople need to be in frequent communication with their home office, and videoconferencing allows just such rapid, effective communication.

Eli Lilly and Company has had considerable success using videoconferencing to keep eight major sales offices in regular contact with headquarters. For Christopher Roberts, former manager of business communication technologies for Eli Lilly, this technology makes sense. He says, "You're able to keep people informed without taking them out of the field."[6]

Sales Force Surveys. As you prepare for a sales conference, here is an idea to consider. Suppose you are bringing in your salespeople from all over the country to one central facility for two days of meetings. Prior to the conference with your sales reps, use a tool called Group Mind Express™ from Catalyst Consulting. Here's how it works: Send an email to each salesperson that includes a link to a site that contains a survey you wrote. When your salespeople go to the site, they answer the questions and the site immediately displays the results to date for the entire survey—showing them where they stand on the issues you raised compared to their colleagues. This allows you to quickly see the concerns that are most important to them. Using this type of tool for surveying your sales force prior to a critical sales meeting will help you zero in on the topics that are of critical interest to them once you actually all come together. This is one way to maximize your twin investments of time and money.[7]

The best leaders know that one-on-one talks can help employees overcome problems.

When you lead by example, everyone wins.

The Sales Manager As a Leader

Pushing yourself to greater heights of leadership is not just a good suggestion—it's crucial for your company's survival. It's not enough to just say, "Keep up the good work." Managers must create a motivational culture that challenges and inspires positive change in their salespeople.[8] The pressure is on everyone in this economy, so managers must be ready to step forward and lead a sales force toward success. One of the keys of leadership is *motivating people*. Sustained motivation comes from day-to-day motivation—and that has to come from sales managers who are leaders themselves.

Sales may be the lifeblood of a company, but some smaller companies don't have a formal sales manager position—and others delegate that responsibility to an already overworked producer, one who may be great at acquiring business but lacks the skill and will to lead others. "Our agency was profitable, but growth was not meeting my expectations," says Ralph Hartwell, founder of the Hartwell Corporation (THC) in Idaho. THC shuffled the sales manager job among various executives, so no one was consistently responsible for setting sales goals, monitoring progress, or achieving results.[9] Hartwell finally recognized the importance of having a solid leader in order to break through to the next level of success. Bob Nelson, author of *1001 Ways to Energize Your Employees*, says, "For today's employees, you can't light a fire under them. You have to light a fire in them."[10] Exhibit 16.3 gives sales managers powerful tips on how to motivate employees and then keep them motivated.[11]

ΔExhibit 16.3

Tips on Motivation

Motivation is Caring *not* Scaring. Fear should never be used as a motivation strategy. It may get managers what they want now, but it will set them up for what they don't want in the future in the form of employee anger, resentment, and lack of enthusiasm and commitment.

Motivation Blossoms in the Right Atmosphere. When employees feel nurtured, appreciated, acknowledged, and respected, they'll give 100 percent of their time, effort, and commitment in return. The job of the manager is to create a work environment that provides employees with the opportunity to attain their goals and experience what they value most in their professional lives.

Walk the Talk. Modeling the behavior leaders want from their salespeople is the most effective way to change any behavior. If they want motivated employees, they need to become a role model for motivation.

The Law of Attraction. The law of attraction states that whatever we focus on we bring to ourselves. If sales managers focus on the lack of motivation in employees, they will find more and more examples of it. When they seek to learn more about motivation and create an atmosphere that fosters it, they will find more examples of motivation in the workplace.

Ongoing Commitment. Motivating employees is an ongoing process because people are continually growing and changing. As they achieve something they want or value, they then seek to achieve more of the same. If motivation is not kept on the managerial front burner, sales managers see the fires in their employees slowly fade and die out.

Despite the widespread use of Total Quality Management techniques in many of today's corporations, a high failure rate of TQM improvement programs exists—60 percent to 67 percent—according to research studies.[12] These failures occurred not because of basic flaws in the principles of TQM, but more so because of ineffective implementation systems. So, what can a sales manager do to ensure his techniques are successful? Here are five leadership skills that a sales manager can use to more effectively put TQM fundamentals into practice.[13]

1. Provide employees with a sense of mission.

2. Create a work environment where salespeople feel free to stretch their talents.

3. Give immediate feedback on what salespeople need to improve on so they don't have to guess.

4. Offer praise and reward in an appropriate way so that individual salespeople are recognized as well as the team as a whole.

5. Help and support employees in developing their talents and careers.

These skills are the basis for the sales manager's approach to the task of sales management. You must remember that *leadership* isn't an event; it is a process. Sales managers must be able to diagnose what their people need and remain flexible enough to provide for those needs.

Based on the leadership skills outlined above, Exhibit 16.4 recommends a new management style. To maximize a team's performance, sales managers must break away from the traditional management style and develop the winning style of management that will help their companies gain a competitive advantage. The idea is to lead, not to simply tell people exactly what to do. You develop people and ask how they think a task should be handled. The winning manager takes the sales force to the next level—after all, they can't accomplish that without the help and support of their salespeople.

Ask yourself, *Why do America's corporate giants invest many hours annually in supervisory and management development?* It's because they recognize that competent and consistent staff supervision is the principal ingredient of an effective and efficient organization; but in order to achieve this, supervisors and managers need to be skilled in communications, planning, scheduling, evaluating job performance, coaching, counseling, team building, handling employee problems and problem employees, resource allocation, and conflict management.[14]

"The key to management lies in always providing value to the people who work under you." This is the definition of strong leadership according to Edward Berube, president of Conseco Insurance Group in Indianapolis.[15] Sales managers serve as champions to the people who report to them.

ΔExhibit 16.4

Traditional vs. Winning Managers

 **Traditional Managers**

1. Stick to their old ways and resist change.

2. See themselves as cops or bosses.

3. Make all the decisions on their own.

4. Are reluctant to share information.

5. Demand action, effort, and long hours.

6. Neglect career-planning discussions and assume company will do that for them.

 **Winning Managers**

1. Thrive on, and relish, change.

2. Think like a coach or team leader.

3. Believe in group decision making.

4. Are eager to share news and information.

5. Expect progress and results to occur.

6. Take initiative for planning own career and assist sales staff in planning theirs.

Adapted from: Dr. Wolf Rinke's book Winning Management: Six Fail-Safe Strategies for Building High-Performance Organizations

The qualifications that produce success for an individual salesperson are not necessarily the same as those needed for success as a sales manager. On one hand, a salesperson must possess a strong sense of self-discipline coupled with a fondness of independence. A sales manager, on the other hand, is continuously involved in interaction with a diverse clientele both inside and outside the organization. The freedom enjoyed by salespeople to arrange and manage their own time and activities is not as likely to be available to the sales manager who is held accountable for the overall effectiveness of a number of salespeople. Managing yourself and your own time is not the same as directing and managing other people's time and energies. Choosing the best salesperson for promotion to sales manager does not always work. A manager's job is to do whatever is necessary to achieve consistent production and growth, both personally and in all members of the sales force, and to build top-performing producers while maintaining a profitable business.

Determining Sales Force Organization

In building and maintaining an efficient sales force, the sales manager performs at least six distinct managerial functions, as shown in Exhibit 16.5. This model serves as a basis for the information presented next and illustrates the complexity of the sales management function.

ΔExhibit 16.5

The Job of the Sales Manager

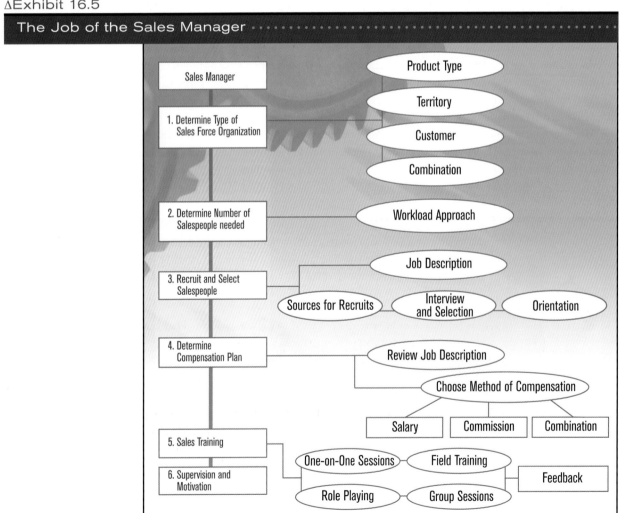

As the exhibit illustrates, the first task that must be performed by a sales manager before the first sale is ever made is determining how to organize his sales team. Organizing the sales force within imposed budget constraints is one of the sales manager's major concerns. No precise rules apply for choosing the organizing strategy to follow. Exhibit 16.6 depicts the three basic types of sales force organization models.

ΔExhibit 16.6

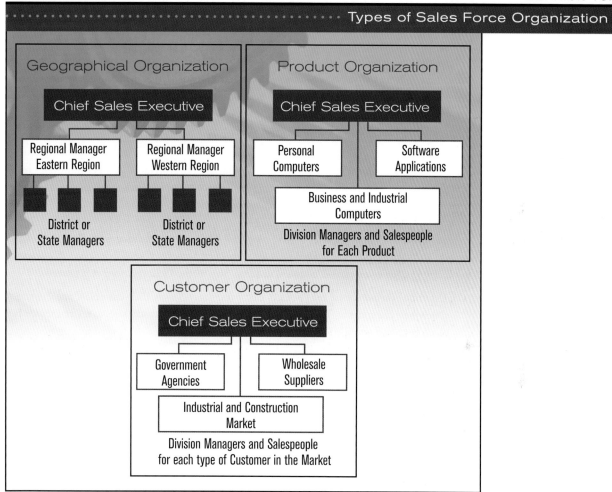

Types of Sales Force Organization

Geographical Organization

Chief Sales Executive

Regional Manager Eastern Region

Regional Manager Western Region

District or State Managers

District or State Managers

Product Organization

Chief Sales Executive

Personal Computers

Software Applications

Business and Industrial Computers

Division Managers and Salespeople for Each Product

Customer Organization

Chief Sales Executive

Government Agencies

Wholesale Suppliers

Industrial and Construction Market

Division Managers and Salespeople for each type of Customer in the Market

Product Organization

When this plan is used, salespeople specialize in the sale of a relatively narrow line of goods or services. This organization is effective in a company that sells expensive, complex, or technical products that require high levels of product knowledge. It is also effective when buying patterns vary greatly among the various parts of the product line. Product organization is expensive because of the time, effort, and human resources needed for specialization.

Bertelsmann AG decided to reorganize their company along strict product lines. According to Michael Dornemann, head of the entertainment division, "If you have a decentralized corporate approach and have too many divisions, it becomes difficult to handle because there are so many overlapping strategic ideas." They now have four clearly differentiated divisions. The move has been enormously successful for them.[16]

Geographic Organization

Salespeople assume responsibility for selling the entire product line within a defined geographical region. This type of organization is probably the most common. If the product line is extensive, this method of organization hampers the salesperson's ability to gain enough detailed product knowledge. If the territory is large, the number of customers and the amount of travel required may cut the amount of service the salesperson can give to each account. The risk exists that such salespeople will choose to concentrate only on the products or services with the highest demand or that are easiest for them to sell.

Customer Organization

Organization on the basis of customer type assigns salespeople to serve a specific type of customer. Some call on industrial accounts, and others call on retail accounts. This method allows salespeople to become knowledgeable about the needs of a given industry or customer type. It also gives the salespeople time to employ personalized sales strategies.

Determining the Size of the Sales Team

The importance of determining how many salespeople to employ can hardly be overemphasized. An understaffed sales force produces sales levels that are too low; over-staffing, however, creates excessive costs and cuts profits. Although simple in theory, determining the appropriate number of people to hire may prove relatively difficult. The problem lies in estimating the impact on the marketplace of adding salespeople.

One frequently used method for determining how many salespeople to hire is called the *workload approach*. This method is based upon determining the total amount of sales work needed, estimating how much one salesperson can do, and then dividing. This method follows a four-step process:

1. Determine the *number of calls* needed. Companies may classify their customers into categories. Often these categories are based on the level of actual sales or potential sales to each customer. Not all accounts will get called on with equal frequency.

2. Determine the *average time necessary per call* and multiply this amount of time by the number of calls to be made to find the total working time needed.

3. Figure how much *actual selling time* (total hours per year) is available for each salesperson (allowing time for travel between appointments and other sales-related activities).

4. Divide the *total working time by the working time per salesperson* to find the number of salespeople needed.

The following formula—based on the four-step process listed above—provides an estimate for the number of salespeople needed:

Sales Force Size = Total Number of Customers and Prospects x Call Frequency x Call Time Required ÷ Selling Time Available for One Salesperson

For example:

Customers	150
Prospects	+600
Total	750

- Call frequency = call on each customer once a month (or 12 times/year)
- Average call time per visit = 45 minutes
- Actual selling time available per year = 4 hours/day x 250 days a year = 1,000 hours

Sales force size = $\frac{750 \times 12 \times .75 =}{1,000}$ $\frac{6,750 =}{1,000}$ 7 salespeople

The more realistic the estimate for each factor, the more accurate the final determination will be. In addition to accurate estimates of these factors, other considerations include the quality of the people recruited: Level of selling skill, personal motivation, experience and product knowledge, initiative, and work habits. All of these factors play a part in whether the estimated levels of sales activity and the estimated results will be reached.[17] The sales manager's ability to determine how many people are needed improves with experience and with knowledge of the people already in the work unit.

Recruiting and Selecting a Sales Force

Building a winning sales force depends in large measure upon the sales manager's effectiveness in recruiting and selecting the best salespeople. The process, like every other selling activity, requires planning and preparation, careful tracking, and efficient carrying out of plans. At least four phases are included in the total process:

Phase I: Determine Requirements for the Position

Finding the right person to fill a sales position is a major concern for every sales organization regardless of size or type. Finding the right person is impossible before you know what qualities are necessary. With all of the communication technology available today to make telecommuting a reality, location is much less important than the qualifications of the candidate.[18] Develop a profile of the candidates who will stand the best chance of succeeding. Make this profile realistic, not idealistic. Planning begins with development of a job description that sets out in written form all of the requirements for a given sales position. The process of writing a job description forces the sales manager to be explicit about what the job requires.

Once the activities are listed, the sales manager can more easily decide exactly what skills and experience a prospective salesperson must have to be considered as a viable applicant. All salespeople are not suited to all sales jobs. Some do an excellent job selling products with low unit value but are unable to close a sale on a big-ticket item. Others do well selling tangible products but have difficulty selling intangibles like insurance or mutual funds. A job description helps to avoid a mismatch between the job and the salesperson. In defining the qualifications for the job, the sales manager should consider four factors:

Educational Requirements. A basic requirement (high school or college degree) and any special training (accounting, liberal arts, pharmacy, computer science, etc.) should be defined.

Experience. Both the length and type of experience required or preferred must be identified. Must past experience be in a particular type of industry? What substitutes are acceptable? Will experience with a competitor be considered? Dartnell's *Survey of Sales Force Compensation* of more than 800 companies in 30 industries reported that companies tend to prefer hiring senior and experienced salespeople over entry-level recruits. Sales managers realize they are not in the training business and don't mind paying more for what they need.[19]

Job Conditions. List any special conditions that affect the job: Seasonal or cyclical demand for the product, low ratio of sales to calls, long absences from home. Make sure the prospective salesperson is able to deal with these conditions both physically and emotionally.

Type of Customers. Determine whether the type of customers to be called on has any bearing on what type of salesperson is needed.

Thorough planning is as important in recruiting a sales force as in any other portion of the selling process. Too often, salespeople are hired for the wrong reasons. They are hired based on a résumé instead of whether or not they have the right values, attitudes, and motivations for a particular company. They're hired based on a "gut feeling" to the exclusion of critical objective evaluation data.

They're hired based on a poorly thought-out set of criteria that doesn't address what the company really needs. Because of these failings, too much time can be spent rehiring, reorienting and retraining new people, instead of turning good hires into great, loyal, long-term sales stars.[20] Without planning, the people you hire may fail to fit into the job you offer them. You not only need good people—you need people who are good for a particular job.

> Leadership: The art of getting someone else to do something you want done because he wants to do it.
> -Dwight D. Eisenhower

Phase 2: Sources for Recruiting

Each sales manager learns through experience the best sources for finding recruits for specific types of sales jobs. Here are six possible sources:

Within the Organization. Occasionally an employee in the production or service portion of the business qualifies for a sales job. Students often take part-time jobs on the maintenance crew or in the office and are eager to enter sales when their education is complete.

Online sources. Companies today use the Internet to locate potential candidates for various sales positions. Numerous websites are established for this explicit purpose, including Monster.com. The professional networking site LinkedIn is also a tremendous potential source of sales recruits.

Competitors. A competing company is a possible source, but caution should be exercised as ethical problems may be involved. Be sure that the salesperson has a legitimate reason for wanting to leave present employment. Take care to evaluate the person's stability, work habits, experience, and attitude toward selling.

Trade and Other Media Advertising. A well-written ad on an online job board or at Craigslist.com produces good prospects. A blind ad asking for an emailed application to be sent to a generic email address saves time by letting you weed out obviously unqualified applicants without taking time for a personal interview.

Schools. Technical schools and night schools, colleges, and universities are potential sources of prospects. Use the placement service in the school for screening.

Employment Agencies. The state employment agency in many cities is valuable. Private agencies are also in the business to find prospects. When using any type of agency, be sure to make the job requirements clear and perhaps set them a little higher than actually required. Get to know the service representative in the agency and you will get better prospects referred to you.

Tips for Effective Hiring

Skip the Learning Curve. Hire someone with experience in the areas specific to your needs.

Choose Marketing Skills Over Sales Skills. Some sales experience is beneficial, but marketing requires different abilities and approaches than does sales.

Hire Charismatic Types. Look for someone with proven leadership abilities and strong communication skills.

Raid the Big Guns. Some of the best training can be found in Fortune 500 companies. So try to attract their best.

Phase 3: Interview and Selection

The interview between the sales manager and the prospective salesperson accomplishes three primary objectives: To give information, to receive information, and to establish a friendly relationship. This applies whether the prospect qualifies for the position or not. The interview process may involve completion of an application form, check of references, personal interview(s), testing, physical examination, and the final decision to hire. Here are some aspects to consider when selecting potential sales team members:

Check References. One effective question that may be asked of former employers is, "Would you consider this person for further employment?" A similar question to put to other references is, "Why do you feel this person would be good in sales?" Some sales managers use the telephone exclusively for checking references. They feel that information may be given on the phone that might never be put into writing in a letter or email.

Ask the *right* questions to get the most out of the interview.

The All-Important Interview. A personal interview can be designed to help the sales manager determine whether a prospect is right for the job. The interview process may require several meetings. One may be used to complete the application form and review it briefly; a second may be a more in-depth interview several days later when the sales manager has had time to check references. Sales managers may use a combination of in-person, telephone, or video interviews to gain the insights they are looking for. Depending on the organization of the company itself, several people other than the sales manager may also interview the applicant. Robert Head, president of Strategic Sales Services Inc., says, "Good hiring procedures for salespeople require a minimum of two interviews, preferably three."[21]

Asking the Right Questions. The session should be used to discover answers to these types of questions:

1. Is the individual actually qualified for the position?

2. How badly does the person want this sales position with our company?

3. Can the candidate demonstrate an understanding of our company's business?

4. Is this individual a problem-solver? Can this person think quickly on his feet?

"Most interviews are a waste of time because the candidate isn't prepared," says Mick Corcodilos, author of *Ask the Headhunter*. He suggests that sales managers ask the job candidates on the phone to come to the interview with solutions to two problems that their company is facing. This challenge stops most of the job seekers dead in their tracks. There is just too much work involved. What a way to reduce the pool of candidates and, at the same time, force those who do accept the challenge to demonstrate an understanding of the job's requirements.

Phase 4: Orientation

All the time and expense of the selection procedure are lost if the new salesperson is not properly integrated into the organization. Of course, the size of the organization affects what is done and how, but in every case a definite program should bring each new salesperson into the company as part of the team and establish for that person a feeling of belonging. The process should include items such as these:

- Introduction to fellow workers
- Office practices
- Company policies
- Vertical communication
- Company-sponsored recreation activities
- Expense account procedures

Determining Compensation

Compensation plans are usually straight commission, straight salary, or a combination of the two.

Straight Commission

A commission is usually figured as a percentage of sales volume. The plan might call for a simple percentage of total gross sales, or it could be based on a percentage of the sales less variable costs. The benefit of the latter plan is that it offers the salesperson concrete incentives for helping to keep selling costs low and therefore emphasizes profit instead of mere volume. The main benefit of a commission plan is the motivation it offers to salespeople for productivity. The disadvantage is that some salespeople are tempted to neglect activities that do not bring in short-term dollars, including service after the sale, helping with installation, and completing needed reports and related paperwork. The straight-commission plan is the plan of choice when aggressive selling is desired.

Straight Salary

At the other extreme is a plan based on a fixed amount regardless of volume. Once more common, today only about 4.5 percent of companies use straight salary as their sole means of compensation.[22] A straight-salary plan gives management the greatest ability to control the activities of salespeople. If the company has an unusual need for post-sale activities, developing new territories, or continuing technical training, salespeople do not feel that they are cutting their own income by giving time to that work. However, a salary plan offers less motivation for intense sales effort than the commission plan. Therefore, a salary plan is the plan of choice when management needs to control salespeople's activities and when aggressive sales activity is not necessary.

Combination Plans

One method to exercise control over sales activities yet retain the incentive value of a commission is a combination of a base salary and a commission or bonus paid on sales above a set level. Another type of combination plan makes use of a commission plus a draw against future commissions earned. This plan protects salespeople in slow seasons or when some outside circumstance lowers productivity temporarily. The company sets a base amount that the salesperson is guaranteed to receive. If commissions earned fall below that figure, a draw is paid to bring income up to the base level. If the salesperson earns commissions above the base next month, the excess is used to repay the draw. Exhibit 16.7 shows how the draw operates.

ΔExhibit 16.7

Sample Combination Compensation Plan

Month	Commissions Earned	Commissions Paid	Draw* Paid (Repaid)	Total Income
January	$1500	$1500	$0	$1500
February	900	900	300	1200
March	1400	1400	(200)	1200
April	1500	1500	(100)	1400
May	1700	1700	0	1700
June	1200	1200	0	1200
Total	**$8200**	**$8200**	**$0**	**$8200**

*Assumes company guarantees a base amount of $1200 per month. Some companies do not require an actual payback as shown in this example. They use the draw as a yardstick for performance.

There aren't many other topics that a professional salesperson or a sales manager is more eager to talk to someone about than sales compensation. With all of the requirements and devices used, compensation plans can be quite complex. They can also bring about unethical behavior. And in many cases they can be very difficult to administer. Especially in today's economy, more salespeople are "job hopping" for a little more money or a change of pace. That explains why companies increasingly entice people with incentives like stock options. The reason? Salespeople are demanding them.[23]

High Price to Pay for Inadequate Plans. Although under compensating salespeople may seem like an attractive cost-cutting strategy for companies in the short run, over time businesses pay the price for underpaying employees in the form of turnover and a general lack of loyalty. In a *CSO Insights* survey on sales compensation performance, 63 percent of companies said that the compensation plan generally drives the selling behavior of sales representatives, and 11 percent said it consistently drives selling behavior.[24] It is obvious that compensation plans greatly impact the performance of salespeople, so companies must work to ensure that the impact is positive. Executives at FedEx Corp realized they needed a new compensation plan for their sales organization because of the volume of complaints coming from field salespeople and sales managers about how confusing and unpredictable the pay program was. In a little more than a year with a new clearly laid-out incentive pay program, there was a dramatic shift in the sales force at FedEx and consequently, much happier salespeople.[25]

> If I had to sum up in a word what makes a good manager, I'd say **decisiveness**. You can use the fanciest computers to gather the numbers, but in the end you have to **set a timetable and act**.
>
> — Lee Iacocca

A TQM-Based Compensation Package

According to Dartnell's Survey of Sales Force Compensation, the importance of profitability is increasing in sales compensation plans. Companies should reward salespeople not only for making sales, but also for achieving corporate sales objectives. Sales managers who do not carefully consider specific marketing and sales objectives almost by default choose dollar sales volume as the incentive criterion. A compensation plan based only on numbers can be detrimental. Rather than satisfy the customer, salespeople are tempted to spend their time focused on exceeding their numbers to maximize their own personal income. A reasonable base salary shows commitment to your sales force.

If the compensation plan is salary-based, it can be structured to reward company loyalty and longevity. Turnover is expensive to a company through training costs and lost sales. It takes a salesperson time to learn the company, its products, policies, and customers. A company with a lot of turnover causes clients to question its stability and may result in business lost to the competition.

Today's sales professionals should be listeners, information gatherers, educators, relationship builders, and the primary sources of customer input to the company. Cultivate a longer-term focus on adding customer value and integrating sales with all other people in the company who impact customers and products. Their pay needs to reflect these expectations. Some approaches involve paying differentiated awards based on strategies concerning customers and products.[26] A Total Quality Management (TQM) based compensation plan includes:

Customer Retention Bonus

Reward the salesperson for maintaining long-term relationships. Retention is a good indication that customers are being satisfied. Hewlett Packard has instituted customer satisfaction into their sales force compensation as they move toward Total Quality Management. According to a survey of 300 top American companies by Handy HRM Corporation of New York, 54 percent of those surveyed tie pay directly to quality standards, including customer satisfaction.[27]

Penetration of Target Accounts Bonus

New, targeted accounts take longer to develop and often do not offer the immediate financial return of established customers. Some salespeople also fear the added rejection that invariably accompanies calling on new prospects. However, gaining the business of target accounts indicates a salesperson's ability better than traditional methods that focus only on volume. A bonus paid for securing the business of targeted individuals or companies will keep salespeople motivated to continue building their customer base and providing their company with expanded growth opportunities.

Company-Wide Performance Bonus

The success of the salesperson is tied to the overall performance of the company. Therefore, the bonus is based on company-wide goals. A national survey reported that 39 percent of companies have annual bonuses for salaried employees tied to company performance.[28] Marshall Industries an industrial electronics company, is evidence that a sales organization can work without commissions and incentives and that a company can grow without volume-based rewards. Marshall has introduced a corporate-wide compensation system that pays everyone—from secretaries to the president—on the same plan, a salary plus a bonus based on the company's quarterly profits. Marshall's 600 inside and outside salespeople are included in the plan.[29]

Robert Rodin, former president and COO of Marshall, says that the change was not a compensation issue, but a quality issue aimed at "aligning our compensation to support customer service." Under the previous commission arrangement, salespeople were "too concerned with their own performance, rather than listening to the customer. Compensation had become an obstacle to world-class quality."

To those who argue that you can't motivate salespeople without commissions, or some form of incentive program, Rodin responds, "You can get people to do anything by offering a reward, but can you get them to sustain it? Can you get them to look at both sides of the sale?"

Other Key Roles of a Manager

Sales Training

Every authority agrees that ongoing sales training is necessary, but measuring the benefits of sales training is a difficult process. In addition, what sales training should accomplish is also not clear, although almost everyone agrees that training is needed in product knowledge and in selling skills.[30] Companies are interested in sales training because they want to increase sales productivity. The emphasis is largely on results. The chairman and chief executive officer of U.S. Steel expressed it this way:[31]

> *We support training and development activities to get results.... We're interested in the specific things that provide greater rewards to the employee, increased return to the stockholder, and enable reinvestment of sales revenue to meet the growing needs of the business. In other words, [we're interested in] those things, which affect the "bottom line."*

Sales managers agree that company training programs should address the purpose of developing in salespeople the characteristics of success. These characteristics usually include the following traits:

1. Listening skills

2. Enthusiasm

3. Empathy

4. Planning skills

5. Personal organization

6. Problem-solving ability

7. Time and territory management

Designing and implementing the sales training program is the sales manager's responsibility. An effective program includes these basic elements:

Field Training and Observation. It is a good idea to have both an experienced salesperson and a manager assist in training new sales reps. Traveling with a senior sales rep to observe selling skills, personality traits, and work habits reveals much about novice sales reps. New reps can also accompany different sales managers to pick out the strengths and weaknesses of each manager and eventually create their own style. Both managers and senior sales reps can impart more wisdom to a newcomer than many training courses might offer.

Unfortunately, sales managers often let sales reports drive their coaching conversations. In sales, performance improvement occurs only through observations—preludes to behavioral coaching. Two important areas of observation are making joint calls and observing telephone or video appointment conversations.[32]

Group Sessions. Sales training sessions that focus on a single topic (such as prospecting, closing, or product knowledge) are valuable in sharpening skills for all members of the sales team. The group training session provides valuable interaction between salespeople and allows individuals to learn from one another. The Cisco WebEx Training Center is a great solution for online training of large groups spread over a wide geographic location.

A common form of training within group sessions is *role-playing*: One trainee assumes the role of salesperson and another trainee or the sales manager plays the role of a prospect. A third person may act as observer to critique the performance. They go through the various steps of the sales process to gain experience in using the sales aids, giving the presentation, asking questions, and handling objections. A session may cover the entire selling process or concentrate on one specific step in the process. The audio or video of role-playing sessions can be recorded for later review.

One-on-One Sessions. The sales manager must be willing to spend time with individual salespeople to give specific feedback and encourage continuing development. One-on-one time can be used to pinpoint individual problems and help the salesperson to develop a program of personal growth to correct any problems discovered.

Interactive Training. Interactive training is a type of learning model where trainees are given audio or video presentations, slide shows, self-tests, and the capability to determine what they want to learn, when they want to learn it. Salespeople using an interactive format will have higher rates of retention, take less time to train, have easier access to information, and have a higher comfort level. Sales managers now have the opportunity to work with one, or one hundred, salespeople in front of a computer to watch and learn new techniques or practice what they do best.[33]

Group training sessions can help bring a sense of unity to your sales team.

Feedback. The sales training program must provide for feedback on performance. When a skill is practiced in a training session, a method for tracking field improvement shows whether the training has been effective. When salespeople see that the training has made a direct impact on their performance and their incomes, they are eager to receive more training and give their best efforts to learning.

The amount of time spent in sales training for recruits and for experienced salespeople varies from industry to industry and also from company to company. Time for training is affected by the complexity of the industry, the commitment of the company to training, and the company's experience with past training programs. The exact procedure also varies as a result of the same factors. Some companies conduct concentrated training for new recruits before they are allowed to go into the field. Others use a mix of training and field experience to help recruits learn by doing. A few still hand the recruit a sales kit and follow the *sink-or-swim* method. The training period for recruits tends to be shorter for manufacturers of consumer products than for manufacturers of industrial products. Service companies including insurance, banking, public utilities, and transportation companies, generally have longer training programs.

> ## The key to successful leadership today is influence, not authority.
> -Ken Blanchard

Supervision and Motivation

A sales manager must see that salespeople call on their accounts with sufficient frequency, prospect for new business, keep up to date on new developments in the general market, and receive continuous training in new product technology or advanced sales techniques. Guiding salespeople in setting realistic goals, offering appropriate incentives to trigger achievement of those goals, and rewarding them for success are the sales manager's responsibility. All of these areas are easy to track with the CRM software available today, as well as the ease of communication provided by smartphones and Wi-Fi access.

Motivation is at the heart of supervision. The sales manager's involvement in motivation is designed to provide an environment within which salespeople can develop the ability to motivate themselves. A sales manager is much like a professional sports coach. John Madden, legendary NFL coach, explained to a reporter his philosophy about motivating football players like this: *"I don't motivate them. I find motivated men and teach them how to play football."*

The principle is clear: If the basic functions of recruiting and selection are successfully performed, training and motivation of the sales force become less of a problem and more of a solution to making more sales—and in turn, profit.

SUMMARY

- The functions of the sales manager differ considerably from those of salespeople although organizations often promote leading salespeople to positions in sales management.

- The sales manager must be both a skillful salesperson and an efficient manager. The sales manager stands between field salespeople and company management.

- The sales manager performs the usual managerial functions of translating the goals of the company into strategies and tactics that the members of the sales department can address through daily activities and seeing that those activities result in the achievement of the department's responsibilities to the company.

- In addition, the sales manager is concerned with helping salespeople develop personally and professionally so that they can make the greatest possible contribution to achievement of the organization's goals.

- Specific tasks of the sales manager include:

  1. Organizing the sales force

  2. Determining personnel needs

  3. Recruiting and selecting salespeople

  4. Designing a compensation plan that motivates salespeople and assures that sales activities will achieve desired goals

  5. Training salespeople to sell the company's product or service effectively

  6. Supervising and motivating salespeople.

REVIEW QUESTIONS

1. List the advantages and disadvantages for choosing a sales manager in each of the following ways:

   a. Promoting the top-producing salesperson in the organization

   b. Lateral transfer of an effective manager from another department (such as finance, advertising, manufacturing)

   c. Hiring someone from outside the organization

2. Are top salespeople automatically likely to be good sales managers? Why or why not?

3. What are the six key functions of a sales manager?

4. How can a sales manager determine how large a sales force should be?

5. What are the most common components of sales training?

6. What does the sales manager need to learn through interviewing a prospective salesperson?

7. What do you consider the most important incentives for salesperson productivity that a sales manager could provide?

8. If a company wants to exercise a great deal of control over the time and activities of its salespeople and does not especially need aggressive selling, what kind of compensation package is most appropriate?

9. If the organization's goal is high-volume sales and management is willing to have salespeople structure their own time and activities, what type of compensation plan is most likely to result in achievement of that goal?

10. What are some of the most easily accessible sources of recruits for positions as salespeople? What are the advantages and the disadvantages of each of these sources?

ROLE-PLAY EXERCISES

The following role-play exercises help build teams, improve communication, and emphasize the real-world side of selling. They are meant to be challenging, to help you learn how to deal with problems that have no single right answer, and to use a variety of skills beyond those employed in a typical review question. Read and complete each activity. Then in the next class, discuss and compare answers with other classmates.

Role Play 16.1 – Analyzing Job Descriptions

You should work independently on this exercise.

Although nearly ¾ of all positions are filled as a result of networking, job descriptions for sales positions are routinely posted online on the websites of individual companies, of job boards, and of recruiting companies. These descriptions are typically written by management and might include very specific requirements expressed in the jargon typical of the type of product or service that is to be sold.

Select a field or industry category in which you are interested. Search for sales positions in that field or category, analyze at least 3 job descriptions, and record what you find.

- How much prior sales or marketing experience is required? Is the experience specific to the field or industry category?
- What is the educational level required or preferred? Must relevant education be focused on a specific field?
- What sort of general characteristics (e.g., excellent communications skills, team-building skills, ease of relating to diverse populations) are required?
- What sort of specialized knowledge (e.g., experience with specific software applications, project management certification, technical or scientific knowledge) is required?

Since these job descriptions pertain to a field or area in which you are personally interested, which requirements as stated in the descriptions surprised you most? How do you plan to fulfill these and the other requirements listed for the positions that you researched?

Role Play 16.2 – The Perfect Sales Manager

For this exercise, the class should be divided into teams of 4 persons each.

On the basis of all the knowledge and experience you have gained in this course, you are about to find yourself working among colleagues in your first sales position. You will probably be a member of a small sales team that reports to a sales manager. As you get to know your colleagues, discussion turns to what makes a really good sales manager. On a periodic visit to your office, the regional director of sales announces to your group that a new sales manager is about to be appointed, and the regional director wants your collective opinion about the qualifications and characteristics that you think should be primary. Now is your big chance: what makes a perfect sales manager?

As a team, discuss the role of a sales manager and decide which characteristics, qualifications, and personality traits you would most like to see in your new manager. Bear in mind the needs of the company, not just the desires of those who must report to the manager. Rank your recommendations in order of importance for the regional director and provide reasons for your selections.

CASE STUDIES

The following case studies present you with selling scenarios that require you to apply the critical skills discussed in the chapter and give you training through simulation, role-playing, and practical learning situations. They are meant to be both engaging and challenging, and like the role-play exercises, don't have one right answer.

Case 16.1 – Musical Chairs

As Vice President for Sales for a major auto supply chain, Leonard Wirt was under a great deal of pressure. After six months on the job, he was due to report to the owners of this privately held company what he thought should be done to improve sales and profitability. Since his recommendations were radical, he knew that this would probably be the toughest sales call of his career.

For the past 55 years, the company had been managed in a very traditional fashion, chiefly by fear. Salespersons, working on strict commission, who failed to meet annual quotas were routinely fired and replaced. Store managers who failed to meet profitability targets were transferred or fired. Because the business required extensive product knowledge about a wide variety of products, district and regional sales managers were traditionally recruited from the top sales performers. But when their districts or regions fell short, heads rolled. Despite all of these changes in personnel, profits continued to sag, and the owners continued to be unhappy.

Based upon his experience and knowledge of more successful approaches to management, Leonard was prepared to recommend sweeping changes.

What changes do you think Leonard should recommend? Which changes should be made first, and why? Which changes would have the most immediate, positive impact on the company's profitability? Which changes recommended by Leonard do you think would be most risky? What sort of quantitative measures, other than overall profitability, should Leonard monitor in order to gauge the success or failure of his initiatives?

Case 16.2 – The New Sales Trainer

Sam has been one of the top salespersons in his medium-size insurance company for about 6 years. He holds a college degree and had previous experience as a high school teacher before getting into insurance sales. Because of his sales achievements and his background in teaching, his vice president has asked him to take over as the new sales trainer for the company. As the vice president put it, "We're not getting enough production out of our sales force, and adherence to company policy has been lax. We need someone who can teach us how to whip our training program into shape." Not especially elegant, Sam thought, but clear.

The typical training program, not including studying for and passing licensing exams, for salespersons at Sam's company is 3 weeks—3 short weeks. To revamp the training program, Sam must develop a curriculum and structure the way in which that curriculum should be presented.

Based on what you have learned in Chapter 16 and the rest of this course, how should Sam address the following issues?

- Which topics should be included in the training curriculum, and why?

- Which topics should be given higher priority and, hence, more time, and why?

- How can Sam hold the attention of new recruits for 3 weeks? What sort of presentation techniques should he employ for more effective retention and learning?

- How can Sam monitor individual progress so that he can address individual trainees' problems before they get out of hand?

ENDNOTES

Chapter 1

1. Conrad Hilton in *Sales Success: 62 Quotes, Special Report*, accessed April 20, 2011, www.eyeonsales.com.

2. Dean M Brenner, "Task-oriented selling," *Advisor Today*. Vol. 98, Is. 12, (December 2003), 62.

3. Susan Hodges," Recommissioning your sales," *ELT*, Vol.15, Is. 2 (February 2003), 22-28.

4. Anonymous, "Surveys Reveal Compensation for Call-Center Sales Professionals," *IOMA's Report on Salary Surveys*. New York: (Sep 2009), Vol 09, Is 9, 2.

5. Anonymous, "Two Surveys Examine Pay for Sales and Marketing Positions," *IOMA's Report on Salary Surveys*. New York: (Jun 2010), Vol 10, Is 6, 9.

6. Simon Bartley, "Seeing is believing!" *Training Journal*. Ely: (Feb 2008), 16.

7. Bob O'Connor, "Business Sense: Training Yourself and Your Staff to Win," *Motor*; (Feb 2007).

8. Dave Hagel, "Why You Need to Hire the Best," *The Canadian Manager*. Toronto: (Spring 2007), Vol. 32, Is. 1, 12.

9. Charles W. Stephens, "Why is Training so Important?" *Industrial Distribution*, Vol. 89, No. 2 (February 2000), 4.

10. See the following sources: D.L. Thompson, "Stereotype of the Salesperson," *Harvard Business Review*, Vol. 50, No. 1, (January/February 1972), 20-29; Robert W. Cook and Timothy Hartman, "Female College Student Interest in a Sales Career: A Comparison," *Journal of Personal Selling & Sales Management*, Vol. 6, (May 1986), 29-34; Michael Swenson, William Swinyard, Frederick Langrehr, and Scott Smith, "The Appeal of Personal Selling as a Career: A Decade Later," *The Journal of Personal Selling & Sales Management*, Vol. 13, No. 1 (Winter 1993), 51; "Sales Strikes Out on Campus," *Sales & Marketing Management* (November 1997), 13; "Selling Sales to Students," *Sales & Marketing Management* (January 1998), 15; Harry Harmon, "An Examination of Students' Perceptions of a Situationally Described Career in Personal Selling," *Journal of Professional Services Marketing*, Vol. 19, No. 1 (Fall 1999), 119-136; Susan DelVecchio, "An Investigation of African-American Perceptions of Sales Careers," *The Journal of Personal Selling & Sales Management*, Vol. 29, No. 1 (Winter 2000), 43-52.

11. Audrey Bottjen, "The Benefits of College Recruiting," *Sales & Marketing Management* (April 2001), 12, and Jack Foster, "A Novel Approach To the Market," *Agency Sales*. Irvine: (Dec 2009), Vol. 39, Is. 11, 10.

12. Laura Mazur, "UK banks must refocus on the personal touch," *Marketing*, (March 4, 2004), 16.

13. Jack Foster, "A Novel Approach To the Market," *Agency Sales*. Irvine: (Dec 2009), Vol. 39, Is. 11, 10.

14. Anonymous, "Power of self-image psychology," *The American Salesman*, Vol. 48, Is. 5, (May 2003), 21.

15. Interview, Josh Hinds, posted September 28, 2006, http://commonground.typepad.com/common_ground/2006/09/if_its_advice_a.html.

16. Mark Haering, "From the Recruiter," *Sales and Marketing Management*, Vol. 155, Is. 5, (May 2003), 55.

17. Roy Chitwood, "Best salesperson in the company should be the CEO," Max Sacks International, accessed August 19, 2007, http://www.max-sacks.com/articles/article0706.html.

18. Abraham H. Maslow, *Motivation and Personality*, 3rd ed. (New York: Harper & Row Publishing, 1987).

19. Steven N. Kaplan, Mark M. Klebanov, and Morten Sorensen, "Which CEO Characteristics and Abilities Matter?" *University of Chicago Graduate School of Business*, August 2008.

20. Julia Angwin, "America Online CEO Makes Strides with Low-Key Style," *Wall Street Journal*. (Eastern edition), (September 2, 2003), B.1.

21. Anonymous, "Sales Departments Are Ready to Spend Money and Hire People in 2011," *PR Newswire*. New York: (Jan 7, 2011), and David J. Cicelli, "Smart Management: Selling Into 2010: A Cause for Optimism?" *Sales&Marketing.com*, posted July 31, 2010, accessed April 20, 2011, http://www.salesandmarketing.com/article/smart-management-selling-2010-cause-optimism.

22. Sherry Siegel, "Selling Your Way to the Top," *Success*, (January/February 1987), Vol. 34, No. 1, 44.

23. Derek Newton, *Sales Force Performance and Turnover* (Cambridge, MA: Marketing Science Institute, 1973), 3; Derek Newton, "Get the Most Out of Your Sales Force," *Harvard Business Review* (September/October 1969), 130-143.

24. Dennis L. Duffy, "Direct selling as the next channel," *The Journal of Consumer Marketing*. Santa Barbara: (2005), Vol. 22, Is. 1, 43, and *Longaberger: An American Craft Company*, accessed April 20, 2011, www. longaberger.com.

25. These traits were gleaned from the following sources: David McClelland, "Hiring Top Performers,"*Success* (May 1994), Vol. 41, No. 4, 34; Brian Azar, "Are You a Master Salesperson," *Personal Selling Power* (April 1992), Vol. 12, No. 3, 27; and "Qualities to Look for When You're Hiring," *Sales and Marketing Management*, (August13, 1995), 84-87.

26. Ralph Waldo Emerson, "Circles," in *Essays: First Series* (1841).

27. Christina Chia, "Controlled enthusiasm fuels inspiration," *Malaysian Business*. Kuala Lumpur: (Sep 1, 2010), 54.

28. Howard Feiertag, "Listening skills, enthusiasm top list of salespeople's best traits," *Hotel and Motel Management*, Vol. 217, Is. 13, (July 15, 2002), 20.

29. Herb Greenberg, "Producers lack key personality traits of successful sales people," *National Underwriter*, (Property & casualty/risk & benefits management ed.), Vol. 107, Is. 47, (November 24, 2003), 11.

30. Tom Cunningham, Dorman Woodall, Willard Scott, and Paul Wheaton, "Training New Hires for Competitive Advantage," *Salesandmarketing.com*, posted November 16, 2010, accessed April 20, 2011, http://www.salesandmarketing.com/article/training-new-hires-competitive-advantage.

31. Tanis Cornell, Phone Interview, October 20, 2007.

32. Anonymous, "Time Management Key to Successful Sales Results, Watson Wyatt Survey Finds," *PR Newswire*. New York: (Oct. 5, 2006).

33. Jim John, "Tough Times Reveal True Sales Professionals," *Salesandmarketing.com*, posted July 31, 2010, accessed April 20, 2011, http://www.salesandmarketing.com/article/tough-times-reveal-true-sales-professionals.

34. Victor M Parachin, "Seven secrets for self-motivation," *The American Salesman*, Vol. 48, Is. 1, (January 2003), 16-21.

35. Geoffrey Brewer, "What Makes Great Salespeople?" *Sales and Marketing Management* (May 1994), 85.

Chapter 2

1. Erick Schonfeld, "Forrester Forecast: Online Retail Sales Will Grow to $250 Billion by 2014," Posted March 8, 2010, accessed April 6, 2011, http://techcrunch.com/2010/03/08/forrester-forecast-online-retail-sales-will-grow-to-250-billion-by-2014.

2. Amy Gahran, "Yahoo's Big Deal with Papers: What About Local Ads?" Posted April 16, 2007, accessed Aug 24, 2007, http://www.poynter.org/dg.lts/id.31/aid.121538/column.htm.

3. Christian Grönroos, *Service Management and Marketing: A Customer Relationship Management Approach, 3rd Ed.* (Chichester: John Wiley & Sons, 2007).

4. Debbie Howell, "Selling trust, expertise hits home with customers," *DSN Retailing Today*, March 27, 2006.

5. "Volkswagen.co.uk: A New Age of Marketing Cars Online" Posted February 2008, accessed April 7, 2011, http://www.ddb.com/pdf/press/current/02-15-08_TribalVW_newAge.pdf.

6. Figure 2.1 created from ideas from the following: Nancy Arnott, "It's a Woman's World," *Sales and Marketing Management* (March 1995), 56; Larry Chambers, "Don't Let Fear Kill Your Sale," *Personal Selling Power*, Vol. 12, No. 6, (September 1992), 36; "Top Sales Reps Prove Their Worth," *Purchasing* (March 22, 1990), 27; and Tony Alessandra, Phil Wexler, and Rick Barerra, *Non-Manipulative Selling*, 2nd Ed. (1987).

7. Barbara Geraghty, *Visionary Selling* (New York: Simon and Schuster, 2007), 240.

8. Robert McGarvey and Babs S. Harrison, "How Tech Hip are You?" *Selling Power* (March 2001), 77.

9. Richard Lee, "Expert touts importance of using social media," *Advocate*, Stamford, Conn: (Mar 20, 2011), C1.

10. Rick Spence, "Resolutions for entrepreneurs to prosper by; Simple steps to give you an edge in 2009," *National Post,* Don Mills, Ont: (Jan 12, 2009), FP.4.

11. Bill Brooks, "The Power of Active Listening," *The American Salesman*, Vol 51, Is. 6, (Jun. 2006), 12.

12. Rhonda Abrams, "Strategies: Make customer retention priority No. 1," *USA Today.com*. Posted May 29, 2009, accessed April 7, 2011, http://www.usatoday.com/money/small-business/columnist/abrams/2009-05-29-customer-retention_N.htm..

13. Hanzo Ng, "After sales service secrets!" *Malaysian Business,* Kuala Lumpur: (April 1, 2009), 54.

14. Manus Rungtusanatham, Jeffrey A Ogden, Bin Wu, "Advancing theory

development in total quality management: A 'Deming management method' perspective," *International Journal of Operations & Production Management*, Bradford: (2003), Vol. 23, Is. 7/8, 918.

15. Gary Salegna and Farzaneh Fazel, "Obstacles to Implementing Quality," *Quality Progress*, Milwaukee: (Jul 2000), Vol. 33, Is. 7, 53.

16. Quint Studer, "How to achieve and sustain excellence: there are seven ways to hardwire excellent outcomes. Do you know what they are?" *Healthcare Financial Management*; (June, 2007).

17. Jude P. Morte, "Special Feature: Best Employers in the Philippines," *BusinessWorld*, Manila: (May 29, 2003), 1.

18. Rose Knotts, "Rambo Doesn't Work Here Anymore," *Business Horizons*, (January February 1992), 44-46.

19. Mark Godson, *Relationship Marketing* (Oxford: Oxford University Press, 2009), 18.

20. W. Edwards Deming, *Out of the Crisis* (Cambridge, MA: MIT, 2000).

21. Margery Weinstein, "How May I Train You? Customer service training programs put the focus on buyer bliss," *Training* (Aug 2006), 29.

22. Rick Medford, "Cut to the Chase: Practical Advice for Successful CRM," *Supply Chain Europe*, London: (Sep/Oct 2007), Vol. 16, Is. 5, 26.

23. Susi Geiger and Darach Turley, "The Perceived Impact of Information Technology on Salespeople's Relational Competencies," *Journal of Marketing Management*, (August 2006), Vol. 22, No. 7, 827.

24. Tom Peters, "Meeting the Dangers and Opportunities of Chaos," *Personal Selling Power*, Vol. 10, No. 6, (September 1990), 49.

25. Adapted from a manuscript by Dr. James C. Cotham, Belmont University, Nashville, TN. First used on March 23, 1995. Actual Date Unknown, "Principles and Concepts of TQM, Competing in the Marketing Wars of the 1990s: Get Better or Get Beaten.

26. Anonymous, "TQM: A snapshot of the experts," *Measuring Business Excellence*, Bradford: (2002), Vol. 6, Is. 3, 54-57.

27. Louise Anderson, "The Bundling Advantage: How Team-based Approach Can Heat Up Sales," *Performance Management*; (January 2006).

28. This section on Team Selling was modified from the following sources: Andy Ferguson, "Sales Departments Claim Marketers Could do Better," *Marketing Week* (September 11, 1997), 28-29; Mark McCormack," Doubles Anyone," *Sales & Marketing Management* (December 1993) 35-36; Tom Murray, "Team Selling: What's the Incentive?" *Sales & Marketing Management* (June 1991), 90; Jack Falvey, "Team Selling: What It Is and Isn't," *Sales & Marketing Management* (June 1990), 8-10; "Team Selling: A Team Approach to Increasing Sales," *Small Business Report*, April 1985), 23-25; and "Calling in the Team," *Professional Selling*, (June 10, 1984), 1-3.

29. Don Green, "Count on strong relationships," *Paperboard Packaging*. Cleveland: (November 2001), Vol. 86, Is. 11, 8.

30. Malcolm Campbell, "How To Become a Top Performer," *Selling Power* (January/February 2000), 61.

31. Anonymous, "Team Marketing: A Simple Approach to Put a Plan Together," *Law Office Management & Administration Report, New* York: (January 2004), Vol. 04, Is. 1, 5.

32. Betsy Cummings, "Done Deal," Sales and Marketing Management, New York: (January 2004), Vol. 156, Is. 1, 16.

33. Henry Canaday, "Flyaway Sales," *Selling Power* (October 2000), 110.

34. Craig A. Martin, "Racial diversity in professional selling: an empirical investigation of the differences in the perceptions and performance of African-American and Caucasian salespeople," *The Journal of Business & Industrial Marketing*, Santa Barbara: (2005), Vol. 20, Is. 6, 285.

35. "USA Quick Facts," *U.S. Census Bureau*, accessed April 9, 2011, http://quickfacts.census.gov/qfd/states/00000.html.

36. Barbara J. Bowes, "The business case for workplace diversity," *CMA Management*, Hamilton: (Dec 2007/Jan 2008), Vol. 81, Is. 8, 14.

37. John Hooker, "Cultural Differences in Business Communication," *Tepper School of Business, Carnegie Mellon University*, December 2008, accessed April 9, 2011, http://web.tepper.cmu.edu/jnh/businessCommunication.pdf.

38. Emily Richwine, "LEHMAN BROTHERS: VALUING DIVERSITY," *Minority Business Entrepreneur*, Torrance: (Nov/Dec 2007), Vol. 24, Is. 6, 22.

39. Ellen Neuborne, "Bridging the culture gap," *Sales and Marketing Management*, New York: (Jul 2003), Vol. 155, Is. 7, 22.

40. Clif Boutelle, "Minority Sales Personnel Have Better Results in Workplaces With Supportive Diversity Climates," *Society for Industrial & Organizational Psychology, Inc.,* accessed on April 9, 2011, http://www.siop.org/Media/News/minority_sales.aspx.

Chapter 3

1. Aragon, Lawrence. "Eugene's Legacy." *Venture Captial Journal,* January 2004

2. N.A. "Say it with pride: I am a salesman!" *Business Line,* April 2004: 1 "Say it with pride: I am a salesman!"

3. Cragg, A.W. "Business, globalization, and the logic and ethics of corruption." *Business Communication Quarterly* 69, no. 2 (2006): 158.

4. McQueeny, Edward. "Making Ethics Come Alive." *Business Communication Quarterly* 69, no. 2 (2006): 158.

5. Black, Tom. *The Boxcar Millionaire: Tom Black's Proven System of Sales Success.* Nashville: Tom Black Center for Selling, 2007.

6. McClaren, Nicholas. "Ethics in Personal Selling and Sales Management: A Reivew of the Literature Focusing on Empirical Findings and Conceptual Foundations." *Journal of Business Ethics* 27 (2000): 286.

7. Wortruba, Thomas. "A Framework for Teaching Ethical Decision-Making in Marketing." *Marketing Education Review* 3, no. 2 (1994): 4.

8. Christians, Clifford G. "A Framework for Teaching Ethical Decision-Making in Marketing." *Journal of Mass Media Ethics* 22, no. 2-3 (Summer 2007): 114.

9. McClaren, Nicholas. "Ethics in Personal Selling and Sales Management: A Reivew of the Literature Focusing on Empirical Findings and Conceptual Foundations." *Journal of Business Ethics* 27 (2000): 286.

10. Bloom, Allan. *The Closing of the American Mind.* New York: Simon and Schuster, 1987.

11. Ellwanger, Adam. "Bloom and His Detractors: The Academic Polemic and the Ethics of Education." *Pedagogy* 5, no. 3 (Fall 2009): 483.

12. Galper, Ari. *Sales Ethics: When Did It Become Okay to Lie?* http://www.unlockthegame.com/SalesEthics (accessed August 23, 2007).

13. Rota, Carlo Patetta. "Rules of behavior: the adoption of a code of conduct is a step toward improving the ethical culture in today's business world." *Internal Auditor,* June 2007.

14. Barnett, Tim and Valentine, Sean "Ethics Code Awareness, Perceived Ethical Values and Organizational Commitment." *The Journal of Personal Selling* 23, no. 4 (Fall 2003): 359.

15. Ingram, Thomas and Schwepker, Charles. "Improving Sales Performance Through Ethics: The Relationship Between Salesperson Moral Judgement and Job Performance." *Journal of Business Ethics,* November 1996: 3.

16. United Professional Sales Association. *The UPSA Ethical Code, Code of Conduct, and Buyer's Bill of Rights.* http://www.upsa-intl.org/index-4-2.htm (accessed April 10, 2011).

17. N.A. "Nice Guys Finish First." *Business Ethics* 7, no. 3 (May/June 1994): 10.

18. Schewpker, Charles H., Good, David J. "Moral Judgement and Its Impact on Business Sales." *Journal of Business Ethics* 98 (2011): 619.

19. Bragg, Arthur. "Ethics in Selling, Honest." *Sales and Marketing Management* 138, no. 7 (May 1987): 44.

20. Blodgett, Mark S. "Source of Business Ethics Convergence: A Review of Global Corporate Websites." *Journal of Knowledge Globalization* 2, no. 1 (Spring 2009): 79-84.

21. Smith, J. Walker. "Selling Doing Good." *Marketing Management,* January/February 2008: 56.

22. Schultz, Howard. *Business Insider: Starbucks CEO Howard Schultz Onward Book Excerpt 2011.* http://businessinsider.com/starbucks-ceo-howard-schultz-onward-book-excerpt-2011-3#ixzz1Jz4QVM (accessed April 18, 2011).

23. Cohen, Andy. "Slowdown Effect: Lack of Ethics." *Sales & Marketing Management,* June 2001: 13.

24. Ferrell, O.C., Ingram, Thomas, Schewepker, Charles. "The Influence of Ethical Climate and Ethical Conflict on Role Stress in the Sales Force." *Academy of Marketing Science Journal,* Spring 1997: 13.

25. Bouville, Mattieu. "Whistle-Blowing and Morality." *Journal of Business Ethics* 81 (2008): 580.

26. Seebauer, Edmund G. "Whistleblowing: Is it Always Obligatory?" *Chemical Engineering Progress* 100, no. 6 (June 2004): 23.

27. Geus, Arie de. "The Living Company." *Harvard Business Review,* March/April 1997: 58.

28. Trent, Karen. "The Dangers of Groupthink." *Teamwork,* June 1990: 1.

29. Strout, Erin. "Doctoring Sales." *Sales & Marketing Management,* May 2001: 59.

30. Perrone, Jasmin and Vickers, Margaret H. "Emotions as Strategic Game in a Hostile Workplace: An Exemplar Case." *Employee Responsibilities and Rights Journal* 16, no 3 (September 2004): 167.

31. N.A. *Calgary Herald: Volkswagen Scandal Deepens.* 2005. http://search.proquest.com/docview/244887025?accountid=39943 (accessed April 11, 2011).

32. Holsworth, Jeanette. "4 Ways to Curb Employee Theft." *Gainesville Biz Report.* http://www.gainesvillebizreportcom/componentcontent/article/61-4waystocurbemployeetheft (accessed April 10, 2011).

33. Schwantz, Randy. "Honesty Turns Out to Be The Best Policy." *National Underwriter (Property & casuality/ ris & benefits management ed.)* 108, no. 4 (February 2004): 33. Seebauer, Edmund G. "Whistleblowing: Is it Always Obligatory?" *Chemical Engineering Progress* 100, no. 6 (June 2004): 23.

34. Hockenull, Terence A. "Weekender Marketing." *BusinessWorld*, August 2004: 1.

35. Katz, D. "All gifts large and small: towards an understanding of the ethics of pharmaceutical gift giving." *American Journal of Bioethics* 3, no. 3 (2003): 39.

36. Lockheed Martin. *Code of Ethics and Business Conduct.* http://actravl.itcilo.org/actrave-english/telearn/global/ilo/code/lockheed.htm (accessed April 11, 2011).

37. United States Office of Government Ethics. *Gifts from Outside Sources.* http://www.usoge.gov/common_ethics_issues/gifts_outside_sources.aspx (accessed April 11, 2011).

38. Tyco. "The Guide to Ethical Conduct and Doing the Right Thing." *Tyco.* http://www.tyco.com (accessed April 11, 2011).

39. Hauserman, Nancy R. "Whistle-Blowing: Individual Morality in a Society." *Business Horizons* 29 (March/April 1986): 4.

40. Bamford, Janet. "When Do You Blow the Whistle?" *Forbes*, October 21, 1985: 168.

41. Wilson, Glenn T. "Ethics, Your Company or Your Conscience." *Working Woman*, 1984: 67.

42. Smith, Jacquelyn. "The Best Companies to Work For." *Forbes.* December 14, 2010. http://www.forbes.com/2010/12/14/best-places-to-work-employee-satisfaction-leadership-careers-survey.html (accessed April 11, 2011).

43. Ligos, Melinda. "Clicks and Misses." *Sales & Marketing Management*, June 2000: 74.

44. Equal Opportunity Commission. *Discrimination by Type.* http://www.eeoc.gov/laws/types/index.cfm (accessed April 11, 2011). (Equal Opportunity Commission n.d.)

45. *Top 20 Sexual Harrassment Cases of All Time.* http://www.hrworld.com/features/top-20-sexual-harassment-cases121307/ (accessed April 11, 2011).

46. Equal Opportunities Employment Commission. *Sexual Harassment Charges.* http://www.eeoc.gov/eeoc/statistics/enforcement/sexual_harassment.cfm (accessed April 11, 2011).

47. Slonik, Claude. "Attoneys advise employers to prevent sexual harassment through policies, training and procedures." *Long Island Business News*, September 15, 2006.

48. Bole, Kristin. "Harassment Training Can Ultimately Be A Money-Saver." *Buffalo Law Journal* 78, no. 21: 1, 14.

49. Brown, Abby. "Is Ethics Good Business?" *Personnel Administrator* 32 (February 1987): 67.

50. Lill, David J. "Issue of Ethics Often Faces Professional Salespeople." *Nashville Business Journal*, April 22-26, 1991: 5.

51. Cummings, Betsy. "Ethical Breach: Sales and Marketing code of conduct is a step toward improving the ethical culture in today's business world." *Internal Auditor*, June 2007.

52. N.A. "Selling and the Law." *Industrial Distribution* 71. (October 1981): 39.

53. Stack, Steven M. "The High Risk of Dirty Tricks." *Sales and Marketing Magazine* 135, no 7 (November 1985): 58

54. N.A. *Uniform Commercial Code.* http://www.law.cornell.edu/ucc/2/article2.htm (accessed April 11, 2011).

Chapter 4

1. Wayne d. Hoyer, Deborah J. MacInnis, *Consumer Behavior 5th Edition* (Mason, OH: South-Western College Pub., 2009), 3.

2. Scott Young, "Measuring Success: Using Consumer Research to Document the Value of Package Design," *Design Management Review*, (Spring 2006).

3. George M Zinkhan, Karin Braunsberger. "The complexity of consumers' cognitive structures and its relevance to consumer behavior." *Journal of Business Research.* New York: (June 2004). Vol.57, Is. 6, 575.

4. For an expanded description of the model, see James F. Engel, Roger D. Blackwell, and Paul W. Miniard, *Consumer Behavior* (Hinsdale, IL: Dryden Press, 1990).

5. Steve Noble, Amy Guggenheim Shenkan, Christiana Shi, "The Promise of Multichannel Retailing" *The McKinsey Quarterly* (October 31, 2009).

6. Alex Jefferies, "Sales 2.0: Social Media for Knowledge Management and Sales Collaboration," *Aberdeen Group* (September 30, 2008).

7. There are 40 squares in the figure.

8. Craig Stimmel, "Building Customer Relations In 2006," *Office World News*, (Nov/Dec 2006).

9. Aron O'Cass. "Fashion clothing consumption: Antecedents and consequences of fashion clothing involvement." *European Journal of Marketing.* Bradford: (2004). Vol.38, Is. 7, 869.

10. Ben Steverman, "Conspicuous Consumption is Back: Subdued fashions of the recession years are fading as wealthy Americans again flaunt luxury purchases," *Bloomberg Businessweek* (January 27, 2011) Accessed April 8, 2011: www.businessweek.com. *Academy of Marketing Science Review*, (2006).

11. Bernardo J. Carducci, The Psychology of Personality: Viewpoints, Research, and Applications 2nd Edition (Chichester, West Sussex, UK: Wiley-Blackwell, 2009), 474.

12. Yinlong Zhang, Karen Page Winterich, Vikas Mittal, "Power Distance Belief and Impulsive Buying," Journal of Marketing Research (October 1, 2010).

13. Betsy Cummings, "Selling Around the World," *Sales & Marketing Management* (May 2001), 70.

14. Julien Cayla, Eric J. Arnould, "A Cultural Approach to Branding in the Global Marketplace," *Journal of International Marketing*, (December 1, 2008).

15. Jeffrey Gitomer. "Where's the Sales Beef? It's Client's Buying Motive." *Boulder County Business Report.* Boulder: (July 23-August 5, 2004). Vol. 23, Is. 16, 6A.

16. James P. Morgan, "Cross-Functional Buying: Why Teams are Hot," Purchasing (April 5, 2001).

17. Geok Theng Lau, Mohammed A Razzaque, Angeline Ong. "Gatekeeping in Organizational Purchasing: An Empirical Investigation." *The Journal of Business & Industrial Marketing.* Santa Barbara: (2003).Vol.18, Is. 1, 82.

18. Michael Cohn, "Relationship Marketing for Your Business," Focus (April 12, 2010).

19. V. Emre Ozdemir, Kelly Hewett, "The Effect of Collectivism on the Importance of Relationship Quality and Service Quality for Behavioral Intentions: A Cross-National and Cross-Contextual Analysis," *Journal of International* Marketing (March 1, 2010).

20. Judith A. Garretson, Scot Burton, "The Role of Spokescharacters as Advertisement and Package Cues in Integrated Marketing Communications," *Journal of Marketing,* Vol. 69, No. 4 (September 30, 2005).

21. Albert Mehrabian, *Silent Messages* (Belmont, CA: Wadsworth Publishing Company 1971).

22. Deb Varallo, *A Dress for Success Seminar*, Belmont University, Nashville, TN, (November, 2006).

23. Yubo Chen, Qi Wang, Jinhong Xie, "Online Social Interactions: A Natural Experiment on Word of Mouth Versus Observational Learning," *Journal of Marketing Research* (April 1, 2011).

24. Stephen M. Nowlis, Baba Shiv, "The Influence of Consumer Distractions on the Effectiveness of Food Sampling Programs," *Journal of Marketing Research* (May 1, 2005).

25. Derek Dean, Caroline Webb, "Recovering from Information Overload," *The McKinsey Quarterly* (January 31, 2011).

26. "INSIGHTations: Bits and Bytes from Around the Blogosphere," (Accessed April 12, 2011) www.marketingpower.com/ResourceLibrary/Pages/newsletters/mr/2010/2/insightations_2.10_aspx#.

27. This section on the voice was adapted from: Jeffrey Jacobi, "Voice Power," *Selling Power* (October 2000), 66; Robert A. Peterson, Michael P. Cannito and Steven P. Brown, "An Exploratory Investigation of Voice Characteristics," *The Journal of Personal Selling & Sales Management* (Winter 1995), 1-16; John H. Melchinger, "Communication-One Key to Unlock Your Sales, " *Personal Selling Power*, Vol. 10, No. 3 (April 1990), 51.

28. Carol Kinsey Goman, Ph.D, *The Nonverbal Advantage: Secrets and Science of Body Language at Work* (San Francisco, CA: Berrett-Kockler Publishers, Inc., 2008) 159. 29. This section was inspired by Alessandra and Wexler, *Non-Manipulative Selling*, 95-113; Gerhard Gschwandt-

ner, *Non Verbal Selling Power* (Englewood Cliffs, NJ: Prentice-Hall, 1985), 3-80; and John T. Molloy, *Live for Success* (New York: Perigord Press, 1981).

30. James Borg, *Body Language: 7 Easy Lessons to Master the Silent Language* (United Kingdom: Prentice Hall Life, 2008), 37.

31. David Lambert, *Body Language 101: The Ultimate Guide to Knowing When People Are Lying, How They Are Feeling, What They Are Thinking, And More* (New York, NY: Skyhorse Publishing, Inc., 2008), 59-60.

32. www.kevinhogan.net Accessed April 11, 2011.

33. Kevin Hogan, *The Secret Language of Business: How to Read Anyone in 3 Seconds or Less* (Hoboken, NJ: John Wiley and Sons, 2008)42.

34. Yun Chu, William F. Strong, Jianyu Ma, Walter E. Greene "Silent messages in negotiations: the role of nonverbal communication in cross-cultural business negotiations," *Journal of Organizational Culture, Communications and Conflict* (July 1, 2005).

Chapter 5

1. David Newton. "Sell to the Psyche." *Kitchen & Bath Business*. New York: (April 2004), Vol.51, Is. 4, 41.

2. Carl G. Jung, *Psychological Types* (New York: Harcourt Brace and Co., 1924).

3. I am indebted to these individuals and their companies for sharing this valuable information with me. For more detail, see David W. Merrill and Roger H. Reid, *Personal Styles and Effective Performance*, (Radnor, PA: Chilton Book Company, 1981); Paul Mok, *Communicating Styles*

Technology (Dallas, TX: Training Associates Press, 1982); Larry Wilson, *Social Styles Sales Strategies* (Eden Prairie, MN: Wilson Learning Corporation, 2000); Tony Alessandra, Phil Wexler, and Rick Barrera, *Non-Manipulative Selling* (Englewood Cliffs, NJ: Prentice-Hall, 1987).

4. John R. Graham, "Four Basic Categories of Prospects," *Personal Selling Power, Vol. 13, No. 8* (November/December 1993), 56.

5. John L. Bledsoe, "How to Improve Your Relationships with Clients- and Your Staff, Too," *The Practical Accountant* (Institute for Continuing Professional Development, 1984).

6. Michael E Rega, Lisa M Clayton. "Recognizing behavioral buying patterns," *Agency Sales. Irvine*: (November 2003). Vol.33, Is. 11, 34.

7. Interpretation Manual for Communicating Styles Technology developed by Dr. Paul Mok, President of Training Associates Press of Richardson, Texas (Dallas: T A Press 1975), 5.

8. Robert F. Kantin and Mark W. Hardwick, *Quality Selling Through Quality Proposals* (Danvers, MA: Boyd and Fraser Publishing 1994), 28.

9. Chet Robie, "Effects of Perceived Selection Ratio on Personality Test Faking," *Social Behavior and Personality*, 2006.

10. Steven I. Miller, Jack Kavanagh, "Emperical Evidence," *4 J.L. & Educ.* (1975), 159.

11. Merrill and Reid, Personal Styles, 88-117.

12. Todd Duncan, "Your Sales Style," *Incentive* (December 1999), 64-66.

13. Hugh J. Ingrasci, "How to Reach Buyers in their Psychological 'Com-

fort Zones,'" *Industrial Marketing* (July 1981), 64; Merrill and Reid, Personal Styles, 88-117.

14. Seth Godin, "The Dating Game," *Sales & Marketing Management* (May 2001), 34.

15. Michael Leimbach, "Sales Versatility: Connecting with Customers Every Time," (Accessed April 22, 2011: www.salesopedia.com/relationships-relationships/2273-sales-versatility-connecting-with-customers-every-time).

16. David Newton. "Sell to the Psyche." *Kitchen & Bath Business*. New York: (April 2004), Vol.51, Is. 4, 41.

17. Tom Hoek, guest lecture at Belmont University, Nashville, TN, March 23, 2006. Mr. Hoek is president of Insurance Systems of Tennessee.

18. Wilson Learning Library, *Versatile Selling: Adapting Your Style so Customers Say Yes!* Nova Vista Publishing: Belgium, 2006.

19. Tony Alessandra, Phil Wexler, and Rick Barrera, *Non-Manipulative Selling* (New York: Prentice Hall, 1987), 112.

20. Rod Nichols, "How to Sell to Different Personality Types," *Personal Selling Power, Vol. 12, No. 8* (November/December 1992), 46; and Malcolm Fleschner, "The Microsoft Way," *Selling Power* (January/February 1998),86.

21. Jeff Thull. "Recognition Smarts," *Incentive. New York*: (September 2004), Vol.178, Is. 9, 120.

22. Bruce Seidman, "The Psychology of the Sale, Part 1," *Salesdoctors.com* (February 14, 2000),2.

23. Patrick Schul and Brent Wren, "The Emerging Role of Women in Industrial Selling: A Decade of Change,"

Journal of Marketing, 56 (July 1992), 38.

24. Henry Cole. "Marketing Real Estate Services: Smart Work versus Hard Work in Personal Selling." *Services Marketing Quarterly.* Binghamton: (2004). Vol. 25, Is. 2, 43.

25. John P Dugan, "Explorations Using the Social Change Model: Leadership Development among College Men and Women," *Journal of College Student Development,* (Mar/Apr 2006).

26. Fredrick A. Russ and Kevin A. McNeilly, "Links Among Satisfaction, Commitment, and Performance," *Journal of Business Research,* 34, 1 (September 1995), 57-61.

27. Judy A. Siguaw and Earl Honeycutt, Jr. "An Examination of Gender Differences in Selling Behaviors and Job Attitudes," *Industrial Marketing Management,* 24 (1995), 46; Robert Sharoff, "She Said, He Said," *Selling* (May 1994), 54-58.

28. Erin A. Cech, Mary Blair-Loy, "Perceiving Glass Ceilings? Meritocratic versus Structural Explanations of Gender Inequality among Women in Science and Technology," *Social Problems, Vol. 57, No. 5* (August 2010), 371-397.

29. Paula Zmudzinski, "Gender Mutters," *Selling Power* (March 2000), 8.

30. Gary Bachelor, "Selling Beyond Gender," *Selling Power* (January/February 1996), 66-67.

31. Sinan Caykoylu, *Cross-Cultural and Gender Differences in Leadership Style Perspectives: a Comparative Study between Canada and Turkey,* (Saarbrücken, Germany: LAP Lambert Academic Publishing, January 7, 2010).

32. Personal Communication with Roger H. Reid (July 21, 2001).

33. Vincent Alonzo, "Role Call: Defining Your Reps' Personality Types Can Open a Window to Motivate," *Sales & Marketing Management* (June 2001), 34-35; Helen Berman, "Selling to Different Personalities," *Folio: The Magazine for Magazine Management* (June 1999), 34-35.

34. Richard Jensen and Roy Spungin, "Analyze Your Prospects to a tee," *Selling Power* (July/August 1997), 80-81.

35. Zenith Training and Development, "The Psychology of Selling Excellence," Accessed August 18, 2007. http://www.zenithtraining.ie/sales-training/.

36. Fran Abrams. "Learning? It's all in the mind." *The Times Educational Supplement. London:* (May 21, 2004), Is. 4584, F8.

37. Gareth Roderique-Davies, "Neuro-Linguistic Programming: Cargo Cult Psychology?," *Journal of Applied Research in Higher Education* (2009), 57-63.

38. Bruce Tuckman, David Monetti, *Educational Psychology* (Belmont, CA: Wadsworth Cengage Learning, 2011), 168.

39. Gareth Roderique-Davies, "Neuro-Linguistic Programming: Cargo Cult Psychology?," *Journal of Applied Research in Higher Education* (2009), 57-63.

40. Reg Connolly, "The NLP Eye Accessing Cues," The Pegasus NLP Newsletter (Accessed April 18, 2011: www.nlp-now.co.uk/nlp_eye_accessing_cues.htm).

41. Kate Burton, Romilla Ready, *Neuro-linguistic Programming for Dummies,* *2nd Edition* (Chichester, West Sussex, England: John Wiley & Sons, Ltd., 2010), 92.

Chapter 6

1. Anonymous, "Study Indicates Sales Professionals Spend Little Time Preparing for Calls; Preparation for Sales Calls Significantly Less than Managers and Buyers Desire," *Business Wire.* New York: (Nov 29, 2005), 1.

2. C.S.M. Currie, R.C.H. Cheng, and H.K. Smith, "Dynamic pricing of airline tickets with competition," *The Journal of the Operational Research Society.* Oxford: (Aug 2008), Vol. 59, Is. 8, 1026.

3. David G. Knott, Jeff Boschwitz, and Decio K. Mendes, "Know Your Company's 'DNA,'" *Best's Review.* Oldwick: (Jul 2004), Vol. 105, Is. 3, 46..

4. George H Walper Jr. and Catherine S. McBreen, "Clients' Knowledge is Power" *On Wall Street,* Feb 2007.

5. Jesse Holcomb, Amy Mitchell, and Tom Rosenstiel, "Cable: Audience vs. Economics," Pew Research Center's Project for Excellence in Journalism, Annual Report 2011, accessed April 25, 2011, http://stateofthemedia.org/2011/cable-essay/.

6. Craig J Coffey. "Differentiating Yourself With Exemplary Service." *National Underwriter.* Life & Health. (August 23- August 30, 2004). Vol. 108, Is. 32, 18.

7. Tate Williams. "The Age-Old Face-Off." *Sales and Marketing Management.* New York: (April 2004). Vol. 156, Is. 4, 64.

8. Marshall Lager, "The Alignment: CRM capabilities and business processes enable technology to shine," *CRM Magazine,* July 2007.

9. Paul and Lauren Gibbons, "Cost Effective IT Training," *Network World*, March 7, 2007.

10. Margaret Driscoll and Saul Carliner, *Advanced Web-based Training Strategies*. San Francisco: (Pfeiffer, 2005)..

11. Anonymous, "WebEx Training Center Wins Three eLearning Guild Member's Choice Awards", *PR Newswire*, June 29, 2007 and Webex.com, accessed April 25, 2011, http://www.webex.com/products/elearning-and-online-training.html.

12. "LDMI Connects With ePath Learning to Enhance Sales Training & Bolster Growth." *PR Newswire*. New York: (August 30, 2004), 1 and ePathlearning.com, accessed April 25, 2011, http://www.epathlearning.com/.

13. From a telephone interview with Paul Goldner on May 16, 2001; and adapted from Erika Rasmussan, "Training Goes Virtual," *Sales & Marketing Management* (September 2000), 108.

14. Denise Bedell, "Know Thy Customer's Behavior," *Global Finance*. New York: (Nove 2005), Vol. 19, Is. 10, 54.

15. Steve Fox, "Android Love: It's Not Just About Phones," *PC World*. San Francisco: (Nov 2010), Vol. 28, Is. 11, 7.

16. Malcolm Fleschner, "Ooh, That Smarts!" *Selling Power* (January/February 2001), 30.

17. Anonymous, "FileMaker Delivers Three Free FileMaker Go Starter Solutions; Manage your contacts, documents, and assests on iPad, iPhone, or iPod touch," *M2 Presswire*. Coventry: (Mar 22, 2011).

18. Anne Stanton. "The "Why" Behind CRM Software." *Infotech Update*.

New York: (March /April 2004), Vol.13, Is. 2, 5.

19. http://www.suradocrm.com/sql_corporate.shtml, Accessed June 27, 2011.

20. Anonymous, "Red Funnel Consulting Upgrades FatStax Sales Productivity App for iPad," *Health & Beauty Close-Up*. Jacksonville: (Mar 31, 2011).

21. Maya Swedowsky, "A Social Media 'How To' for Retailers," *Salesandmarketing.com*. Posted July 31, 2010, accessed April 27, 2011, http://www.salesandmarketing.com/article/social-media-how-retailers.

22. Barbara Giamanco, "6 Tips for Driving Social Sales Success," *Salesandmarketing.com*. Posted March 10, 2011, accessed April 27, 2011, http://www.salesandmarketing.com/article/6-tips-driving-social-sales-success.

23. Facebook Press Room, accessed April 27, 2011, https://www.facebook.com/press/info.php?statistics; and Justin Smith, "December Data on Facebook's US Growth by Age and Gender: Beyond 100 Million," *InsideFacebook.com*, posted January 4, 2010, accessed April 27, 2011, http://www.insidefacebook.com/2010/01/04/december-data-on-facebook's-us-growth-by-age-and-gender-beyond-100-million/.

24. Anonymous, "#numbers," Twitter blog, posted March 14, 2011, accessed April 27, 2011, http://blog.twitter.com/2011/03/numbers.html, and Maggie Shiels, "Twitter co-founder Jack Dorsey rejoins company," *BBC News*. Posted March 28, 2011, accessed April 27, 2011, http://www.bbc.co.uk/news/business-12889048.

25. Anonymous, "LinkedIn Reaches 100 Million Members Worldwide," *Business Wire*. New York: (Mar 22, 2011).

26. Tamara Chuang, "Apple debuts budget computer and capitalizes on iPod success," *Knight Ridder Tribune News Service*. Washington: (Jan 11, 2005), 1.

27. M.G. Siegler, "The Mac Versus PC Debate Has Never Been Clearer," TechCrunch.com, posted Jul 23, 2009, accessed April 26, 2011, http://techcrunch.com/2009/07/23/the-mac-versus-pc-debate-has-never-been-clearer/.

28. Anonymous, "Gap Inc. Updates Investors on Strategies to Regain Market Share and Expand Internationally," *Business Wire*. New York: (Oct 15, 2009).

29. Brian Quinton, "General Mills Tests Using Groupon to Drive Trials, Coupon Use," *Promo (Online)*. Danbury: (Apr 26, 2011).

30. Anonymous, "Author Presents Six Strategies for Motivating Employees," *Healthcare Financial Management*. Westchester: (Nov 2010), Vol. 64, Is. 11, 26.

31. Robert McGarvey and Babs S. Harrison,"Easy as Pie," *Selling Power* (March 2000), 116.

32. The sections of this chapter dealing with motivation and goal setting were taken largely from Paul J. Meyer's *Dynamics of Personal Goal Setting, Dynamics of Personal Leadership*, and *Dynamics of Personal Motivation* (Waco, TX: Success Motivation, 1991, 1992, and 1993, respectively).

33. James Wilkins, "The 'why' is what drives positivity," *Conference and*

Incentive Travel. London: (Mar 2011), 16.

34. Paul Werlin, "Seven Keys to Self-Motivation," *Bank Investment Consultant.* New York: (Aug 2010), Vol. 18, Is. 8, 25.

35. Gladeana McMahon, "A question of coaching," *Training Journal.* Ely: (Mar 2011), 68.

36. Rajen Devadason, "Thermometer or thermostat?" *Malaysian Business.* Kuala Lumpur: (Jan 1, 2011), 58.

37. Donna L. Cohen, "Plan Your Way to Success and Increase Sales," *Agency Sales.* Irvine: (Oct 2006), Vol. 36, Is. 10, 36.

38. Valentino Sabuco, "What's Really Important to You?" *The Saturday Evening Post.* Indianapolis: (Jul/Aug 2007), Vol. 279, Is. 4, 46.

39. Paul J. Meyer, *Dynamics of Personal Goal Setting*, Lesson 5 (Waco, TX: Success Motivation, Inc., 1984), 2.

Chapter 7

1. Farber, Barry. "Get On Track." *Entrepreneur* (February 2000): 138.

2. Stanton, Travis. "*Myths of Lead Management.*" Exhibitor Magazine. http://www.exhibitoronline.com/exhibitormagazine/sep10/research-lead-management.asp (accessed April 26, 2011.).

3. N.A. "Why Sales Leads Fall Through The Cracks, And How SFA Can Make The Difference." *Customer Interaction Solutions* (July 2006).

4. Zemanski, Renee. "Developing New Leads." *Selling Power* (March 2000): 34.

5. Beveridge, Dirk. "Qualifying Your Prospects." *The American Salesman* 36, no 6 (June 1991): 6-9.

6. Meyer, Paul J. *Sales Training Material for Distributors of SMI International, Inc.* (Waco, TX).

7. Prashad, Sharda. "Tailored Sales Pitches Work Best." *Toronto Star* (October 20, 2005).

8. Cates, Bill. "Referrals 101." *Selling Power* (October 2000): 56.

9. Zalz, Cliff. "Building Relationships." *Business Marketing* (August 1992): 34.

10. Twining, Michael. "Million To Win." *Selling Power* (March 2000): 50.

11. Libin, Richard F. "Bring Back This Lost Art Form." *Ward's Dealer Business* (Feb 2007).

12. Weiss, Wendy. "Why Make Cold Calls?" *Sales and Service Excellence* (June 2010).

13. Stewart, Irby F. "Golden Opportunities." *Selling Power* (March 2001): 62.

14. N.A. "The Medium and the Message." *Direct Marketing* 56, no 9 (January 1994): 27.

15. Deutsch, Ryan. "Social Media as a Direct Marketing Channel." *destinationCRM.com* (Oct 2009). http://www.destinationcrm.com/Articles/Web-Exclusives/Viewpoints/Social-Media-as-a-Direct-Marketing-Channel-56357.aspx (accessed April 27, 2011).

16. Gitomer, Jeffrey. "Networking Not Working? Try Smart-working." *Dallas Business Journal* (January 2000): 43.

17. Greenwald, John. "Sorry, Right Number." *Time* 142, no 11 (September 1993): 66.

18. Amodio, Michelle. "Are There Suitable/Affordable/Adequate Technologies For Small To Medium- Sized Call Centers?" *Customer Inter@ction Solutions* (Nov 2006).

19. Canto, Eduardo Javier. "Survey Says: Where the Sales Are." *Sales & Marketing Management* (June 2001): 18.

20. Adedia.com staff. "A well-designed website can be your personal sales assistant." http://www.adedia.com/articles/2010/01/07/website-sales-assistant (accessed May 25, 2011).

21. Internet Marketing Strategy Diva. "Tips for creating successful sales websites." http://www. internetmarketingstrategydiva.com/2010/01/29/tips-for-creating-successful-sales-websites (accessed April 27, 2011).

22. Yener, Nail. "Common Characteristics of Successful Direct Sales Sites." http://www.nailyener.com/common-characterisitics-of-successful-direct-sales-websites (accessed April 27, 2011).

23. Google. "Google AdSense." http://www.google.com/adsense/www/en_US/tour/tools.html (accessed April 26 2011).

24. Cummings, Betsy. "In Their Shoes." *Sales and Marketing Management* 156, no 10. (October 2004): 36.

Chapter 8

1. "The Preapproach & Telephone Techniques," accessed April 29, 2011, http://www-rohan.sdsu.edu/~renglish/377/notes/chapt08/.

2. Kenneth L. Fields, "There's no substitute for telephone prospecting," *American Agent & Broker.* St. Louis: (Mar 2010), Vol. 82, Is. 3, 26.

3. Michael Crom, "How to improve on sales calls," *Gannett News Service.* McLean: (Sep 28, 2006), 1.

4. Long Island Business News Staff, "When it comes to sales, preparation is key," *Daily Record and the Kansas City Daily News-Press,* Jan 7, 2006.

5. Jack Kwicien, "Improving sales management effectiveness: outreach; Three business development strategies can make a big difference in your success," *Employee Benefit Advisor*. New York: (Oct. 2010), Vol. 8, Is. 10, 60.

6. Chad Kaydo, "Lights! Camera! Sales!," *Sales & Marketing Management* (February 1998), 111.

7. Rich Wilkins, "Visualize Your Success," *Professional Selling Power*, Vol. 13, No. 1 (January/February 1993), 69.

8. Jhan R. Dolphin, "Early Birds: Preparation is key to sales success," *Light Truck and SUV Accessory Business & Product News*. Fort Atkinson: (Mar 2008), Vol. 21, Is. 2, 14.

9. Kate Maddox, "Lead management takes cooperation," *B to B*. Chicago: (Dec. 11, 2006), Vol. 91, Is. 17, 3.

10. G. Berton Latamore, "Perfect Match," *Selling Power* (September 2000), 150-155.

11. Marcia A. Reed-Woodard, "What you look like online," *Black Enterprise*, Jan 2007.

12. George N. Kahn, "Without Ammunition," *The Smooth Selling Series* (New York: George N. Kahn Co., 1976) 3.

13. Jennifer Keim, "Eric Kline: Be a confident sales rep," *HME News*. Yarmouth: (Oct 2007), Vol. 13, Is. 10, 82.

14. Adapted from John J. Franco, "Ring Up More Telephone Sales with Well-Trained Personnel," *Business Marketing*, Vol. 71, No. 8 (August 1986), 84; and "Telephone Closes Are Up," *Personal Selling Power*, Vol. 14, No. 4 (May/June 1994), 20.

15. Susan Greco, "The Need for Speed," *Inc.*, April, 2007.

16. "Getting Past the Gatekeeper," *Selling Power* (July/August 2000), 56; Jan Gelman, "Gatekeeper," *Selling*, Vol. 2, No. 1 (July/August 1994), 54-56; and Nanci McCann, "Protocol," *Selling*, Vol. 1, No. 9 (May 1994), 79; Jack Foster, "Maximizing FACE TIME with Customers," *Agency Sales*. Irvine: (Jul 2010), Vol. 40, Is. 7, 40.

17. Anonymous, "Really Simple Systems Survey: Majority of Small Companies Use Social Networking in Everyday Business," *Health & Beauty Close-Up*. Jacksonville: (Apr 29, 2011).

18. Craig Fisher, "How to recruit effectively using Twitter," *Recruiter (Online)*. London: (Apr 26, 2011).

19. Heather Baldwin, "5 Tips to Get the Most from Your LinkedIn Profile," *SellingPower.com*. Accessed April 29, 2011, http://www.sellingpower.com/content/article.php?a=9428&nr=1.

20 Heather Fletcher, "Please Try This Call Again; Next Time With More Integration," *Target Marketing*. Philadelphia: (Apr 2011), Vol. 34, Is. 4, 7.

21. Wendy Weiss, "Top Ten Tips for Terminating Telephone Terror," *The American Salesman* (December 2000), 15-17.

22. Susan McGinnis, "Smart Talk: Make an impression," *HME News*. Yarmouth: (Feb 2011), Vol. 17, Is. 2, 19.

23. "Voice Concerns," *Personal Selling Power*, Vol. 13, No. 7 (October 1993), 44.

24. "Making a Telephone Investment," *Professional Selling*, Vol. 22, No. 5 (March 10, 1984), 1-2.

25. Jeffrey Jacobi, "Voice Power," *Selling Power* (October 2000), 66.

26. Anonymous, "Contact Management Software synchs with wireless devices," *Product News Network*, March 27, 2006.

27. David Lill, "From phone to face-to-face," *Selling Power* (January/February 1998), 46-47.

28. Barry Z. Masser and William M. Leeds, *Power-Selling by Telephone* (West Nyack, NY: Parker Publishing Company, 1982), 56.

29. Shafiroff and Shook, *Successful Telephone Selling*, 36-37.

30. John Boe, "Selling is a Contact Sport: Keys to Effective Phone Calling," *The American Salesman*. Burlington: (Nov. 2010), Vol. 55, Is. 11, 12.

31. "Sixteen Ways to Improve Your Telemarketing Effort," *Personal Selling Power*, Vol. 12, No. 7 (October 1992), 42.

Chapter 9

1. Dolak, Dave."Sales and Personal Selling." http://www.davedolak.com/c-mktg5.htm (accessed November 9, 2004).

2. Engleberg, Isa N. and Wynn, Dianna R. *Think Communication*. Toronto: Allyn & Bacon, 2011. 110; Morton, Brain. "Be prepared to make a good, quick first impression." *Ottawa Citizen* (May 23, 2007): 1.

3. Laidman, Jenni. "Make it Count." *The Tennessean* (June 21, 2001): section D, 1-2; Kahn, George N. Kahn. "The Impression You Make." *Smooth Selling* 62 (1967): 2.

4. Anonymous, "Home staging assists sellers." *USA Today* (in Collaboration with the Society for the Advancement of Education) (April, 2007).

5. L.R., Vithyaa. "Importance of customer service." *Business Times* (October 19, 2004): 1.

6. Isabel Lee. "Art of selling one's skills crucial in clinching job," South China Morning Post. Hong Kong: July 17, 2004. pg. 5.

7. Leotta, Joan. "Dressed to Sell." *Selling Power* (October 2000): 89.

8. Alessandra, Anthony J. and Wexler, Phillip. *Non-manipulative Selling.* Reston, VA: Reston Publishing, Inc 1979: 87-93.

9. Frankel, Lois. *The Thin Pink Line.* Feb 25, 2009. http://thethinpinkline.com/?s=dress+and+credibility (accessed May 2, 2011).

10. Hayes, Jerry. "Do You Look Like a Doctor?" *Optometric Management* (Jul 2006).

11. N.A. "Attire Guide: Dress Codes from Casual to White Tie." April 13, 2010. http://www.emilypost.com/everday-manners/your-personal-image/69-attire-guide-dress-codes (accessed May 2, 2011).

12. Puente, Maria. "How NOT to dress for work." *USA TODAY* (November 2006).

13. Lackie, Dave. "Mute about suits; Many men have no idea how to dress properly, and they're afraid to admit it." *National Post* (December 31 2010).

14. Modified and adapted from the following sources: Ligos, Melinda. "Does Image Matter." Sales & Marketing Management (March 2001): 53-56; Green, Leo "Ask an Expert: Five Do's and Don'ts for Dressing Down," CA Magazine (January/February 2001): 11; Brewer, Geoffrey and Kaydo, Chad. "Dressing for Success." Sales & Marketing Management (August 2000): 104.

15. Shemek, Pat. "Super Duper Difference." *Selling Power.* (July/August 2000): 56.

16. Solnik, Claude. "Immaculate receptions: The art of greeting clients to your firm." *Long Island Business News* (Jul 21, 2006).

17. Huling, Emily. "Leading from the Front Line." *Rough Notes* (Mar 2007).

18. Lydia, Ramsey. "Seal the Deal Sales Technique." http://sbinformation.about.com/od/sales/a/ucsaletechnique_2.htm (accessed November 9, 2004).

19. Johnson, Dorothea. "Five Tips for International Handshaking." *Sales & Marketing Management* (July 1997): 90.

20. Porter, Henry. "Opening for Every Occasion." *Sales Management* 109, no 9 (October 30,1972). 6-8.

21. Witsman, Karl. "No More What's His Name Again." The American Salesman, Vol. 32, No. 2 (February 1987), 25.

22. Adapted from "Here's an Easy Way to Remember Your Customers' Names." *Master Salesmanship.* Concordville, PA: Clement Communications, Inc.. (1979): 3; and McCann, Nanci. "When You Forget a Prospect's Name." *Selling* (March 1994): 101.

23. Mok, Paul P. "CST Influencing Model" from *CST: Communicating Styles Technology.* Dallas: T.A. Press, Inc. (1982): 13.

24. Holmes, Chet. "The Ultimate Sales Approach." http://www.success-magazine.com/the-ultimate-sales-approach/PARAMS/article/1099/channel/22. (accessed May 3, 2011).

Chapter 10

1. Jim Scheer, "Asking Good Questions," *Office World News,* Jan/Feb 2006.

2. Ginger Trumfio, "Underlying Motivation," *Sales & Marketing Management* (June 1994), 71.

3. Kristen des Chatelets. "Asking the Right Questions." *Dealerscope. Philadelphia* (June 2004). Vol.46, Is. 6, 26.

4. Terrence A. Hockenhull. "Weekender: Marketing." *BusinessWorld. Manila* (January 9, 2004), 1.

5. George Ludwig. "Earn Your 'Doctor of Selling' Degree." *National Underwriter. Life & Health. Erlanger* (August 23-August 30, 2004).Vol.108, Is. 32, 50.

6. Art Sobczak, "Proposal Worthy," *Selling Power* (June 1997), 56; and Tim Connor, *The Soft Sell* (Crofton, MD: TR Training Associates Int'l., 1981), 64.

7. Andrew Rudin, "Just the Facts! – How Asking the Right Questions Will Yield the Right Answers," *SalesVantage.com* (2010) Accessed May 4, 2011 www.salesvantage.com/article/897/Just-the-Facts-How-Asking-the-Right-Questions-Will-Yield-the-Right-Answers.

8. John O'Toole, "The Want Makes the Sale," *Selling* (June 1994), 43.

9. Camille P. Schuster and Jeffrey E. Davis, "Asking Questions: Some Characteristics of Successful Sales Encounters," *Journal of Personal Selling and Sales Management,* Vol. 6, No. 1 (May 1986), 17.

10. Anonymous, "Probing Skills Course Aims to Educate the Learner about the Role of Questions in Various Situations and the Importance of Asking the Right Question at the

Right Time," *Business Wire,* Jan 17, 2006.

11. Information gathered from the Outside Technologies, Inc. website at www.outsidetechnologies.com and from Andrew Rudin, "Just the Facts! How Asking the Right Questions Will Yield the Right Answers," *SalesVantage.com* (2010) Accessed May 4, 2011 www.salesvantage.com/article/897/Just-the-Facts-How-Asking-the-Right-Questions-Will-Yield-the-Right-Answers.

12. Anthony J. Alessandra and Phillip S. Wexler, *Non-Manipulative Selling* (Reston, VA.: Reston Publishing Co., 1979), adapted from 54-57.

13. Tim Connor, *The Soft Sell* (Crofton, MD: TR Training Associates Intl., 1981), 67.

14. The Sales Hunter Video Podcast, "Repeat the Key Question, Selling is all about asking better." *PyroTV.com,* July 12, 2007.

15. Neil Rackham, *SPIN Selling* (New York: McGraw-Hill), 1988.

16. Information gathered from Transworld Systems, Inc. website www.transworldsystems.com (Accessed May 2, 2011).

17. Rackham, Ibid, 89.

18. Todd Youngblood, "Let Customers Sell Themselves," *Selling Power* (March 2001), 52.

19. William Kendy, "Probing For Real Customer Needs," *Selling Power* (January/ February 2001), 26.

20. Steve Atlas, "When and How to Use Your Favorite Close Effectively," *Selling Power* (September 2000), 48.

21. Jim Scheer, "Closing sales," *Office World News, May/Jun 2006.*

22. Warren Greshes, "Prospecting Skills III," *Warren Greshes Video, Brightcove.com;* Accessed 8/6/07.

23. W. Brown, "Listen Up," *Professional Safety,* Vol. 54, Issue 4 (April 2009), 8.

24. Jan Flynn, Tuula-Riitta Valikoski, Jennie Grau, "Listening in the business context: Reviewing the state of research," *International Journal of Listening,* Vol. 22, Issue 2 (2008), 141-151.

25. Joseph DeVito, *Human Communication* 10th Edition (New York, NY: Longman, 2008).

26. Briggitta Brunner, "Listening, communication, & trust: Practitioners' perspectives of business/organizational relationships,"*International Journal of Listening,* Vol. 22, Issue 1 (2008), 73-82.

27. N. Nicholson, "Listening and Learning," *Communication World* (July 2007), 2.

28. Roy Chitwood, "High tech can't beat out high touch of sales," *Executive Sales Training and Development* (Accessed May 4, 2011) www.maxsacks.com/articles/austin13.html.

29. Jonathan Steele, "Active Listening: Mastering This Skill and Master Communication," *Speechmastery.com* (posted April 1, 2011) Accessed May 4, 2011 www.speechmastery.com/activelistening.html.

Chapter 11

1. Brooks, Bill. "What is the Difference Between What Customers Need and What They Really Want." *The American Salesman* (January 2001): 3-5.

2. Canton, Dr. James. *Technofutures: How Leading Edge Technology Will Transform Business in the 21st Century.* Hay House 1999.

3. DiResta, Diane. *Knockout Presentations.* Chandler House Press (1998).

4. Engler, Bill. "Marketing Magic Inspired by P.T. Barnum." http://www.marketingprofs.com/6/engler1.asp?sp=1#split (accessed May 23, 2006).

5. Wilson, Bill. "Quick Tip: Preparation Time." http://www.presentation-pointers.com/showarticle/articleid/195/ (accessed September 1, 2007).

6. Hoover's White Paper Series. "How to Convert Prospects to Sales Faster With Pre Call Planning." http://www.whitepapercompany.com/pdfs/Appum-Hoovers.pdf (accessed May 3, 2011).

7. Hoover's White Paper Series. "How to Convert Prospects to Sales Faster With Pre Call Planning." http://www.whitepapercompany.com/pdfs/Appum-Hoovers.pdf (accessed May 3, 2011); Schultz, Mike and Doerr, John. "Sales Call Planning: What to Know Before Every Sales Call." http://www.whillsgroup.com/insights/articles/sales-call-planning-what-to-know-before-every-sales-call (accessed May 3, 2011).

8. Arbel, Tali. "Proceed with Caution: Presentation Roadblocks, Even the most seasoned salespeople know it: Presentations cause anxiety." *Sales and Marketing Management.* http://www.presentations.com/msg/content_display/sales/e3i778b0e5af917c-8c6b92ad42115694838# (accessed January 02, 2007).

9. Hannan, Mack. "The Three C's of Selling: A Sure Cure for the Salesman's Curse." *Sales & Marketing Management* 10 no 7 (May 1976): 93.

10. Women's Business Center. "Features and Benefits."http://www.onlinewbc.gov (accessed November 23, 2004).

11. Trumfio, Ginger. "Underlying Motivatio." Sales & Marketing Management. (June 1994): 71.

12. Taylor, Robert F. *Back to Basic Selling.* Englewood Cliffs, NJ: Prentice-Hall (1985): 75.

13. Modified and adapted from: U.S. Census Bureau, Current Population Reports, 1993.

14. Kahn, George N. "You're on Stage." *Smooth Selling* (1975): 2.

15. National Sales Development Institute. *10 Steps to Greatness in Selling.* Waterford, CT: The National Sales Development Institute (1980): 10-12.

16. Wright, Greg, interview by Lill. (July 10, 2007).

17. Tracy, Larry. "Preparing A Presentation, The Tell 'Em and 3-1-2 Method." http://www.presentation-pointers.com/showarticle/articleid/216/ (accessed August 23, 2007).

18. Drews, Tom. "How to Design and Deliver Effective Virtual Sales Presentations." http://www.slideshare.net/gotomeeting/how-to-design-and-deliver-effective-virtual-sales-presentations (accessed May 4, 2011).

19. Marks, Ronald B. "Dramatize Your Presentation or Lose the Sale." http://www.advancedsselling.com (accessed November 20 2004).

20. Holcombe, Martha W. and. Stein, Judith K. "How to Deliver Dynamic Presentations: Use Visuals for Impact." *Business Marketing* 71, no 6 (June 1986): 163-164; Kern, Richard. "Making Visual Aids Work for You." *Sales & Marketing Management* (February 1989): 46-49.

21. Alexander, Bob. "How Laptops Put You in the Driver's Seat." *Personal Selling Power* 10, no 2 (March 1990): 53.

Chapter 12

1. Boe, John. "Overcome objections and close the sale." *Agency Sales* 33, no. 9 (September 2003): 29.

2. Pell, Roger. "The Road to Success is Paved with Objections." *Bank Marketing* 22 (1990): 16.

3. Feiertag, Howard. "Finding out reasons for objections is key to overcoming them." *Hotel and Motel Management* 217, no 18 (October 2002): 14.

4. Boe, John. "Overcome objections and close the sale." *Agency Sales* 33, no. 9 (September 2003): 27.

5. Redmond, Thomas M Jr.. "Prospect objections can be overcome." *National Underwriter* 106, no 2. (June 2002): 19-20.

6. Kaiser, Robert. "A couple of ideas for overcoming hidden objections." *National Underwriter* 106, no 18 (May 2002): 30-31.

7. Pollock, Ted. "How good a closer are you?" *The American Salesman* 48, no 6 (June 2006): 18.

8. Huisken, Brad. "Busting the sales busters, Part II," *JCK* 174, no 3 (March 2003): 66-67.

9. Lake, Michael. "Overcoming objections is the key to sales," *Hudson Valley Business Journal* (March 2008): 26.

10. Huisken, Brad. "Busting the sales busters, Part II," *JCK* 174, no 3 (March 2003): 66-67.

11. Gitomer, Jeffrey. "Make Objections obsolete to pave your way to sales."

The Central New York Business Journal (December 2006): 21

12. Campbell, Kim Sydow and Davis, Lenita. "The Sociolinguistic Basis of Managing Rapport When Overcoming Sales Objections." *Journal of Business Communications* 43, no 1 (January 2006): 45

13. Huisken, Brad. "Busting the sales busters, Part II," *JCK* 174, no 3 (March 2003): 66-67.

14. N.A. "How do you address Objections? Here's a few ideas." *Life Association News* (November 1996): 16-18.

15. Atlas, Steve. "Listening for Hidden Objections." *Selling Power* (June 2000): 36.

16. N.A. "Customer Objections: Do You Have the Answers?" *Professional Selling* 22, no 5 (March 1984): 3.

17. Anderson, Wilma G. "Nine mistakes to avoid when marketing to seniors." *National Underwriter* 107, no 20 (May 2003): 22.

18. Roberts-Phelps, Graham. "Objections Are Opportunities to Sell." *Personal Selling Power* 12, no 8 (November/December 1992): 34.

19. Gitomer, Jeffrey. "Attitude is the one-word definition of success." *Fort Worth Business Press*" (September 15-21 2008): 28.

20. Brooks, Bill. "Are you responsive enough for your prospects and customers?" *The American Salesman* 48, no 2 (February 2003): 21-23.

21. Kasper, Jim. "Objections: Questions in Disguise." http://www.salesvantage.com (accessed September 10, 2007)

22. Brooks, Bill. "Time, budgets and excuses...how do you overcome them?"

The American Salesman 47 no, 1 (January 2002): 13-15.

23. Weiss, Wendy. "Eliminate Objections: And close more sales this year." *Sales and Service Excellence* (January 2010): 4.

24. Graham, John R. "How to sell more when others are selling less." *The American Salesman* 48, no 2 (February 2003): 15-20.

25. Ramsey, Robert D. "How to pitch a new idea." *SuperVision* 65, no 3 (March 2004): 8-9.

26. N.A, "How To Control Your Sales Appointment, How salespeople can get and keep the power all throughout their selling interaction."http://www.5min.com/Video/How-To-Control-Your-Sales-Appointment-1185 (accessed July 17, 2007).

27. Farneti, David. "Opening Doors And Establishing Winning Sales Relationships." *Agency Sales* 34, no 2 (February 2004): 28-30.

28. Natenberg, Todd. "Overcoming Objections." http://www.selfgrowth.com/articles/Natenberg4.html (accessed September 1, 2007).

29. Russell, Frederic et al. *Selling: Principles and Practices* (New York: McGraw-Hill, 1982): 321; and Rasmusson, Erika. "The Pitfalls of Price-Cutting." *Sales & Marketing Management* (May 1997): 17.

30. Gross, T. Scott. "The Service Factor." *Selling Power* (October 2000): 45.

31. Weiss, Wendy. "The Price Is Right? How to handle a customer's objections to price of an item." *American Salesman* 46, no 1 (January 2001): 6.

32. Chadha, Rhadika. "Sellers of stuff: Salespeople should be trained to meet the demands of the ever-changing marketplace to stay abreast of competition. How do you distinguish your brand from the competition?" *Businessline* (January 22, 2004): 1.

33. Kendy, William F. "Handling the Price Objection." *Selling Power* (September 2000): 41.

Chapter 13

1. Brian Tracy, *The Art of Closing the Sale*. Thomas Nelson, 2007.

2. Gerhard Gschwandtner, "On Closing the Sale," *Personal Selling Power*, Vol. 17, No. 5 (July/August 1987), 6.

3. Anonymous, "Closing the sale can be tough, but guidelines can ease the way," *San Fransisco Chronicle*, Wednesday, December 28, 2005; Page C-4.

4. Paul H. Green, "Closing A Sale," www.multiplex.com/Greensheet, July 9, 2001.

5. Jeffrey Gitomer, "A funny thing happened to me on the way to closing a sale," www.insiderbiz.com, July 15, 2001. Jeffrey Gitomer is author of *The Sales Bible* and *Customer Satisfaction is Worthless, Customer Loyalty is Priceless*.

6. NBC's *The Celebrity Apprentice*, Season 4, 2011.

7. Jim Duerr, Personal Interview, September 26, 2011.

8. Anonymous, "The Truth About Getting Prompt Buying Decisions," *The American Salesman*. Burlington: (Jul 2010), Vol. 55, Is. 7, 21.

9. Selling Power Editors, "Persistence Leads to Success: Just Ask Gerhard Gschwandtner and Joe Sugarman," *Selling Power*, sellingpower.com, (January 5, 2004).

10. Graham Roberts-Phelps, "Make Persistence Pay," *Personal Selling Power*, Vol. 14, No. 4 (May/June 1994), 68.

11. Dr. Seuss, *Green Eggs and Ham* (New York: Random House, 1960)

12. Dave Kahle, "Closing the Sales," *The American Salesman*. Burlington: (Feb 2010), Vol 55, Is 2, 3.

13. John Boe, "Some Will, Some Won't, So What!" *The American Salesman*. Burlington: (Jan 2011), Vol 56, Is 1, 22.

14. Adapted and modified from "Sometimes I Say No," SellingPower.com (November 24, 2004), Pam Lontos, "Rejection Conditioning," *Selling Power* (June 1997), 78; and Tom Reilly, "Salespeople: Develop the Means to Handle Rejection," *Personal Selling Power*, Vol. 7, No. 5 (July/August 1987), 15.

15. Ted Pollock, "How Good of a Closer Are You?" *The American Salesman*. Burlington: (Apr 2010), Vol 55, Is 4, 22.

16. Steve Beagelman, "The Art of Closing the Sale in 10 Easy Steps," *Franchising World*. Washington: (Feb 2008), Vol 40, Is 2, 52.

17. Anonymous, "Sales Technique Nonverbal communication: Body language matters," *Travel Trade Gazette*. Tonbridge: (Nov 30, 2007), 38.

18. Phil Sasso, "Listening in for more sales," *Professional Distributor*. Fort Atkinson: (Dec 2007), Vol 15, Is 9, 18.

19. Steve Atlas, "Listening For Buying Signals," *Selling Power* (March 2000), 38.

20. Keith Rosen, "How to Avoid a Prolonged Close," http://www.allbusiness.com/sales/selling-techniques-

closing-sales/4001385-1.html, Accessed July 23, 2007.

21. Adapted and modified from "Read the (closing) signs," *Selling Power* (September 1997), In the SELLING IDEAS section of the magazine, 108; and Adapted from William J. Tobin, "Watch for the Right Signal," *Telephony*, Vol. 197, No. 15 (October 8, 1979), 114-115.

22. William Kendy, "Body of Knowledge," *Selling Power* (March 2001), 68.

23. Jeanne Pritt, "Fifteen Secrets to Closing A Sale," *The Profit Zone Newsletter* (July 1998). From "The Profit Zone" at www.profitzone.com.

24. Iain Macfarlane, "Techniques to Improve Sales Success Rate," *Wisconsin State Journal*. Madison: (Aug 1, 2005), 8.

25. http://changingminds.org/disciplines/sales/closing/ownership_close.htm. Accessed June 24, 2007.

26. Andy Cohen, "Are Your Reps Afraid to Close?" *Sales & Marketing Management* (March 1996), 43.

27. James O'Hara, "The Silent Barriers to Closing the Sale," *Selling* (May 1997), 9.

28. http://changingminds.org/disciplines/sales/closing/never_best_time_close.htm. Accessed June 26, 2007

29. http://changingminds.org/disciplines/sales/closing/123_close.htm Accessed June 28, 2007

30. "Closing Tips," *Selling Power*, sellingpower.com, November 2004.

31. Susan DelVecchio, James Zemanek, Roger McIntyre, Reid Claxton. "Updating the Adaptive Selling Behaviours: Tactics to Keep and Tactics to Discard," *Journal of Marketing Management.* (September 2004), Vol.20, Is. 7, 8, 859.

Chapter 14

1. Brian Tracy, "Customer Retention Driving Profits Through Giving Customers Lots of Reasons to Stay," http://www.1000advices.com/guru/customer_retaining_4life_bt.html, Accessed September 1, 2007.

2. Kim Kinter, "No. 1 In Customer Satisfaction," *Selling* (April 1994), 98-100; and Daniel V. Byrne, "Delivering on a Guarantee: Perfect Service, No Exceptions," *Nation's Business* (August 1991), 6.

3. Ginger Trumfio, "Anything for a Client," *Sales & Marketing Management* (June 1994), 102; and Kate Bertrand, "In Service, Perception Counts," *Business Marketing* (April 1989), 44.

4. Andrea V. Hernandez, "Not settling for 'good': Phenix City Chick-fil-A crew embraces 'second-mile service' policy," *Knight Ridder Tribune Business News*, Washington: (Sep 26, 2006), 1.

5. Anonymous, "Do the Right Thing," *Professional Builder*, Newton: (December 2003), Vol. 68, Is. 12, 76.

6. Boone, Elisabeth "From Better to Best: The Power of Benchmarking," *Rough Notes*. May 2007. FindArticles.com. 04 Sep. 2007. http://findarticles.com/p/articles/mi_qa3615/is_200705/ai_n19431629. And Anonymous, "Hylant Group's Annual Meeting Outlines Strategic Growth Plan," posted April 8, 2010, accessed April 12, 2011, http://www.hylant.com.

7. Paul R. Timm, *Customer Service: Career Success Through Customer Satisfaction* (New Jersey: Prentice-Hall, 1988), 45.

8. Julie Monahan, "Small Businesses Want Products, Advice, More," *American Banker*, New York: (May 18, 2004), Vol. 169, Is. 95, 3.A.

9. John Tschohl, "Exceptional Service-The Secret Weapon," *The Selling Advantage* (July 29, 1991), 2.

10. Susan Spielberg, "Pennies for their thoughts: Customers rewarded for feedback," *Nation's Restaurant News*, New York: (March 28, 2005), Vol. 35, Is. 13, 1.

11. Anonymous, "REI Earns Top 10 Ranking on FORTUNE's Best Places to Work List; Marks REI's Ninth Consecutive Year on List," *Business Wire*, New York: January 9, 2006, 1, and Anonymous, "Recreational Equipment, Inc; REI Posts 2007 Revenues of $1.3 Billion and 8.2 Percent Comp Store Sales," *Energy & Ecology Business*, Atlanta: (Jan 14, 2008), 150.

12. Matt Nitzberg, "Putting the Shopper in Your Shopper Marketing Strategy," *Shopper* Marketing, posted June 17, 2009, accessed April 14, 2011, http://www.dunnhumby.com/admin/files/6-09_ShopperMktg_Nitzberg.pdf.

13. Helen Edwards, "Slavery doesn't pay," *Marketing*. London: (May 26, 2010), 18.

14. Brett Stevenson, "Million Dollar Customers – they're all around you!" *Dealer Marketing Magazine*, posted June 3, 2010, accessed April 14, 2011, http://dealermarketing.com/columns/from-the-publisher/2012-million-dollar-customerstheyre-all-around-you.html.

15. Kevin Freiberg and Jackie Freiberg, "Nuts! Southwest Airlines' Crazy

Recipe for Business and Personal Success," 1996. Adapted an insert in *Selling Power* (September 1997), 103

16. Daniel Yee, "Chick-fil-A cooks up recipe of customer loyalty," *Deseret News* (Salt Lake City), Sep 18, 2006.

17. "Get More From Current Customers," in the Selling Ideas section of *Selling Power* (October 2000), 62.

18. Susan Spielberg, "You want fries with that?" *Nation's Restaurant News*. New York: (Oct 4, 2004), Vol. 38, Is. 40, 86.

19. William Kendy, "How to Move the Customer to a Higher Purchasing Level," *Selling Power* (June 2000), 33-34.

20. Kathleen Cholewka, "CRM: Calling All Customers," *Sales & Marketing Management* (May 2001), 25-26.

21. Todd Beck and Anne Smith, "Four Keys to Customer Loyalty," *The Catalyst*, Spring 2006.

22. Marc Hochstein, "A Subprime Servicer Aiming for Friendly," *American Banker*, New York: (June 4, 2004), Vol. 169, Is. 107, 1.

23. Steve Atlas, "Focus on Solutions," *Selling Power* (March 2001), 40.

24. Angi Semler, "Cranking up Customer Service," *Automotive Body Repair News*, Cleveland: (June 2004), Vol. 43, Is. 6, 30-35.

25. Ray Dreyfack, "Good Complaints," in the Selling Ideas section of *Selling Power* (March 2000), 54.

26. Karl Albrecht and Ron Zemke, *Service America! Doing Business in the New Economy* (Homewood: Karel Albrecht International, 2008), 7-8.

27. Frederick H. Reichheld, "Learning from Customer Defections," *Harvard Business Review* (March/April 1996), 56-59; and Charles W. L. Hill and

Gareth R. Jones, *Strategic Management Theory*, (South-Western College Pub, 2009) 118.

28. Anonymous, "Community. Loyalty. Lifetime Value," posted January 14, 2008, accessed April 14, 2011, http://www.ibm.com/ibm/ideasfromibm/us/library/pdfs/IFI_Retail_011408.pdf..

29. "Turn Conflict with a Customer Into a Selling Opportunity," *Personal Selling Power*, Vol. 12, No. 8 (September 1992), 73.

30. Dr. Ken Blanchard, "Mistake Proof," *Selling Power* (January/ February 1998), 42; and "Do You Deliver on Your Promises?" *Professional Selling*, Vol. 22, No. 10 (May 25, 1984), 4.

31. Terence A. Hockenhull, "Weekender: Marketing," *BusinessWorld*, Manila: (June 13, 2003), 1.

32. Anthony Urbaniak, "After the sale - what really happens to customer service," *The American Salesman* (February 2000), 14-17.

33. Anonymous, "Social Media Success Stories," posted 2009, accessed April 15, 2011, http://www.slideshare.net/kholzapfel/social-media-success-stories and Jeremy Twitchell, "From Upstart To $1 Billion Behemoth, Zappos Marks 10 Years," posted June 16, 2009, accessed April 15, 2011, http://about.zappos.com/press-center/media-coverage/upstart-1-billion-behemoth-zappos-marks-10-years.

34. Geoffrey Brewer, "How to Stay in Touch," *Sales & Marketing Management* (February 1998), 109.

35. Julie Puckett, "A Quick Thank-You," in the Reader To Reader Hot Tips section of *Selling Power* (September 2000), 60.

Chapter 15

1. Michael Jackel, Sabine Wollscheid, "Time is Money and Money Needs Time? A Secondary Analysis of Time-Budget Data in Germany," *Journal of Leisure Research* Vol. 39 Issue 1(2007), 77.

2. David Morrison, "Setting Boundaries on Commitments," *Public Management*, Vol. 92, Issue 3 (April, 2010), 20.

3. Laura Vanderkam, *168 Hours: You Have More Time Than You Think,* (New York, NY: Penguin Group, May 2010).

4. Laura Vanderkam, *168 Hours: You Have MoreTime Than You Think*.

5. "Time Management Tips for Busy College Students," *Daily Herald (Arlington Heights, IL)* July 18, 2010: 4, *Questia*, Web, April 29, 2011.

6. John Adair, Melanie Allen, *Time Management and Personal Development* (London, England: Thorogood, 2003), 26.

7. John Adair, Melanie Allen, *Time Management and Personal Development*, 9.

8. Steven Berglas," Chronic Time Abuse," *Harvard Business Review,* Boston: (June 2004), Vol. 82, Is. 6, 90.

9. Roger Leslie, "Time Management," *Listen*, Hagerstown: (May 2004), Vol. 57, Is. 9, 20-21.

10. Anonymous, "Will the Piles Ever Go Away?" *USA Today*, New York: (March 2004) Vol. 132, Is. 2706, 8

11. Tom Cox, "7 Rules of Extreme Time Management," *Oregon Business Journal* (April 20, 2011).

12. Anonymous, "Get on Top of Your Time Management," *Pulse*, Tonbridge: (April 5, 2004), 38.

13. Information gathered from the following:Cromwell Schubarth, "Small Business Tech Use is Growing," *San Jose Business Journal* (April 28, 2011) and, Kent Bernhard, Jr., "A tectonic Tech Shift," *Portforlio.com* (April 28, 2011), Accessed April 29, 2011 www.portfolio.com/business-news/2011/04/28/ipad-use-leads-to-technology-shift-by-small-business-owners.

14. Sue Shellenbarger, "Managing Workplace Distractions," *The Wall Street Journal* (February 23, 2011).

15. Rick Davis, "All systems go: a systemized approach to selling can lead to organizational success". *Prosales.* Jan 2006. FindArticles.com. 06 Sep. 2007. http://findarticles.com/p/articles/mi_m0NTC/is_1_18/ai_n16005254.

16. Jane Collingwood, "Organization Strategies for ADHD," *Psych Central* (April 29, 2011)Accessed April 29, 2011 www.psychcentral.com/lib/2011/organization-strategies-for-adhd/.

17. Jane Collingwood, "Organization Strategies for ADHD.

18. William F. Kumuyi, "Setting and Scoring Your Goals: Goals are Stated Ambitions; and All Leaders Know They Must Set Them and Follow Them Up till They Are Accomplished. For, Failure to Set Goals Reduces Leadership to Management by Chance and Hunches-A Sure Recipe for Corporate Disaster," *New African* July 2008, *Questia*, Web, April 29, 2011.

19. Collingwood, "Organization Strategies".

20. Peter Taylor, "The Art of Productive Laziness," *Industrial Management*, Vol. 51, Issue 4 (July/August 2009), 18+.

21. Melinda Ligos, "Cutting Meetings Down to Size," *New York Times*, (Late Edition, East Coast). New York: (January 11, 2004), 3.10.

22. Anonymous, "The Secrets of Time Management," *Agency Sales*, Irvine: (May 2004), Vol. 34, Is. 5, 40-41.

23. Stephen Rush, "From Baseball to Business," *Nation's Business* (October 1996), 50.

24. Taken from an article by David Lill, "Time to Spare," *Selling Power*, (May 1997), 72-73.

25. Renee Zemanski, "Time Management: How to make effective use of your time on the road," *Database101.com* (November 16, 2010)Accessed April 29, 2011 www.database101.com/wordpress/2010/11/time-management-how-to-make-effective-use-of-your-time-on-the-road/.

26. Steve Atlas, "When the Customer Isn't Right," *Selling Power* (January/February 2001), 32.

27. For a more thorough discussion on "How to Run Your Territory Like a Business," See the booklet Territory Management, Bureau of Business Practice, Inc. (1989), 6-16.

28. Richard Oppenheim, "Is That a Computer in Your Pocket?," *Searcher*(February, 2009), *Questia*, Web, April 29, 2011.

29. "TerrAlign4: Sales territory mapping software," *Product Landing Page* (Accessed April 28, 2011: www.terralign.com/products/terralign4.html).

30. John Cook, "Concur to buy mobile travel startup TripIt for up to $120M," *Puget Sound Business Journal* (January 13, 2011).

31. Rich Bohn, "Territory Management Better Sales," *Sales & Field Force Automation* (April 1998), 76.

32. See these sources for more information on computer mapping systems: Niklas Von Daehne, "The Technology Edge," *Success* (May 1994), 53-54; Charles Lee Browne, "On the Road Again," *Personal Selling Power* (March 1994), 36; George W. Colombo, "Putting Sales on the Map," *Selling* (July/August 1994), 27-29; Thayer C. Taylor, "Mapping Out a Strategy," *Sales & Marketing Management* (February 1994), 51-52.

33. Krishna K Havaldar Vasant M Cavale, *Sales and Distribution Management: Text and Cases* (Tate McGraw Hill Education, 2007).

34. Anonymous, "Personal Selling: Time and Territory Management," (Accessed April 29, 2011) www.sykronix.com/tsoc/courses/sales/routing.htm.

Chapter 16

1. Dan Cullin, "How Much Does it Really Cost to Hire the Wrong Salesperson?" http://www.ssstars.com/content/news/Hiring_Cost.htm, assessed May 26, 2011.

2. John Sullivan, "Cost Factors and Business Impacts of Turnover," *Chicago Job Resources*, chicagojobrescource.com, accessed November 12, 2006.

3. Sara Calabro, "Meaningful Rewards," *Sales and Marketing Management.* New York: (Mar 2005), Vol. 157, Is. 3, 26.

4. Anonymous, "How to Become an Innovative Sales Manager in 4 Virtual Steps," *Selling Power* white paper, available at http://www.selling-power.com/microsite/?mid=151&sp_src=sponsored_link.

5. From email communication with Dr. William Barnett, April 2011.

6. Erika Rasmusson, "Setting Your Sights on Videoconferencing," *Sales &*

Marketing Management (September 1997), 106.

7. Mary Boone, "The E-Vangelist: Face Time," *Sales & Marketing Management* (June 2001), 29.

8. Kathleen Cholewka, "Seven Signs You're Failing as a Manager and How to Avoid Them," *Sales & Marketing Management* (March 2001), 42.

9. Boone, Elisabeth, "Sales Management: Choices and Challenges," Rough Notes. Dec 2006. FindArticles.com. 09 Sep. 2007. http://findarticles.com/p/articles/mi_qa3615/is_200612/ai_n17193461.

10. Audrey Bottjen and Eduardo Canto, "Pep Talks That Inspire Reps," *Sales & Marketing Management* (June 2001), 66.

11. "Streetwise Tips on Motivation," *Streetwise Managing People,* accessed May 3, 2011, http://www.businesstown.com/people/motivation-advice.asp.

12. Quint Studer, "How to achieve and sustain excellence: there are seven ways to hardwire excellent outcomes. Do you know what they are?" *Healthcare Financial Management.* June 2007. FindArticles.com. 09 Sep. 2007. http://findarticles.com/p/articles/mi_m3257/is_6_61/ai_n19311760.

13. Melissa Campbell, "What Price Sales Force Satisfaction?," *Sales & Marketing Management* (July 1994), 37.

14. John E. Baer, "The cost of inadequate leadership: ineffective management carries a hefty price tag for the typical 120-bed nursing home." Entrepreneur.com. Posted Sept 2006, accessed May 3, 2011, http://www.entrepreneur.com/tradejournals/article/162791500.html .

15. Julie Strugeon, "Wanted: Successful Sales Manager," *Selling Power* (September 2000), 114.

16. Malcolm Fleschner, "Perfect Pitch," *Selling Power* (November/ December 1997), 25.

17. For a more detailed example and discussion of this useful approach, see Mark Johnston and Greg Marshall, *Sales Force Management.* (Irwin: McGraw-Hill 2010).

18. Anonymous, "How to Become an Innovative Sales Manager in 4 Virtual Steps," *Selling Power* white paper, available at http://www.selling-power.com/microsite/?mid=151&sp_src=sponsored_link.

19. George O'Brien, "Talent Search," *BusinessWest.* Chicopee: (Aug 18, 2008), Vol 25, Is 7, 16.

20. Gary Duncan, "Poor Hiring Often Leads to Astronomical Turnover Costs," *Denver Business Journal,* (March 12, 2004).

21. Robert G. Head, "Select Salespeople Systematically," *Personal Selling Power,* Vol. 13, No. 4 (May/June 1993), 68-69; and Geoffrey Brewer, "Mind Reading: What Drives Top Salespeople to Greatness?" *Sales & Marketing Management* (May 1994), 86.

22. Anonymous, "2010 Sales Compensation & Performance Management: Summary of Metrics," accessed May 3, 2011, www.varicent.com/docs.

23. Michele Marchetti, "What a sales call costs," *Sales and Marketing Management.* New York: (September 2003), Vol. 152, Is. 9, 80.

24. Henry Canaday, "What Are You Worth," *Selling Power* (January/February 2001), 83.

24. Anonymous, "2010 Sales Compensation & Performance Management:

Summary of Metrics," accessed May 3, 2011, www.varicent.com/docs.

25. Andy Cohen, Jennifer Gilbert, Melinda Ligos."Extreme Makeovers." *Sales and Marketing Management.* New York: (May 2004), Vol.156, Is. 9, 36.

26. Patricia Zingheim, "Are your salespeople out of line?" *Selling Power* (July/August 2000).

27. Susan Greco, "The Customer Driven Bonus Plan," *Inc* magazine (September 1995), 89; Kerry Rottenberger and Richard Kern, "The Upside-Down Deming Principle," *Sales & Marketing Management* (June 1992), 39-44

28. Todd Nelson, "Employee Compensation Likely to Change," *The Tennessean,* Section E (October 1, 1992), 4.

29. "Selling Without Commissions," *Sales & Marketing Management* (June 1994), 97.

30. Churchill, Ford, Walker, *Sales Force Management,* 486.

31. Edgar Speer, "The Role of Training at United States Steel," *Training and Development Journal,* Vol. 30, No. 6 (June 1976), 18-21.

32. Jack Hubbard, "Making coaching part of the performance culture's DNA: Part 1". *The RMA Journal.* (Sept 2006), Vol 89, No 1, 72..

33. See Cisco WebEx Training Center for an example of interactive training, http://www.webex.com/products/elearning-and-online-training.html.

INDEX